Focusing on

JESUS

Daily
Christ-centered Thoughts

Jim Fowler

C.I.Y. Publishing
P.O. Box 1822
Fallbrook, CA 92088-1822
www.Christinyou.net

FOCUSING ON JESUS

Daily Christ-centered Thoughts

Published by
C.I.Y. Publishing
P.O. Box 1822
Fallbrook, California 92088-1822

ISBN 10 digit – 1-929541-61-9
ISBN 13 digit – 1-978-929541-61-4

Printed in the United States of America

FOREWORD

In this compilation of daily readings, I have attempted to strike a balance between theological thoughts and practical topics dealing with our Christian lives. In that I was theologically trained in several disciplines and institutions, it is always my temptation to form my thoughts in theological categories and vocabulary, but since 1973 when the presence of the Spirit of Christ became a living reality in my life, the practicum of theology has become the more vital concern, focusing particularly on the reality of the indwelling presence of the living Christ. "Christ in You" is the biblical moniker of the ministry I have been engaged in for over twenty-five years.

Let me explain up front that this is not a typical fluffy, feel-good religious devotional intended only for a euphoric moment in the morning or evening. These daily thoughts will make you stop and think, ponder and reflect, on the fullness of the life of Jesus within you. I make no claims to being an accomplished writer. I simply write what I think in my own colloquial manner. I am aware that I employ many passive verbs and construct run-on sentences, but I am somewhat comforted in knowing that the apostle Paul did likewise. Not an excuse for lackadaisical writing, I admit!

The thoughts in these daily articles came rather spontaneously in the midst of daily life. There was no agenda or systematic plan for their layout in a book. Rather randomly, I would think of a topic, usually when awakening in the morning between 4 and 5 am. As that thought germinated, it would often grow into a daily reading. These brief articles (approximately 300 words) were then posted on my Facebook page. When there was insufficient time to ponder a topic, I would jot the idea in a list that I kept on the desktop of my computer, and come back to it later to see if it might be a thought that could be expanded so others could enjoy or benefit from such. Some thoughts, topics, subjects, and ideas grew out of books and articles I read, while others were sparked by messages I listened to or conversations with others – even the observation of the absurdity of so much religious activity. For the most part, there is no rhyme nor reason for the order of the readings. The book is not systematically organized, though a few readings were placed on particular days of the year that have a special emphasis.

The reader will find in these readings many comments that are critical of institutional religion. These are but the negation that is necessary to point to the positive realization that we must focus on **JESUS**. As my friend, Burt Rosenberg, quipped, "You have to know what AIN'T, in order to know what IS." The reader should allow the negative exposés to be the springboards to a positive consideration of the contrast with the character and continuous activity of Jesus Christ.

I do not expect all readers to agree with all of the thoughts in this volume. In fact, I hope that few will. The Christian community needs to avoid Xerox-thinking, wherein everyone thinks the same, dresses the same, and conforms to one another. We need to agree to disagree without being disagreeable, and thus to enjoy our unity in Christ in the midst of the diversity of Christian thought and practice.

The reader will notice that I usually attempt to document a thought with scriptural citation or reference. I believe that the inspired scriptures of the new covenant literature (*New Testament*) are the primary objective source to learn of God's historical revelation of His Son, Jesus Christ. I believe that the Holy Spirit is the divine agent who brings enlightenment to our human minds to understand the written text of the inspired scriptures. May the divine Spirit likewise bring enlightenment to your thinking as you read these daily readings during the year. The reader is encouraged to look up the scripture references cited in the readings to determine for yourself the validity of what is written, in like manner as did the Bereans who were "examining the Scriptures daily to see whether these things were so" (Acts 17:11). It has been suggested by some readers that these brief, and sometimes provocative articles, can serve as interesting discussion-starters for Christian study groups. Some pastors may even use the thoughts in these daily articles as sermon-starters.

Will I continue to write brief articles such as these? I do not know, but the answer is "probably." Over a four-year period, I have become accustomed to putting my daily thoughts in written form. One fellow quipped, "Jim Fowler has never had a thought that was not committed to writing." So be it! Now in my seventies, I appreciate the absence of any deadlines for speaking or publication, and have learned to "rest" in my La-Z-Boy recliner, waiting to see what God might bring to mind.

May God bless and enlighten (Eph. 1:18) your thought processes as you read these "Daily Christ-centered Thoughts."

Jim Fowler
2019

Table of Contents

Words of Appreciation

Every writer draws from the well of previous reading and conversations. I have especially benefitted from the input of W. Ian Thomas, Norman Grubb, Frank Viola, and many others.

There are numerous people to whom I am grateful for their comments on these daily readings as they appeared on the Facebook page, "The Issue is Jesus," throughout the years of 2018 and 2019. Don Burzynski often commented, as did Matthew and Michelle Morizio, Dan and Sarah White, John and Terri Russin, Muriel Ruppert, Kenneth and Jeanie Grief, Mary C. Wilkinson, Lawrence Lenk, Russ and Margaret Previte, Don Nugent, and many others too numerous to mention. Thank you, my friends, for your encouragement. Thank you, Dave Hook, for giving this volume a final read.

There are some friends here in my hometown of Fallbrook, CA who have been very encouraging during the past two years. In particular I want to mention Art Deming, who just recently graduated to glory. He would call every few weeks to excitedly share how he had benefitted from a reading in the previous book of readings, *The Issue is Jesus*, and would ask for more copies to give to friends. He was looking forward to reading this new volume. Bill Hoganson was equally encouraging whenever I saw him in the care home where he resides.

A special word of thanks to my dear wife, Gracie, for your patience with me during the many months of writing these readings – for those many mornings when I got out of bed early to write – for those many times when I appeared to ignore you because I was concentrating on the next thought and attempting to put it into words. Thank you for putting up with me for fifty years of marriage. I love you!

Jim Fowler – 2019

JANUARY 1

PERSONAL RESOLUTIONS

As we commence a new year, it has become a cultural tradition for people to make personal resolutions articulating their resolve to refrain from attitudes and actions of the past, as well as initiate goals for new attitudes and actions for self-betterment in the new year. Seldom do we take the time to evaluate whether such resolutions are self-motivated. Are our resolutions self-focused or other-focused? Genuine *agape*-love is by definition other-focused. We must beware of falling into the humanistic trap of self-improvement, thinking that our works of performance are going to make us better Christians.

We do not want to become "Little Jack Horners" sitting in a corner saying, "Oh what a good boy am I!" Self-improvement is not the method of Christian discipleship; it is the procedure of humanistic self-help betterment that leads only to pride and arrogance. Self-resolve is not what leads to sanctification and maturity in the Christian life, but faithful receptivity of the activity of divine life in our behavior. Yes, change is often necessary in the lives of Christians, but the effective change-agent will not be our self-resolve, but reliance on the grace-activity of God via the Son, **JESUS**, and the power of His Spirit.

If you are making personal resolutions at the beginning of the year, you might want to evaluate whether they are motivated by self-concern and personal achievement, by means of self-improvement. Or are they motivated by the Spirit of the Lord **JESUS** in order to allow Him to be and do all that He wants to be and do in your life this year? If the Lord is in control of your personal resolutions, they will usually be other-oriented, with the intent to love others (Jn. 13:34,35), to pray for others (James 5:16), to take time to help the less-fortunate, and to give to those God prompts you to give. "Do not merely look out for your own personal interests, but also for the interests of others" (Phil. 2:4).

JANUARY 2

SPIRITUAL, BUT NOT RELIGIOUS

Those who have a vested interest in their religious organizations become quite agitated, to the point of almost having a coronary attack, when they hear people say, "Well, I am interested in pursuing what is spiritual, but not interested in religion." Such a statement sends shivers down their arthritic religious spines, for they know that such sentiment will lead to the decline and demise of their beloved institutions. More particularly, the rotted foundations of their religious houses of cards will be exposed, leaving their previously prestigious positions evacuated, and their inflated retirement plans bankrupt.

Frankly, I think that such expressed attitudes are indicative of a divinely orchestrated move of the Spirit, designed to change the course of God's people and their relationships with God and with others. Yes, I know that the word "spiritual" can have a myriad of meanings, and can lead people into a maze of spiritualized mysteries, but I trust the Spirit of God to orchestrate the process of drawing people to Himself via the Son, Jesus Christ. These people, the SBNRs (spiritual, but not religious), are not necessarily pursuing narcissistic independence (as they have been charged), but they are definitely not interested in a closed-minded club of like-minded people who are more interested in themselves, their beliefs, their traditions, and their meetings than the "others" of the world who are needy and hurting.

I am encouraged when I hear people say they are desirous of being involved in the "spiritual, but not the religious." They do not want to go into the dead-end cul-de-sac of religion, but are open to pursue the leading of the Spirit in their lives, despite the fact that it might be non-traditional and violate the religious mantra, "We've never done it that way before!" Because **JESUS** is alive by the Spirit in His receptive people, the newness of the Spirit must be allowed to blossom as He wills.

JANUARY 3

WHAT IS NORMAL?

The high school student was explaining to me how difficult it was to live consistently as a Christian youth in the context of the contemporary high school environment. "I don't want to be weird, or stand out like a sore thumb," he explained. *"I just want to be normal*, and fit in with the prevailing youth culture." I explained to the young man, "It sounds to me that you are not wanting to be 'normal,' and are wanting to simply be 'average;" just wanting to conform to the median thought and behavior of your fellow students." This led to an extended discussion of the difference between desiring to be "normal" and seeking to be "average."

To be "average" is to be the median between the best and the worst – the center point between the high and the low. To be "normal" is to correspond with a standard or "norm" by which the activity or object is to be evaluated. In the discussion that ensued, the young man agreed that his desire was to avoid being different than his peers, to avoid having to take a stand that would make it obvious that he was choosing to operate on the basis of Christian values instead of the prevailing world values, particularly in reference to the vocabulary of his conversations and participation in crude jokes with sexual innuendoes.

Continuing our conversation, we discussed what "normal" behavior and conversation might be for a teenage Christian youth in today's culture. The norm, the standard, for human behavior, whether youth or adult, is the person and life of Jesus Christ. Jesus was man as God intended man to be, allowing God the Father to live through Him (Jn. 14:10) at every moment in time for thirty-three years. That is "normal" humanity. **JESUS** is the norm for Christian character and behavior, that is to be lived not in the attempted imitation of Jesus, but in the dynamic out-living of the life and character of **JESUS** in our daily lives.

JANUARY 4

LIVING ON TWO PLANES

We are not referring to eroded geographical plains, or to aeronautical planes, but to levels of existence and function. All people live on two planes, but there are many who are unaware that they participate on a functional plane beyond the temporal operations of life in their physical body. The majority of Christians seem to think that when they became a Christian, they added another plane of being in their lives, that they added a spiritual dimension to their obvious physical function. Such thinking is a fallacy. All human persons live on both a spiritual and physical plane of existence, for God created human beings with both spiritual and physical functionality.

Those persons who are spiritually unregenerate, and not Christians, function by "the spirit that works in the sons of disobedience" (Eph. 2:2). They are unaware of such spiritual function because "the natural man cannot understand spiritual things" (I Cor. 2:14); "the god of this world has blinded the minds of the unbelieving" (II Cor. 4:4). Christians, however, spiritually regenerated with the indwelling Spirit of Christ (Rom. 8:9,16), with the "mind of Christ" (I Cor. 2:16), can appraise spiritual things (I Cor. 2:15), and should have an awareness that the Spirit of God is working in their lives as they respond by faith.

Many Christians, however, are dragged down by their prior development of "fleshly" patterns of selfish and sinful thought and behavior. Failing to keep their focus on the sufficiency of God's grace in the presence of the living Lord **JESUS**, they revert to a monocular viewpoint that sees and operates merely from a temporal and physical perspective, whereby they function no differently than an unregenerate person. Christians need to recognize that the Spirit of Christ supersedes the "flesh" tendencies of our soul (cf. Gal. 5:16-24), and the spiritual plane provides the character by which we live on the physical plane.

JANUARY 5

YOU CANNOT LIVE THE CHRISTIAN LIFE

This may be a surprising or shocking statement to some Christians, who have long been admonished by their pastors and leaders to live a Christ-like life, and have been given a myriad of procedural "how tos" in order to accomplish the task in accordance with the expectations of their ecclesiastical authorities. The truth of the matter is that only Christ can live the Christ-life! He lived that life out perfectly in physical form during His redemptive mission on earth, and desires to do so again by His Spirit in Christian people, Christ-ones, in every age. He wants to re-present His life in our human form today.

In 1691, some friends of Congregationalist pastor, John Gammon, compiled some excerpts from his teaching in a book entitled, *Christ, a Christian's Life: A believer's life derived from Christ and resolved into Christ.* Though seldom known or read today, that book became a classic volume whereby many Christians recognized that the Christian life is not a performance of self-effort to "be like Jesus," but must be derived from the presence and activity of the living Lord Jesus within a Christian individual. The Christian life is a derived life – not a self-enacted life of performance attempting to conform to an ideal.

Sincere Christians, after having given their best effort to conform to the prescribed standards of Christ-like attitudes and behavior, have thrown up their hands and declared, "The Christian life is an impossible life!" They are right. Living the Christian life is impossible if one is attempting to generate and enact such by his own power. You cannot live the Christian life – only **JESUS** Christ can. It has rightly been said, "The greatest sin of Christian people is trying to live the Christian life." The living Lord **JESUS**, living in, through and as us, stands ready to supply the divine grace-dynamic to live out His life and character in our behavior as Christ-ones (Christians).

JANUARY 6

IT'S NOT WHAT WE DO, BUT WHAT HE DOES!

Reformed theology emphasizes divine action rather than human action in the personal interaction of God and man. Explanation of Christian thought influenced by Augustine of Hippo (A.D. 354-430) and John Calvin (A.D. 1509-1564) often emphasizes the sovereign action of God to the extent that it denies there is any legitimate active response on the part of man to what God has done in the Savior, Jesus Christ. Though such thinking should be commended for recognizing that human persons can do nothing to save themselves from their fallen predicament, and the action of salvation must commence with and be completely enacted by God, it fails to account for genuine personal relationship made possible by God's creation of human beings as personal beings with freedom of choice and response-ability to freely enter into a divine-human spiritual relationship and union by receiving the presence and activity of God within the human spirit by faith.

Yes, the divine impetus of Christian conversion must be by divine initiative. "For by grace are you saved through faith" (Eph. 2:8). But, the ongoing sanctifying process of the Christian life must also be enacted by the divine dynamic of God's grace, received by human faith. "As you received Christ Jesus, so walk in Him" (Col. 2:6). "Having been reconciled, you shall be saved by His life" (Rom. 5:10). The divine initiative of grace and the human receptivity of faith are the two sides (divine and human) that come together to allow for ongoing relationship between God and man. We must never think that it is our human performance that accomplishes God's purposes, either in redemptive regeneration or in the sanctifying manifestation of Christ's life in the Christian life. God took the initiative of grace to send His Son, **JESUS** Christ, to be the Savior and Lord of our lives, and we have the opportunity to be receptive to such by faith. It's not what *we* do, but what *He* does!" Our response-ability is to make the choice of faith that simply receives His grace-action.

JANUARY 7

NO MAN IS AN ISLAND

In 1624, John Donne published *Devotions upon Emergent Occasions*, a volume of metaphysical poetry. In "Meditation XVII" there is one non-rhyming verse of seven lines wherein Donne explains that "no man is an island." Likening humanity at large to a continent of land, he indicates the necessary interconnectivity of all the parts of the landmass, emphasizing that the isolation of a detached island does not serve the greater objective of the whole. His point is that we humans need each other, and when the bell tolls for the death of just one individual there is a diminishment of the entirety of human society.

In the analogy of a connected continental landmass to the whole of human society, Donne sought to explain the essential importance of every clod of earth that comprises an entire continent, like unto the essential importance of every individual to the whole of human social interaction. In contrast to the humanistic tenets of individual insignificance and the striving self-sufficiency to prove that our lives have meaning, Donne was stating that every person is an essential component of the whole of humanity, functioning in conjunction with the larger mass of mankind. The loss of one man, "for whom the bell tolls," diminishes the whole.

Donne's thesis holds true when considering the Body of Christ, the Church, also. We need each other. *No man is an island.* We are part of a functional whole. God created us as social creatures, and did not intend that any Christian should be an isolated and insular "lone-ranger Christian," claiming no need to interact in oneness and unity with others. The function of the entire Body of Christ requires every Christian acting conjointly (cf. I Cor. 12:12-25) in relational union. The presence of the living **JESUS** in each Christian holds the body together in unity, and overcomes all facets of death as His life and His corporate Body are eternal.

JANUARY 8

INTO THIN AIR

Jon Krakauer wrote a book entitled, *Into Thin Air: A Personal Account of the Mt. Everest Disaster*, published in 1997. It became a best-selling non-fiction book, and was later adapted into a movie, *Everest*, in 2015. Krakauer, an outdoor enthusiast and journalist, was participating in an attempt to climb Mt. Everest in May, 1996, when a "rogue storm" struck the team while attempting to summit the mountain. Eight climbers died that day, and there was much controversy in the climbing community about how the competing guide agencies were commercializing the Mt. Everest experience, and putting their customers at risk.

Moving from the arduous ascent of the tallest physical mountain on planet earth (29,029 feet), we might compare and contrast such a climb into the "thin air" of the earth's upper atmosphere with the spiritual ascent into the "thin air" of God's presence and function. Many Christians seem content to live in the lowlands of Christian experience, complaining of the fog as well as the high heat and humidity. There does not seem to be any competition among elite spiritual guides seeking to direct willing Christian participants into the higher altitude of knowing God in an intimate personal way and appreciating what it means to "live by the Spirit" (Gal. 5:25).

In contrast to the saints of old, who considered it to be the Christian's objective to know God in an ever-deeper intimacy, contemporary Christians seem to be content with a shallow experience of contemporary excitement, singing repetitive phrases while raising or clapping their hands as the full extent of what is deigned to be worship. May God prompt more of His people to pursue the adventurous spirituality of venturing into the "thin air" of intimate personal communion with God, reverently participating in eucharistic appreciation of the "good grace" of God in the living presence of the Lord **JESUS** Christ.

JANUARY 9

ETERNAL WEIGHT OF GLORY

We were "created for His glory" (Isa. 43:7), and are instructed to "do all to the glory of God" (I Cor. 10:31). The Creator God designed human beings to derivatively express or image His all-glorious character in our human behavior. The apostle Paul used a phrase that explains how our "momentary light afflictions" (the circumstances of life) are intended to lead to "an eternal weight of glory" (II Cor. 4:16-18). The phrase likely keys off of the Hebrew word for "glory" (*kabod*), that conveyed the concept of "weightiness" or "heaviness;" figuratively referring to the impact, importance, significance or honor of something or someone.

We must explore what "the eternal weight of glory" means for Christians today. How do the difficulties, hardships and sufferings of the present life produce for us an "eternal weight of glory"? When we participate in the "unseen" perspective that Paul referred to, we become aware that the Spirit of God is exerting the pressure of His grace to conform us to Christ (cf. Rom. 8:29). The "weight of glory" is akin to the relational embrace of a divine "bear-hug," whereby God is pressing us into Himself, compressing everything into the singular reality of the life of **JESUS**, so we can truly experience "Christ in us, the hope of glory" (Col. 1:27).

This present sanctifying experience of glory does not preclude that "the eternal weight of glory" also looks forward in hope to a yet to come reality of heavenly glory, a place of glorious perfection where the hindrances and afflictions of this earthly life are superseded in the eternal presence of the Triune God. The temporary weight of our present problems cannot be compared to the weightiness of perfect and eternal divine action. As Paul writes elsewhere, "The sufferings of this present time are not worthy to be compared with the glory that is to be revealed us" (Rom. 8:18), when we are "face-to-face" with **JESUS**.

JANUARY 10

BEWARE OF SEEKING NOVELTY

There is a grave form of idolatry that has been perpetuated in the American churches for many decades. Though seldom identified, this idolatrous pursuit is a chasing after and adoration for innovation, for novelty, for the latest new thing that holds promise for advantage and advancement. Such a quest for novelty is not a new problem. When Paul went to Athens, his spirit was provoked, observing that the city was "full of idols" (Acts 17:16). Luke, the author of Acts, parenthetically remarked, "all the Athenians ... used to spend their time in nothing other than telling or hearing *something new*" (Acts 17:21).

The churches of America today clamor after the newest programs and techniques to achieve the greatest statistical growth in comparison and competition with others. The cultural historians would no doubt point out that part of the American dream has always been to be on the "cutting edge" of invention in order to stay ahead and compete. To that one must add the distinctive American philosophy of pragmatism that espouses "whatever works," combined with the humanistic incentive of "Just do it!" The churches of America must beware of bowing down to the "god of novelty" as they espouse the latest fads of worship, follow the newest ideas from the best-selling Christian book list, and seek to employ the innovative methods of growth that a popular church has utilized. Church growth procedures are vacuous compared to our need for "growing in the grace and knowledge of our Lord and Savior, Jesus Christ" (II Pet. 3:18).

Innovation and invention is particularly questionable when attempting to adjust orthodox theology into novel ideas hitherto unknown. Rather than novelty in thought or action, Christians should develop single-focus on the living Lord **JESUS**, and concentrate on the newness of life in Him, with the expression of His divine character in Christian behavior.

JANUARY 11

THE ISSUE IS JESUS

I read a report of an occasion that occurred at Oral Roberts University years ago. The campus chaplain, Tommy Tyson, was scheduled to speak in chapel, and he had chosen First Corinthians 1:30,31 as his text:

"But by His doing you are in Christ Jesus, who became to us wisdom from God, and righteousness and sanctification, and redemption, so that, just as it is written, 'Let him who boasts, boast in the Lord.'"

Standing before the student body in the chapel, Chaplain Tyson took a deep breath and began,

"I do not believe in redemption. I do not believe in healing. I do not believe in deliverance. I do not believe in salvation."

It was as if the air was sucked out of the room, as the faculty and student body gasped. After a brief pregnant pause, Chaplain Tyson continued, "Here is what I do believe: I believe in a Personal Redeemer, a Personal Healer, a Personal Deliverer, a Personal Savior; I believe in Jesus."

What was the chaplain trying to say? Genuine Christian belief is in the Person of **JESUS** Christ, not in human systematizations about various doctrinal or theological subjects. The text clearly states that it is "in Christ Jesus" (in spiritual union with the living Lord Jesus) that we participate in His wisdom, His righteousness, His sanctification, and His redemption. Therefore, our only boast is in the Lord Jesus Christ."

It is imperative that Christians put aside their persistent bickering about ideological doctrines, and focus their attention on "growing in the grace and knowledge of our Lord and Savior **JESUS** Christ, giving Him the glory" (II Pet. 3:18).

JANUARY 12

WHO IS MY ENEMY?

In the dialogue that preceded Jesus' telling of "The Parable of the Wounded Traveler" (Lk. 10:25-37), a Jewish lawyer asked Jesus what was necessary to inherit eternal life. "What does the Law say?" Jesus asked. The lawyer correctly quoted Deut. 6:5, "You shall love the Lord your God with all your heart, soul, mind and strength," adding "and your neighbor as yourself" (Lev. 19:18). "Do that, and you shall live," Jesus said, knowing quite well that the lawyer could not do so without the provision of the indwelling Spirit of God's grace. Recognizing that he was indicted by his own recitation of the Law, the lawyer quickly responded with a technical question, "Who is my neighbor?"

Religionists, in general, are usually attempting to self-justify their elitist attitudes and lack of compassion for others who do not think or act like they do, and are not really interested in finding a human neighbor in need. They are more concerned with determining, "Who is my enemy? Who are those I do not feel obliged to love because they think differently, act differently, and worship differently?" For the Jewish people of the first-century region of Judea, some of their foremost untouchable enemies were the impure Samaritan half-breeds to their north. So, Jesus told a parable about a Samaritan traveler who fell among thieves.

Religion has been more interested in identifying their enemies than their neighbors in need of compassion and love. There are many religiously polarized peoples who have developed a mind-set of grudging hostility that transcends the centuries and generations: Jews vs. Christians. Christians vs. Muslims. Catholics vs. Protestants. Methodists vs. Baptists. Conservatives vs. Liberals. Who is our enemy? Our real spiritual enemy is Satan (cf. Acts 13:10), with his power of death (Heb. 2:14; I Cor. 15:26); not those we have demonized because they have a different belief-system or morality code than we do.

JANUARY 13

WE ARE NOT *CALLED TO BE "LIKE JESUS"?*

Let me make this clear and unequivocal: The new covenant literature nowhere encourages anyone to be "like Jesus" by attempting to conform to His perfect behavior. Such would be an inculcation to engage in the impossible. The call to "be like Jesus" is an unbiblical and unorthodox misunderstanding of the gospel that fails to comprehend the death and resurrection of Jesus; fails to appreciate the integral tie between the physical Jesus of history and the continuing Spirit of Christ (cf. I Cor. 15:45) in Christian lives; and fails to grasp the dynamic of divine grace whereby God empowers the Christ-life in Christ-ones.

There is so much conversation and preaching in the churches today about being "like Jesus." The incentive to be "like Christ" is a constant pry bar used by religious leaders to attempt to leverage Christian people into performance-based conformity to the perfection of the behavior of Jesus, as determined by the teachers of a particular religious group. Such a behavior incentive simply reveals that Christian thought in general often has an underlying premise that is essentially deistic, wherein Jesus is a detached and distant model of yesteryear, whose ideal behavior is to be emulated and reproduced.

The essential reality of the Christian gospel is the present-living Christ. It is not the remembrance of a long-ago historical Jesus. It is not the speculation of what is allegedly supposed to occur in Jesus' name in the future. The resurrected and living Lord Jesus is the single reality of Christian truth. If Jesus is not alive by the Spirit (cf. I Cor. 15:45) within a receptive individual, then despite their epistemic belief-system, and despite the moralistic conformity of their behavior, such a person is not participating in the redemptive and restorative reality (cf. Rom. 8:9) that God made singularly available in and through His only-begotten Son, **JESUS** Christ.

JANUARY 14

CHRISTIAN MIND-GAMES

Head-games, mind-games, power games. They are the subtle psychological games people play to make themselves look superior, and the other person inferior. Some people view the whole of human life (even Christian life) to be but a competitive sport of one-up-man-ship wherein they maneuver and manipulate to overpower the other person, psychologically, socially, financially, even spiritually. Religion is just one of the arenas where such human games are often played, and the competition therein is particularly intense because the issues are regarded to be of eternal consequence to the contestants.

Ananias and Sapphira may have been playing mind-games when they attempted to "lie to the Holy Spirt" and "test the Spirit" (Acts 5:1-11), apparently attempting to engage in the one-up-man-ship of appearing more "spiritual" and generous than they truly were. Christians play mind-games, seeking to convince themselves and others that their doctrinal belief-system is more orthodox and biblical than that of others. The mystery of prayer is particularly susceptible to mind-games as people attempt to make deals with God, "I'll do this, if You'll do that;" or revert to the guilt of surmising that one's prayers were not answered in the manner desired because the one praying did not have sufficient faith.

Whenever Christians fail to appreciate the immense love and grace of God in Jesus Christ, they will inevitably revert to a legalistic religious mind-set of human performance, where they will play mind-games that attempt to bring God down to their level through anthropopathic attribution. They will falsely imagine that they can manipulate God and others, utilizing ulterior motives and exploitation to achieve their own ends. All such gamesmanship is contrasted with the simple grace-based relationship wherein God in Christ provides everything necessary to be what God desires us to be.

JANUARY 15

EARLY CHRISTIAN WORSHIP

It is a safe assertion to say that there were no megachurches or super-churches in the early centuries of the Church of Jesus Christ. The Christians, gathering together in the context of much persecution from the imperial Roman authorities, local politicos, and religious elitists (even Jewish pogroms to exterminate Christians, cf. Acts 8:3; 13:50; 14:19; Gal. 4:29) – the Christians often had to "go underground" (literally and figuratively) in order to fellowship together, to love one another, and to encourage one another to stand firm in their faith in the One who they believed to be the Son of God, the singular Lord and Savior of mankind.

Compelled by their simple faith in Jesus Christ, their gatherings were uncomplicated by elaborate formal liturgies, mandated orders of service, or required positions of hierarchical leadership necessary for participation. The Christian community engaged in informal and spontaneous interaction as they worshipped their Lord and Savior, encouraging one another to re-present the life and character of the Lord Jesus Christ in every facet of their personal lives. They encouraged one another (Heb. 10:25) as they shared how the Christ-life was being lived out in their lives in the practical situations of daily life.

The early Christian assemblies were Spirit-directed encounters, rather than the strict, predictable and monotonous "services" often offered in churches today. Believing that the Spirit of the living Lord Jesus lived within every Christian person, each could minister to another by the "manifestations of the Spirit" (I Cor. 12:7). When they gathered together "each one had a psalm, or a teaching, or a personal revelation, or a tongue, or an interpretation" (I Cor. 14:26), and by the supervising grace of the Spirit of God, their entire time together served as a time of edification and up-building of their faith in the living **JESUS**.

JANUARY 16

"WE LEPERS..."

Josef De Veuster was born in 1840 in Belgium. He became a Roman Catholic priest, and took the name "Father Damien" from the third century, Saint Damian, of Syria. His heart for missions brought him to Hawaii in 1864, where he volunteered to be assigned to the leper colony on the island of Molokai. Leprosy (Hansen's disease) was regarded as very contagious and incurable, a perspective dating back at least nineteen centuries to the time of Jesus (cf. Lk. 17:11-18). Willing to become a leper to gain the lepers to Christ, Father Damien lived with them, worked with them, ate with them, and worshipped with them.

Eleven years after going to Molokai, Father Damien realized that he, too, had contracted leprosy. Standing before his quarantined congregation, Father Damien began his next homily, "We lepers...," indicating his complete identification with the people he was serving. He was now one of them in every way, including ostracism, quarantine, and the death sentence of this terrible disease. The leprous congregation knew that Father Damien, in likeness to His Lord Jesus Christ, had "become one of us, to heal our infirmities" (cf. Isa. 53:5), a complete ministry of intercessory identification, laying down one's life for others.

It was necessary that Jesus become one of us, fully human, to accept and endure the likeness of our "sinful flesh" (Rom. 8:3), in order to effect our deliverance and salvation. Gregory Nazianzus (A.D. 329-390), one of the Cappadocian fathers of the early Church, once wrote, "the unassumed is the unhealed," indicating that Jesus identified with our humanity in every possible way to become the Savior of mankind and to restore humanity to be "man as God intended man to be." "He (**JESUS**) Himself partook of flesh and blood, that He might render powerless him who had the power of death, that is the devil" (Heb. 2:14), as only He, the God-man, could do.

JANUARY 17

PERFECTIONISM

Most have known people who might be labelled "perfectionistic." They seek to do everything correctly and perfectly, without mistakes. Their standard of excellence is commendable, but they seldom seem to enjoy their successes because they are so self-critical of any imperfections. They set the bar too high – higher than they, or anyone else, can achieve. Such a mind-set is self-destructive; these people drive themselves crazy. Driven by a self-absorbed narcissism, a form of OCD (obsessive, compulsive disorder), they are so fearful of disapproval or failure, they seldom appreciate the good in anything.

Many such persons are to be found in religious communities. Beginning with the idea of a Perfect God, they have been instructed that God expects them to perform in perfect accord with His perfect character. Since God's acceptance of them is thought to be determined by their performance achievements, they soon recognize their inabilities and failures (aka "sins") and identify themselves as losers (aka "sinners"), filled with guilt and shame for their imperfections. Eventually, they focus only on the negatives, becoming judgmental of themselves and others, even hypocritical procrastinators to avoid more failures.

God is indeed perfect, but does He expect perfect behavior of His created beings? When God gave the Law to the Israelites, He knew full well they could never perfectly keep it by their own effort. Perfection of human behavior is not the objective. But did Jesus not say, "Be perfect, as your heavenly Father is perfect" (Matt. 5:48)? Yes, but what is the source of perfect character in human behavior? Only the Perfect God, via the "Perfect One," **JESUS** Christ, can empower the expression of His perfection. Christians, made spiritually perfect (Phil. 3:15) by the presence of Christ within, are to derive His perfect character in their behavior (cf. I Tim. 1:16; I Jn. 4:12).

JANUARY 18

PERFECT MISTAKES

Cheryl Walterman Stewart tells of the time when her uncle, Paul Nybakken, was packing used clothing in wooden crates to send to orphanages in China. On the way home from the church building, he reached into his shirt pocket and realized that his new eyeglasses were missing. He replayed the events of the day in his mind, and figured they must have fallen into one of the crates he had nailed shut, and were on their way to China. Times were tough during the depression, and Paul was a bit upset that he would have to buy another pair of eyeglasses, especially since they were having a difficult time feeding six children already.

Sometime later, the director of the Chinese orphanage was visiting the churches in America, and came to Paul's small church. The missionary thanked the people for their faithful support. "But most of all," he went on to say, "I want to thank you for the eyeglasses you sent last year. The government authorities came through and destroyed everything at the orphanage, including my eyeglasses. I could conceive of no way to replace my spectacles. Then your crates arrived, and in one of them was a pair of eyeglasses laying on the top of the clothing. When I tried them on, it was as though they were custom-made for me. Thank you for being a part of that miracle."

The congregation listened, but thought that the missionary must have confused their church with another. They didn't recall sending any eyeglasses. But Paul, sitting in the back of the sanctuary, had tears running down his cheeks, knowing that God had used him in an inadvertent but miraculous way. He prayed, "Lord **JESUS**, thank you for letting me lose my glasses, even though I was quite aggravated when it happened." Christians need to remember that "all things work together for good for those who love God" (Rom. 8:28). Even so-called accidents and losses can serve God's purposes, and become "perfect mistakes."

THE SHOOT-OUT AT THE O.K. CORRAL?

There have been many conflicting reports about what occurred at (or near) the Old Kindersley (O.K.) Corral in Tombstone, Arizona Territory on the afternoon of October 26, 1881. The town of Tombstone was so named because Ed Schieffelin, an amateur rock collector, had been told by his buddies that the only thing he was going to find in the rugged mountains was his own tombstone. He found silver instead. The silver-mining boomtown of Tombstone exploded in population in 1879, and like many frontier towns was characterized by raucous lawlessness. There was no love lost between the so-called "lawmen" and the renegade "cowboys," who were mostly just bandits. The thirty-second shootout just off Fremont Street, near the O.K. Corral, became the subject of much debate and legend.

I see some ecclesial similarities to this Old West incident. For centuries, we have observed gathered confines of mediocrity called "churches." They have not been conclaves of excellence and righteousness – but not hell-holes of hate, either. Everything was just "okay" as the church-goers went about their business of attempting to be nice to nice people, and thus preserve the status-quo of religiosity. The restrictive fences of religious rules and regulations kept the sincere people corralled into their respective holy huddles of denominated impiety.

The legalistic Law-men attempted to maintain order in the community, but the boomtown phenomenon of megachurches revealed rampant unruliness. The greed for silver created much animosity; so much so, that the younger "cowboys" were setting their aims for the Law-men. The turmoil was brought to a head in a deadly shootout at the "okay" corral, and when the smoke settled, the death-toll was legendary. All that exists today is a cemetery of tombstones, the R.I.P. assembly, and there is not much life in the religious graveyard.

JANUARY 20

GOD HATES RELIGION

Religion in any form is repugnant, offensive and reprehensible to God. God hates religion! The Triune God of Father, Son and Holy Spirit desires that all persons might come and participate in His loving community, but there is only one way to do so, and that is through the faith reception of the living Lord Jesus in a dynamic and vital interpersonal relationship. The accoutrements of religious "pomp and circumstance" have no place in the initiation or development of genuine relationship and intimacy with the living Lord Jesus; in fact, they will inevitably be a hindrance to personal knowledge of God in Christ.

Even in the religious structure of the Law-covenant that God designed for the Jews, the natural tendency of fallen man was to formulate a myriad of strictures to bind people in ever-tighter strait-jackets of "self-made religion" (Col. 2:23). The prophet Amos expressed God's disdain for all such religion when he spoke for God, "I hate, I reject your festivals, nor do I delight in your solemn assemblies. Even though you offer up to Me burnt offerings and your grain offerings, I will not accept *them*; Take away from Me the noise of your songs" (Amos 5:21-24). God hates and rejects the religion that binds people in pious self-effort, thinking they are doing something for God.

God's desire is that all human beings might be restored to the fullness of their intended humanity by the presence and function of **JESUS** within the spirit of every person. God's redemptive and restorative grace-action in the Person of His Son, Jesus Christ, is the divine new covenant arrangement whereby the triune God seeks to draw all mankind into intimate spiritual relationship with Himself. Yet, even Christ-ones, legitimate Christians, still seem to have the natural tendency to reduce the dynamic of Christ's life into religious regulations that are an abomination to God. God hates religion in every form.

THE VALLEY OF THE DRY BONES

The imagery of "the valley of the dry bones" has captured the imaginations of teachers and song-writers for centuries. James W. Johnson wrote the song, "Dem Dry Bones," (first recorded in 1928), explaining how Ezekiel connected the foot bone to the ankle bone to the shin bone to the knee bone to the thigh bone to the hip bone..., etc. "Dem bones, dem bones, gonna walk around; now hear the word of the Lord." A more contemporary reference to the "dry bones" was released in 2015 by Lauren Daigle, entitled, "Come Alive (Dry Bones)."

> As we call out to dry bones, "Come alive, come alive!"
> We call out to dead hearts, "Come alive, come alive!"
> Up out of the ashes, let us see an army rise.
> We call out to dry bones, "Come alive!"

Ezekiel first saw the vision of the dry bones (Ezek. 37:1-14), and recognized it as a portrayal of the condition of the nation of Israel. He had previously been given a prophesy of the rebirth of the nation (Ezek. 36), the fulfillment of which was eventually realized in the "holy nation" (I Pet. 2:9) of God's chosen people participating in the light of Christ.

Ezekiel's vision of "the valley of the dry bones" is often interpreted today as an image of the condition of the contemporary church – lifeless when it comes to a vital spiritual re-presentation of the living Lord Jesus. The vision goes on to indicate that God is going to breathe life (cf. Gen. 3:7) into the dry rattling bones. The breath (*pneuma*) of the Spirit must enter into the persons represented as skeletons, reinvesting them with the very life of God in human persons. This restoration from death to life cannot be accomplished by human ingenuity via reconstruction and revitalization plans (even revivals), but must be enacted by God enlivening people with the life of **JESUS** Christ.

JANUARY 22

PHILOSOPHICAL PONDERINGS

Everyone has good times and bad times, but it is the bad times that are the best times because they lead us into the crises of despair and doubt. In despair, we recognize our inability, and are led to repentance, exclaiming "I can't; only He can!" Doubt is a cul-de-sac wherein we recognize the only way out is to let Him do what He wants to do – the receptivity of His activity – the essence of faith. Despair and doubt are the springboards of repentance and faith, so the best bad times toss us back to the ultimate Good of God, who exclaims, "Let the good times begin!" His grace-dynamic is the life of the party.

Walking in the daylight of the sun is often regarded as the safest course of action. Perhaps not! In the daylight of the sun we choose our own course, and determine the safe actions of self-preservation. Such self-determination is the wide path that leads to death. Could it be that walking in the darkness brings us into the ultimate security of entrusting our souls and bodies to the light of the Son and the eternal safety of His life? As we live life forward, it may not seem so, but the 20/20 hindsight of God's directional leading allows us to advance trustfully into the darkness, not knowing what God is up to in our lives.

The past is water under the bridge. The future is but soap-bubbles of speculation. We must live in the present moment of the "now." To attempt to do otherwise is to build our lives on the shifting sands of "coulda been" and "wanna be." The divine One who gives meaning to all of life identifies Himself as the first-person singular in the continuous present of the "I AM," thus indicating that we can only meet and relate to Him where He is, in the "now." We cannot meet and relate to God *en masse* in the anonymity of a group, but only person-to-person and heart-to-heart as individuals, desirous of present-tense participation with the Divine who makes each moment come alive.

CHRISTIANITY IS CHRIST

I never cease to be amazed at the pathetically low spiritual I.Q.s that are so evident in the Christian community at-large. The institutional church has perceived itself to be primarily an educational institution to teach doctrine and ethics, but if the churches were held accountable to meet even a modicum of "learning outcomes," they would fail miserably and be subject to immediate closure. If you were to conduct an exit poll of those exiting the churches, and ask them only one simple question, "What is Christianity?" it would reveal an astonishing ignorance of what the church and the Christian life is all about.

Christianity is not a weekly ritual of going to the religious filling station to get recharged or refueled with enough spirit-gas to empower one for the next week. Christianity is not an entertainment venue wherein to experience the "fellowship of excitement." Christianity is not to be connected with any particular cultural features, nor any traditional religious worship rituals. Christianity was never intended to be a religion with accompanying doctrinal belief-systems, nor a system of morality with codified behavioral standards. Christianity is not an –ism of human thought, nor an ecclesiastical institution.

Christianity is Christ, the risen and living Lord **JESUS** dwelling within the human spirit of receptive individuals in order to re-present His life and character in the behavior of those identified as Christ-ones, and collectively in the Body of Christ, the Church. Paul explains that "the mystery of the gospel is Christ in you, the hope of glory" (Col. 1:27). Christianity is Christ-in-you-ity! "If any person does not have the Spirit of Christ *in their spirit*, they are none of His, *i.e. not a Christian*" (Rom. 8:9). On the other hand, the individual who has received **JESUS** Christ will experience "the Spirit *within* bearing witness with their *human* spirit that they are a child of God" (Rom. 8:16).

JANUARY 24

EXOUSIA

When Jesus spoke, the audience was "amazed at His teaching, for His message was with authority" (Lk. 4:32). The word "authority" is translated from the Greek word *exousia*, that is etymologically derived from two Greek words: *ek* = "out of"; *ousia* = "being." The audience recognized that Jesus had within Himself the power, dominion, and authority to make the declarations He was making. "Out of His own Being" as the very Son of God, He could speak and act with Divine authoritative power to implement what He was saying. He could do what He did because He was who He was. Out of His own Being, He acted as God.

When Jesus was giving final instructions to His disciples, He commissioned them, saying, "Go therefore and make disciples of all the nations, baptizing them in the name of the Father and the Son and the Holy Spirit, teaching them to observe all that I commanded you; and lo, I am with you always, even to the end of the age" (Matt. 28:19,20). He prefaced that commission by declaring, "All authority has been given to Me in heaven and on earth" (Matt. 28:18). The word "authority" once again translates the Greek word, *exousia*, because He was asserting that "out of His own divine Being," He could commission and control.

In defense of his life and ministry before King Agrippa at Ceasarea Maritima, Paul explained that on the road to Damascus he was knocked down, and the voice of the living Lord Jesus gave him his personal commission: "I am sending you to the Gentiles that "they may turn from darkness to light and from the dominion (*exousia*) of Satan to God, that they may receive forgiveness of sins" (Acts 26:18). Paul's words reveal what genuine spiritual conversion entails, a radical exchange from deriving "out of the spiritual being" of Satan, to deriving "out of the spiritual being" of God in Christ.

JANUARY 25

THESAURUS

Most readers are familiar with and have used Roget's *Thesaurus*. Many logophiles (those fond of words) regard Roget's *Thesaurus* as one of the three most important books ever printed in the English language (the *Bible*, Webster's *Dictionary*, and Roget's *Thesaurus*). Those three books have long been important to my studies, though now I access them digitally on the internet.

Dr. Peter Mark Roget (1779-1869) was a physician, scientist, and philologist who developed the *Thesaurus* early in his life (1805), but did not publish the book until forty-seven years later (1852). His objective was not just to identify synonyms and antonyms, but he sought to build a structure of all the categories of contrasts and opposites within the English language. Modern editions of Roget's *Thesaurus* have sometimes abandoned Roget's structure to simply put the synonyms and antonyms in dictionary form, but this sacrifices the foremost value of Roget's work. Roget's original structuring of English words into contrasted classification categories is a masterpiece of thought-organization and will prove valuable to all who are interested in the broad spectrum of contrasting human concepts.

The word *thesaurus* is a transliteration of the Greek word for "treasure," and Roget used it to entitle his "treasury of English words." The same Greek word is used in the biblical text of II Cor. 4:7 – "we have this *treasure* in earthen vessels, that the surpassing greatness of the glory may be of God and not of ourselves." What is the "treasure" that Paul referred to as inhabiting our physical bodies? The treasure (the *thesaurus*) in our earthen vessels is the Spirit of the living Lord **JESUS**, who gives reality and meaning to our being, revealing that we do not live for our own glory and self-aggrandizement, but to express the glorious character of God unto His glory.

JANUARY 26

AN ECCENTRIC INDIVIDUALIST

If you are not acquainted with Soren Kierkegaard (1813-1855), I want to take this opportunity to introduce you to this unique Christian brother. Born in Copenhagen, Denmark, his appearance, thoughts and actions were out of the ordinary. Most of his contemporaries thought he was weird, and most Danes to this day do not want to claim him as one of their own. The family name, Kierkegaard, means "church yard," and the grounds of many European churches were grave yards, so he was caricatured and parodied as a "dead head." The truth of the matter is, he was a spiritual giant of the Christian faith. Read a few of his written words, and see what you think:

- It belongs to the imperfection of everything human that man can only attain his desire by passing through its opposite." (*Journals*)
- This is one of the most crucial definitions for the whole of Christianity; that the opposite of sin is not virtue, but faith. (*The Sickness Unto Death)*
- Whether it is a help or a torment, I want only one thing, I want to belong to Christ, I want to be a Christian. (*Practice in Christianity*) •
- Life can only be understood backwards; but it must be lived forwards. (*Journals*)
- You cannot get the truth by capturing it, only by its capturing you. (*Journals*)
- Christendom in comparison with the Christianity of the New Testament is just playing Christianity. (*Attack on Christendom*)
- We are strangers and pilgrims in this world"! A Christian in the New Testament sense is literally a stranger and a pilgrim, he feels himself a stranger, and everyone involuntarily feels that this man is a stranger to him. (*Attack on Christendom*)
- God creates out of nothing. Wonderful you say. Yes, to be sure, but he does what is still more wonderful: He makes saints out of sinners. (*Journals*)

I warn you! Kierkegaard is not an easy read, but there is much to be mined in his writings, particularly in his *Journals.*

FEAR OF DEATH?

Many people (including Christian people) are quite uncomfortable speaking about death. It did not used to be that way. A century or two ago, people found the topic of death quite natural and socially acceptable, and discussed it at length. The topic of sexuality, however, was quite taboo and shunned from civil conversation. Now, we have turned it around the other way: the topic of sexuality is splattered on the billboards of our public media, and we openly discuss sexually aberrant behaviors as alternative lifestyles. Human dying has become the modern taboo and the verboten subject of our conversations today.

Many people have a deep fear of death and dying, and will go to great lengths and expense to attempt to find a way to avoid the inevitable. Most are aware of the common myth of Ponce de Leon and his alleged search for the "fountain of youth," to avoid or at least forestall death. A doctor advised me recently that "everyone wants to live longer," and was taken aback when I responded that longevity of physical life was not necessarily my objective, and I would therefore not need to purchase his touted life-extending products. The professionals of the world do not know what to do with someone who is not afraid to die.

The Son of God became a human being, in the person **JESUS**, accepting human mortality for the express purpose that He might die a death He did not deserve, to overcome the consequences of the death that all other human beings deserved due to sin. This He did, "that through death He might render powerless him who had the power of death, that is, the devil, and might free those who through fear of death were subject to slavery all their lives" (Heb. 2:14,15). Jesus accomplished the "death of death," and explained, "he who believes in Me will live even if he dies" (Jn. 11:25), and come to the place where "there will no longer be any death" (Rev. 21:4).

JANUARY 28

THE DOORWAY OF DEATH

What comes to your mind when you think about physical death? Is it walking off of a precipice into the great unknown? Is it like walking into a dark cave, and seeing a bright light. Many have shared their "near-death experiences" in articles, books and speeches. I really do not care to see or hear any more of them; they are irrelevant to me. I want to form my own personal images based on God's revelation (scriptural and personal). There will be a continuum of the life that I derive from the risen Lord Jesus, the eternal life that "cannot die." I will continue to be the "new creature" that I am in Christ, but I will be living in a new context without the hindrances of this world.

I imagine the doorway between physical death and heavenly existence something like this: I walk through a set of double-doors into an immense brightly lighted room. "Wow! I have never been here before. I like what I see. These are going to be some nice "digs.". Everything seems to be so perfect in this place. So many people interacting in harmony as they lovingly engage with one another. But it is that one Person that stands out in the entire room, as every person orients their attention to the One who is the source of all light and life. The presence of JESUS makes this place heavenly."

From this perspective, physical death is nothing to fear. I continue to live after the old physical body-house crumbles, deriving spiritual life from the One who is life (Jn. 11:25; 14:6). This allows the doorway of death to be an inviting and exciting opportunity to make a move to a new neighborhood, to participate in a change of scenery. Jesus doesn't change! My life "in Jesus" doesn't change. What changes then? Only the environmental context – from the earthly to the heavenly, and God accommodates that change by giving me a new house (II Cor. 5:1), suited to the neighborhood where I will be living forever.

IS HUMANITY PERMANENTLY SINFUL?

When God created human beings, male and female, He declared, "It is very good!" (Gen. 1:31). God was pleased with the being and function of the human creatures He had created. There was, and still is not, anything wrong with our humanness, which has three levels of functionality (spiritual, psychological – mental, emotional and volition – and physiological), allowing us to be choosing creatures capable of responding and relating to God by deriving God's character in our human behavior to the glory of God (cf. Isa. 43:7).

In the fourth century, Augustine developed a perverted form of Christian thought that explained that when Adam first sinned in the garden of Eden, the entirety of humanity became inherently corrupted, defiled, depraved, and defectively incapable of functioning as human beings (essentially subhuman), including the inability make free choices to respond to God's loving actions in Jesus Christ. This was theologically referred to as "original sin" that made all human beings inherently sinful – an intrinsic condition of fallen humanness that could never be resolved even when an "elect" person was made to become a Christian.

If a human being is permanently, inherently sinful (as so much of Christian theology maintains; cf. *Westminster Confession of Faith*), then the Christian gospel has been gutted of the freely chosen personal relationship that is promised through the Person of **JESUS** Christ and the power of the Holy Spirit. There is no opportunity for a spiritual exchange whereby an individual can be transformed from the spiritual condition and identity of being a "sinner" to the regenerated spiritual condition of being a "saint" by the indwelling presence of the "Holy One," the risen and living Lord Jesus. The apostle Paul wrote, "If any person is in Christ, he is a new creature; old things have passed away, behold, all things have become new" (II Cor. 5:17).

JANUARY 30

PARADIGMS

I woke up this morning thinking about "paradigms." No, not about a "pair of dimes" in my pants pocket that together constitute one nickel short of a quarter! I was thinking about the structure and formation of human thinking. Our English word "paradigm" is based on two Greek words: *para* = alongside; and *deigma* = to show or demonstrate. Human beings have different patterns by which they collect and connect common threads of thought into concept-bundles.

We all have multiple categories wherein we have developed clusters of paradigmatic opinions. These will include established attitudes about political issues and orientation (Republican or Democrat), educational philosophies and objectives, and general ideological preferences (whether progressive or conservative). In addition, most persons have a religious and/or spiritual paradigm of convictions about God and worship, as well as a scientific paradigm of how knowledge of the world around us is to be collected, and a social paradigm of how society should be regulated, including an economic paradigm of the best methods for doing business (capitalism or socialism).

Paradigms are not necessarily set in concrete. Human beings are certainly capable of changing their attitudes and opinions. When different evidence and ideas are set before us, we can compare them with our concept-bundles (paradigms), and perhaps engage in a "paradigm shift" to another perspective. The apostle Paul certainly had a radical paradigm shift when he moved from persecuting Christians (cf. Acts 22:4; 26:15; I Cor. 15:9) to become the "apostle of grace" to preach the grace-dynamic of the Christian faith in the living Lord **JESUS**. Our particular individual collection of paradigm clusters forms our "worldview," the perspective by which we evaluate everything transpiring in the world around us.

JANUARY 31

WORLDVIEW

There is much discussion these days about analyzing and developing one's worldview, the individual and collective perspectives by which we approach everything that is transpiring in the world around us. Our worldview is a composite of our philosophical perspectives and established attitudes, our paradigms of thought that become the prism through which orient ourselves to our environment.

The perspective of natural man, the secular or humanistic worldview, generally fails to take God into account when evaluating what is transpiring in the world. Humans are regarded as independent beings, rather than derivative creatures designed to derive their being and function from the Creator God. Employing deified human reason, humans are regarded as the final arbiters of collective progress toward utopian objectives.

There are some who advocate a "Christian worldview," but this usually comprises an amalgamated "Christian-religion worldview," that is actually a secular worldview with a veneer of Christian terminology varnished over humanistic perspectives.

Instead of what the religionists call a "Christian worldview," I would encourage Christian people to develop a "Christ in you as your Life worldview," that recognizes that the risen and living Lord Jesus dwells within the spirit of a Christian, and everything we think and do as a Christian should derive from the "mind of Christ" (I Cor. 2:16) within us. As Christ-ones (Christians), we view the world-system as the antithetical antagonist of the kingdom of Christ. Recognizing that Satan is "the ruler of this world" (Jn. 12:31; 14:30; 16:11; II Cor. 4:4)), we view the fallen world from a "Christ-perspective," and operate within that world from the grace-dynamic of the activity of the risen Christ operating through us.

FEBRUARY 1

WHEN DOING RIGHT IS WRONG

Christian religion, like all religion, is built upon the false premises of the "believe right" and "do right" performance of mankind in order to "be right" before God. The old-covenant Jewish religion of law-performance was instituted to reveal the inability of the Hebrew people to "do right" in a manner pleasing to God. They ended up "doing what was right in their own eyes" (Deut. 12:8; Judg. 17:6; Prov. 21:2) – i.e. self-righteousness. Christian religion is rampant with such "do right" performance righteousness. Christians are encouraged to study their Bibles to find the "right thing to do," and then "do it" obediently. No wonder Christian people are afflicted with a prevailing attitude of defeatism!

The apostle Paul wrote, "if righteousness *comes* through the Law, then Christ died needlessly" (Gal. 2:21). If righteousness before God can be generated by our performance, i.e. self-righteousness, then the vicarious death of Jesus Christ on the cross for the sins of all mankind in order to make human beings righteous was an unnecessary redundancy. As one pastor stated, "if a man can make himself righteous by what he does or does not do, then Jesus died *for the fun of it*!" The very thought of such should make any genuine Christian person cringe!

Paul's confidence was "not in having a righteousness of his own derived from the Law, but the righteousness which comes from God on the basis of faith" (Phil. 3:9). God is righteous (Isa. 45:21), and He sent His Son, "the Righteous One" (Acts 22:14). In receiving the Spirit of Christ, we are "made righteous" (Rom. 5:19; II Cor. 5:21) and given the grace-dynamic to express the righteous character of Christ as we are "filled with the fruit of righteousness which comes through **JESUS** Christ" (Phil. 1:11). "The righteousness of God is revealed from faith to faith" (Rom. 1:17), and such faith is the deriving of righteous spiritual condition and behavioral expression from the living Christ.

FEBRUARY 2

WHY DID JESUS COME TO EARTH AND DIE?

The standard answer among Christians is that Jesus came to earth as a human being to die and save us from our sins. That is true. It is not inaccurate. The angel told Joseph, for example, that "you shall call His name Jesus, for He will save His people from their sins" (Matt. 1:21). Jesus explained the purpose of His death during the last supper with His disciples, "My blood is poured out for the forgiveness of sins" (Matt. 26:18). At the core of the truths of the Christian faith is the fact that Jesus died on the cross of Calvary as the divine Redeemer and Savior in order to take the death-consequences of human sin upon Himself.

Allow me to push the envelope a little farther, and state, "Jesus came to earth as a human being and died on the cross in order to save us – yes, from our sins, but also *from our righteousness*." That is a truth that many Christians have not considered. They have not expanded their concept of sin to include every expenditure of self-effort that attempts to perform acts of human righteousness before God. One of the primary sins of Christians is to conceive of Christianity as a religion wherein they are to commit themselves to the performance of righteousness – self-righteousness! – the opinion that we can self-generate and perform righteous character that satisfies God.

God is not pleased and thrilled with our human self-righteousness. God told Isaiah (64:6), "All your righteous deeds are as a dirty rag" (the side-note in many bibles indicates that this Hebrew word means "a menstrual cloth"). Paul explained that the righteousness that comes from performing the Law, he counted as "dung," desiring instead "the righteousness that comes from God on the basis of faith" (Phil. 3:6-9). "Christ is the end of the performance of righteousness to everyone who believes" (Rom. 10:4), for the Righteous One, **JESUS**, "manifests His righteous character by faith" (Rom. 6:13).

FEBRUARY 3

TRINITARIAN MONOTHEISM

Many people attempt to lump together the monotheistic religions of the world, often indicating that the religions of Judaism, Islam and Christianity all believe in and worship the same singular monotheistic God. Deeper awareness of the uniqueness of the Christian faith reveals that Jesus and the New Testament writers definitively explained the singularity and unity of the Godhead in the relational interaction of the diverse personages and functions of the Father, Son and Holy Spirit. Such "Trinitarian monotheism" is the unique theology of the Christian faith.

The early councils of the Church sought to explicate this uniqueness of Christian thought in standardized creedal statements in order to protect and preserve the clarity of Christian theological understanding. At the Council of Nicea (A.D. 325), Athanasius (from Alexandria, Egypt) prevailed over Arius (from Libya) in the assertion that Jesus is the *homoousion* (from Greek *homo* = same; *ousia* = being), i.e. the same co-essential Being as the Father God. Arius was contending that Jesus, the Son, was brought into being by the Father ("there was a time when He was not; then he was begotten and became a son"), and was henceforth *homoiousion* (Greek *homoi* = similar; *ousia* = being), i.e. of similar being to God the Father. (Thus, the dictum about an "*i*ota of difference.") The interpretation of Arius was determined to be heretical, and not Christian understanding.

The Nicene Creed was amended in A.D. 381 at the Council of Constantinople to clarify that the Holy Spirit was equally part of the essential relational oneness of the Trinitarian God. When the Nicene Creed is repeated in the worship of contemporary Western churches, it is the revised version that is utilized. It is important for Christians to continue to affirm the co-essentiality of Father, Son, and Holy Spirit, for if **JESUS** is not God, there is no eternal salvation for mankind.

FEBRUARY 4

IS THE CHURCH A BUILDING?

Many teachers have declared that "the church is not a building." We need to consider the etymology of some Christian terminology. The word most commonly translated into English as "church" from the Greek new covenant literature is the word *ekklesia*, meaning "an assembly of people called out to consider an issue of public interest together." The word was used for the assembly of the Hebrews "in the wilderness" (Acts 7:38). Luke used the word for the public gathering, a town meeting, of the Ephesians (Acts 19:32). There is no record of the Greek word *ekklesia* used in early historical or biblical writings to refer to a religious church building. It was always an assembly or a gathering of interested persons.

The English word "church," as used for several centuries now in our English New Testaments to translate the Greek word *ekklesia*, is etymologically derived from the Germanic word *kirche*, that did refer to a church building, and was the basis of the Scottish word for a church building – "kirk." So, etymologically the English word "church" *does* have reference to a building, despite the common protestations to the contrary.

We would be better served if we avoided the word "church," and translated the Greek word *ekklesia* throughout the New Testament as "the assembly," or as William Tyndale did in the first English New Testament (A.D. 1526) as "congregation." Why was it changed to "church" in later English translations? Because the Anglican ecclesiastical authorities insisted on maintaining the usage of the word "church" to preserve their institutions, and the elevated status of their positions in the minds of the people. The instructions to the translators of the *King James Bible* in A.D. 1604 mandated that the ecclesiastical word "church" be used instead of the word "congregation." What a mess we have made in referring to the collective "Body of **JESUS** Christ."

FEBRUARY 5

AN EVANGELICAL MISEMPHASIS?

In their evangelistic endeavors, evangelicals often tell distraught and seeking souls, "The solution to your problems is to go to church, and there you will find peace for your soul." I find that to be a misleading misstatement. Should we rather be telling persons fraught with the pain of their problems and concerned about their relationship with God, "Jesus is the only Savior who can make a person safe from the dysfunction of sin in order to experience the freedom of deriving life and character from God?

Perhaps the zeal and zest for evangelism in some evangelical churches is a misplaced emphasis, concealing improper objectives to build an elitist empire that strokes some pastor's ego, and wins denominational accolades for the highest percentage of growth and highest membership numbers. Is evangelism to be regarded as a procedural methodology for building churches? After Peter confessed Jesus as the promised Messiah, Jesus said, "Upon this rock (of confessed faith and receptivity of Me), I will build My *ecclesia* (My congregation and assembly of Christ-ones), and the Satanic onslaught will not prevail or overcome them" (Matt. 16:18 paraphrased). Jesus said that HE would build His *ecclesia* (His collective spiritual Body that we have traditionally called "His Church), and that not via procedural programs of evangelistic persuasion.

Religious teachers have often referred to what is called the "Great Commission," using Jesus' words as a mandate for evangelism? "As you are going (wherever your life might take you), encourage people to be followers and learners of Christ (disciples), ...and lo, I am with you always" (Matt. 28:19,20 - paraphrased). Is this really a dictate for evangelistic extension and church-building, or is it consistent with the words of St. Francis of Assisi, "Share Christ wherever you go, and if necessary use words." We are to re-present **JESUS** in all that we do.

FEBRUARY 6

DO HUMANS HAVE A SIN-NATURE?

Reference to one's "sin-nature" in Christian conversations is almost universal. Christians of every stripe and denomination refer to one's "sin-nature," despite the fact that the phrase cannot be found in any properly translated version of the Bible (ex. not in KJB, ESV, or NASB). The *Encyclopedia of Philosophy* suggests that the word 'nature" is so imprecise and ambiguous that it is best avoided in all philosophical and anthropological discussions. So where did Christian conversation latch on to this phrase "sin-nature"? Once again, it traces back to the misconceptions about "original sin" by Augustine in the fourth century.

Augustine's teaching of "original sin," a thesis wherein sinfulness is attributed to all humanness via the seminal transmission of sin through every generation from Adam onward, pervades Christian thought. Thus, it is alleged, sin became intrinsic to "human nature," and human beings can never be saved or relieved from such condition, or restored to God's intention.

Despite the abundance of references to "human nature, sin nature, Adamic nature, fallen nature, old nature, new nature," etc. in the vocabulary of Christian religion, there are no equivalent phrases in the original text of the Greek New Testament. Neither is the phrase "old man" (Rom. 6:6; Eph. 4:24; Col. 3:10) equivalent to the phrase "sin-nature." Some have mistakenly translated the Greek word *sarx*, meaning "flesh," as "sin-nature" (cf. Rom. 7:18,25 - NIV). The "flesh that sets its desire against the Spirit" (Gal. 5:17) is better understood as the residual patterns of sin-tendencies, the "fleshly desires" or "desires of the flesh" (cf. Eph. 2:3; II Pet. 2:10,18) that remain in the soul of regenerate persons. Biblical usages of the word "nature" seem to indicate that we were spiritually "by nature, children of wrath" (Eph. 2:3), but by spiritual regeneration Christians have become "partakers of the divine nature" (II Peter 1:4) – **JESUS** Christ in us!

FEBRUARY 7

TRUST

I recall several occasions in the parenting process when one of our children (we had five children) would complain when I would not allow them to participate in some activity they wanted to be involved in with their friends. "Why do you not trust me?" they would question. I would explain that "trust" is something that is built upon a foundation of reasonable expectation that a person will act in accord with the pattern of previous behavior. "Trust is built on a track-record" is the phrase that my children heard me say on numerous occasions. They were seldom content with my explanation, for the myopic short-sightedness of youth does not want to allow for the time it takes to build a pattern of behavior (especially after a breakdown in consistency).

As Christians, we are God's children and are now called to trust God. There is no problem with "track-record" when it comes to God. God is faithful. He is "the same yesterday, today, and forever" (Heb. 13:8). The Psalmist writes, "Your faithfulness is throughout all generations; You established the earth, and it stands" (Ps. 119:90). Paul writes, "God is faithful, through whom you were called into fellowship with His Son, Jesus Christ our Lord" (I Cor. 1:9).

Christians are to develop the subjective confidence that trusting God's way and God's grace is the best way for our lives. But, like my children, we have the tendency to want to "go our own way" and "do our own thing." Solomon writes, "Trust in the LORD with all your heart and lean not on your own understanding (Prov. 3:5). We either trust God, or we trust in ourselves and the world around us. "There is a way that seems right unto man, but the end thereof is death" (Prov. 14:12). When we trust in ourselves, we eventually and inevitably run into the wall of our own insufficiency, having to say, "I can't; only You can; I'll trust You." Such trust is essential to any genuine relationship of love.

PERSONAL IDENTITY

From the beginning of time, human beings have been asking, "Who am I?" and "Why am I?" A natural tendency of mankind is to attempt to identify their identity by what they do in life. "I am a carpenter" or "I am a doctor" – their identity is formed by their career. Others seek to find their identity in their associations. "I belong to this fraternity or sorority" or "I am a member of Who's Who in America." Many try to build their identity on their monetary assets. "I am a multi-millionaire" or "My portfolio is well invested." "I live in a mansion, and drive a Maserati." Still others try to construct their identity on their physical or mental abilities. "I am a star athlete." "I was valedictorian of my class."

All of these foundations of personal identity can fail a person. Careers terminate as we grow older. Friendship and associations can sour and turn into rejection. Monetary assets can decline quickly in a recession. Physical property can burn or be blown away. Physical and mental abilities diminish with natural aging. If these should occur, does one lose their identity? If we suffer the loss of all these things, do we draw a blank when we ask, "Who am I?" or do we have a personal identity that can withstand the loss of all physical, social, and material considerations?

The deepest sense of personal identity is to be found in spiritual, not physical or psychological criteria. In the core of one's being, in the spirit, we have the possibility of a permanent identity that can transcend the externalities of life. This is not a self-sovereign identity ("I am someone because I am me!"), but a spiritually derived identity based on the presence of an indwelling spirit, either "the spirit that dwells in the sons of disobedience" (Eph. 2:2) or the Spirit of God in Christ (cf. Rom. 8:9). For the Christ-one, the Christian, our identity is formed by the spiritual presence of the living Lord **JESUS** in our human spirit. Christ is the basis of the Christian's personal, spiritual identity.

FEBRUARY 9

ARE YOU SUPERSTITIOUS?

Everyone probably has a few superstitious inclinations – some reservations or suspicions about certain actions, objects, ideas or people. Common cultural superstitions include an aversion to walking under a ladder, observing a black cat, carrying a rabbit's foot, knocking on wood, crossing one's fingers, or what might happen on Friday the thirteenth. Some athletes wear a "lucky" piece of clothing; brides perpetuate the superstition of wearing "something old, something new, something borrowed, something blue," and catching the bride's bouquet is superstitiously regarded as a sign that you are the next to be married.

Superstitions are often connected to magical ideas of cause and effect – a linear thought-process that reasons "*if* one does this, *then* that might/will happen." By such irrational reasoning, superstitious people think that by their "works" (what they do or do not do) they can maintain control over their lives – that "luck" will be on their side. Christians do not believe in "luck;" they believe in God's providential action through the Son, Jesus Christ. The apostle Paul wrote, "Have nothing to do with silly myths (old wives' tales believed by the gullible), but train yourself in godliness (derived from God)" (I Tim. 4:7)

Religious people are particularly susceptible to pious superstitions: putting rosary beads on the mirror to keep one from car accidents; believing that if they have a "quiet time" by reading the Bible and praying, God will be pleased and bless them; attending church services and participating in the Eucharist as a "means of God's grace"; acquiring theological knowledge to "have the mind of Christ." Paul may have had such in mind when he wrote of the elementary principles of the world, "do not handle, do not taste, do not touch, things destined to perish" (Col. 2:20-22). Christians should eschew superstitious thoughts and actions, and derive all from the living Lord **JESUS**.

CONSPIRACY THEORIES

Yes, Satan is the "ruler of this world" (Jn. 12:31; 16:11). Yes, the devil is up to no good; he is the Evil One (II Thess. 3:3; I Jn. 2:13,14)! But it seems that many Christians are giving the diabolic deceiver too much credit, and failing to recognize that by the finished work of Jesus Christ, He has "disarmed the rulers and authorities" (Col. 2:15) of evil, and "destroyed the works of the devil" (I Jn. 3:8), having gained the victory over Satan on the cross. Yes, he is still an adversary and "prowls around like a roaring lion, seeking to devour" (I Pet. 5:8) and deceive (II Jn. 1:7; Rev. 12:9), and he seems to have deceived many gullible Christians to superstitiously speculate about conspiracy theories.

Conspiracy theories are speculative interpretations that the events of the world are being manipulated by powerful people for evil purposes. They are often fear-mongering falsehoods, similar to the "chicken little syndrome" of paranoid claims of coming catastrophe (i.e. "the sky is falling"). The attraction of sharing conspiracy theories is the pride of people who think they have figured out behind-the-scene secrets, and have a "special knowledge" of what is going on. They are just focusing on the negative of Satan's evil, rather than on the positive of God's good.

The Bible does record some incidents of conniving conspiracy (cf. II Samuel 15:12; Acts 23:12) among men, but the foremost conspiracy is on the spiritual plane where Satan conspires to counter and negate all that God does in **JESUS** Christ by the Spirit. Christians must recognize that "Greater is He who is in you, than he who is in the world" (I Jn. 4:4). God is in charge! "The gates of hell" (Matt. 16:18) will not prevail against what God is doing. Isaiah explained, "Do not call conspiracy everything that these people call conspiracy; do not fear what they fear, and do not dread it. The Lord Almighty is the one you are to regard as holy, he is the one you are to fear" (Isa. 8:12,13).

FEBRUARY 11

"LOVERS OF SELF"

In his advice to his young associate, Timothy, the apostle Paul explains that "difficult times will come," first mentioning that there will be those who are "lovers of self" (II Timothy 3:2). Without getting into any discussion of whether these are the "last days," we do observe that the narcissistic attitude, "It's all about me; I have to look out for #1 – myself," is obviously rampant in our culture today. There has been a progressive increase in the me-ism wherein people of all ages are encouraged to "be assertive" and "be all you can be." Some have speculated that twenty percent of people today may be "pathological narcissists," as identified by the American Psychiatric Association (*DSM-5*).

Selfishness is not a new phenomenon. It began with the first human couple in the Garden of Eden when they disobediently chose to go their own way by eating from the "tree of the knowledge of good and evil" (Gen. 2:9). In rejecting God's plan that they should be derivative creatures partaking of the "tree of life" (divine life), they chose the Satanic alternative (and lie) of setting themselves up as their own center of reference whereby they could allegedly self-determine what is "good and evil" on the basis of their own self-centered, narcissistic whims and desires. Narcissism is named after a Greek mythological creature, Narcissus, who thought himself so lovely that he stared at his image in a pool and committed suicide due to unrequited love.

Narcissists are usually obsessed with the way they look, exaggerate their own achievements, think their way is always right, and always want their own way. They are controlling, unpredictable, hypocritical, and self-righteous. Before we throw too many stones, it must be admitted that we all have areas of self-concern and residual patterns of selfishness identified as "the flesh" (Gal. 5:16,17). The Spirit of **JESUS** in the Christian instills humility and prompts interest in others" (Phil. 2:3,4).

FEBRUARY 12

SPIRITUAL ABSTRACTIONS

Since spiritual realities are beyond the parameters of empirical observance and scientific evaluation, they are often regarded as unverifiable abstractions of speculative mythology by the scientific community. The foremost fallacy of the scientific method is to claim they seek to know (Latin *scientia*) what is real, yet they self-limit their search to the physical and material world, making the absurd assertion that if anything is not empirically observable by the five physical senses of human beings it does not exist. Thus, God, angels, and even love, are projected as hypothetical and nonexistent. The physical is the only reality.

Spiritual realities are no less true or real, but exist in another sphere of understanding. The Christian gospel pertains to the spiritual realities of how the God who is Spirit (Jn. 4:24) sent His Son, Jesus Christ, in tangible human form (Jn. 1:14; Phil. 2:7,8) in order to restore the relational presence of His divine presence in mankind. One young child, who could only conceptualize spiritual abstractions in concrete terms, said, "I opened the door and let Jesus come and live in my heart, and then I threw away the key." Children and many contemporary adults often require some sense of tangibilizing in order to formulate and conceptualize spiritual realities in their minds.

The natural tendency of fallen man is to externalize, to deal with tangibles rather than intangibles, to conceptualize in the concrete rather than the abstract. The question has been asked: "Are the ordinances of baptism and the Lord's Supper tangibilized and externalized activities, designed to accommodate the natural tendency of mankind to need such concrete signposts and recollections to convey abstract concepts of God's overwhelming and participatory presence?" Religion tends to inculcate additional physical activities to bring the spiritual abstractions of Christianity into tangibilized form and routine (i.e. ritual).

FEBRUARY 13

THE CHURCH GROWTH MOVEMENT

What is known as "the Church Growth Movement" dates back to the 1960s, and was spawned by the missiological thinking of Donald McGavran, who founded the School of World Mission at Fuller Theological Seminary in Pasadena, California in 1965. As a third-generation Christian missionary, he saw the ineffectiveness of traditional mission endeavors that often established a "mission station or compound" in a foreign location, and then ventured out of their "bunker" to share the gospel message with persons outside of the walls. He recognized the sociological importance of building social and relational bridges with the people, in order meet them where they are and allow the gospel to relate to their real cultural and personal needs.

Taking his mission experience as a springboard, McGavarn sought to apply some of the same principles of cultural relevance to how American churches share the gospel. The church of Jesus Christ is not to be isolated in separated bomb-shelters where people gather in their holy huddles of like-mindedness. The Church Growth Movement degenerated, however, when American leaders emphasized methods, formulas, procedures and techniques that led to numerical success: "Just-get-'em-in-the-doors," and count the "warm bodies," evaluating church growth by attendance numbers. Church success was evaluated statistically – by the big Bs of buildings, budgets and baptisms.

Christianity is not cultural inattention or accommodation. Christianity is the reality of the living **JESUS** functioning in the lives of people within any cultural context. Beyond just converting people, the church must pay attention to God's intent for the restoration of humanity by the development of character derivation among Christian people, allowing the life and character of the Lord **JESUS** Christ to be expressed in behavior. That needs to be our missional intent in the church today.

FEBRUARY 14

"LOVE IS FROM GOD"

We have a rather loosey-goosey understanding of "love" in contemporary English usage. We love cars and clothing, food and friends, movies and marriage partners; and, of course, we love God, country, and all our family members, etc. What's the difference? First, we must recognize that the highest level of love is not a self-generated human sentiment or feeling. It is a volitional choice to express divine love, the highest good of another person, without thought of what we get out of it.

The Greek language of the New Testament had at least four different words to describe "love." The word *storge* was utilized for familial love, the affection of parent for child, child for parent, and other family interactions. A second word, *phileo*, referred to the deep friendship of brotherly love, and is the root of Philadelphia, "the city of brotherly love." The Greek word *eros*, from which we get the English word "erotic," pertained to a self-satisfying, often physical love, including sexual love. The highest form of love was expressed in the Greek word *agape*, used to explain God's love, a pure unselfish and unconditional love always extended outwards for others.

Christians are commanded to love (*agape*) others as God loves us (cf. Jn. 13:34). How can we do that? It is only possible for a human being to love another as God commanded when that person knows God and His character of love. Every Christian has "the love (*agape*) of God poured out within their heart by the Holy Spirit who was given to them" (Rom.5:5), and can express God's love as "the fruit of the Spirit" (cf. Gal. 5:22). The apostle John explains, "let us love (*agape*) one another, for *love is from God*; and everyone who loves is born of God and knows God" (I Jn. 4:7). Love is from God (*ek Theos*, "out of God," derived from God), and is only "brought into being" in us by the presence of **JESUS'** life and character in a spiritual new birth.

FEBRUARY 15

IS CHRISTIANITY A RELIGION?

The predominant opinion of people you might ask this question of would probably affirm that Christianity is a religion. The popular understanding is that Christianity is categorized as one of the major religions of the world, as any textbook of world religions would explain. There is no doubt that there is a phenomenon called "Christian religion," but the question that must be asked is whether God ever intended for Christianity to be a religion. Jesus did **not** say, "I came that you might have a religion, and practice it more faithfully." Rather, He said, "I came that you might have life, and have it more abundantly" (Jn 10:10).

From the perspective of a natural man who does not understand spiritual things (I Cor. 2:14), Christianity is a religion as etymologically defined from the Latin *religare*, meaning "to bind or tie" to something (an idea, object, institution, etc.). The Christian religion certainly binds people to ethical rules and regulations, and worship rituals. From the perspective of God's intention to spiritually restore humanity through the Person and work of His Eternal Son, Jesus Christ, Christianity is not religion, but the opportunity to receive the divine presence of the Son of God into one's spirit in order to be humanity as God intended.

To properly identify Christianity, it is necessary to disconnect Christianity from religion and understand the integral connection to the Person and life of Jesus Christ. A Christian is a "Christ-one," identified as being "in Christ." Christianity is best understood as Christ-in-you-ity. Only by the indwelling Spirit of Christ can one understand the spiritual reality of Christianity. (Rom. 8:9; I Cor. 2:11-13; II Cor. 13:5). Christianity is the Person of the risen and living Lord **JESUS**, dwelling by His Spirit in the human spirit of a person receptive to such spiritual reality by faith. There is no genuine Christianity without a personal and experiential relationship with the living **JESUS**.

FEBRUARY 16

RELIGIOUS PROGRAM SPECIALISTS

A leader in a major Christian parachurch organization was explaining her responsibilities in the ministry-organization. She was designated as the "Program Specialist," tasked with the development of the most effective methods and programs to implement and manage the projects that were determined to be the objectives of the organization. I was appalled and had to suppress my gag-reflex, to think that so-called "Christian ministry" was being conducted with a big-business model of humanly conceived objectives, utilizing humanistic management methods to accomplish their projected results of success.

The humanistic world-system is all abuzz about analyzing which methods, techniques, and procedures will best achieve the successful completion of their self-projected goals. So much time and energy is spent in developing project management methodologies to calculate and design the best "programs" to arrive at the goals that they have designated as self-determined "success." Christian ministry, however, cannot be conducted on the world's success methods. Genuine Christian ministry will operate exactly 180 degrees opposite from the humanistic models. Yet, the contemporary churches roll out "program" after "program" to implement and achieve what they have self-designated to be their standard of statistical "success."

The Body of Christ was never intended to operate with self-determined objectives or self-generated planning and orchestration as the means of accomplishment. Christian success is not to be measured by statistical numbers. Christian ministry is Holy Spirit conceived and achieved. Christian ministry is to be derived ministry – not what we think we can do for God, but what the living Lord **JESUS** prompts and directs that we engage in, and empowers to accomplish by His Spirit. The Body of Christ is not goal-oriented, but God-oriented.

FEBRUARY 17

LOVE BEYOND REASON

Bob was my roommate in college. He was a year older than I was, but was taking five years to finish, and I was doing it in four years. We did many things together, including buying a boat and skiing on the lake, as well as taking a trip to Canada and the 1967 World's Fair in Montreal, continuing on to New York City, Washington D.C., St. Louis, and back to Kansas. When we graduated from college, Bob joined the U.S. Navy, and I went to Edinburgh, Scotland for seminary. When I returned from Scotland and became a youth pastor in a large church, I gave Bob's address to one of the college girls in the youth group. They began corresponding, and a year or two later were married. They lived in California, and it was only a few more years before I moved with my wife and children to the Golden State also.

In January, 2016 Bob was working at a print shop in Del Mar, and just half an hour before quitting time he slumped over his desk and quit breathing. He was in cardiac arrest. The paramedics arrived within minutes and transported him to Scripps Hospital in La Jolla. They cooled his body to keep his brain from swelling. I sat with his wife at the hospital and rehab center every day for almost a month. Many days, I wondered whether he would live. He survived with only a few cognitive difficulties, and came home to be with his wife. Then, just a few weeks later, his wife collapsed of a heart attack, and died a few days later. I stood with him during her dying days, assisting him in the decision to remove life support, and then conducted her memorial service.

To this day, I still try to spend time with Bob every couple of weeks. He has a few memory problems, but we run errands, go for car rides and hikes, and even went to a NASCAR race. Over and over he exclaims, "I can't believe you have stood with me all the way. Why?" I usually reply, "That's what friends are for – love doesn't have to have any reasons."

FEBRUARY 18

RELIGIOUS BUSY-NESS

We have all heard the expression of being as "busy as a bee." A brief observation of a honey-bee hive reveals a buzz of frenetic activity, but despite its looking like confusing chaos, it is a well-organized cooperative effort toward God's intended objective for such bees – to produce honey.

Many people in our modern world live very busy lives. People are rushing and hurrying and trying to find meaning in their lives. Some of them are engaging in busy-ness trying to fill the empty spaces inside of them. Others seem to be deceived in thinking that because they are busy, they are doing what they should be doing, confusing activity with accomplishment. There is a mind-set in the world that equates activity with significance, rushing with meaning, and busy-ness with productivity. The busier one is, the more important and successful one must be.

Then, in the midst of all that, such a person may be introduced to religious activity. Religion seeks to get people "involved" and "committed" in "religious busy-ness." To what end? Often the end objective is simply to build the statistical numbers of the organization, and enhance the reputation of the pastor-leader. Such results-oriented busy-ness produces nothing but "dead works" (Heb. 6:1; 9:14). "There is a way that seems right unto man, but the end thereof is death" (Prov. 14:12; 16:25).

The apostle Paul explained that he was "not like a man running aimlessly" or "fighting like a man beating the air" (I Cor. 9:26). There is a world of difference between someone who is shadow-boxing and someone who is "fighting the good fight" (I Tim. 1:18; II Tim. 4:7) The "good fight of faith" (I Tim. 6:12) is being receptive to engagement in what God wants to do in and through us. The activity is what **JESUS** wants to do by the empowering of His Spirit to express His character in us to His glory.

FEBRUARY 19

RELIGIOUS WORKERS

I overheard a couple of young pastors conversing about all they were doing as they engaged in their endeavors of "working for the Lord." There was no sense of their being instruments of the living Christ to allow Him to minister through them by the "gifts of the Holy Spirit" (I Cor. 12:1,4,9). Rather, with an air of false humility, they were proudly boasting of all they were accomplishing, seemingly thinking that God, as well as all their parishioners, should be extremely pleased with their efforts. It was all I could do to quell my reaction that regarded them as somewhere between pathetic and appalling.

These fellows weren't genuine "ministers" of the gospel; they were merely humanistic do-gooders, camouflaged in the guise of professional, clerical religiosity. Now we must admit that these types of persons do accomplish some "good works" for the good of humankind, but what they do is often driven by self-promotion and their own feel-good motivations. There is a great chasm of difference between the "relative good" connected to "the tree of the knowledge of good and evil" (Gen. 2:9,17) in the Garden of Eden, and the "absolute good" that is derived only from the character of God as He expresses His divine goodness.

John explained, "the one who does good is of (Greek *ek* - derives what he does from) God" (III Jn. 11). "Absolute good" is only derived from God. It is not a character trait we can generate or produce as a human virtue in our human endeavors. The rich young ruler came to Jesus inquiring, "Good Master, what must I do to inherit eternal life?" (Mk. 10:17; Lk. 18:18). Jesus responded, "Why do you call me good? No one is good except God alone" (Mk. 10:18). If you are not willing to recognize that I am God, and that all divine goodness is derived from God, then don't address Me with your religious accolades of goodness. Genuine good is only determined by its source in the character of God.

FEBRUARY 20

CHRISTIANS AND SUFFERING

Let's face it! Physical life involves suffering. It is impossible to live in the context of this world-system without experiencing personal suffering. Suffering is a collateral part of the cosmic spiritual battle between God and Satan, good and evil. Fallen humanity operates with the rejective character of Satan, and this issues forth in suffering for those affected by such. Jesus explained, "In this world, you will have tribulation" (Jn. 16:33). "If they persecuted Me, they will persecute you" (Jn. 15:20). Paul wrote, "we kept telling you in advance that we were going to suffer affliction" (I Thess. 3:4).

Some have argued that human suffering is an argument against a loving God. How can an all-loving, all-powerful God allow suffering? I would argue, however, that human suffering verifies the loving grace of God, whereby we can appreciate that we are free choosing creatures, with an opportunity to rely on and derive all from God in the midst of difficult times. We are drawn into prayerful communion with God in the midst of suffering, and learn to recognize the possibility of intimate personal relationship with God and others. In the midst of community, we see our need to "bear one another's burdens" (Gal. 6:2).

Instead of viewing suffering as something to eschew or decry, Christians should appreciate what God is doing in the midst of human suffering. Many who have suffered greatly, have in retrospect said, "It was the best thing that could have happened to me! I learned so much in the midst of the pain." Suffering compels us to evaluate what is most important beyond the temporal and physical. As Paul wrote to the Corinthians, "Momentary, light affliction is producing for us an eternal weight of glory beyond all comparison" (II Cor. 4:17). After just being pummeled with stones, Paul said, "Through many tribulations we must enter the kingdom of God" (Acts 14:22).

FEBRUARY 21

DOING THINGS FOR JESUS

Many sincere Christians have been taught that it is their duty to "live like Jesus," "love like Jesus," "work for Jesus," and "serve Jesus." They often sing the chorus:

> Living for Jesus, a life that is true;
> Striving to please Him in all that I do;
> Living for Jesus wherever I am;
> Doing each duty in His holy name...

It may come as a shock to many such Christians, but they need to be told: "**STOP** trying to be like Jesus! **QUIT** trying to live the Christian life. **CEASE** all of your religious busyness. Cut it out! Jesus is not in the business of employing more workers for His taskforce."

Religion (yes, Christian religion) has, for the most part, presented a false gospel to people. Beginning with the humanistic premise that human beings are "independent selves" who can appropriate the benefits of Jesus for themselves and act on their self-resolve, they continue with a deistic "separated concept" of the Christian being stuck here on earth, and Jesus is somewhere else (up in heaven? ...imprisoned within the walls of the church building?). Then, they admonish these poor Christian dupes to work their hearts out attempting to do what they never can do. "Doing things for Jesus" is simply self-righteousness. God is not impressed with a dirty Kotex (cf. Isa 64:6) or a pile of human feces (Phil. 3:8), both of which represent death (cf. Prov. 14:12; 16:25). Everything you do, thinking you are doing something for Jesus, is a hindrance that mucks up His re-presentation in you.

Jesus doesn't need anything done for Him. He is the dynamic of all good things. Christian activity is always and only Christ in action. **JESUS** simply wants to live out His life in you.

JUDGMENT

Many people do not want to think of God as a Judge engaging in judgment. But to fail to do so is to make God less than His human creatures. The Greek word for "judgment" is *krino*. The word means "to decide, to determine, to distinguish, to discern, to draw a conclusion, to separate between ideas, to judge or adjudge between alternatives." Humans engage in critical, analytical thinking every day, making judgments about various options and alternatives all the time. The creature (mankind) is not more capable, having more abilities, than the Creator God. God made pre-determinations and makes determinations all the time. God is a choosing and volitional Being.

God has determined that His objective for His created beings is to manifest His character. We are created for His glory (Isa. 43:7), for consistency with Who He is – His character. In that same pre-determination is the obverse – God hates, and does not wish to tolerate, that which is inconsistent with Who He is – sin is everything contrary to Who God is! God graciously and lovingly determined that the consequences for all such sinful inconsistency would be taken voluntarily and vicariously by His Son, Jesus, at the cross (Jn. 5:22). All sin, and all sinners, have been judged in the death of Jesus on the cross. Judgment has been enacted in the death of Jesus (Jn. 12:47), and is certainly not something that Christians need to presently fear. Yes, when we die, "then comes judgment" (Heb. 9:27), but this is simply the divine determination of those who have received by faith what Christ has done for them, and those who have rejected such.

Divine judgment has been accomplished by Jesus in His death on the cross of Calvary. God predetermined and predestined that it should be that way – that the entire restoration of humanity would occur by His judgment of sin in **JESUS** as our substitute, and His determination to place His life in mankind once again!

FEBRUARY 23

CHRISTIAN FAITH AND HUMAN ACTION

The Christian faith is not about what you do, or don't do. "Well, we have to do something," is the retort of activistic peoples. "We are capable people, and we are not looking for hand-outs. We want to get the credit for what we have done." The grace of God is a hard pill to swallow for the modern world. It goes against the sacred work-ethic that we have pragmatically inculcated in our Western culture. Despite that philosophical incongruity, the Christian faith is not another religious performance and conformity club. Becoming or being a Christian is not in any way based on what a human does, either in one's initial faith-reception or in the continuing faith-reception (cf. Col. 2:6) of the on-going Christian life. Christian faith is about what Jesus, the Son of God, has done, and desires to continue to do in any person who will allow Him by their receptivity to live out His life in human form every moment of every day.

The only human action advocated by Christian teaching should be the action of receiving (cf. Jn. 1:12; Gal. 3:2) the "good news" of the living Lord Jesus, the receptivity of the Spirit of Christ (cf. Rom.8:9) into one's human spirit (cf. I Thess. 5:23), whereupon the individual has "Christ within, the hope of glory" (Col. 1:27). When the living Jesus dwells within the Christian (cf. Gal. 2:20), the grace-provision of the life and character of living Jesus within is the dynamic by which they are enabled to live the Christian life, which is simply the eternal life of the risen Lord and Savior re-presented in the contemporary world today.

The Christian faith is not about what we do or don't do. It is about what **JESUS** has done by taking the death consequences of our sins, and what He continues to do as the living Lord to re-enact His life and character in and through us as Christians. Our response-ability is simply to receive God's divine grace and say "Thank you, Lord **JESUS**."

FEBRUARY 24

ARE YOU PLAYING THE ROLE OF A CHRISTIAN?

Perhaps the most quoted of William Shakespeare's writings are the words from "As You Like It," where the character Jacques says, "All the world's a stage, and all the men and women merely players; they have their exits and their entrances, and one man in his time plays many parts." The ancient Roman poet, Juvenal, wrote more than a millennium earlier, "All of Greece is a stage, and every Greek's an actor." The concept of human beings playing roles and acting out parts in the over-all drama of life is an age-old image. But the question we want to address is whether our actions in the drama called "Christianity" are simply a dramatic role that the Christian plays for the expected applause of God or the audience of humanity around us?

If Christian living is simply a performance of play-acting an assumed role of a projected personage, then we are simply hypocrites going through the motions of acting out a charade. Is that what Christian living is all about – the pretense of a masquerade wherein we are "faking it" to present a spurious and deceptive "play" of "Christianity?" If so, it is time for Christians to take off their costumes, make-up and masks, and exit the stage because it has been an absurdly poor performance in the amateur dramatic production called "church."

Conceiving of the Christian life as a dramatic role is a totally illegitimate and inadequate image. The living out of our Christian faith is not a *role* we play, but the *reality* of the risen and living Lord Jesus living out His life in and through the Christian. Christ-ones (Christians) are to allow the living Christ within them to manifest His life (II Cor. 4:10,11) in their bodily behavior. Christian living is the re-presentation of the life and character of **JESUS** in our mortal bodies to reveal the risen and living Lord to those who might observe us. May the world around us observe the reality of the life of **JESUS** in our behavior as Christians.

FEBRUARY 25

DO YOU WANT WHAT YOU DESERVE?

Let us consider a sequence of three basic words. The first word is "**justice**." From the Latin *justitia* (meaning "fair" and "righteous"), the philosophical concept of justice refers to an impartial, even-handed, attribution of what is deserved or due. When justice is served, the one whose fate is being determined will "*get what they deserve.*" If the context is social justice, then the focus will be that everyone "get what they deserve" in social equity and fairness. If the context is legal justice, the objective of good law-based governance is that the lawbreaker should be sentenced in such a manner that they "*get what they deserve.*"

The second word in our sequence of thought is "**mercy**." The Greek playwright, Sophocles, wrote, "there comes a point where justice becomes injurious," and when such occurs it is time to consider mercy. When mercy is administered instead of justice, the person under consideration "*does not get what they deserve.*" Perhaps on the basis of kindness or compassion, juridical mercy may grant leniency, clemency, pardon or forgiveness, even without reason. Jesus said, "Blessed are the merciful, for they shall receive mercy" (Matt. 5:7). God's character of mercy is exhibited socially in "works of mercy" for the unfortunate.

To complete our triad of words, we shall consider the word "**grace**." Grace is a distinctively Christian concept and action. "Grace and truth were realized through Jesus Christ" (Jn. 1:17). Often defined as the "free, unmerited favor of God," the necessary implication is that a person "*gets what they do not deserve.*" Grace is better explained as the dynamic expression of God's action via His Son, **JESUS** Christ. Eastern Orthodox Christians refer to grace as the "divine energies" of God in Christ, sufficient for the entirety of Christian living. Grace has been misunderstood by many Western Christians because they separate the gift from the Giver – grace is not a commodity dispensed by the church.

FEBRUARY 26

DON'T DANCE WITH DIOGENES

Diogenes of Sinope, aka Diogenes the Cynic, was an early Greek philosopher, who lived approximately four hundred years prior to Jesus. To say that Diogenes was eccentric is an understatement. He was expelled from his hometown of Sinope (in the northeast part of what is now Turkey) for defacing currency that his father, a banker, was producing. Henceforth he set out to deface social and political currency, challenging established customs and rules. With great disdain, he eschewed the vanity and artificiality of social values and institutions. He was consistent in acting out what he taught, living as a homeless panderer in Athens and sleeping in a large clay jar at the temple of Cybele. Citizens of Athens considered him a public nuisance, for he would violate social custom by eating in public, embarrassing public speakers like Plato, even urinating, and defecating in public. The one teacher he seemed to appreciate was Antisthenes, a student of Socrates, who taught asceticism and austerity of life in the avoidance of earthly pleasures. To act out his thinking, Diogenes would carry a lighted lantern in broad daylight, explaining that he was "looking for an honest man, but could find nothing but cheats, rascals and scoundrels."

Anecdotal references indicate that he lived and acted "like a dog." His comment: "I play up to those who give me something; I bark at those who refuse; and I set my teeth in rascals." Considered as one of the founders of the philosophical school of Cynicism, it is interesting that the Greek word for cynic is *kunikos*, meaning "dog-like," from *kuon*, the Greek word for "dog."

Cynical skepticism that distrusts all human and societal motivations is merely a negative disposition of unbelief. God has called Christians to be "the light of the world" (Matt. 5:14), not cynical ascetics with aversions to the world. The character of **JESUS** Christ is not cynical, but positively hopeful for all mankind.

FEBRUARY 27

LIKE MOTHER, LIKE DAUGHTER

Many a young man has been advised that if he wants to know how his young girlfriend will turn out when she grows up to be a woman, he should carefully observe his girlfriend's mother. There is an old proverb that says, "Like mother, like daughter." In fact, that proverb is quoted in the Bible. Ezekiel 16:44 – "everyone who quotes proverbs will quote this proverb concerning you, saying, 'Like mother, like daughter.'" The context for this quote is not very flattering, however. Ezekiel is voicing God's indictment of the nation of Israel for her unfaithfulness, drawing the analogy of successive generations of harlotry and whoredom – a negative example of "like mother, like daughter."

Such reference does not forestall the fact that the proverb can be utilized in a positive manner to encourage a daughter to follow in the footsteps of her godly mother. Proverbs 31 mentions a godly woman who "opens her mouth in wisdom, and the teaching of kindness is on her tongue. She looks well to the ways of her household, and does not eat the bread of idleness. Her children rise up and call her blessed." (31:26-28). A wise and godly mother will always desire that her daughters observe her life and faith, and make similar determinations to be godly women who are spiritual daughters of God "in Christ."

From the biblical usage of the proverb, "like mother, like daughter," we must lament the fact that many mothers have not provided exemplary models for their daughters to follow in their footsteps, and many daughters have grown up to display similar negative personality traits as their mothers. But, what higher aspiration could a Christian mother have than to provide a derived imaging of the character of God, hoping that her daughters would make similar determinations of faithful receptivity to allow the Lord **JESUS** Christ to live out godly character in their lives as Christian wives and mothers?

FEBRUARY 28

THE RELIGIOUS RAILROAD

In the seventeenth century (1678), John Bunyan wrote an allegory of the Christian pilgrimage, entitled *The Pilgrim's Progress*. In the nineteenth century (1843), Nathaniel Hawthorne wrote a short parody of Pilgrim's journey, entitled "The Celestial Railroad." Hawthorne's story has Pilgrim riding a train over the same terrain mentioned by Bunyan, but the character identified as "Evangelist" is now changed to "Mr. Smooth-it-away," who represents the smooth-talking preachers that soft-pedal the dangers, gloss over the terrors and doubts of life, and attempt to paint over the trials encountered on the Christian journey.

Allow me to be so audacious as to attempt a reverse parody of Bunyan's story. Like Hawthorne, I will draw a mental picture of a railway ride, but on "The Religious Railroad" many unsuspecting souls have been railroaded into boarding a railway coach that is not destined for the "celestial city," but is headed in the opposite direction. The passengers being "taken for a ride" have presented their "church membership certificates" as boarding passes, and have heard the authoritarian conductor yell, "All aboard the Southbound Express!" The initial part of the journey is smooth and comfortable as the passengers get to know each other, and are enjoying their ride together. Then, passing through "the Slough of Despond," the passengers are not despairing of their sinful wrongdoing, but are becoming agitated and miserable about the unfulfilled promises in the glossy travel brochure for the journey. This is no luxury journey of grace, for the passengers are all recruited to stoke the fires, man the stations, and otherwise contribute their works (and currency) to the forward motion of the train. When they arrive at the City of Vanity, they excitedly disembark for an excursion of folly in Vanity Fair. Sufficiently diverted and entertained, the unsuspecting passengers reboard the train for the continuing journey, the terminus of which is an unbearable cauldron of misery.

FEBRUARY 29

THE PRAYER OF FAITH

James, the brother of our Lord Jesus, referred in his epistle to the efficacy of "the prayer of faith" (James 5:15 - KJV), to set in motion God's healing action for one who is sick. What constitutes a legitimate "prayer of faith"? Is it merely conjuring up enough desire and resolve until we are convinced that God will do what we are asking to heal and bring health to one we know and cherish? That sounds more like a "prayer of positive thinking" than "the prayer of faith." How might we identify and define, then, an effectual "prayer of faith," so contemporary Christians might engage in and implement what James referred to?

Such a "prayer of faith" is beyond the mere subjectivism of hopeful "Pollyanna" optimism. Genuine prayer is never an attempt to project our will upon God, to convince Him to do what we want Him to do. He is not a "push-button God." We cannot "twist God's arm" to get our human desires fulfilled. The "prayer of faith" is not a specific and particular kind of prayer, nor a prayer technique to make prayer more effectual. It is simply communion with God that expresses our willingness to rely on God's power and wait for God's timing to enact whatever God wants to do in a particular person's life and situation.

A different translation reads, "The prayer offered in faith will restore the one who is sick, and the Lord will raise him up" (James 5:15 – NASB). Prayer is not telling God what to do. Prayer involves the submissive recognition that only God's healing power can heal what needs restoring in a human being, whether it be physical, psychological, social, or spiritual. Faith is simply human receptivity to God's activity. In prayer, we are willing to engage in communion with God, listening to His heart of loving compassion and relational concern for others, and relying on what He wants to do by His Son, **JESUS**, in the power of the Spirit. The "prayer of faith" opens our hearts to God's grace-action.

MARCH 1

"SIZE DOESN'T MATTER"

By definition, a megachurch is a Protestant Christian church averaging more than 2000 persons in attendance every Sunday. In the past, there have been examples of large churches, such as Charles Spurgeon's Metropolitan Tabernacle in London, and Aimee Semple McPherson's Angelus Temple in Los Angeles, but the main thrust for the development of megachurches took place in the latter part of the twentieth century, with an emphasis on statistical success. Megachurches usually have a pastor with a strong personality and charisma, and most hold multiple services each week to accommodate the crowds.

The sociological advantage of megachurches is the fact they attract people with a numerical aura of success, as well as the multiplicity of programs available. Smaller churches are usually unable to compete with the megachurches, and accuse them of stealing their sheep. Leadership principles in a megachurch are often patterned after complex big-business management systems. To facilitate relational dynamics in such large numbers of participants, most megachurches schedule small-group gatherings to encourage interactive conversation.

Contrary to popular opinion, size doesn't matter. On the Day of Pentecost there were 3000 people who responded to Peter's preaching. A congregation of Christians may have 30 or 30,000, but there comes a point where the size, the number of participants, demands a change in organizational and operational structure to keep the group connected and engaged in vital interaction. A megachurch requires a sociological restructuring in order to maintain relational interaction among the participants. The question will always be: given the size of the group, are they able to maintain spiritual intimacy with the living Lord **JESUS** and with one another in the Body of Christ, despite the number of participants in their gathering?

MARCH 2

THE BLUEPRINTS

Every physical building requires blueprints, and perhaps models, in the preliminary preparation for construction. The spiritual community known as the "church" is also pictured as a building. "You (Christians), as living stones, are being built up as *a spiritual house* for a holy priesthood, to offer up spiritual sacrifices acceptable to God through Jesus Christ" (I Pet. 2:5). The spiritual house of the People of God also required blueprints and preliminary models to prefigure and project what was to come in the eventual construction of the intended building of "God's household of faith" (Eph. 2:19; Gal. 6:10).

What Christians refer to as the Old Testament scriptures is the sheaf of blueprints for what God was planning to build upon Jesus Christ in the new covenant. God gave the nation of Israel the patterns of the tabernacle, the worship tent (Exod. 25:9), prefiguring patterns for the new covenant tabernacling of Jesus (Jn. 1:14), dwelling in His people. David also had plans when he began to build the temple, the "house of the Lord" (I Kings 6:1), prefiguring that Christians would individually (I Cor. 6:19) and collectively (I Cor. 3:16) comprise the "temple of the Holy Spirit" in the new covenant of Jesus Christ.

Jesus explained that on the rock of faith in Him, like that exhibited by Peter, He would "build His church" (Matt. 16:18), a spiritual dwelling place for His presence in His people. Only the divine Builder can build His spiritual building; it cannot be constructed by the best efforts of humans. Jesus is the foundation, as well as the "chief cornerstone" (I Pet. 2:6,7) of the house of God, and Christians are stones (I Pet. 2:5) positioned on Jesus. We need to see how the Old Testament is the New Testament *concealed*, and New Testament is the Old Testament *revealed*. Christians must see **JESUS** in the blueprints of the old covenant and in the reality of the spiritual house, the Church.

MARCH 3

PITFALLS OF TODAY'S CHRISTIAN RELIGION

When one steps back to get a broad view of the panorama of Christian religion today, it appears we have fallen into the quicksand and sacrificed our Christian foundations. This did not happen overnight, but has been developing in various patterns of thought for centuries. The Enlightenment has gradually killed off the Christian theological explanation of God with its thesis of self-regulating naturalism. Evangelicalism long ago buried the Christian understanding of created humanity, by capitulation to humanism. When the Christian understanding of God and man collapses, our structure of thought has no divine foundation.

Christian thought today has become an advocacy of "Evangelical Humanism." From the time of Augustine in the fourth century, anthropological formulation within Christian thought has been skewed by a dualistic understanding of a human being comprised of only body and soul, failing to appreciate the physiological, psychological and spiritual function of humanity. Denying the ability of fallen humanity to exercise freedom of choice to respond to God's redemptive action, Christian thought accepted the humanistic premise that human beings function as "independent selves," anthropologically ignorant of the derived being and action of humanity.

In practical Christian living, Christians generally function as "Practical Deists." Their concept of God is that of a distant and detached deity, who having set all things in motion now sits back to gaze on his experiment, not knowing how it will turn out. Casting their prayer petitions at an abstract, far-removed power in the sky, the religious view of God has been an objectified and separated concept of a transcendent "god" who does not interfere in human enterprise. Christian thought has been fearful of the internal and immanent presence of Christ indwelling the Christian's spirit and functioning as the Lord of one's life.

MARCH 4

EXISTENTIALISM

"Existential" is a word bandied about by many intellectual and philosophical types of academic persons, who seem to think they know what it means. Among Christian persons the word is often freighted with a negative connotation of relativism or a subjectivism that creates its own reality. Existentialism, as a term is rooted in the word "existence;" and the core of such thought is that human existence is not to be explained in abstract academic concepts and theories, but must commence in the recognition that each thinking subject discovers a sense of "being" within their inner thoughts, feelings and actions as human individuals.

Existential thought often commences with negative observation of the surrounding world-system. For Kierkegaard (1813-1855) it was existence in the midst of "anxiety" concerning the choices that humans must make. For Camus (1913-1960) it was the "absurdism that life is void of meaning." For Sartre (1905-1980) it was the "condemnation of human freedom" and having to face human responsibility. Existentialism deals with every individual's attempt to find a sense of identity and meaning in the midst of a fallen world-system that does not make sense and produces no sense of harmony or love among mankind.

The Danish thinker, Soren Kierkegaard is often credited as being "the father of existentialism," but he did not approach the subject of human existence in the same sense as the unbelieving Frenchmen, Camus and Sartre. From a Christian perspective, Kierkegaard recognized the objective God-created existence of each individual, but emphasized the subjective contemplation of life necessary for arriving at the truth of one's personal sense of meaning and identity beyond sterile explanations of rationalism. In the midst of our rationalistic Western culture, Kierkegaard explained that an individual must make "a leap of faith," in total abandonment to the reality of the unseen, **JESUS** Christ.

MARCH 5

THE IMPORTANCE OF THE INDIVIDUAL

The Danish thinker, Soren Kierkegaard, wrote: "the individual – that is the decisive Christian category." He was not advocating isolated individualism, nor a system of self-realization or self-effort whereby one self-actualizes one's being. He was not an "atomist" who viewed Christian faith as opposed to collective Christian assembly – He just wanted the church to be what the church was supposed to be, "the Body of Christ." He did not believe the church was meant to be an institutional "Establishment" of Christendom that haughtily projects they have "a corner on God," as was prevalent in his day.

It is only as an individual that we enter into personal relationship with Jesus Christ, a "simple life" in communion with God, and then collectively comprise the assembly or congregation of *ekklesia* with others. The "group," the "crowd," the "Church gathering" is not where our identity is to be formed, for our real self-awareness is discovered in union with God in Christ. A single human individual "in Christ" gives reality to all that Jesus Christ came to bring by His life. This is in sharp contrast to all forms of socialism and ecclesiasticism that seek to herd human beings into "movements" and "denominations."

An individual's real sense of spiritual being and personal freedom can only come into fruition in relationship with God through Christ. In the inner subjectivity of communion with Christ we discover truth, i.e. the reality about ourselves and everything else that relates to us. All the philosophical arguments about Christianity get us nowhere. "If we receive the witness of men (all the historical and theological arguments), the testimony of God (to our spirit-heart) is greater. Those who believe in the Son of God (**JESUS**) have the testimony within" (I Jn. 5:9,10), i.e. "the Spirit bears witness with our spirits that we are children of God" (Rom. 8:16)."

MARCH 6

YOU DON'T FIT?

Do you sometimes feel like you are "the odd person out"? ...like a square peg trying to fit in a round hole? ...as if you just don't fit in the social groups you used to be comfortable in? ...like you are an anomaly or an incongruity? You are not alone. Many serious and sincere Christians have that same sense of irregularity or non-belonging. God created us with a God-given need and desire to socially interact and belong together with others, and share ourselves with others. But no person or group of people can fulfill our deepest need of belonging, for that relational oneness is only found in "belonging to the Lord Jesus Christ" (Gal. 5:24).

The Christian does not fit in the social milieu of the world. We are "in the world, but not of the world" (Jn. 17:11-18). The world-system of evil, wherein the Evil One is the ruler (Jn. 14:30; 16:10), operates with the character of selfishness and sinfulness. Such is the character and action that we have repudiated in our acceptance of Jesus Christ as our Lord and Savior. Though we physically exist in the cosmos of human life on planet earth, we know we are an anomaly that does not fit and must not adapt to the ways of self-serving worldliness. Instead, we are to be "salt" (Matt. 5:13) and "light" (Matt. 5:14) to the world around us.

The most difficult sense of irregularity comes when maturing Christians realize they "do not fit" in the institutional Church, the very place where they thought they were made to fit. The Church in our modern culture has so degenerated as to be but an enclave of worldly religiosity. The spiritual saint recognizes that many who are called Christians do not share a deep sense of spiritual awareness. Maturing Christians will feel like they are living in a wilderness among non-like-minded people. A Christian must learn to accept that other people cannot meet their needs, and only in union with **JESUS** Christ can we traverse the path that God has designed for us – and it may be quite socially solitary.

MARCH 7

PERSPECTIVE

When an artist first sets a canvas on the easel, and before she ever commences to paint the first stroke, she must first determine the perspective from which all objects in the painting will be oriented. This usually requires a horizon line or "eye-level" to give a sense of dimensional axis and depth of field, as well as selecting the angle of the light source to regulate brightness and shadow angle. The viewpoint of the viewer of the art should be aligned with the viewpoint of the artist who created the work in order to have a correct perspective of what the artist was intending to convey.

God's great creative work also had an initial perspective that began with a predetermined horizon line from which all other objects and action were to be oriented. The Divine Artist pre-horizoned (Greek *prohorizo* – "predestined") His cosmic masterpiece so every object and person in His creation should be aligned with His Son, Jesus Christ (Eph. 1:5). As He continued His masterpiece, He carefully crafted His work of redemption to emphasize the focal point of His love in the divine Son, born as a man and dying on a cruel cross, thereby giving the critical vertical and horizontal dimension to the relational picture.

We, the viewers and participants, are now obliged to discover a viewpoint whereby our perspective aligns with the grace-perspective of the Creator-artist, so we can properly appreciate the finished work of God's creation and redemption. Such appreciation of the Artist's work requires us to have a contextual frame of reference whereby we put ourselves in the relational picture, and experientially begin to see things as God sees things. When our perspective is in alignment with God's perspective, we begin to see and participate in what God is doing – not just with 20/20 hindsight of the historical past, but the continuous presence of the living **JESUS** drawing us into God's masterpiece.

MARCH 8

PERCEPTION AND REALITY

In the so-called "postmodern" era of thought, personal feelings and subjectivity of thought have been elevated to preeminence, considered to have primacy in consideration of what is important and real. In the preceding "modern" era, when scientific method reigned supreme, empirical observation of physical phenomena by our human senses was the criteria by which one could establish scientific "laws" about reality. Both of these epistemological periods of naturalistic thought based their perception of reality on human sensory evaluation. Modernism posited that the physical world is the only reality, and our objective sensual perception of the natural world allows us to know definitively what is real. Postmodernism asserts that reality is in the eyes of the beholder, that reality is individuated in the subjective sensory perception of how each person experiences their reality, i.e. "perception is reality."

Differentiation must be made between "sensual perception" wherein we become aware of something by our physical senses of seeing, hearing, etc., and "mental perception" whereby we understand the meaning of what we have sensed and develop a determination of reality. We must also recognize the distinction between perception of what is outside of ourselves – objective to us, and perception of our internal feelings and thoughts – subjective within us.

Christian thought recognizes the existence of both physical and spiritual reality. Such reality exists apart from and prior to any human perception of such. This objective reality, personal and physical, can reveal itself to human sensory perception, and be subjectively appreciated. The Self-existent God has revealed Himself in His created order, and by the redemptive revelation of His Son, **JESUS**, who identified Himself as the divine Reality – "I AM the way, the reality, and the Life" (Jn. 14:6).

MARCH 9

TRIPLE FUNCTION

Christian teaching through the centuries has had an inadequate anthropological explanation, ever since Augustine transferred his Platonic and Manichean concepts of body-soul dualism into his teaching about human functionality. The apostle Paul wrote to the Thessalonian Christians, "Now may the God of peace Himself sanctify you entirely; and may your spirit and soul and body be preserved complete, without blame at the coming of our Lord Jesus Christ" (I Thess. 5:23). "Spirit" and "soul" and "body" refer to a tri-level human function, and Paul prays that God might be allowed to cause each level to function as He intends.

Spirituality, the study of human spiritual function, has been so neglected in much Christian thought (especially Protestantism). That is to be expected, since they misunderstand the function of God's Spirit in the human spirit. Paul clearly states, "If anyone does not have the Spirit of Christ (*in their spirit*), they do not belong to Christ (Rom. 8:9). If they do, "the Spirit bears witness with our spirit that we are a child of God" (Rom. 8:16).

Psychology, the study of the soul (or psyche) has been an educational discipline since the nineteenth century, but has predominantly been explained from a humanistic perspective that fails to take account of how the divine presence and character of God in one's spirit affects the mental, emotional, and volitional attitudes and actions in the soul. Christian religion has not understood that humans derive character from Christ within.

Physiology, the study of our physical, bodily function is not focused on anatomy, but on behavioral expression within Christian teaching. Whereas legalistic religious teaching is concerned with the "thou shalts" and "thou shalt nots" of behavior modification, genuine Christian teaching focuses on the character of **JESUS** manifest in our behavior (cf. II Cor. 4:10,11).

MARCH 10

BLAME

Stuff happens! Who is to blame? The Aristotelian-based logic of the Western world always seems to require the attribution of blame for whatever happens. The linear cause-and-effect premise of thought requires a cause to be blamed for every effect, and that cause may be mechanical or personal. When a character element is included, i.e. good or evil, then the personal cause to be blamed often comes down to either the good God or Satan, the Evil One. God is the essential cause of all things, because He is the Creator of all things, but He is never the blameworthy or culpable cause of evil, for such is contrary to His character.

The Western world of thought seems quite incapable of accepting the premise of divine providence or divine mystery – that what God is doing in His creation may be beyond the human logic principle of cause-and-effect. The finite understanding of humanity will never comprehend the infinite Being or ways of God. "His ways are past finding out" (Rom. 11:33). Human logic will never figure out Theo-logic. The humanistic premises that elevate the human mind as the final arbiter of truth and reality, preempt all consideration of God's supremacy and control of all things. Divine omnipotence is replaced with human reason as the final arbiter and initiator of all actions.

The fallen world of mankind is always seeking a culpable culprit to blame for what is happening in their lives. Unwilling to accept responsibility or blame themselves, a source-cause must be identified on which to affix the blame. In conjunction with Adam and Eve, many seek to blame another person for their action and seek to get off the hook of responsibility for their actions. Beyond that, human beings will attempt to blame social forces, fate, heritage, spiritual causes, etc. When sufficient blame has been placed on the scale to attempt to balance personal guilt, they will then feel "justified" – but righteousness is only in **JESUS**.

MARCH 11

BESETTING SINS

Since the publication of the *King James Bible* in A.D. 1611, English-speaking Christians have referred to "the sins that so easily beset us" (Heb. 12:1), and to the repetitive patterns of sinful behavior that we often succumb to as "besetting sins." Other English translations refer to "the sins that hangeth on" (Tyndale), hamper us, distract us, ensnare us, entangle us, assault us, trip us up, won't let go, and we so easily fall into." Every Christian knows experientially about these habituated tendencies we are individually vulnerable to engage in time and time again, despite our efforts to stop, put away, or overcome.

Paul wrote, "If any person is in Christ, the old has passed away, behold, all has become new" (II Cor. 5:17). Really? That is true in terms of our spiritual condition, but the Christian retains the residual fleshly patterns of sinfulness in the desires of the soul. So, how do we deal with these habituated and individuated weaknesses and propensities to particular sins? No amount of will-power and human self-effort will overcome these sometimes obvious, sometimes secret, tendencies to engage in selfish and sinful character expression that does not evidence (thus misrepresents) the character of Christ who lives within us.

Some refer to this conflict in the soul of the Christian as "spiritual warfare," whereby our fleshly lusts wage war against the soul" (I Pet. 2:11). Paul does indicate, "The flesh sets its desire against the Spirit, and the Spirit against the flesh; for these are in opposition to one another" (Gal. 5:17), but Christians are not called to fight against the flesh patterns. In the same passage that mentions "besetting sins," we are told to "look to **JESUS**, the author and finisher of our faith" (Heb. 12:2). In repentance, we are to transparently say to God, "I can't deal with this area of sin; You can, by the power of your Spirit; and by faith, I choose to submit and allow you, **JESUS**, to be Lord of my life in this area.

MARCH 12

DERIVATIVE HUMANITY

The Creator God is the Self-generative source and sustenance of all created things. He does not derive anything from another, from any source external to Himself, and is therefore not dependent or contingent on anyone or anything. His creation, particularly humanity, is not self-generative; they are not little self-creative gods. Human creatures are intended to derive all being and character from the Creator-God, i.e. to be dependent and contingent on God. Created with freedom of choice, they have the response-ability to make faith-choices of receptivity to the activity of God in their lives. When thus availing themselves to God's presence and manifestation, they function as the derivative human beings God created them to be.

When the original couple chose to listen to the humanistic lie that they could "go it alone," and be their own source of action, they soon learned they had been duped, and discovered that they were now deriving from the character and activity of the negative spirit-source, from the Evil One, from Satan. Human beings are always derivative creatures, making either/or choices of character derivation from one spirit-source, or the other – either/or. Every human being is spiritually indwelt by, and deriving from, either God or Satan. There is a "spirit that works in the sons of disobedience" (Eph. 2:3), whereas the Spirit of God in Christ is at work in the Christian (Phil. 2:13).

Day by day, we derive the spiritual character of our behavior, either selfishness and sinfulness from Satan, or righteousness and godliness from God in **JESUS** Christ. Humans do not produce character from their own inherent source – they do not generate righteousness out of themselves, nor do they generate sinfulness out of themselves. Human beings are always derivative creatures, in contrast to the humanistic premise so prevalent in our world that humans can be the source of their own activity.

MARCH 13

GOD IN THE BOX

As youngsters, we thought it the height of hilarity to call an establishment and ask, "Do you have Bud in the bottle? ...do you have Red Man in a can? ...do you have Jack-in-the-Box? If you do, you need to let him out!" We never thought of calling local churches to advise them that they should let God out of the stained-glass-window boxes of their church buildings, although it would have been a much more appropriate request. Religion, in general, has a tendency to box God in the parameters of their narrow and limited perspectives of thought, their inadequate theological explanations, or their particular ritual motions.

God is not a "genie in a bottle," who at the behest of certain magical religious incantations will come out of the bottle and grant the wishes of the one making requests. God, being infinite and eternal, is beyond the confines of space and time, and cannot be confined in any box of anthropomorphic conceptualizations, any box of performance standards, any box of religious or legalistic "believe right," or "do right" ground rules. God just doesn't fit in any of the man-made boxes of thought, behavior, worship practices, ecclesiastical prejudices, etc. God cannot be limited, used, or manipulated in any way.

Despite our boxes of doctrinal purity, requiring a particular "statement of faith" ... Despite our boxes of moral conformity, requiring definite "thou shalts" and "thou shalt nots" ... Despite our boxes of contingency expectations, making bargains with God expecting Him to grant certain benefits if we are faithful ... Despite our boxes of religious excitation, wherein we desire to be blessed, inspired, ecstatic, or euphoric ... God cannot be confined in any religious box. The living Lord **JESUS** will break out of every box wherein humans might attempt to confine, entrap or domesticate Him. He is alive by the Spirit, and always operates in the freedom of His own Being and divine empowering.

MARCH 14

LIFE FORMS

All life is not the same kind of life. Life comes in various forms. There are three types of life mentioned in the New Testament, the life of the body, the soul, and the spirit, and these loosely correspond to three different Greek words:

Physical life. The Greek word referring to physical life is *bios*. We see this word in the word "biology," which is the study of physical life in plants, animals, and humans. Likewise, a "biography" is a written document of a person's physical life. "Symbiosis" refers to living things living together in dependence. When the doctor orders a "biopsy," it is the removal of living tissue for diagnostic examination. *Bios* can refer to one's life-span, as well as to the character of the life that one lives. Luke writes of "the pleasure of this life (*bios*)" (Lk. 8:14).

Psychological life. The Greek word from which we get "psychology" is *psuche*, which has been transliterated into English as "psyche," referring to the mental, emotional, and volitional functionality of the human soul. Older psychology textbooks usually explained that psychology was the "study of the soul." Other derivative English words include psychosis, psychosomatic, and psychiatry. Jesus said, "Whoever wants to save his life (*psuche*) shall lose it" (Matt. 16:25).

Spiritual life. The Greek word for spiritual life in the New Testament is *zoe*. Science used this word to refer to "zoology," the study of animal life in the zoo, as distinct from plants and humans. In the Greek New Testament, however, the word *zoe* refers to spiritual life, eternal life, the divine life of the Son of God. Referring to **JESUS**, John begins his gospel, "In Him was life (*zoe*), and the life (*zoe*) was the light of man" (Jn. 1:4). Jesus declared, "I am the way, the truth, and the life (*zoe*); no man comes to the Father but through Me" (Jn. 14:6).

MARCH 15

THE SUBLIME

Most people have had moments when they have been transported into a realm of thought or imagining, perhaps akin to having a dream or vision, that is paranormal. Can you recall having a beyond the ordinary, "out of this world" experience that elevated your consciousness into a state of awareness beyond the cares of this natural world? The English word "sublime" is derived from two Latin words: *sub* = under, up to; *limen* = threshold, limit. In such an experience, we are lifted up to the limits of our normal human apprehension, and we enter into an exhilarating and perhaps euphoric, heavenly encounter.

Numerous philosophers have speculated about the sublime. Religion has attempted to orchestrate the sublime in the architecture of cathedrals, the pageantry of worship, the magnificence of music, the persuasiveness of preaching. But the spiritual sublime derives only from the Divine. God alone can reveal Himself and His sublime heavenly presence and character. Many Christians can attest to experiencing a *kairos* moment in the midst of *chronos* time when "heaven came down and glory filled my soul" – when they beheld a glimpse of God's glory, and were intoxicated with a spiritual "high" in the divine presence.

May I suggest that such sublime experiences should be more common and ordinary for those who are walking with **JESUS**. Those in spiritual union with the living Lord have the opportunity and the privilege of experientially uniting in the heavenlies with our "Beloved," the lover or our souls. We, too, can meet Him on the Mt. of Transfiguration, as did Peter and John. We, too, can be lifted up to the "third heaven," as was Paul. God desires to reveal Himself to us in repetitive personal revelations "beyond what we might ask or think" (Eph. 3:20), inviting us into the intimate fellowship of the *pleroma* fullness of His abundant life, as we are receptive to such grace by faith.

MARCH 16

A RIGHT TO HAPPINESS?

"Does everyone have a basic right to happiness?" That is the question I asked many people in my informal, unscientific survey. The overwhelming majority of those who answered the question responded, "Yes, of course, everyone has a basic right to happiness." Really? Perhaps they were thinking of the phrase in the *United States Declaration of Independence* that states, "all men are created equal, and are endowed by their Creator with certain inalienable rights; among these are Life, Liberty, and the pursuit of Happiness." Note carefully: our guaranteed rights include the "pursuit of happiness" – not happiness itself.

Happiness is an elusive concept. *The Canadian Charter of Rights* and *The Universal Declaration of Human Rights* both state the rights of "life, liberty, and the security of the person." Perhaps that is what Thomas Jefferson meant when he drafted the *U.S. Declaration of Independence*. Likely so, in which case personal happiness had to do with well-being, thriving, and the possibility of bettering oneself. But contemporary usage of the word "happiness" usually refers to a subjective state wherein a person perceives that they are getting what they presently want, and therefore have positive pleasurable thoughts and emotions.

The etymology of the word "happy" evidences an origin in the Old Norse/English word "*hap*," which meant "chance." Observe other words using that root concept: happen, happening, happenstance, haphazard, perhaps, mishaps, and hapless. Happiness is the chance good fortune that by the luck of the draw you get what you want. Neither our government or the Bible can guarantee the right of such happiness. The Christian gospel, on the other hand, promises blessedness (cf. Matt. 5:6-12) and joy (John 15:11; 16:24), for those willing to reject selfish desires of personal pleasure, and instead accept and derive all their well-being from the living Lord **JESUS** Christ.

CHRISTIANITY IS NOT MORALITY

The majority of people would probably surmise that religion, including the Christian religion, involves a moral objective of changed behavior. The general public thinks that Christianity is foremost concerned with morality. Alongside of the psychological model that advocates "behavior modification" via positive and/or negative reinforcement, many think Christian thought is focused on rules and regulations of right and wrong, do this – do not do that; thou shalt – thou shalt not. Religion, in general, does indeed operate on codified behavioral regulations, but Christianity is averse to all legalistic standards of behavior.

The foundation of morality is the morés, the acceptable cultural values and expectations of a particular social unit or society. In other words, their morality is based on subjective principles of propriety and acceptability of performance of various external behavioral actions. Such socially determined morality lacks an absolute, objective foundational standard. It lacks any sense of spiritual source and provision, depending only on the alleged self-effort of human performance to conform. The inability to adequately perform in full accord with the social moral expectations inevitably fosters pretense, and hypocrisy.

C.S. Lewis explained that for the Christian, "morality is a joke!" Morality looks only at the external behavioral results, and fails to consider the internal spiritual source of character. Christian behavior is based on the foundational indwelling presence of **JESUS** Christ in the human spirit, whereby the grace-provision and dynamic of God's character is energized and empowered within and through the Christian. C.S. Lewis also wrote, "any good in the Christian comes from the Christ-life within." Instead of changed external behavior, Christianity points to an exchange of spiritual source and character, whereby the life of **JESUS** is "manifested in our mortal flesh" (II Cor. 4:10,11).

MARCH 18

CHRISTIAN MISUNDERSTANDING OF SIN

One would think that if any peoples should understand the meaning of "sin," it would be Christians, who have (in the past anyway) relentlessly harped on human sinfulness. But the truth of the matter is that historically Christians have misunderstood what is involved in the reality of sin for many centuries. Beginning with Augustine (4th cent.) Christians have often considered sin to be an intrinsic pollution and corruption within humanity (the anthropocentric view of sin). In conjunction with depraved humanity, there has been the perspective that sin is defined by human beings committing wrong actions, contrary to the character of God (the moralistic and behavioral view of sin). Others have focused on sin as the violation of God's Law, affirming that "the power of sin is the law" (I Cor. 15:56), and "sin is lawlessness" (I Jn. 3:4) – (the legalistic view of sin). These explanations of sin all "miss the mark" of the most basic biblical understanding of sin.

Sin is not to be legally defined by law prohibitions. Sin is not to be anthropocentrically defined as the intrinsic rottenness of humanity. Sin is not to be moralistically defined as the wrong actions of human behavior. Christians must understand that sin is to be ontologically defined as the character derived from the being (Greek *ontos* = being) of the spiritual personage of Satan, the Evil One. The apostle John writes, "The one who practices sin is of (Greek preposition *ek*, meaning "out of" in terms of source or origin) the devil; for the devil has sinned from the beginning" (I John 3:8). By an exchange of spiritual source in the human spirit, a receptive individual can experience spiritual regeneration and union with **JESUS** (I Cor. 6:17). The only alternative to Satan's character expression of sin-expression in human beings is the presence and function of the Spirit of Christ (Rom. 8:9), the "Righteous One," who supersedes all sinful character in the manifestation of His character of righteousness in the Christian.

MARCH 19

LEARNING TO OBEY

Every young child must learn to obey their parents. That is part of parental responsibility, to teach a child obedience in the various contexts of life (home, school, government, etc.). Such instruction initially requires a rule-based obedience for the safety of the child: "don't run out in the street; don't touch the hot stove; don't hit your sibling." Parents determine the boundaries that the children are expected to obediently fit within. Beyond the rule-based expectations of obedience, parents will want to teach their children a relational obedience wherein the children develop a commitment to a loving interpersonal family.

Contrary to what many people think, obedience is not primarily "keeping the rules." In the law-based old covenant of God with the Hebrew people, law-keeping was a foremost emphasis that the Jewish people had agreed to do, saying, "We can do it!" (Exod. 24:7). They could not. They did not. The people of Israel were disobedient (Rom. 10:21; 11:30-32), and "these things happened as examples for us" (Heb. 10:6,11), that Christians might learn obedience from the negative example of the disobedience of the Jewish people under the old covenant.

Turning to the new covenant arrangement of God with His people, the operational principle is not legal performance of the law by rule-keeping, but relational listening to the indwelling presence and voice of God. The Greek word for "obedience" throughout the New Testament is *hupakouo* (*hup* = under; *akouo* = to listen, the word from which we get "acoustics"), meaning "to listen under." We are informed that Jesus "learned obedience through the things that He suffered" (Heb. 5:8). As a human being, the Son learned to "listen under" the voice of the Father, particularly in the difficult times of trial and suffering. Likewise, it is in the troubles of life that Christians learn how to faithfully obey by listening to **JESUS** in relational reliance and derivation.

MARCH 20

FROM REALITY TO ACTUALITY

There are numerous spiritual realities that are true of every Christian from the occasion of their spiritual regeneration, when they become a "new creature" (II Cor. 5:17) in Christ. When we receive the Spirit of Christ into our human spirit, we become "children of God" (cf. Rom. 8:9,16). We are "sons of God through faith in Christ Jesus" (Gal. 3:26). Christians are no longer "enemies of God" (Rom. 5:10), but the "people of God" (I Pet. 2:10); no longer "sinners" (Rom. 5:8) in spiritual identity, but "saints" (Rom. 1:7), "holy ones" by the presence of the Holy One in us; no longer "unrighteous" (Rom. 1:29), but made "righteous" (II Cor. 5:21) by the presence of the Righteous One forming our identity; no longer "alienated and hostile" toward God (Col. 1:21), but "reconciled" to God (II Cor. 5:18,19). The spiritual reality is that Christians are "forgiven" (Eph. 1:7), "accepted in the Beloved" (Eph. 1:3) with "no condemnation" (Rom. 8:1), and "sealed with the Spirit" (Eph. 1:13) in spiritual union with Christ (I Cor. 6:17). That is our spiritual reality, by the presence of the One who is Truth (Jn. 14:6).

Translating those spiritual realities into the experiential actuality of daily living is a process for every Christian. Yes, we have inner conflict between the "flesh" (Gal. 5:17) and the desires of the Spirit. Yes, we are tempted by the diabolic tempter (I Cor. 10:13) to express sinful character, and thus behave contrary to who we have become in Christ. Yes, we are responsible to "stand firm" (Phil. 4:1), to "abide" (Jn. 15:4-9), to "be filled with the Spirit" (Eph. 5:18), to "walk by the Spirit" (Gal. 5:16,25), and "to conduct ourselves in the grace of God" (II Cor. 1:12), as we are "saved by His life" (Rom. 5:10), recognizing that "greater is He who is in you, than he who is in the world" (I Jn. 4:4). The actuality of our out-living of **JESUS**'s life will not be perfect (Phil. 3:12), and we will have our failures and laments (cf. Rom. 7:14-25), but such behavioral actualities do not diminish the spiritual realities.

THEOLOGICAL EMPHASES

Theology is the study of God. The word "theology" is derived from two Greek words: *theos* = God; *logos* = words, logic, study of. Human beings have long made attempts to know about God using the best of human reasoning and logic, and consequently have attempted to explain their conclusions in the words of many theological books. The problem is that human logical reasoning never arrives at an adequate explanation of God, and never leads a person to know God in a personal and experiential relationship. God can only be known as He reveals Himself, and His particular historical and personal Self-revelation is by His Son, Jesus Christ.

There have been many varieties of humanly reasoned theology:

Biblical theology – the study of how various biblical authors portray God in their writings. How is Pauline theology differentiated from Johannine theology, or the theology of James, or even the comments of Jesus in the gospels?

Historical theology – the study of the ever-changing conceptions of God and His ways throughout the history of the Church, explaining the viewpoints of historical theologians, and different segments of the Church, ex. Roman Catholic and Protestant theology.

Philosophical theology – the study of the logical arguments whereby men have attempted to arrive at the God-conclusion, and the attempted explanation of why God has acted as He has in all of His creative and redemptive endeavors.

Systematic theology – the study of the explanations of God's Being and actions systematically and topically organized.

Dogmatic theology – the study of how theology has been formulated in the dogmas and doctrines of the church.

The knowledge of God is best summed up in the statement of **JESUS**, "If you have seen Me, you have seen the Father" (Jn. 14:9).

MARCH 22

THE MOST PREVALENT SIN OF CHRISTIANS

If you were asked to name the most prevalent sin among Christian people, what would be your answer? No doubt, some would say "hypocrisy," pretending to be what you are not – pretending to be perfect, or pretending to have a depth of spirituality that is betrayed by behavioral manifestations. Others might choose "gossip" as the most prevalent Christian sin, for much Christian conversation does involve talking about other people and their problems. Another choice for the most obvious sin of Christians might be "materialism," for Christians have certainly succumbed to the consumerism so prevalent in the world. Still others might name the "pride" of knowing the truth and being right as the foremost sin of Christians.

These are but a few of the Christian sins that might be identified as the most pronounced or most prevalent. Believe it or not, the answer that is herewith being proposed as "the most prevalent Christian sin" is fostered and encouraged by the religious preachers – in fact, hardly a week goes by that the pulpiteers do not browbeat their congregations to engage in this endeavor, regarding it to be a virtue rather than a sin, and regarding it to be the highest objective of being a Christian believer. What a travesty. When sin is regarded to be virtue, when humanistic self-effort is called sanctification, what egregious apostasy.

So, what am I suggesting to be the most prominent and pervasive sin among Christians? I am suggesting that being committed to, and trying to live the Christian life by means of conforming to specific behavior patterns, engaging in religious disciplines, participating in church rituals, and being involved in the legalistic activities of a church organization is sin contrary to God's intent. Only **JESUS** can live the Christ-life – He has done so perfectly during His redemptive mission on earth, and desires to do so again in and through Christians in whom His Spirit lives.

MARCH 23

GOD'S EXPECTATIONS

Religious persons who view obedience to God as conforming to behavioral rules, and keeping God's Law (including the unwritten and unspoken laws of their church authorities), often think that God has high expectations for their performance. In response to what they consider to be God's expectations of them, these religious persons are very diligent to engage in "good works" and the busy-ness of what is called "the work of the Lord" (which is religious-speak for church involvement that is but the human works of a deceived believer). Imposing such expectations is what keeps the religious organization from total collapse.

GOOD NEWS for Christians: God has no expectations for you to perform or conform in any way. That is why "there is now no condemnation for those who are in Christ Jesus" (Rom. 8:1). Christians are "created in Christ Jesus for good works which He prepared beforehand that we might walk in them" (Eph. 2:10), "equipped in every good thing to do His will, working in us that which is pleasing in His sight, through Jesus Christ" (Heb. 13:21). God is the dynamic of His own demands. He never asks anything of us, but that He has provided everything necessary to behave like the Christ-ones we have become. The onus is never on human beings to muster up performance that meets the alleged expectations of God. It is what God does, not what we do.

Oh yes, we sin and manifest character contrary to the character of God. Many Christians then engage in excessive confession and apologies. "Oh, God, I've done it again. Oh, God; You won't believe what I have done this time." God's reply, "I did not expect anything else out of you. The only thing you can do apart from Me is sin! What grieves Me the most is that you keep trying to do what only I can do. You seem to think that your performance can replace or supersede My grace. Relax and let Me be your life. You can't; only I can live righteously, live godly, live the Christian life."

MARCH 24

ASSET OR LIABILITY?

When I was in high school, I took a course in bookkeeping. Later, in college, I took a course in economics. I decided that I did not want to become a "bean-counter/bookkeeper." But these courses were not a total loss, for I soon saw that many Christian people seem to view God as the Big Bookkeeper in the heavens, who is balancing His asset and liability columns. Many Christians, in their valuation of themselves, tend to view themselves as God's liability. If they had to write themselves in on God's ledger sheet, they would put themselves in the negative column, as a detriment to God's cause! What a sad personal indictment.

In truth, every Christian should reckon themselves to be God's asset. God paid a dear price for you. He paid the price of sending His only begotten Son (cf. Jn. 3:16), who, in turn, paid the price giving His life on the cross for us (cf. Gal. 2:21). Paul makes it clear: we have been "bought with a price" (I Cor. 6:20; 7:23). In the economic world, when an object is purchased, it immediately becomes an asset. Since we have been objectively purchased by the blood of Jesus, we are God's asset whether we feel like it or not. Our subjective evaluation of where we stand with God is often skewed, making us feel like we are a liability to God based on our misrepresentation in sinful behavior.

When Christians subjectively view themselves as God's liability, they tend to revert to various performance endeavors in their attempts to "measure up" to God's expectations, trying to earn a place in God's plus-column, falsely believing that God views them as a failure. On the other hand, when Christians believe they are God's asset, not because of anything they have meritoriously done, but because they were "bought with a price" by the death of **JESUS**, they are free to live by the victorious life of the risen Lord, allowing Him to manifest His character and thus manifest what an asset they are "in Christ **JESUS**."

MARCH 25

I AM DYING

If I were to approach a friend and declare, "I am dying!", they would probably respond, "Oh dear, what happened? Were you in an accident? Did you contract a disease? How long do the doctors indicate that you have to live?" Such a direct statement is often taken with the shock of having suffered a personal tragedy that will lead to imminent physical death. My surprising statement did not say that I was near physical death, or about to meet my demise in death, but used a continuous present participle, the word "dying." Do you remember what your grammar instructor said, "Participles usually end with –ing"?

In this case, I was using an on-going present participial verb to refer to a process that is true of every human person from the time they are born. From the moment of our birth, our physical bodies are beginning to die. In fact, scientists inform us that approximately three hundred million cells in our human body die every minute, and most are replaced immediately by the God-designed generative principle called human life. As we get older, a few less cells are replaced every day. What we need to see is that living and dying are part of an integrated dialectic, both of which are part of our human living here on earth.

What did the apostle Paul mean when he told the Corinthians, "I die daily" (I Cor. 15:31)? Some would say that Paul was extolling the need to "die to self" and subjugate our selfishness every day. That is doubtful. The context of his comment seems to indicate that his physical body was being pummeled by various forms of physical persecution on a daily basis. He was being beaten, stoned, having to face wild animals and harsh conditions, and all these took a toll on his physical body. Was he afraid that his body might die physically? No, he explained to the Philippians, "for me to live is Christ, to die is gain" (Phil. 1:21). Living and dying are part of God's plan for every person, including **JESUS**-followers.

MARCH 26

NATURAL MAN

Christian teaching often refers to the designation of a "natural man." This phrase, only used one time in the Christian New Testament, deserves closer evaluation and definition. The apostle Paul explains that "a *natural man* does not accept the things of the Spirit of God, for they are foolishness to him; and he cannot understand them, because they are spiritually appraised" (I Cor. 2:14). This is contrasted with the designation of "*spiritual men*" just three verses later in I Cor. 3:1, contextually defined as one who has "received the Spirit who is from God, so that we may know the things freely given to us by God" (I Cor. 2:10-13).

These contrasting designations in the original Greek language of the New Testament are *psuchikos anthropos* (soulical or soulish man), usually translated "natural man," and *pneumatikos anthropos* (spiritual man). As noted above, a "spiritual man" is a human being (whether male or female) who has received and is indwelt by the Spirit of Christ, and "led by the Spirit" (Rom. 8:14) by listening to the Spirit. Conversely, a "natural man" is a spiritually unregenerate human being (male or female), "devoid of the Spirit of God" (Jude 19), but energized by "the spirit that works in the sons of disobedience" (Eph. 2:2).

Some Christians have mistakenly indicated that a "natural man" is an individual who operates from his self-generating soul (cf. *psuchikos anthropos* – soulical man). Such a humanistic premise fails to recognize the necessary spiritual source of all derived human behavior. Utilizing the same Greek word *psuchikos*, James the Lord's brother writes of a "wisdom that does not come down from above (from God), but is earthly, *natural*, demonic" (James 3:15). A natural, unregenerate person is energized by a diabolic spiritual source that energizes selfish and sinful patterns of "flesh" that are opposed to the Spirit (Gal. 5:17). A Christian is no longer a "natural man," but identified by **JESUS** living within.

MARCH 27

PERSONAL RESPONSIBILITY

There is much conversation these days about personal responsibility. Some want to deny personal responsibility, while others want to emphasize personal responsibility. The arenas wherein such discussions transpire include:

Social law assumes personal responsibility: What did the perpetrator do; how did it violate the law; what is the legal consequence?

General philosophy addresses the moral responsibility of mankind as moral agents, considering how an individual adapts to the morés of a social group.

Christian theology argues whether the "sovereignty of God" implies a divine determinism that disallows human free-will, taking away personal responsibility.

Psychology considers personal issues of compulsion, obsession and addiction along with mental illness, concluding these are diseases and sickness beyond individual responsibility.

Postmodern thought tends to deny the responsibility of the individual "invisible man," focusing instead on collective social responsibility.

Christian thought has historically explained that God created human beings as responsible choosing creatures with the freedom of choice (rather than free-will) to respond to God with choices that have consequences. The English word "responsibility" is a contraction of the two-word phrase "response-ability," implying a human ability to respond with receptivity of God's activity. This removes any implications of a responsible duty to perform or conform in accord with required obligations, while recognizing our personal faith-response to God's grace in **JESUS** Christ.

MARCH 28

FULL DISCLOSURE

In the world of business finance, "full disclosure" refers to a complete accounting of all the finances of a business, wherein no pertinent information of assets or liabilities is concealed from a potential buyer or auditor. The business of the institutional church has often lacked such full disclosure, and has been protected from being open and transparent by laws allowing non-profit institutions to keep their business dealings secret from public scrutiny. Hence, religious institutions are notorious for having hidden agendas, for failure to disclose comprehensive financials, and for not reporting assets and liabilities.

In the world of sales, the principle of "truth in advertising" is an important issue designed to guard against deceptive, misleading, and inaccurate explanation of the product or its function. Advertisers are required by law to disclose factual information, and provide evidence of such facticity and veracity when asked, to avoid fraud being perpetrated on unsuspecting consumers. But there does not seem to be any oversight agency governing the claims that religious groups make about the product they are selling, peddling, merchandising, hustling, huckstering (II Cor. 2:17) with insincere and mercenary motives.

An indictment of Christian religion would reveal both an absence of "full disclosure" in the church and a violation of "truth in advertising" in the presentation of the gospel. In the proclamation of the Christian "good news," religious institutions and preachers often offer a watered-down version, a half-gospel that sells the true gospel short. It is common knowledge that a half-truth is a whole lie. Yes, it is true that the gospel of grace in Jesus Christ is free, but at the same time it will cost the recipient everything they are and have. That is why Dietrich Bonhoeffer, the twentieth-century martyr wrote his book, *The Cost of Discipleship*, challenging the "cheap grace" of religion.

DINING WITH THE DEVIL

This is the title of a book written by Os Guiness, who was at one time associated with the Christian apologist, Francis Schaeffer. I recall listening to him teach when I visited the L'Abri Fellowship in Huemoz, Switzerland in 1970. The book, *Dining with the Devil* (1993), subtitled "The megachurch movement flirts with modernity," is an early critique of the "church growth" megachurch phenomenon that began to mushroom in the late twentieth century churches, and continues as the *modus operandi* of successful and touted American churches to the present.

When the leaders of local churches get caught up in the "spirit of the age" with a quest for statistical advantage and bragging rights among the evangelical "powers that be," they are on the slippery slope to sacrificing what the community of faith was meant to be. The church is not an organization to be patterned after contemporary business-models. The pastor of a church is not equivalent to the CEO of a corporation. Worldly methods of marketing tools and management theories, employed with the objective of statistical power and control are incompatible with and antithetical to the growth of the living Body of Christ.

The Church is singularly unique as the dynamic organism of Christ-indwelt people, wherein the living Lord **JESUS** is the personal dynamic for the manifestation of His life and ministry in His people. For this reason, the organizational procedures and practices of contemporary business-models will never suffice for the growth and development of the Body of Christ. The time-honored understanding of the priesthood and ministry of all believers is too often sacrificed on the altar of pastoral popularity and statistical growth in attendance and monetary contributions. If the focus is on end-results, and the interests and needs of the "seeker" audience, rather than focusing on the living reality of **JESUS**, then the Church has been "dining with the devil."

MARCH 30

SPEAKING IN TONGUES

Throughout the history of the Christian faith, there have been references to Christian people speaking in language-forms that those who heard them did not comprehend. The biblical evidence begins with Jesus commissioning His disciples to preach the gospel, adding that those who heard would "speak in new tongues" (Mk. 16:17). This was fulfilled on Pentecost when the Holy Spirit descended and "every man heard them speak in his own tongue/language" (Acts 2:6). Gentile believers in the house of Cornelius spoke in tongues (Acts 10:46), and several people spoke in tongues in Ephesus (Acts 19:6). The most extended passage of instruction concerning "speaking in tongues" occurs in Paul's epistle to the Corinthians (I Cor. 12,13,14).

The phenomena of "speaking in tongues" has been a topic of much discussion and debate throughout the history of the church. The manifestation of this phenomenon was emphasized by those known as Pentecostals, beginning early in the twentieth century. Later in the same century, "speaking in tongues" was exhibited by the neo-Pentecostals or Charismatics. Many of the leaders in the mainline traditional churches objected to such contemporary "speaking in tongues" and taught cessationism, the theory that the spiritual gifts ceased in the apostolic era after the death of the original apostles of Jesus, and was no longer a viable or acceptable Christian expression.

There is no reason to denounce or demean those Christian brethren who have found a meaningful worship experience (private or public) in the practice of "speaking in tongues." The same Holy Spirit that prompted such speaking in the first century is the same Spirit who is alive and operative in Christians and the church today. When the practice of "speaking in tongues" exhibits the supernatural to unbelievers, or glorifies the Lord **JESUS** in Christian people in an edifying manner, praise God!

THE PASTOR'S WIFE

The pressure placed on pastor's wives in some religious circles is pathetic and abominable. The congregants of many local churches traffic on the abilities of the pastor's wife, often thinking they are getting a "two-for-one" special when they hire a new pastor. The pastor's wife is often expected to "minister" musically (if she has musical talents), to teach women's bible classes, lead the annual vacation bible school, teach children's Sunday School classes, counsel women with problems, and all that regardless of how many young children she might have in the home (her primary ministry), or whether she is vocationally employed in a career of her own, or is working to "make ends meet" at home.

My wife, Gracie, is very gifted musically. She plays piano, organ, oboe, flute, etc. She has a university degree in music education and training in both vocal and instrumental conducting. Despite being gifted and trained, she will not be "guilted" into playing in churches because they think she should play for free "as a ministry." She is also gifted as a teacher, presently serving as a full-time college professor, but will teach in the context of the church only when she believes God is calling her to do so. She jealously guards her freedom "in Christ" to be led of the Spirit, and to avoid being "railroaded" by religious people or groups that want to "use" her.

Every pastor is responsible to protect his wife from unwarranted and unwanted "opportunities to serve" in the local congregation. She must be allowed to be her own person as a "child of God," who listens to the direction of the Spirit (cf. Rom. 8:14) as she allows the life of the living Lord **JESUS** to be manifested in her life (cf. II Cor. 4:10,11). Any pressure from local parishioners who would seek to "play Holy Spirit" in the life of the pastor's wife should be resisted and rebuked. The pastor's wife should be allowed the freedom to be just that, to just be a wife serving as the helpmate of her husband who has been called to be a pastor.

APRIL 1

TERRORISM

"What has become of this world?" exclaimed the older gentleman as he viewed the latest media broadcast of terrorist tactics meant only to terrify innocent people. Throughout the history of humanity there have been "wars and rumors of wars" (Matt. 24:6), and such conflict can be expected until the end of time. Fallen mankind has often engaged, and will continue to engage, in violence against other people based on political, national, cultural, economic, religious, and ideological issues. But the phenomenon of indiscriminate terrorism intended to intimidate an entire group of people has increased in modern times.

The rules of engagement in warfare used to have basic parameters which included an acceptable use of force and violence against a specific identified opponent. Terrorism, however, is a form of asymmetric warfare that will use any means possible to terrorize people indiscriminately. They have used such tactics as suicide bombings and mass poisoning to attack and kill innocent and defenseless people. Terrorism is the warfare of the weak, who are unwilling or unable to stand up and engage in conflict *tête-à-tête,* head-on.

It has been said, "One man's terrorist is another man's freedom fighter." What does that mean? In the late twentieth century there were religious anti-abortion terrorists engaged in bombing abortion clinics and shooting medical doctors who performed abortions. They thought they were fighting for the freedom to be pro-life, and in their "zeal without knowledge" (Rom. 10:2), they were willing to allow the end to justify the means. Fundamentalist religion often creates extremist zealots and terrorists, so committed to their ideological belief-system they are willing to defend such even to the point of dying and killing others and destroying the property of those with whom they disagree. Such actions do not express the character of **JESUS**.

APRIL 2

HEALING

Human bodies are complex organisms, and subject to many diseases, injuries, and even unexplainable ailments. Since most individuals will suffer some or many of such maladies, there is a great interest in physical healing among the human community. The medical profession looks back to Hippocrates as "the father of medicine," and looks forward to the promise of empirical science in developing medicines that will increasingly bring healing to sick bodies. There are some who think that physical science and medicine are the only legitimate means by which to consider physical healing in the modern world.

Many others, however, believe that the materialist model of physiological healing can be supplemented, if not supplanted, by subjective or supernatural healing methods. Some espouse humanistic self-healing via meditation and mental processes. Many, in various religions, believe that the spirit-world, including God, can heal physiological, psychological and spiritual problems in human beings. The Christian faith also believes that God who created human bodies has the power to restore and heal those bodies by the supernatural power of the Holy Spirit sought through prayer and the laying on of hands (cf. James 5:14).

Jesus certainly engaged in divine healing during His time on earth, on occasions mentioning the effectiveness of such via the sufferers' faith-receptivity (Mk. 5:34; 10:32; Lk. 19:10). The apostle Paul mentions the spiritual giftedness of healing (I Cor. 12:9). As with many spiritual gifts and empowerings, healing has been misused and abused by "faith healers" and by those who claim that there is a divine right of universal healing for all Christians in the atoning work of **JESUS** Christ on the cross, citing Isaiah, "by His scourging we are healed" (Isa. 53:5). The Christian must not deny that there can be healing by natural medical means, as well as the supernatural intervention of God.

APRIL 3

WORSHIP

Contemporary concepts of worship among American Christians tend to be centered on lively, enthusiastic group-singing of repetitive choruses. Song leaders with praise bands are often utilized to work the audience into an orgy-like frenzy, using emotive hype to encourage the participants to a level of group excitation, accompanied with hand-raising and bouncing (which one observer called "pogo-sticking for Jesus"). Driving down the freeway, I saw a large banner (perhaps 200 feet long) attached to a church building with the words emblazoned on it, "The Fellowship of Excitement." If human excitement is our objective, then it is not worship!

The English word "worship" is etymologically derived from the old Anglo-Saxon word *weorthscipe*, meaning "worth-ship," referring to the ultimate worth of the character of God. True worship is not man-centered (to get our emotions worked up; to get "high on Jesus") or event-centered (together at a particular time and place), but God-centered. Legitimate Christian worship is *derived from* and empowered by God's grace, Spirit-inspired, and Christ-actuated. Christian worship is *directed to* the triune God in adoration, admiration, reverence and veneration of the value and worth of the character of God and His action.

JESUS is the subject and object of Christian worship. The Christ-life in the Christian will always express the "worth-ship" of God's character. Every action in the life of a Christian should be an act of worship. Everything? Yes, whether cooking meals, cleaning toilets, driving the automobile, disciplining the children, or intimate times with our spouse. This despite Martin Luther's comment, "It is impossible to have spiritual thoughts about what you do with your mate in bed." We have to ask ourselves: "Is there anything that I am engaged in that does not glorify God and express the worth-ship of His character?" If so, we must evaluate whether we are allowing **JESUS** to be our life in that area.

APRIL 4

SACRAMENTS

The triune God is singularly and absolutely holy and sacred. The very word "holy" implies that God is "set apart" from everything that is not Him. What God is, only God is! God alone is worthy of our worship and reverence. Religions, however, attribute holy and sacred significance to various actions, objects and persons. This was true in the Judaic religion of the Old Testament where the temple, objects used in the temple, and the actions of the priests in the temple were described as "holy" because of their association with the worship of God. Likewise, in the ensuing Christian religion, various actions, objects and persons have been identified as "holy," i.e. priests, scripture, Holy Baptism, Holy Communion, etc., because of their connection to the Holy God.

The Christian religion has called some of these rites and actions "sacraments," from the Latin *sacer* (sacred or holy). The Roman Catholic Church and some Protestant churches identify seven sacraments – Baptism, Eucharist, confirmation, penance, matrimony, holy orders, and anointing the sick – sometimes regarded as "essential for salvation." Other Protestant churches have two "ordinances," baptism and Lord's Supper, while others emphasize only the internal significance. The Eastern Orthodox churches refer to these actions as "mysteries," emphasizing the unknowable reality of what God is doing in human lives. The Church, as a whole, has defined a "sacrament" as "a visible action signifying an invisible spiritual reality."

Liturgical brethren, who attach great meaning to the religious sacraments, are sometimes shocked when I declare, "I am the sacrament of God; I am the visible expression of the invisible character of God." Every Christian, as a "saint, a holy one of God" (I Cor. 1:2), is indwelt by the Holy presence of the triune God, and is intended to visibly image the invisible character of God in Christian behavior, thus becoming living sacraments of God.

APRIL 5

IT'S FRIDAY, BUT SUNDAY IS COMING

S.M. Lockridge (1913-2000) was an African-American pastor at a Baptist Church in San Diego, CA. He is best known for a sermon he preached, entitled "He's My King," in which he emphasized, "It's Friday, but Sunday's Comin'." He took the Passion narrative of Jesus' crucifixion on Friday and pointed out the betrayal, mockery, suffering, and death of Jesus, as well as the despair, forsakenness, defeat and hopeless response of the disciples. Repeatedly, he countered the dire situation of Friday with the phrase, "but Sunday's Comin'," emphasizing the victory of resurrection with the joy and elation of the disciples on Easter.

Many preachers have adapted Pastor Lockridge's sermon and emphasized the psychological sorrows that many people experience on the figurative "Fridays" of life. Many are still mocking Jesus. Many are rejecting Him, and yelling, "Crucify him!" Many suffer from brutality and betrayal. Many are discouraged, hopeless, and filled with grief. Many suffer from guilt and shame. Many are desperately hanging on, looking for a coming future day when things will get better, when they will feel "happy," and have a positive outlook on life. Yes, and many of these suffering "Friday despair" call themselves "Christians."

May I suggest that it is more biblically and theologically correct to flip the entire narrative. The victory of the gospel story is better presented as "It's Sunday; Friday is Done." The redemptive work of Jesus is completed and accomplished. From the cross, Jesus declared, "It is finished!" (Jn. 19:30). Jesus' sacrificial death accomplished everything necessary for the entire restoration of humanity, not just in the future but right now! The living Lord **JESUS** is our present and real hope (cf. I Tim. 1:1). He is our victory, our peace, our assurance, our grace-provision. Christians can have an entirely different perspective than the world around them. Christians are to live on the Sunday side of the cross!

APRIL 6

RESURRECTION "NOW"

When the topic of "resurrection" is considered in Christian teaching, it is usually used to emphasize "Resurrection **THEN**" (in the past), or "Resurrection **WHEN**" (in the future), but seldom to emphasize "Resurrection **NOW**" (in the present). Christian religion tends to emphasize the *past* and the *future*, to the neglect of the *present*. Often there is an emphasis on the fact that our *past* sins are forgiven, and our *future* destiny is assured, but the *present* provision for living the Christian life is sidestepped. Our *past* is forgiven; our *future* is assured; but the *present* is the "pits"! It seems that the best that the Christian religion can offer is that we are just "hanging on for dear life" on the rickety roller-coaster ride of present existence, hoping for a rapture to relieve us from the ruckus, and awaiting death to depart unto heaven.

I am not content with a religious message that has both ends covered (past and future), but does not have an adequate message of hope and provision for the **NOW** – the present! A message of *past remedy* and *future reward*, without the fullness of a *present reality* that allows one to live life to the fullness in Jesus Christ is a static and sterile message of what "has been" and what "will be" without any NOW. It is but a religious sandwich with nothing in the middle – no meat – no substance! It is a religious method that leaves a vacuous void right where we need it most – right **NOW**! It is a message that leaves people in the "black hole" of religion, constantly compressed into the conformity of restrictive performance, hoping they won't get "left behind."

The "good news" of the Christian gospel is that the Resurrection-Life of the risen and living Lord Jesus is the vital and dynamic presence within the Christian that provides a centrifugal action that allows the character of Christ to be expressed in Christian behavior – right **NOW** – in every circumstance of our present lives. Resurrection **NOW**!

APRIL 7

WHY DO YOU DO WHAT YOU DO?

Little Jack Horner sat in the corner, eating his Christmas pie.
He stuck in his thumb and pulled out a plum, and declared,
"Oh, what a good boy am I!"

Was Jack a "do-gooder" who did what he did so others would see him and praise him in like manner as he heaped self-praise upon himself? Was he seeking self-aggrandizement? Of the basic journalistic "W-questions": who?, what?, when?, where? and why?, WHY is the most important. The "why" explains the purpose and objective of the course of one's action.

Many people's "why" is self-oriented: money, attention, fame, power, pleasure. The "why" of our action will usually be based on the "who" of our sense of identity. The "why" of our action should not be used to establish the "who" of our identity. Who you perceive yourself to BE will be the basis of "why you DO what you DO." Our contentment should be in Being, rather than in Doing and accomplishing. If there is no clear "why" motivation, then our focus will be on "who," it's all about me; or "what," on profit, praise, and self-glory instead of God and other people.

People who do not have a clear "why" for what they do, often have expectations of "atta boy" or "atta girl" commendations, recognition, pats on the back, and achievement certificates. They often feel unappreciated, disgruntled, or get their feelings hurt if no one jumps in to help them. Feeling rejected, they begin to complain about their plight and withdraw from involvement.

Why do you do what you do? Paul wrote that we are to "do all to the glory of God" (I Cor. 10:31). We are to engaged in what God wants to be and do in us. Since "God is love" (I Jn. 4:8,16), what He wants to do in us will likely be for others, and will manifest the character of **JESUS** in our every action (II Cor. 4:10,11).

APPRECIATING PRODIGALITY

The parable that has long been known as "The Parable of the Prodigal Son" (Lk. 15:11-32) has also been called by other titles. Some people are shocked to hear it referred to as "The Parable of the Prodigal Father." A common meaning of the word "prodigal" refers to a wasteful, profligate, imprudent, and depraved spendthrift, as was exhibited by the younger son. But the root of the word "prodigal" is the Latin *prodigus* meaning "lavish, extravagant, bounteous, or generous." The father in the parable, representing God the Father, is extravagantly lavish and generous in expressing His loving appreciation that the younger son has returned home after his wayward escapades. He throws a party for all the farmhands and family friends, kills the prize steer for prime steaks, and makes the returning son the celebrity honoree of the occasion.

The elder of the two sons in the story despised both the negative prodigality of his younger brother, as well as the positive prodigality of his father. The older son prided himself on his loyal religious duty. "For so many years I have been serving you" (Lk. 15:29). He was acting the part, going through the motions, expecting to get his reward from the estate in the end. The rebellious debauchery of the younger brother and the joyless religious duty of the older brother caused them to be equally self-absorbed. Both had contempt for the loving character of their father, who desired relational bonding of love with them both.

The parable is primarily about the prodigious and lavishly extravagant grace of God the Father, expressing His limitless love for all of His sons (and daughters) – for all of us. "All that is mine is yours," the father explains to the elder son (15:31). In like manner, "God has blessed us with every spiritual blessing in heavenly places in Christ **JESUS**" (Eph. 1:3). Do we appreciate the lavish and extravagant prodigality of our Father God?

APRIL 9

THE BONDAGE OF RELIGION

The world seems to have no end to the perversions in which people will engage, be they relational, religious, sexual, social, etc. Religion, in particular, has a seemingly endless variation of strange and bizarre deviances and distortions, partly because religion has no established norm of practice and behavior – people will do anything in the name of religion. The etymology of the word "religion" traces back to the Latin words *religare* and *religio*. These words referred to binding or tying one thing to another. Human anatomy, for example, refers to a "ligament" that ties or binds bones to bone or a bone with cartilage.

Religion, throughout human history, has tied or bound people in ethical rules and regulations, as well as rituals of acceptable practice as defined by the religious authorities. To be fair, there is a positive side where one can refer to being bound in personal devotion to the God that one worships. By and large, though, the bondage of religion, though facilitating meaningful social ties, has been detrimental to peoples' experiencing the relational freedom that Jesus Christ intended to bring in Himself. Jesus said, "You will know the truth and the truth will set you free" (Jn. 8:32). "If the Son makes you free, you will be free indeed" (Jn. 8:36).

Based on the etymology of the word "religion," some have explained that religion is a form of pscho-spiritual BDSM (bondage, domination, sadism, masochism). Satanically inspired religion has attracted power-hungry and materialistic leaders who seek to dominate the lives of other people by binding such followers in rules, regulations and rituals. They seem to thrive on sadistic practices that cause pain to the followers, and encourage masochistic involvement (i.e. "give until it hurts;" "keep serving until you burn-out and become a martyr.") The bondage of religion is a perversion that is contrary to God's intent for a love relationship with humanity through the Son, **JESUS** Christ.

APRIL 10

THERE'S NOTHING YOU CAN DO *FOR JESUS*

Christian people are constantly talking about all that they are *doing for* Jesus. They have been repetitively challenged to "live *for* Jesus," "give your all *for* Jesus, "burn-out *for* Jesus," "lay down your life *for* Jesus," to "work *for* the Lord, Jesus," "step out *for* God," "make a difference *for* God." It would appear that God and His Son, Jesus, are extremely helpless beings, weak, disabled, debilitated, dependent, and impotent. They seem to need everything done *for* them. That is what religion specializes in, incentivizing people to *do* this or that *for* God and the Son, Jesus; getting people involved in performance, "go, go, go and do, do, do *for* Jesus. Try harder; do more *for* Jesus!"

God, the Father, the Son, and the Spirit, does not need anything done *for* Him. Jesus is God. God is Independent, All-powerful, Almighty, Sovereign, and Self-generative. God does not need anything done *for* Him. Everything God does He does out of His own character and Self-empowering. He does what He does because He is who He is. What are you going to *do* for Someone who is, has, and does everything? How are you going to assist Him? God is not seeking people to join His taskforce.

We human beings, on the other hand, are dependent and derivative creatures. Humans cannot *do* anything out of themselves. They derive character and energizing out of a spirit-being source (either God or Satan). It is not God who is dependent and needy of our *doing* anything *for* Him. Jesus said, "Apart from Me, you can do nothing" (Jn. 15;5). All we can do *for* God, *for* **JESUS**, is to cease all our impotent efforts to *do* anything *for* Him. Our response is simply "Thank You Lord, I will accept what You have done on my behalf; by faith I am willing to be receptive to Your continued grace-activity in my life. Our human response of faith is not something we *do for* Jesus, for which He should be thankful that we are "on board," on His work-force.

APRIL 11

STOP TRYING TO BE "LIKE JESUS"

We have all heard the fallacious religious mandate and incentive that Christians are to strive to be "like Christ." Yet, not once in the entire New Testament is there an inspired call or admonition to "be like Jesus" or to "be like Christ" (only in human-added religious headings - cf. Phil. 2). Jesus is the God-man, divine and human. Inherent within Himself is the exclusive divine power to manifest godliness and the character of Christ. We are human creatures, incapable of being "like God" or "like Jesus." The only possibility to manifest godly character, as it was for Jesus as a man also, is to derive such by the receptivity of faith.

Religion specializes in inculcations for Christians to engage in what they are incapable of doing, to keep people busy striving to do what they cannot do. Such activity keeps religious people dependent on the religious organization and leaders, constantly involved in attendance and monetary giving in an attempt to achieve the impossible. Only Jesus can "be like Jesus." He desires to be Himself and manifest His life and character in our human behavior (cf. II Cor. 4:10,11). The only question is: will we allow Him to be our life and act out His life using the vehicles of our bodies? He is not asking that we do anything; just receive.

Religion does not understand and will never accept the dynamic gospel of God's Grace in Jesus Christ by the Spirit. It would put religion out of business! Religion is always focused on performance-based admonitions for human activity – what man is supposed to do, rather than on what God has done and is doing. The gospel of God's grace pertains to what God does, not what we are supposed to do. The living Lord Jesus wants to be all and do all in the Christian. That is what it means for Jesus to be Lord of our lives. **JESUS** wants to be Himself, as He is allowed to live out His life and character in every Christian person. Jesus will appreciate that you cease trying to mime what only He can do.

APRIL 12

FRANKLY, I DON'T GIVE A DAMN!

In the epic Civil War drama, *Gone with the Wind* (1939), Scarlett O'Hara tearfully asks Rhett, "Where shall I go? What shall I do?" Rhett Butler, matter-of-factly replies, "Frankly my dear, I don't give a damn!" He had done all he was going to do to win her love. As for me, I have done all that I ever intend to do to keep the religious institution afloat and operational. No amount of pleading, cajoling or manipulative "guilting" will dissuade me from walking away and giving up on religion and its shenanigans. That is where our freedom in Christ begins, when we cease striving to control or even participate in a go-nowhere endeavor.

We all have situations in our lives where we have come to the end of our rope. We are ready to cease striving to resolve the situation in ways that most would consider favorable. God is in control. My seeking to be in control of the situation will not contribute to a God-honoring solution. So, we choose to back-off, perhaps throw up our hands, and exclaim, "Frankly, I don't give a damn!" There's nothing wrong with that. In fact, I should think that God is extremely excited that we have come to the end of ourselves, our own endeavors and works, and we are willing to entrust ourselves to whatever God wants to do.

All the religious inculcations to engage in religious activities to accomplish something *for* God are fruitless. It's a go-nowhere, dead-end endeavor. One might as well beat their head against a wall as to repetitively engage in religious activities. If the religious institutions go "down the tube" and "peter-out" and dwindle into oblivion (which many are already doing), I don't give a damn. It is my opinion that old dinosaurs should be allowed to go extinct and disappear. I don't give a damn about religion, but my participation with God through union with my Lord **JESUS** is priceless. Religion emphasizes faith in religion, but Christians are called to put their faith in God through **JESUS**.

APRIL 13

WHEN FAITH AMOUNTS TO NOTHING

James was a very practical man. He didn't engage in speculative and theoretical theology; his focus was on behavioral outcomes. Because of this, he is often charged with emphasizing "works" instead of grace. In fact, the venerable reformer, Martin Luther, so misunderstood the epistle of James that he questioned its canonicity and referred to it as an "epistle of straw," unable to reconcile Paul and James on the correlation of faith and works. Paul wrote, "For by grace are you saved through faith; not of works" (Eph. 2:8). James wrote, "Faith without works is useless" (James 2:20) and "dead" (James 2:26) – nothing!

It does not appear to me that there is an irreconcilable antinomy between what Paul and James wrote in the inspired scriptures. Perhaps the apparent dichotomy is in the semantic meaning of the words they used. "Faith," for example has different connotations. It can mean mental assent to the veracity of factual data, and James explained, "the demons believe and quake" (I2:19), but it did them no good. But both James and Paul seem to have realized that "faith" has a more dynamic new covenant definition of "our human receptivity of God's activity." The faith-response to Christ will necessarily have behavioral outcomes.

The concept of "works" also has more than one meaning. Paul was certain that religious "works" could not to be considered as having meritorious saving significance before God. We are not saved by our front-loaded works! James was just as convinced that without the back-loaded concept of "works" as the outworking of the life of the indwelling **JESUS**, then the dynamic definition of "faith" is made null and void. Faith amounts to nothing if we fail to recognize that God's grace-activity is part of the definition. Christian faith is not passivism or acquiescence; by definition, it allows for the inevitable active expression of God's grace in the behavioral outcomes of the Christian life.

APRIL 14

TAINTED EVANGELISM

To address the modern methods of evangelism prevalent among Christians today is akin to an iconoclastic attack on one of the most revered evangelical idols of our day. I am emboldened to do so after reading the words of Christoph Blumhardt, a German spiritual leader, written over a century ago to his son-in-law who was a missionary in China. His words are so prophetic of what would develop more fully in modern religious practice. With great wisdom, Christoph Blumhardt (1842-1919) wrote, "Aggressive attempts at evangelizing do not spring from the love of God, but from the spirit of business."

Often taking their miscue from questionable religious interpretations of the so-called "great commission" in Matt. 28:19,20, many evangelical groups have developed aggressive methods of evangelism. That text is not an imperative mandate to go and share the doctrines of the institutional church, but employs a participial verb best translated, "As you are going about your daily life, use the opportunities to share your faith and introduce others to what it means to be a follower of Christ."

Many religious groups, especially in America, have advocated forms of evangelism that fail to express the love and concern of God. They are often merely a propaganda activity of "works" with an incentive to earn points before God. Such activity is no longer a sharing of the "good news" of the reality of the living Christ, but an engagement in human endeavors of productivity that allegedly enhance the false numerical success of the institutional church by manipulating their uncomfortable victims to repeat a creedal mantra they do not understand. Christians may share the life of **JESUS** that has transformed their own lives, but the objective is not to dump information on unsuspecting victims, and then gloat about their successes like frontiersmen of old making notches on their rifles for picking off another prey.

APRIL 15

"ONE SPIRIT WITH HIM"

As a Christian, you are so one with the Spirit of the living Lord Jesus that there should be no explanation of you apart from Him. That doesn't mean that you ARE Him, and can strut around say "I AM Jesus!" Though our spiritual relationship with Jesus is so tight that we are called "Christians," i.e. Christ-ones, that does not mean that we are essentially the God-man, the Son of God. Our identity as Christ-ones is a derived identity, always dependent on the distinct divine other, i.e. on the one and only Christ whose spiritual Being and presence forms who we are in union with Him. Apart from Him, I am and can do nothing (cf. Jn. 15:5).

Writing to the often misrepresentative Corinthian "Christ-ones," the apostle Paul explains, "the one who joins himself to the Lord is one spirit with Him" (I Cor. 6:17). In like manner as the union of a man and woman in marriage is a "one flesh" union, so our spiritual union with Christ is a "one spirit" union. In the marital union, the husband and the wife retain their distinction as individual persons. The man does not become the woman, nor does the woman become the man. In marriage, we are not *essentially* one, but we are *relationally* one. In like manner, the spiritual oneness-union of the believer with Jesus, we are not *essentially* one with Christ, but we are *relationally* united and identified with the Spirit of the living Christ – so much so that we, as Christ-ones, cannot be adequately identified or explained apart from who **JESUS** is as Lord in and through us.

Such spiritual union of the Spirit of Christ with the Christian's human spirit is an overlooked and missing component in much contemporary Christian understanding. Most Christ-ones have not assimilated the awareness that they are spiritually "one with Jesus" to the extent that they can say, "Christ is my life" (Col. 3:3,4); "it is no longer I who lives, but Christ lives in me" (Gal. 2:20) – as me! Christ-ones have "one spirit" union with **JESUS**.

A MATTER OF CONTROL

I was sitting with a man as we ate breakfast together. His life was a pattern of obsessive, compulsive, and addictive forays into self-destruction. He had just come down from one such binge, and I asked him why he repetitively kept going back to alcohol and drugs, knowing that such actions always led to misery. His response was surprising, "It is my attempt to be in control." The answer seemed ironic, since the addictive behaviors always seemed to be controlling him, and causing him to be "out of control." After I questioned such, he explained that he had such a controlling wife that he felt like he was never in control of anything, but when he drank or snorted, he felt like he had control to make such a decision, even if it was self-destructive.

This man and his wife were engaged in a vicious cycle. The wife was a devoted Christian woman who was continually trying to keep the family under control by protecting the children from the erratic excesses of the obsessive husband. Yes, she had some "control issues," and tended to disallow her husband to take the lead in family matters, but the husband's excuses for his abuses certainly did nothing to provide stability in the family. There was an uncontrolled struggle for control in the relationship.

God did create human beings as choosing creatures with freedom of choice, so we do, in one sense, have the ability or power to control the decisions we make. We are self-determinative by the choices that we make. In a more overarching spiritual sense, though, every human being is a derivative creature who is being controlled by a spiritual source, either God or Satan. Our choices are receptive choices to derive either positive (righteous) or negative (evil) character from a spirit-source. Those who have received the Spirit of the living **JESUS** into their spirit as Christ-ones have the continuing choice to allow **JESUS** as Lord to be in control of their lives and the decisions they make.

APRIL 17

LAW VERSUS GRACE

When some Christians think of the "law," their mental picture is the tablets of stone that Moses brought down from Mt. Sinai. When historicized and objectified in such thinking, such Christians often fail to see the contemporary implication of "law" in their Christian lives. An expanded perspective of "law" allows us to recognize the general concept that "law" always pertains to "human doing" and performance – a "do-right religion." This allows us to see that legalistic efforts to please God by our human doing are antithetical to the new covenant of grace wherein Jesus has (and still does) perform everything necessary.

A similar misconception of "grace" resides in the minds of many Christians when they conceive of "grace" as an unmerited favor of an "eternal-life package" that we receive as an inheritance when we choose to believe in the historical Jesus. Such a static event and experience-centered perspective of "grace" fails to appreciate the dynamic of God's grace invested in every Christian by the indwelling presence of the living Lord Jesus in order to live out the Christ-life in a moment-by-moment, day-by-day re-presentation of Christ's life and character. Grace is the present dynamic of the risen Lord Jesus by the Holy Spirit.

So, what do these misconceptions of contrasting activity lead to in Christians' lives today? When Christians focus on "law," they are bound by different varieties of "believe-right" and "do-right" religion which only frustrate. Only by receiving God's dynamic grace of **JESUS** living His life out through us can the Christian rest secure in the peace of divine sufficiency. Attempting to perform "the letter of the law" is deadly (cf. II Cor. 3:6). The Spirit of grace, on the other hand, is enlivening as **JESUS** empowers and manifests His life in the behavior of our mortal bodies (cf. II Cor. 4:10,11). Do not settle for the bondage of law-based religion, but revel in the freedom of God's grace-dynamic day-by-day.

APRIL 18

"YES, LORD!"

On occasions, I have explained to others that my prayer language only has two words: "Yes, Lord!" What more does one need in their communication and communion with God? Since "Jesus is Lord," a foremost declaration of Christians from the beginning of the Christian faith, implies that Jesus is in control of our lives, the responsibility of a Christian is not to attempt to "call the shots" and live their life in self-sufficiency. The indwelling living Lord Jesus is to direct our lives as "sons of God ... led by the Spirit (Rom. 8:14). We prayerfully "listen under" God's leading in obedience and respond with, "Yes, Lord, I will act in accord with your directive by Your grace-empowering."

Peter was progressively learning how the new covenant of grace in the living Lord Jesus was to become operative. While on the rooftop of Simon the Tanner in Joppa (Acts 10:9-16), God lowered a sheet filled with God-created animals, some of which were non-kosher in his Jewish religious tradition. When advised to kill and eat these animals, Peter responded with self-righteous religious indignation, "By no means, Lord..." He apparently did not yet see the incongruity of his response. If Jesus is the operative Lord of our lives as Christ-ones, it is not our place to "call the shots" and say "No" to God's direction in our lives.

The only appropriate response of a Christ-one is to obediently "listen under" the inner promptings of God's Spirit and prayerfully respond with, "Yes, Lord. Whatever you say!" We are only responsible to be and to do what God directs and desires to be and do in us today. We do not take our instructions from any other, not even the religious leaders of the ecclesiastical institution in which we might participate. As Peter rightfully explained earlier to the religious authorities, "We must obey God rather than men" (Acts 5:29). "Jesus is Lord" (I Cor. 12:3; Phil. 2:11), and this is the functional basis of all Christian action.

APRIL 19

THE MYSTERY IS CHRIST

The apostle Paul writes in his epistles, "the mystery is Christ" (Eph. 3:4; Col. 2:2; 4:3). What does he mean? The Greek word *musterion,* that we translate as "mystery," does not refer to an enigmatic and puzzling conundrum, or to a secretive "who-dunnit" thriller. The Greek word, as Paul uses it, pertains to something that was "once concealed, but is now revealed" in Jesus Christ (cf. Rom. 16:25). Notice that Paul indicates that the mystery IS Christ; not a separated and detached message *about* Jesus. Jesus IS the full reality of all that God wants mankind to know and experience for relational restoration.

Throughout the history of Christian thought, a different connotation of "mystery" has often appeared. The Gnostic concept of "mystery" seeks a lofty and esoteric awareness of the "deep things of God" that the uninitiated cannot fathom or appreciate. Many Christian people love to engage in mystical musings of alleged spiritual abstractions that seem to be beyond normal human thinking, the paranormal. They revel in lofty metaphysical discussion of elevated awareness of spiritual concepts, and the result of such is but a puffed-up pride (I Cor. 8:1) of knowing things that others cannot understand.

It is possible to love ideas more than one loves Jesus. If **JESUS** is not the heart and essence of all that you are thinking of, meditating on, and living out, then whatever you have it is not the Christian gospel. The issue is **JESUS**. The risen and living Lord Jesus Christ IS the once concealed, now revealed reality of God. The divine Son of God became a man in the incarnation, who by death, resurrection and ascension has Himself been made available to all mankind for full restoration. There is no mysterious secret beyond how the historical Jesus became the experiential Jesus via the "mystery of the gospel" (Eph. 6:19), comprised of "Christ in you, the hope of glory" (Col. 1:26,27).

GOD'S PROVISION FOR CHRISTIAN LIVING

The primary thing the old covenant lacked was the provision and empowering to fulfill what God asked Israel to do in the Mosaic Law. That didn't take God by surprise. He planned it that way! The purpose of the Law was to expose the inability of God's people to keep the Law and thus manifest the character of God. The failure of Israel, despite their proclaimed intents of "we will do it!" (Exod. 24:7), "You can count on us!" was a foregone conclusion from the beginning. They were set-up for failure! God knew that the Jewish religion was just a preliminary stepping-stone for the restoration of humanity in Jesus.

Some find it difficult to believe that God would set up a religious system, like the Jewish Law-religion, knowing full well that human beings were incapable of the kind of obedience required to keep God's requirements in such a system. But that was God's all-wise way to give fallen mankind the time to be fully convinced that the way of human performance "works" inspired by Satan was a bankrupt dead-end system that could never please God. The message of the old covenant was, "You don't have what it takes! Keep looking for what does work!"

The new covenant of God in the person of Jesus Christ is the good news that we are given the provision to express the character of God in human behavior when we receive by faith the grace-dynamic of the indwelling Spirit of Jesus Christ within the human spirit. Everything that God desires of mankind is provided by the divine grace-action of **JESUS** living in the Christian, the empowering of His Spirit. We have what it takes in Jesus – the provision to be man as God intended man to be. "God has blessed us with every spiritual blessing in heavenly places in Christ" (Eph. 1:3). "His divine power has granted to us everything pertaining to life and godliness" (II Pet. 1:3). "All things belong to you" (I Cor. 3:21) – full provision for Christian living.

APRIL 21

REALLY?

No one would have dreamed up a religion that began with the premise that the Creator of the universe sent His Son to the humans on planet earth in the form of an infant boy born in a sheep-stall and wearing diapers, identifying Him as the deliverer and savior of mankind. From a purely logical perspective, it does seem rather far-fetched, don't you think? Then, that Son, after He has grown to adulthood, constantly declares that He eschews all religion, and tells the leaders of the prevailing Jewish religion of the region where He resided, "You are of your father, the devil who is a perpetual liar and a murderer" (Jn. 8:44).

Yet, apart from the incarnation, Christianity is a meaningless story with very little content. "Ain't it nice to be nice to nice people?" is not a message that gives meaning to life, or heals the physical and social brokenness of the human race, or inspires people to lay down their lives to share it with others, or produces hope for something more than we now have. The physical incarnation of Jesus serves as the historical and biblical *"stake in the ground"* that exposes and invalidates the false spiritualization of Christianity, that is evidenced in so many fanciful and mystical speculations of Christian thought through the centuries.

The God-man born under such humble circumstances was subsequently indicted for sedition and subjected to a criminal's death of Roman crucifixion. Who would start a religion centered around a man who was executed by governmental authorities for insurrection, and then claim that his death was really a divine triumph and victory? The message of a criminalized Christ, a murdered Messiah, is a hard-sell, even if they claimed that He arose from the dead. It is no wonder that the Christian gospel, with its narrative of incarnation, crucifixion, and resurrection, was from the beginning considered moronic and scandalous (I Cor. 1:18-25). **JESUS** alone is Savior and Lord – Really!

APRIL 22

TWO CATEGORIES OF MANKIND

In the narrative where Jesus encounters Nicodemus in John 3:1-15, we can perceive two categories of mankind. Nicodemus was "a man of the Pharisees," as religious as religious could be, yet as spiritually ignorant and unregenerate as natural man can be. Nicodemus came to Jesus, cognizant that Jesus had a heavenly component of God that was not present in his own life. He saw the presence and the activity of God in Jesus, comprising a second category of mankind beyond his own experience. Jesus "cut to the chase," and said, "Unless one is born from above, he cannot see and experience the heavenly kingdom of God" (3:3).

There are only two categories of mankind, the unregenerate and the regenerate, the natural and the spiritual (cf. I Cor. 2:14-3:1). The only way to make the transition from natural to spiritual is to "be born from above" as Jesus said to Nicodemus. The Spirit of God must be received and allowed to indwell the spirit of a human being. Jesus pictures this as a "new birth" whereby the divine life of God is "brought into being" again in the spirit of a human being, as was true of mankind at creation, but was repudiated and forfeited when the original couple made the choice to reject the derivation of God's life, and became sinners.

The spiritual dimension of restored humanity is not an "add-on" to the physical that occurs when a person is "born again" and becomes a Christ-one (Christian). All human beings have both physical and spiritual existence. There is, however, an exchange of spiritual indwelling content that occurs at spiritual regeneration, when "the spirit that works in the sons of disobedience" (Eph. 2:2) is exchanged for "the Spirit of God" (Rom. 8:9) in Christ. Such newness of spiritual life by the indwelling of Jesus Christ causes a receptive individual to become a "new creature" in Christ (II Cor. 5:17), who is "born of the Spirit" (Jn. 3:8) and comprehends "heavenly things" (3:12).

APRIL 23

IS SATAN OPERATIVE IN PEOPLE?

While many do not believe in spiritual beings and limit all reality to the natural physical world, many others throughout the world believe in and experience spiritual realities. Most religions of the world espouse the awareness of spiritual beings and activities, but increasingly people are rejecting the metaphysical tenets and practices of religion. Spiritual presence and activity does not necessary have to be couched in religion. Many who have eschewed religion are deeply involved in spirituality. Differentiation must be made, however, between evil spiritual activity and the spiritual action of a good and righteous God.

Throughout Christian history, Christians have recognized that the spirit of Satan is "alive and well on planet earth" (cf. Hal Lindsey), but asserted that "the Spirit of truth" (Jn. 15:26; 16:13) embodied in the risen and living Lord Jesus, the life-giving Spirit (I Cor. 15:45), is the antithesis of and conqueror of "the spirit of error" (I Jn. 4:6). The Christian gospel is the glorious reality of "the Spirit of Christ" (Rom. 8:9) bringing divine life into the spirit of a receptive individual with the expectation that such a Christ-one (Christian) might be "strengthened with power through His Spirit in the inner man" (Eph. 3:16) to live out the Christ-life.

Christians have been reticent, however, to accept that Satan and his power is operative in those who are not Christians. Is it because they do not want to offend unbelievers? Scripture is clear that the fallen world of mankind is "in the Evil One" (I Jn. 5:19), caught "in the snare of the devil, held captive to do his will" (II Tim. 2:26), and "the prince of the power of the air is the spirit working in the sons of disobedience" (Eph. 2:2). W. Ian Thomas writes, "As godliness is the consequence of God's activity to reproduce Himself in you, so all ungodliness is the consequence of Satan's activity to reproduce the devil in you" (*Mystery of Godliness*, pg. 86). Yes, Satan is operating in non-Christians.

APRIL 24

THE PERFORMANCE SLIDE

As children, many of us loved the "slipper-slide" on the local playground. It was so exhilarating to climb the steps, sit on the top, put our hands in the air, and let gravity pull us to the bottom as we squealed with laughter. The taller the slide the better. We used to take waxed paper from mom's cupboard to make the slide more slippery. As time has marched on, it seems that some Christians never progressed beyond their love for the "slipper-slide." Like wax on smooth metal, many Christians are drawn to the playground of religion, willing to climb higher and higher to participate in the performance slide of religious activity.

Why do so many Christian people seem to gravitate to performance-oriented requirements and techniques as the *modus operandi* of the Christian life? Why are regenerated people so willing to accept and submit to the rules and regulations of religion? Why are those who call themselves Christians so susceptible to legalism and the meritorious "do good" mentality of attempting to maintain a right relationship with God? Paul asked the Galatian Christians, "you who want to be under law, do you not listen to the law" (Gal. 4:21) and its binding performance requirements? "As you received Christ Jesus the Lord, so walk in Him" (Col. 2:6). It's a faith-walk, not a DO-walk!

An answer to the above stated questions seems to be that there is an element of selfish performance pride patterned in the fleshly desires of mankind (even after they become Christians), whereby they want to get credit for their accomplishments. They want their "works" to count for something in the sight of God. They want to think that they can co-operate with God in His endeavor of salvation and sanctification. How sad that so many Christians just can't quite accept that Jesus has "paid it all," that Jesus has done everything that needs doing in His "finished work" of **JESUS** Christ. "It is finished!" (Jn. 19:30). There is nothing more to DO!

APRIL 25

GULLIBILITY

I am constantly amazed at the gullibility of people who appear to be rational individuals, but are willing to accept the most outlandish explanations of phenomena, and turn to most bizarre untested procedures to treat their medical and human needs. These are often people who fully assent to the empirical basis of scientific investigation and accept the humanistic theories of human sufficiency for all matters of life, and are often quite condescending in their attitudes toward what they perceive to be the incredulous gullibility of Christian people who believe in a God who has made Himself known in Jesus Christ.

They likely debunk the mythology of the Greeks and Romans, with their consult of the oracle of Delphi in prescientific days as speculative superstitions, but the credulity by which they believe propositions totally unsupported by any evidence is nothing short of incredible. Many are susceptible to far-fetched conspiracy theories, both historical and modern. They are prone to believe in ancient aliens from other planets, extraterrestrial beings who visited in "unidentified flying objects" (UFOs) to explain natural and historical phenomena. If they are religious, they may project such thinking to futurist "left behind" theories.

When it comes to the physical healing of their bodies, these same people will fall for almost any promised pills and procedures to cure their ailments. Modern "snake-oil peddlers" (often religious) are always available to offer fraudulent solutions such as ion therapy, acupuncture, biofeedback, aromatherapy, chelation therapy, as well as homeopathic or chiropractic treatments and faith-healing. Fallen mankind is perpetually searching for something beyond themselves, something metaphysical to meet their needs, and willing to take ill-advised actions. Spiritually, the historical and experiential evidence is quite sufficient to support personal belief in **JESUS** Christ as the Savior of mankind.

DOUBLE INCLUSION

In the fields of theoretical mathematics and computer programming, reference is made to "double inclusion," usually seeking the avoidance of such. These fields are beyond my expertise, but within the biblical explanation of the relationship between the living Christ and the Christian there does seem to be reference to an essential double inclusion. The scriptures refer to both our being "in Christ," and Christ being "in us." This spiritual double inclusion has been a source of confusion for many Christians, as many find it difficult to understand whether the function of the preposition "in" is equivalent in both phrases.

Of these two phrases, reference to Christ being "in the Christian" is lesser used, but no less important for understanding the Christian condition. Paul explained that "the mystery of the gospel is Christ in you" (Col. 1:26,27). "It is no longer I, but Christ lives in me" (Gal. 2:20). "Do you not recognize that Jesus Christ is in you?" (II Cor. 13:5). The preposition "in" is used in this instance in its primary meaning of location within another object. The Spirit of the living Christ dwells within the spirit of a receptive Christian. But this is more than static location, and will necessarily refer to the functional expression of His life.

The more prominent of the two phrases in the New Testament is reference to the Christian being "in Christ," "in the Lord," and "in Him." Paul wrote, "If anyone is *in Christ,* he is a new creature" (II Cor. 5:17). "There is no condemnation for those who are *in Christ Jesus*" (Rom. 8:1). We desire "to present every man complete *in Christ*" (Col. 1:18). Many Christians find it difficult to conceptualize the Spirit of Christ as a location within which Christians are placed. Our being "in Christ" might be viewed as inclusion in a functional spiritual union with the living Christ, whereby He serves as the means and instrumentality of manifesting His life. Think of "in Christ" as "in union with Christ."

APRIL 27

DOES GOD DAMN ANYONE?

"Damn it" (or "dammit") is one of the most-used expletives among the general public. In its verb form, it has an understood subject being God, i.e. "God damn it." In common adjectival form, it can be applied to almost anything, i.e. a "God-damned *whatever*." Most who use the word never consider the content of what they are saying. The words become the verbal punctuation of our conversations, likely evidencing limited vocabulary. The word "damn" has a base meaning of requesting God to condemn someone to hell, or reference to God's having adjudged someone/thing as damnable. Truly a "curse word."

We will consider the theological question, "Does God ever damn anyone to hell?" It is imperative that we begin with the character of God, the essential being of God. John writes, "God is love" (I Jn. 4:8,16), meaning He seeks the highest good and well-being of all created humanity. God is for us, and not against us! God wants us to live and enjoy life to the fullest. Jesus said, "I came that you might have life, and have it more abundantly" (Jn. 10:10). The divine, spiritual life of God in Christ is to be lived out in the practicality of everyday life on earth as the positive lubricating character of all social interactions in human community.

God is in the empowering grace business; not in the damning business. God is far more concerned about commending and encouraging us, than condemning us. "God is the one who justifies; who is the one who condemns?" (Rom. 8:33,34), asked Paul. To the woman discovered in adultery, Jesus said, "I do not condemn you" (Jn. 8:11). Let it be clearly stated, God does not damn anyone to hell! You can, however, "condemn yourself" (Rom. 2:1) and stand "self-condemned" (Titus 3:11), by your choice to reject God's love in **JESUS** Christ. "God did not send the Son into the world to condemn the world, but that the world might be saved through Him" (Jn. 3:17).

APRIL 28

BROKEN RELATIONSHIPS

It has been stated that the two causes of all broken personal relationships are (1) selfishness, and (2) lack of communication. In pondering that assertion, I have questioned whether the two can be boiled down into one unified explanation for the cause of all failed relationships. Is not the failure to communicate indicative of the fact that one person selfishly considers the other as not worth taking the time and effort necessary for genuine communication – to talk to or listen to the other? In that case, selfishness becomes the one attitude and action that sabotages personal relationships that are meant to be lubricated with love that seeks the highest good of the other without selfish concern.

The norm of all interpersonal relationships is the interactive love of the triune God – the mutual, interpenetrating love of the Father, Son and Holy Spirit. The Trinity is an eternally perfect personal love relationship, despite that fact that it is a love-triangle. "God is love" (I Jn. 4:8,16). Since love is always reaching out to another, the three-fold God determined to send the Son to identify with human creatures, inviting them to participate in the divine love relationship by reception of and union with the living Spirit of Christ. Such presence and function of the loving triune God is the basis of all proper human love relationships.

What is the antithesis of love? Some have indicated that the opposite of love is hate, bitterness, or intense animosity toward another. Others have identified the alternative to love as indifference or apathy, the failure to "give a damn" about the other. I am suggesting that the opposite of love is personal selfishness. Whereas God's character is love, the character of the diabolic antithesis to God (the devil or Satan) is selfishness. Satan is at work in the midst of all broken relationships, exhibiting the self-oriented and self-absorbed character that he commenced with: "What's in it for me? I want to be number one!"

APRIL 29

CAN CHRISTIANITY BE FUNNY?

Have you ever met some of those killjoy Christians who seem to think that God is a humorless God who sits alone up in heaven looking down on what's happening among men on earth, and interjecting periodically, "Are you having fun? Cut it out! Get serious!" Why do we see so many joyless Christians, sitting in the church pews without smiles and looking as if they have just been sucking on a dill pickle? No enjoyment whatsoever! Some people just don't seem to have a "funny bone," and are unable to enjoy a good chuckle. Or perhaps they have been listening to the religionists who advocate the solemnity of graveyard religion.

Now, I agree that life in Christ is a serious matter, but what happens along the way can be very humorous and funny. I enjoy the humor of life, and I like to laugh. People have commented that I have a distinctive laugh, similar to Vizinni's laugh in *The Princess Bride* movie. My response, "Inconceivable!" I have offended people with my propensity to laugh at situations and see levity in much of what happens in life. Sorry, but I'm not really sorry! Early in my Christian life, I read Elton Trueblood's book, *The Humor of Christ,* and realized that much of what Jesus was saying to His disciples, and in His parables, was humorous.

Organized Christianity is so constricted and narrow-minded, and those who participate in it are often incapable of seeing just how funny they are when they "get their panties in a bunch." I think it is hilarious the extent to which some religionists take themselves so serious as to be unable to see how ridiculous they are. I do not appreciate humor that is vulgar, or that is insensitive to people's differences (physical, mental, religious), and is demeaning of others who are different. Meanwhile, I will continue to laugh at the various forms of humor in the teaching of **JESUS**, as well as the humor provided by fellow Christians who have no idea how absurd and outlandish their attitudes and behavior really are.

APRIL 30

CENTER OF REFERENCE

This article is not intended to consider a library full of books. In recent times, libraries are often called "centers of reference," or "resource centers," but this article will explore a more philosophical and theological perspective of examining the "center of reference" of human thought processes. All human thought necessarily has an organizing point of reference (or focal point) to which all subsequent thinking is related.

When mankind was first created, the intent was that God should dwell in the spirit-center of a human being and be the "center of reference" for all that each individual thinks, feels, decides and does. The Satanic temptation of mankind was to reject the theocentric center of reference, and allegedly to become one's own egocentric center of reference; "to be like God, knowing good and evil" (Gen. 3:5). It was a lie, for human beings are derivative and dependent creatures who necessarily draw from a spirit-source for their being and function. When mankind rejected God's intent and experienced a negative spiritual exchange in the spiritual core of their human being, mankind in general was duped into thinking that they were their own center of reference, when in reality Satan was "the spirit working in the sons of disobedience" (Eph. 2:2).

Collectively, human thought in general maintained the idea that God should be the center of reference for many centuries. But from the time of the Enlightenment (18th century), there was a change from a theocentric reference point in human thought to a humanistic reference point for all human considerations.

The gospel proclaims that by Christ's redemptive action it is possible for human beings to experience a spiritual exchange by receiving the Spirit of **JESUS** Christ in their spirit, allowing Him to be the "center of reference," the Lord of one's life.

MAY 1

RIGHTEOUSNESS

All legitimate discussion of righteousness must begin with the character of God – His essential righteous and just Being, the basis of His righteous actions. "All His ways are just; righteous and upright is He" (Deut. 32:4). "Your righteousness, O God, reaches to the heavens" (Ps. 71:19). "There is no other God besides Me, a righteous God and Savior" (Isa. 45:21). God is the foundation of all Righteousness.

Religion too often casts righteousness into moralistic or ethical rightness of behavior in conformity with determined codes of acceptability. "Righteousness is doing what is right in the sight of God," is a common religious inculcation. Solomon did write, "I walk in the way of righteousness, in the midst of the paths of justice" (Prov. 8:20), but mere behavioral righteousness so quickly degenerates into performance "works" of righteousness.

Reacting to the ecclesiastical "works" of expected behavioral righteousness in the Roman Catholic Church, the Protestant Reformers sought to emphasize relational right-ness with God by employing an emphasis on "justification." Their emphasis, however, veered off into an overly objectified legal paradigm of a divine judge declaring, imputing, and reckoning an individual to have a status and standing of righteousness before God in the heavenly courtroom. Merely a legal righteousness.

The triune God desires a personal relationship of righteousness with all mankind, whereby His righteous character indwells the human spirit by His presence and function within us. In spiritual identification, the Christian actually becomes the righteousness of God (Rom. 5:19; II Cor. 5:21; Eph. 4:24) because **JESUS** Christ, the divine "Righteous One" (Acts 3:14; 7:52; 22:14) is present in our spirit as our new identity, and desirous of manifesting His righteous character in and through our behavior.

MAY 2

CHRIST IS OUR LIFE

Most Christians would aver that Jesus Christ is their Savior and Lord, and assert they have received eternal life from the living Lord Jesus. They have been regenerated in a spiritual new birth, i.e. born again with the "life from above," which is the life of the One who declared, "I AM the way, the truth, and the life" (Jn. 14:6). Many Christians, however, think of Jesus as the guarantor of a spiritual deposit of eternal life received as a down payment for the future experience of eternal life in heaven. Few Christians understand the implications of the indwelling Lord Jesus who lives in them in order to live out His life as their life.

What did Paul mean when he referred to "Christ who is our life" (Col. 3:4)? In the previous verse, he explained to the Colossian Christians, "Your life is hidden with Christ in God" (Col. 3:3). The human spirit of the Christian is united with the Spirit of the risen and living Christ in a spiritual union of oneness. "The one who is joined to Christ is one spirit with Him" (I Cor. 6:17). The Christian has the privilege of being so identified and united with the living Jesus that our spiritual identity is that of a Christ-one, and we live out of the empowering His Spirit formed in our spirit, able to say as did Paul, "For me to live is Christ" (Phil. 1:21).

It is important that every Christian mature to the point of realizing there is no other way to explain me apart from Him. The essence of who I am as a Christ-one (Christian), has no other explanation other than that the living **JESUS** Christ is my life. He inhabits and occupies my spirit so thoroughly that "I am complete in Christ" (Col. 1:28), and "it is no longer I who lives, but Christ lives in me" (Gal. 2:20). It is in that process of unified identity with **JESUS** as our life that we "reign in life through the One, Jesus Christ" (Rom. 5:17), and enjoy participating in the new humanity that "came to life and reigned with Christ for a thousand years" (Rev. 20:4).

MAY 3

GRACE-DYNAMIC

Grace is the divine reality that can only be understood by someone in whom the Spirit of the living Christ dwells, lives, and provides spiritual appraisal (I Cor. 2:10-16). A person must know Jesus personally to know grace. "Grace and truth came into being in Jesus Christ" (Jn. 1:17). In the old covenant, the Hebrew people recognized God's favor and lovingkindness, but the grace of God in Jesus is only realized in the new covenant. To know Jesus, living and active in your life, is to know grace. Grace is **JESUS** alive in you and living out His life through you. Grace is the dynamic activity of God in Christ by the power of the Holy Spirit.

Religion has traditionally failed to understand the dynamic of divine grace in Christ Jesus. Failing to be aware that Christianity is the living Christ lived out in Christ-ones (Christians), religion has tended to view grace as a static substance or commodity conveyed to adherents to grant them a shot of "go-juice," a turbo-boost to cause them to perform as better members of the church. Participation in the Eucharist has been touted as the primary "means of grace" or process of acquiring more of this "magic bullet" of empowerment to fulfill the obligations of performance that the ecclesiastical authorities encourage.

How does one know if God's dynamic grace is operative in their life? The "fruit of the Spirit" (Gal. 5:22,23) is the active character of Christ. Jesus told His disciples, "If you have seen Me, you have seen the Father" (Jn. 14:9). In like manner, when the character of Christ, the "fruit of the Spirit," is evidenced in a Christian's behavior, one can be sure that the root of such fruit is the dynamic grace of God in Jesus Christ. Grace is God in action, doing what God does in perfect consistency with His character. God can do nothing other than act in dynamic grace via the actions of the Son, **JESUS** Christ, as energized by the Holy Spirit. There is no Christianity apart from the dynamic grace of God.

MAY 4

"LOVE YOUR NEIGHBOR AS YOURSELF"

In light of various scriptural admonitions to avoid self-interest (cf. Phil. 2:3,4), and the caution of being "lovers of self" (II Tim. 3:2), what does this phrase mean? Quoting from the old covenant law (Lev.19:18), Jesus refers to this statement as part of the "greatest commandment" (Matt. 22:39; Mk. 12:31; Lk. 10:27), and illustrates the meaning in the parable of wounded Samaritan traveler. Many have misused this statement, using it in conjunction with humanistic pop-psychology as a call to self-love in order to have a positive self-image. That is definitely not the intended meaning of this dictum.

There is no call or command in these verses to "love yourself," but there does seem to be an acceptance of and accommodation to the natural self-concern and self-preservation that all human beings have for their own well-being. There is a basic God-given desire to live and to be socially engaged with others. Human beings are not naturally suicidal or non-social. We have a natural inclination for self-preservation. If we come across a bear on the hiking path, our instinctual response is to back away, leave the scene, and save our own skin. There is nothing wrong with that. This statement utilizes a simile that encourages our love for another to be as intense and spontaneous as our natural self-concern for our own well-being.

Only by God's grace can we seek the well-being of another, our neighbor, in like manner, and to the same extent that we protect our own well-being. When we understand that divine *agape* love seeks the highest good of another, without any consideration of what we get out of it, we can allow such love to be expressed in our attitudes, affections, and actions by the dynamic of God's grace (Rom. 5:5; Gal. 5:22). As **JESUS** lives out the character of God's love in our Christian behavior, undue self-love will be overcome by His love for others.

MAY 5

BELIEVE-RIGHT, DO-RIGHT RELIGION

Perhaps the greatest aberration of Christianity is when it is misrepresented as a "believe-right" and/or "do-right" religion. Yet, this is exactly what is advocated by the churches of Christian religion week after week. Focusing on and deifying their distinctive belief-systems, the innumerable denominational groups consider their churches to be educational institutions to propagandize and indoctrinate additional people with the proper and acceptable doctrines they espouse. Belief-systems are "a dime a dozen," and epistemological investigations will never establish ultimate truth and knowledge.

In like manner, performance-based religion will never be able to formulate and codify an ethical system of propriety and morality that will produce righteousness. Although the old covenant Jewish religion was built on the Law-code of "thou shalt" and "thou shalt not," it was incapable of incentivizing the righteous character of God in human behavior. "Israel, pursuing a law of righteousness, did not arrive at that law" (Rom. 9:31). The performance of law never arrives at life or righteousness (Gal. 2:21; 3:21). All that performance-based "do-right" religious rules can produce is temporary external behavior modification.

Christianity is Christ – the Spirit of the risen and living Lord **JESUS** dwelling in the human spirit of a receptive person in order to function as the Life of that person. Such a Christ-one (Christian), allowing Jesus to live in and through them, allows the "mind of Christ" (I Cor. 2:16) to "renew their (human) mind" (Rom. 12:2), in order to have Spirit-directed beliefs and thinking. Such a Christ-one also allows the indwelling Spirit of Christ to be the active agency of activity that glorifies God. God equips "us in every good thing to do His will, working in us that which is pleasing in His sight, through Jesus Christ" (Heb. 13:21). Jesus Christ in the Christian creates correct belief and action.

DIVINE DESIGN OF DERIVATIVENESS

God created all things to operate and be sustained by deriving from His divine supply. The Psalmist wrote, "The heavens declare the glory of God; the firmament shows His handiwork" (Ps. 19:1). Human beings were the highest of God's created order, designed as relational, choosing creatures, capable of deriving the spiritual character of God in their behavior. Paul wrote, "From Him and through Him and to Him are all things" (Rom. 11:36). "From Him" is translated from the Greek preposition *ek*, meaning source, origin or derivation. Humans are to designed to derive all things *ek Theos*, "out of God."

In a New Age newspaper, an article declared, "derivativeness is tyranny." Consistent with their humanistic premise that "every man is a god unto himself and master of his own fate, not to be controlled by any other," especially deriving from God, the authors understood that Christian thought was based on the premise of God's design of derivativeness, and were attempting to deny such. In one sense, this was encouraging because they understood God's divine intent, and were rejecting it. On the other hand, they were using the age-old suggestion of Satan to the couple in the garden of Eden, "Derivativeness is tyranny."

The most discouraging part is that Christian religion, in general, has not understood or taught God's design of derivativeness. Operating on a homogenized premise of "evangelical humanism" whereby human functionality is regarded to be deriving from man's best effort and performance, this is often phrased in the false premise that "God helps those who help themselves." Human performance-based religion has failed to grasp that God provides the sustenance and supply for all He has created. God's intent for His people in the redemptive new covenant is that Christians should derive all from the divine presence of the Spirit of **JESUS** living in their spirit, to express God's character.

MAY 7

FAITH MISCONSTRUED

Faith is a basic biblical concept that is a major building block of Christian thought. It is amazing, then, how the understanding of "faith" has been misconstrued by being pushed to the extremes of theological thinking. On one side of the theological divide, the Pelagian-Arminians have misconstrued faith as a contributive "work" of man. On the other side, the Augustinian-Calvinists have misconstrued faith as a "gift" of God. It is important to find a biblical balance that recognizes God's gracious creation of mankind with freedom of choice, as well as the human choice of faith that an individual can make to receive Jesus as Lord.

One form of religion has twisted the word "faith" to be a human "work," whereby an individual is required to muster up enough confidence in order to trust the object of one's faith, and surrender to such in reliance. This is often illustrated by having enough faith to sit on an untested chair. Having enough courage to trust and rely on a rickety chair is not the same as faith in God. It ends up being merely "faith in faith." Those who over-emphasize "faith" tend to focus on what man does, rather than on what God has done and is doing. Christian faith is a response to what God does, not a focus on what human beings do.

Another religious perversion is to identify "faith" as a gift of God given only to a select few identified as the "elect." Ephesians 2:8,9 does read, "For by grace you have been saved through faith; and that not of yourselves, it is the gift of God; not as a result of works, so that no one may boast." It is not the "faith" that is the "gift of God," but God's salvation. Reference to the "faith of Christ" in Galatians 2:20 (KJV), is better understood as human "faith in Christ." Faith is the privilege afforded to human beings to respond to what God has made, and continues to make available by His grace through the Son, **JESUS** Christ. Faith is human receptivity of God's activity; our availability to His ability.

AVAILABILITY

For many years, I have appreciated a song written by Dick Anthony (1971). Some dear friends, Dick and Diana Busby, often sang this song as a duet, and it became a much-requested song in their repertoire. Of the many musicians I have known and heard, this couple had an unsurpassed spiritual depth to use their talent to minister to people's hearts through music. The words of this song, "Available," are powerful:

> Available for God to use me,
> Available if God should choose me;
> If it be here or there,
> It doesn't matter where...

Availability to God's direction and utilization is an essential part of Christian faith. In fact, faith has been defined as "our availability to God's ability," or "our receptivity to God's activity." The dictionary defines "availability" as "the quality of being able to be used, accessed, or utilized, without restriction."

Our availability implies that we willing to "submit ourselves to God" (James 4:7). Like "clay in the potter's hand" (Jere. 18:6), we want to be pliable, willing to be formed and utilized as God sees fit. When Isaiah was being commissioned as a prophet, his availability was evident: "Then I heard the voice of the Lord, saying, 'Whom shall I send, and who will go for Us?' Then I said, 'Here am I. Send me!'" (Isa. 6:8). The absence of openness and availability to God to be and do everything He desires in us, to go wherever He might direct, represents a lack of trust and faith in God.

When functioning as Christ-ones (Christians), **JESUS** Christ is to be Lord of our lives. We are not "calling the shots," or serving as His counselor (Rom. 11:34); rather, He directs our lives as we are available in faith to all that He desires and empowers.

MAY 9

FIRST WORDS

First words are important. Those who are parents probably remember that time when their child was jabbering in baby-talk, but getting ready to say their first word. Would it be "ma-ma" or "da-da" or "no-no"? Parents often go gaga over the first words that their child utters, whether really intelligible or not. Salespersons are trained to recognize that their opening words can set the tone for the entire sales experience. Public speakers know the importance of the first words of introduction of their speech. The young man who is approaching a young lady often practices his first words of greeting carefully to impress.

As one opens the *Gospel According to Mark*, it should be noted that the first words from the mouth of Jesus are, "The time is fulfilled, and the kingdom of God is at hand; repent and believe in the gospel" (Mark 1:15). These are important first words, for they connect the whole of the scriptures. "The time is fulfilled," the occasion that was expected in the prophecies of the Old Testament. "The kingdom of God is at hand," the promised kingdom wherein God would reign in His people. "Repent," change your minds and actions about your superiority and ability to please God. "Believe in the gospel," be receptive to the good news of God that has been incarnated in the Person who stands right before your eyes.

First words often require additional explanation for the hearer to fully comprehend the content and meaning of what is being said. Jesus' first words to His Jewish audience certainly required additional years of proclaiming the content of the gospel, and explaining the entirely new paradigm of thought necessary to grasp the new covenant reality in Himself. This would entail the abandonment of their religious belief-system and their legal morality code, in order to recognize that Truth is in a Person – in **JESUS** Christ, the promised deliverer, savior and Messiah.

BELIEVING IS RECEIVING

The human action of believing has always been regarded as the necessary response to the gospel of Jesus Christ. When the Philippian jailor asked, "What must I do to be saved?", Paul replied, "Believe (*pisteuson*) in the Lord Jesus, and you will be saved" (Acts 16:31). In modern times, the word "believe" has been trivialized. It has degenerated into a shallow mind-exercise of mental acceptance of an idea whereby the idea becomes a settled opinion (whether valid or not). In religious thought, it often means to join the consensus of a particular group by signing the membership card or other such initiation.

Scottish author, William Barclay, referring to the Greek words *pisteuo* (to believe) and *pistis* (belief or faith), explains, "the first element in faith is what we can only call receptivity, ...not receptivity of facts or the significance of the facts, ...but the receptivity of the Person of Jesus Christ" (*The Mind of Saint Paul* - 112). This is quite evident in John's gospel, "As many as *received* Him, to them He gave the right to become children of God, even to those who *believe* in His name" (Jn. 1:12,13). Believing is receiving! But this is not merely receiving information; this is receiving the personal Spirit of the living Lord Jesus.

Genuine believing-receptivity of Jesus is more than a casual, "Okay, I'll take it; count me in." Receiving the personal presence of the Spirit of Jesus is more like, "I'll bet it all; I'm all in;" it is the personal surrender of total involvement in One other than yourself. Receiving **JESUS** is receiving the One who will become your essential identity, your Life (Col. 3:4), your hope (I Tim. 1:1), your "all in all" (Eph. 1:23). Paul explained, "It is no longer I who live, but Christ lives in me" (Gal. 2:20). Our faith-receptivity is ongoing in the Christian life. "As you received Christ Jesus the Lord, so walk in Him" (Col. 2:6), i.e. by faith, the receptivity of His character and activity in every situation, at all times.

MAY 11

WHAT DO YOU WORRY ABOUT?

All human beings have some degree of worry in their lives, even if it is couched in the "concerns" of life for which they are responsible. There seems to be a sliding scale from the everyday "concerns" of life to being maxed out in "panicked anxiety" over the events of one's life. The English word "worry" is derived from the Old English word *wyrgan*, meaning "to strangle" or "to choke." The Greek word translated "worry" in the New Testament is *merimnao*, meaning "divided mind." When we worry, we have a divided mind over what we should do, and this strangles and chokes clear thinking and responsible choices.

The apprehensive uneasiness of mind and contorted emotions that we experience when we worry is an indication that we are assuming a responsibility that is not necessarily ours to assume. We are failing to recognize that God is bigger than any problem we might have, and loves us enough to seek our highest good in every situation. Worry preempts the receptivity of faith in God and His sufficiency for the situation. Worry is a form of humanistic self-orientation that thinks, "It's up to me to take care of this situation. If I don't take care of this problem, nobody will." In that regard, worry is a form of practical atheism.

In His Sermon on the Mount, Jesus said, "Do not be anxious for your life, what you shall eat, or what you shall drink; nor for your body, what you shall put on. ...your heavenly Father knows that you need all these things" (Matt. 6:25-34). The apostle Peter wrote, "Cast all your anxiety on Him, because He cares for you" (I Peter 5:7). The apostle Paul reminded the Philippians, "Be anxious for nothing, but in everything by prayer and supplication with thanksgiving let your requests be made known to God. And the peace of God...shall guard your hearts and minds in Christ **JESUS**" (Phil. 4:6,7). The world around us says, "Don't worry; be happy!" The gospel declares, "Exchange your worry for faith."

RECEIVING JESUS

When Christians are asked what they received when they became a Christian, they often answer by mentioning the "things" they received. They refer to the blessings and the benefits of the forgiveness of sins, of eternal life, and a reconciled relationship with God. These answers are not improper or inaccurate, but these "things" do not stand alone, and must not be detached from the One in whom they are all incorporated and embodied. What we have received in order to become a Christ-one (Christian) is not just some "thing," but some One, i.e. the risen and living Lord Jesus Christ who has come to live in our spirit.

Yes, we have received "forgiveness of sins" (Acts 10:43; 26:18), the "word of God" (Acts 8:14; I Thess. 1:6; 2:13; James 1:21), a "blessing from God" (Heb. 6:7), and "the promise of an eternal inheritance" (Heb. 9:15). The Christian has received "the gospel" (I Cor. 15:1), which entails "mercy" (II Cor. 4:1) and "grace" (Jn. 1:16; Rom. 1:5; 5:17), the "gift of righteousness" (Rom. 5:17), "reconciliation" (Rom. 5:11) with God, and "adoption as sons" (Rom. 8:15; Gal. 4:5) in "a kingdom that cannot be shaken" (Heb. 12:28). We have received "the Holy Spirit" (Jn. 20:22; Acts 2:38), with His "anointing" (I Jn. 2:27) and "power" (Acts 1:8).

All of these "things" are "in Christ Jesus." **JESUS** is the "Word of God" (Jn. 1:1,14), the Forgiver of sins (Matt. 9:2; Mk. 2:5), the blessing of God (Eph. 1:3), and eternal life (Jn. 17:3; Rom. 6:23). **JESUS** is the gospel (II Thess. 1:8), the Righteousness of God (I Cor. 1:30; II Pet. 1:1), the King who reigns in the kingdom (Jn. 3:3; 18:36; II Pet. 1:11), and the One who reconciles (Rom. 5:11) us to God, functioning as "the life-giving Spirit" (I Cor. 15:45). When we "receive Christ Jesus the Lord" (Jn. 1:12; Col. 2:6), we receive the fullness of God (Matt. 10:40; Eph. 3:19) – everything that God has to give to mankind (Eph. 1:3; II Pet. 1:3). All things belong to the Christian (I Cor. 3:21-23) in Christ.

MAY 13

SELF-DISCIPLINE

Are Christians encouraged to engage in self-discipline? Or, are we to submit to the discipline of God the Father in our lives? The answer to both questions is a qualified "Yes!" Christians should generally be cautious of inculcations that use words with the prefix self-, for these are usually laden with the humanistic philosophy of the world, implying that it is what we do by human performance that makes us better and brings us to the desired end of self-betterment – such words as self-help, self-realization, self-fulfillment, self-development, self-improvement. We see them all the time; these words are everywhere.

Paul's words to Timothy, however, encourage, even command, a type of self-discipline (with a difference). He wrote, "Discipline yourself unto godliness" (I Tim 4:7). This is not humanistic self-discipline, but an emphasis on the continuing freedom of choice and responsibility that Christians have to exercise faithful receptivity. Our discipline does not create godliness, for godliness is only the result of God manifesting His godly character in our behavior. "Great is the mystery of godliness" (I Tim. 3:16), wrote Paul. "His divine power has granted us everything pertaining to life and godliness" (II Pet. 1:3).

Writing to the Christians in Colossae, Paul "rejoiced to see their good discipline, and the stability of their faith in Christ" (Col. 2:5). But he also writes of the discipline of God in Christ Jesus. "We are disciplined by the Lord, so we will not be condemned along with the world" (I Cor. 11:32). "Those whom the Lord loves He disciplines; He disciplines us for our good, so that we may share His holiness" (Heb. 12:6-10). The risen Lord Jesus Himself said, "Those whom I love, I reprove and discipline" (Rev. 3:19). It is important to remember that discipline is not punishment. Discipline (both the Lord's discipline, and our self-discipline) is the process of forming disciples of Jesus Christ.

MAY 14

"IN CHRIST"

What does it mean to be "in Christ"? The prepositional phrases "in Christ," "in Christ Jesus," "in the Lord," "in Him," "in whom," etc. are used approximately 164 times in the New Testament scriptures. This is a core tenet and reality of Christian thought and faith. But many Christians have expressed their confusion concerning what these phrases mean in the practicality of Christian living today. The import of these phrases is immense, for they lead us into the full import of our being encompassed within the Spirit of the living Lord Jesus, whereby all that He is in His Divine Being is available to be expressed as us.

Some have called the reality of being "in Christ" a "positional truth" that transcends the real experience of a Christian today. I object to such a marginalization of this important biblical reality. To be "in Christ" is an actual spiritual truth that contemporary Christians deserve to realize and experience in their personal lives. Christian teachers have been selling Christians short by failing to explicate these phrases in a meaningful and practical manner. In large part that is due to Christian leaders having never personally experienced what it means to be in spiritual union with the living Christ manifested as the "Spirit of Christ."

These phrases are not simply explaining a locative sense of spatial location, as if the Christian is in "the Jesus box." The spiritual reality of being "in Christ" is best understood as being "in union with Christ," in the manner expressed in I Cor. 6:17 – "the one who is joined to the Lord is one spirit with Him." Try reading the phrases like this: "If anyone is in *union with* Christ, he is a new creature" (II Cor. 5:17). "By His doing you are in *union with* Christ Jesus" (I Cor. 1:30). "In *union with* Christ all will be made alive" (I Cor. 15:22). "We are created in *union with* Christ Jesus for good works" (Eph. 2:10). "You are all one in *union with* Christ Jesus" (Gal. 3:28).

MAY 15

TO THE PREACHERS

Many parishioners and those serving on pastoral search committees have exclaimed, "Good preachers are hard to find." The question then becomes, what constitutes a "good preacher/pastor?" When Jesus was called a "good teacher," He explained that "no one is good apart from God" (Lk. 18:18). A good pastor-teacher is one who knows God, not just theology about God, but has a genuine personal and intimate knowing-relationship with God through the indwelling presence and union with the Spirit of Christ, and allows his life and ministry to be empowered by the dynamic of the Holy Spirit.

The objective of a pastor/preacher is to preach the living Jesus he personally knows. "We do not preach ourselves, but Christ Jesus as Lord" (II Cor. 4:5). "We preach Christ crucified" (I Cor. 1:23). If the preacher's message does not assist the congregation to understand how the risen and living Lord Jesus relates to their daily lives, then it is not Christian preaching. The purpose of preaching is not merely the recitation of historical details of scripture, nor is it theological explanations of factual data. I recall hearing a sermon that did not mention the name of Jesus even once until the obligatory closing prayer ended, "in Jesus name."

Preachers, pastors, ministers (whatever they are called in your tradition) must be humble enough to recognize that they are just human beings like everyone else. They are not celebrities to be revered. Though expected to be models of spiritual maturity, and sometimes occupying an elevated pulpit that looks down on the "laity," the preacher must be honest and transparent. Admission of personal faults, failures and weaknesses, allows the people to identify with their shepherd. Warned not to "lord it over" the flock (I Pet. 5:3), pastors must avoid "pastoral authority" and attempts to dictate, intimidate or manipulate. The objective is simply to share **JESUS** in one's proclamation and life.

THE PRELUDE TO GRACE

In musical parlance, a prelude is a short piece that precedes and serves as an opening, preface or overture to other music. In other contexts, prelude refers to the preliminary lead-in or preparatory precursor to what is to follow. In the biblical narrative, the Law of the old covenant Jewish religion serves as the preliminary prelude to the focal event of the revelation of God's redemptive and saving action in Jesus Christ to implement the new covenant gospel. The Old Testament Law served as the prelude to the grace embodied in Jesus Christ in the New Testament. "Grace was realized in Christ Jesus" (Jn. 1:17).

Oftentimes the topics of law and grace are viewed as polarized opposites, set in contrast to one another, law versus grace. There is indeed such a dichotomy, but it is equally necessary to understand the sequential correlation of the two. The covenant of law serves as a requisite stepping stone to orient us to the destined objective of God to provide His grace provision in His Son, Jesus Christ. Though often critical of Law, Paul does not indict the Law as entirely useless, for he explains, "the Law is holy and righteous and good" (Rom. 7:12). The Law served its purpose as the contrasting paradigm to God's grace in Christ.

In like manner as children must first learn to accept parental boundaries, and hear the "No, No" of parental limitation before they can appreciate the freedom of adulthood, so God's people first needed to understand their inability and insufficiency by attempting to keep the Law in order to appreciate the provision and sufficiency of God's grace in Jesus Christ. Though we are often critical of legalistic religion, we must admit that it does serve a constructive purpose to reveal insufficiency. The Law of the Jewish religion served God's historical and theological purpose as the preliminary launch-pad of the new covenant provision of **JESUS** Christ, as the prelude to God's grace.

MAY 17

ADDICTION

Addiction is not a new phenomenon in the personal and social history of mankind. Whether it be addiction to chemical substances (alcohol, drugs, nicotine), or various activities (gambling, overeating, sexual involvement, gaming, religion), or addiction to personal pursuits (success, performance, correctness, knowledge), these have been evident in humanity from ages past. Natural man has a propensity to fixate on objects and activities in a selfishly obsessive, compulsive and addictive manner. In order to address the issue of addiction, we have to recognize how complex and far-reaching this problem really is.

Historical observation reveals a wide variety of attempts to address addiction problems of humanity. Societies have tried legislating substances and activities with prohibition. Then there was the moralism of "Just say No!" Humanistic advocacy of self-help, self-discipline, self-healing has also been suggested. Various psychological methods of rehabilitation and recovery have been promoted. Physiological approaches suggest a "disease model," perhaps a brain disease, treated with pharmacology. Social reorientation is another suggested remedy, with the substitution of religion or an anonymity group (ex. AA, NA, FA, SA).

These many approaches reveal the complexity of addressing human addiction. The entirety of human function must be taken into account, the physical, psychological, mental, emotional, social, spiritual, etc. There is a sense in which everyone has areas of addictive behavior. Everyone is addicted! Everyone has patterns of the "flesh," and "besetting sins." The problem of addiction must be addressed from the inner spirit of an individual to the outer manifestations and social implications. The Spirit of Christ within can overcome the "spirits" of self-orientation and self-indulgence, and support us externally and socially in a loving community of *ecclesia*, the Body of Christ.

MAY 18

SELFISHNESS

While still a young man, approximately twenty years old, I remember suggesting to my college roommates, "The essence of all sin is selfishness." Over fifty years later, I have not been persuaded otherwise. The opposite of God's love, the outward flow of His character seeking the good of others, is the character of the Evil One emphasizing inward self-centered concern for one's own advantage, profit or pleasure – "me, me, me" – without regard for another. The fall of mankind into sin brought about the self-serving character of egocentricity and narcissism.

The Evil One's character is selfish sinfulness. Lucifer pompously declared, "I will make myself like the Most High" (Isa. 14:14), and became the Satanic deceiver, soliciting mankind in temptation to implement his character of self-centeredness and "selfish ambition" (Rom. 2:8; Phil. 1:17; James 3:14,16). He tempted the first couple to be "like God," their own self-center of reference. Thereby, the human race began to derive the selfish and sinful character of the devil in all they were and did. When we sin, we derive such from Satan, *ek diabolos* (I Jn. 3:8). The theological teaching of Augustine attempted to mitigate such explanation by positing that sin and selfishness were embedded in the total depravity and corruption of human being and function. Not true! The source of all the selfishness of sin is derived from Satan.

The selfish pride of mankind has been operative ever since the world of mankind fell "into the Evil One" (I Jn. 5:19), "the spirit that works in the sons of disobedience" (Eph. 2:2). Satan masquerades his activity by using all the self-prefixed words that infiltrate our humanistic vocabulary – self-oriented, self-absorbed, self-serving, etc. But God "is able to humble those who walk in pride" (Dan. 4:27), and those who are "in Christ" are encouraged to "do nothing from selfishness or conceit, but regard one another as more important than yourselves" (Phil. 2:3).

MAY 19

WHEN SATAN TAKES CONTROL

When one visits with criminals incarcerated in prisons for violent crimes, and they are asked to explain why they did what they did, their responses often use terminology like "a blanket of blackness came over me," or "the beast took control of me." Serial murderers have explained that "a powerful force overcame me" and "I made a pact with the devil." They often refer to being possessed or oppressed by a "power of darkness" or an "evil force" in the midst of their being blinded by rage and fury, overcome by hate and murderous revenge, until they lost control of their rational decision-making responses.

In our psychologized culture, such comments are analyzed as paranoid schizophrenia or other forms of mental and emotional dysfunction, without any willingness to entertain an explanation of the negative spiritual empowering of a diabolic Evil One. Bible-believing Christians, however, should be quite aware of the spiritual forces that are vying to control the minds and emotions of human beings in order to manifest their contrasting character of either goodness or evil in human behavior. Scriptures are clear that there is an ontological being of Satan who seeks to counter the character and activity of God in Christ.

Most people are aware of times when anger and vengeance filled their minds and emotions, and they were tempted to act out in violent and injurious ways toward other people. We must "be sober and vigilant, because your adversary, the devil walks about like a roaring lion, seeking whom he may devour" (I Pet. 5:8). By God's grace in **JESUS** Christ, Christians have been given the provision to "resist the devil" (James 4:7), and "stand against the wiles of the devil" (Eph. 6:11), giving him no place (Eph. 4:27) to actuate his evil character in our behavior. Temptations to evil character and action will come to all persons, but by God's power we can choose to disallow Satan to take control.

MAY 20

ANYTHING LACKING IN YOUR CHRISTIAN LIFE?

I have encountered Christians who were decrying that "there's something missing in my Christian life." Unable to identify what was missing, they maintained that there was a void inside of them causing them to be unsatisfied and unfulfilled. Maybe you can identify with this feeling. If these persons are genuine Christians, having received the Spirit of Christ (cf. Rom. 8:9) into their spirit, having become "new creatures in Christ" (II Cor. 5:17) with everything spiritually "made new," then "in Him, they have been made complete" (Col. 2:10), and there is no spiritual deficiency. They have everything God has to give – **JESUS**.

But, we must differentiate between a person's spiritual plenitude and psychological maturity. Spiritually, God "has blessed us with every spiritual blessing in the heavenly places in Christ" (Eph. 1:3), "granted us everything pertaining to life and godliness," (II Pet. 1:3), and "all things belong to us" in Jesus Christ. We "are not lacking in any gift" (I Cor. 1:7), "lacking in nothing" (James 1:4). Yet, despite all this magnanimity of God's grace in Jesus Christ, many Christians are not aware of their spiritual riches (Eph. 1:7; 2:7; 3:8). In the minds and emotions of their soul, they do not understand their spiritual abundance.

This necessary growth in awareness of the sufficiency of **JESUS** is true in every Christian. It is the growth process (II Pet. 3:18) of "maturity" and recognizing our completeness. Paul explains his ministry as "teaching every man...so we may present every man *complete* in Christ" (Col. 1:28), "praying earnestly that we may *complete* what is lacking in your faith" (I Thess. 3:10; II Cor. 13:9,11). "Let us press on to *maturity*" (Heb. 6:1), until we attain...to a *mature* man, to the measure of the stature which belongs to the fullness of Christ" (Eph. 4:13). Though perfect in spiritual condition (Phil. 3:15), we are all in the process of being perfected (Phil. 3:12) to the fullness of mature understanding.

MAY 21

SUCCESS

The humanistic world-system has dangled the carrot in front of us. They have convinced modern man that the objective of human life here on earth is "success." However, no one seems able to clearly define what success entails. Is success measured by the cumulative value of physical and monetary assets? Is success measured by arriving at the top of the heap of positional advancement in the social pyramid? Is success measured by achieving celebrity status in a particular self-chosen endeavor? All of these pseudo-success paths may well serve as a stepping-stone to the most important success a person can experience.

I am suggesting that human success is measured by failure, and discovering how to respond to that failure. The fallen human race was designed to fail! Such statements sound so absurd and counterintuitive to the humanistic premises of the worldview that pervades modern thought today. But, human beings were never intended to be successful as self-sufficient gods ruling themselves and others. To be successful human beings, every person must come to the end of themselves, and recognize that they do not have what it takes in themselves to be and do what the world and its religion indicates we should be to be successful.

Yes, we are failures, falling short of God's design for humanity, i.e. "sinners." To come to that awareness is an essential step in becoming a successful human being. As in the many anonymity groups, we must begin by admitting, "I can't; only He can; I choose to let Him be and do whatever He chooses to be and do in me." Such an attitude is called "repentance," a change of mind concerning our ability to "pull off life" successfully, and a consequent change of action that allows God's grace to come into action in our life to be "all in all" in us (Eph. 1:23). Human success is in recognizing our inability and failure, and knowing who to turn to, **JESUS**, in order to be man as God intended man to be.

THE TUNING NOTE

My wife is a professional oboist. She began playing oboe when she was twelve years old. One of the distinctives of the oboe is that this is the instrument that traditionally gives the tuning note for the entire orchestra. When you attend an orchestral concert, you will hear the oboe play a prolonged note, likely an A440, and all of the other musicians tune their instruments to that standard pitch. This tuning note allows the symphony (Greek *sun* = together; *phōnē* = sound) to produce a unified sound in tune with each other. Without a standardized tuning note a symphony becomes discordant cacophony (*kakos* = bad; *phōnē* = sound).

This musical observation is analogous to the necessary standardization for functional interaction of the human race. The cosmic symphony of human life also has a tuning note that allows all the instruments to function in conjunction with one another. The perfect pitch tuning note for man to function and interact as God intended is the person and character of **JESUS**. If He is not the tuning note for the social symphony of mankind, human interactivity will inevitably produce the bad noise of cacophony, failing to play in conjunction with one another. This scenario has certainly played out on the world stage again and again: "every man did what was right in his own eyes" (Judg. 17:6; 21:25).

Random relativism of self-determined resonance will never produce the confluent harmonies necessary for a full symphonic unity of sound or socialization. Every component part must relate to, be aligned with, and consonant with the tuning note of the divine character of **JESUS**. Just as the A440 tuning note is not a tangible entity, the intangible reality of the Spirit of Christ can only be heard by one who is spiritually attuned to "the sound of His voice" (Jn. 10:16,21). **JESUS** is to be the tuning note for our personal lives, as well as the social interactions of the *ecclesia*, the church, the Body of Christ.

MAY 23

JDHD – A SERIOUS EPIDEMIC

The Western world is suffering from a plethora of dire health epidemics. A neurological phenomenon has been labelled ADHD (Attention Deficit/Hyperactivity Disorder), characterized by problems with concentration, memory, and impulsiveness in both children and adults. ADHD is caused by neurological connectivity and communication issues in the neurons of the human brain, and is transmittable via hereditable genetics. A corollary phenomenon in Western religion might be labelled JDHD (Jesus Deficit/Hyperactivity Disorder). Lacking spiritual connectivity and communication with God, much Christian religion evidences a deficient attention on Jesus and engagement in hyperactive religious endeavors without constructive purpose.

What are the observable characteristics of JDHD? Foremost is the inattention of such persons to intimate relationship with the living Lord Jesus. They are easily distracted with irrelevant church busyness that occupies their short attention-spans. An aversion to thinking deeply about spiritual things leaves them vulnerable to poor judgments and reactive impulses toward others and inconvenient situations. Difficulty with managing their emotions is expressed in impatience, irritability and anger, with a propensity to moodiness and depression. Misdirected hyperactivity distracts their own focus and that of others.

The options for overcoming JDHD include "exercising oneself unto godliness" (I Tim. 4:7), by taking manageable personal steps of "setting one's mind on things above" (Col. 3:2). Such Christians require the focus of "fixing their eyes on **JESUS**, the author and perfecter of faith" (Heb. 12:2). A deep relational connection and interactive personal communication with **JESUS** through intimate prayer will allow the "Jesus deficit" to be transformed into a "Jesus abundance," as they recognize the fullness of their identity in Christ, and all that belongs to them in Jesus Christ.

"THE DRAW"

The promoters were sitting around the table discussing what they wanted to use as "the draw" to entice the public to attend their proposed event. Should they book a celebrity, or a popular music group, or a well-known comedian as a headline act that would serve as a source of attraction for the public to buy tickets to their production. The advertisers were similarly attempting to determine what appealing product should be promoted, either with claims of excellence or exaggerated claims of effectiveness, or alternatively made available at an inexpensive price as a "hook" to *draw* and bring in the customers to their sale.

"The draw" to Jesus Christ is completely antithetical to these worldly techniques of enticing, inducing and eliciting a response. Jesus told the grumbling Jewish leaders, "No one can come to Me unless the Father who sent Me *draws* (Greek *elkuo/elkuso*) him" (Jn. 6:44). There must be a divine invitational draw to bring people into participation with the triune God. After entering Jerusalem prior to His death, Jesus said, "I, when I am lifted up from the earth (*resurrection*), will *draw* (Greek *elkuo/elkuso*) all men to Myself" (Jn. 12:32). Jesus is the divine One who draws, and He is "the draw" in Himself. "The draw" is not something peripheral to Him, not a heavenly destination, not spiritual benefits, not involvement in the church. "The draw" is just the person and character of Jesus Christ.

Religion often fails to recognize the spiritual "draw" of Jesus. Instead, they adopt and adapt the methods, strategies and programs of the world's promoters and all their publicity gimmicks. They use Jesus as an attraction to summon people to their particular religious product, promising some thrill or excitement. God's divine *draw* is **JESUS** alone! He continues to draw people to Himself, as He re-presents His life and character in the behavior of His Christ-ones (Christians).

MAY 25

GOTCHA!

This colloquial expression for "I got you" has become quite common in English dialogue since the last quarter of the 20th century. It was used as the title of a less than successful movie in 1985. College students in the 1980s played a game called "Gotcha!" that utilized paintball guns and the element of a surprise attack. The term is used when someone pulls off a successful prank or trick, and also when someone is caught red-handed doing something they weren't supposed to be doing. In computer programming it is used of a construct that is counterintuitive and may not produce the desired effect. Golfers have used the exclamation to irritate a partner who is preparing to drive his ball from the tee. It is also used to acknowledge apprehension of what another person has stated; "Gotcha!"

In our Christian pilgrimage, there are oftentimes "gotcha" moments wherein we know that Jesus has gotten our attention concerning what He wants to do in our lives. Or it may be the recognition that God has intervened in our lives in a way that we were not anticipating. Many Christians can look back over their lives and identify specific times when God in Christ by the Spirit has gotten ahold of their lives, their thinking, their affections, in a way that changed the trajectory of how the rest of their life would play out. The One who "has the whole world in His hands" can orchestrate a personal "gotcha" that changes our life.

Peter must have had a "gotcha" moment when Jesus busted him about his triple denial of knowing Jesus, and the cock crowed three times. Paul, no doubt, experienced a "gotcha" revelation when he was knocked down on the road to Damascus and heard the living Lord Jesus confront him about his persecution, and he went on to surrender his life to Jesus. Can you remember a "gotcha" moment in your life wherein God acted to get your attention or to take hold of your life in genuine discipleship?

MAY 26

FROM THIS POINT ON

It is not of much interest to me how you got to where you are, i.e. how you came to receive Jesus Christ as your personal Lord and Savior. Your theological trajectory to becoming a Christ-one may have been via a charismatic experience, or via deterministic Reformed election, or via performance-based Arminianism, or even via the liturgical sacramentalism of Roman Catholicism. Whatever means by which you became a Christ-one, our primary concern must now be how we proceed from this point onwards, from where we are in our spiritual condition to the objective that God has for every Christian to manifest Christ's life.

When Christians understand the glorious spiritual condition that is theirs "in Christ Jesus," i.e. the fullness of their spiritual identity as Christ-ones, they can proceed to allow the life of Jesus to be lived out in behavioral manifestation. Christians can then begin to *behave* like who they have *become*. The transition from one's initial spiritual regeneration when the Spirit of Christ came into our human spirit in a spiritual rebirth, must be followed by the ongoing sanctification process whereby the indwelling life of Jesus Christ is allowed to be lived out in the behavioral manifestations of our Christian lives.

Concerning this perfecting process of sanctification, Paul wrote, "Not that I have already obtained it or have already become perfect, but I press on so that I may lay hold of that for which also I was laid hold of by Christ Jesus. ...forgetting what lies behind and reaching forward to what lies ahead, I press on toward the goal for the prize of the upward call of God in Christ Jesus" (Phil. 3:12-14). Likewise, he encouraged the Hebrew Christians to "leave the elementary teaching about the Christ, and press on to maturity" (Heb. 6:1). From this point on, we must press on to allow the *indwelling* life of **JESUS** to become the *out-lived* life and character of **JESUS** in our behavior.

MAY 27

A THEOLOGICAL DISCUSSION

Some Christian brothers were having a "discussion" whether salvation in Jesus Christ involved alleviation, abrogation, or amelioration. The questions under consideration were, "Does the redemptive action of Jesus' death on the cross *alleviate*, diminish, mitigate and attenuate the problem of man's sin?" or "Does the death of Jesus on Calvary's hill *abrogate*, rescind, annul and do away with the consequences of man's sin?" or "Does the vicarious death of Jesus for the sins of mankind *ameliorate* and rectify man's sinfulness, to the extent that human beings experience atonement and reconciliation with God for eternity?"

Do you want to jump in and participate in this discussion? If you do, be forewarned that the discussion will turn on the semantic definitions of some of the words being discussed, as well as some of the theological presuppositions of the participants. Does salvation *alleviate* the emotional pain of human sinfulness? Does salvation *abrogate* the legal consequences of sin before God's Law? Does salvation *ameliorate* and improve a human being's right standing with God? One participant argued that alleviation of emotional pain was not the issue of salvation. Another fellow contended that legal consequences were not the issue. Still another, thought that amelioration involved self-improvement that makes a person more spiritual by engaging in religious endeavors and duties. Do you want to weigh in?

Throwing my hat in the discussion ring, I will declare that Christianity is not about human self-improvement. Self-help is antithetical to Christian thought. It is not what we do, but what God does on our behalf via **JESUS** Christ. In addition, the legal paradigm of sin in reference to the Law has been done away with in the new covenant of **JESUS** Christ, including all the legal nuances of "justification." By God's grace we are forgiven and "made righteous" by the presence of the Righteous One, **JESUS**.

MAY 28

DENOMINATIONAL DISTINCTIVES DIMINISHING

Denominations, by definition, are denominated by their differences. "We believe this; you believe that." "We do this; you do that." It's all part of the "believe-right, do-right" religious environment. If there were not some distinctive differences in doctrine or practice, then why would one group come into being on a different corner of the community from others, unless it was based only on personality differences? And why do some denominational groups have such animosity, even hatred, for other groups who think or act differently, even charging the others with being heretical or cultic, causing rifts and alienation?

I am pleased to report that in my recent observations, denominational distinctives seem to be diminishing. Who would have thought that I would be fellowshipping with congregations as diverse as Presbyterians, Baptists, Assemblies of God, Anglicans, Lutherans, Seventh Day Adventists, Roman Catholics, and Independents, etc.? As I worship with these groups having different denominational labels, I discover that they have very similar worship patterns which seem to be merging into what might be called a common evangelical emphasis on Christian worship of the triune God of Father, Son, and Holy Spirit.

This is as it ought to be. The Spirit of the living God seems to be orchestrating a unity in the Body of Christ. Not a legal merging of institutional denominations. Not an ecumenical amalgamation of creedal statements. Not regulated policies of polity and procedure. Yet, despite the differences of thought and practice, these are being set aside as of secondary importance. Even in the churches of the New Testament, the early Christians had differences of opinion, but "in Christ" they could agree to disagree as long as they agreed that their commonality was to be found in the Person and work of the living Lord **JESUS**. May we all be denominated only as being Christ-ones! Christians only!

MAY 29

THE CHRISTIAN "MEME" CULTURE

Social media on the internet has been barraged of late by a plethora of Christians who seem to think that they are witnessing to the gospel by posting a variety of photos, images, and colorful backgrounds with textual statements superimposed. These textual excerpts may be quotes from various authors, short quips, jokes, or often scripture quotations. Once they are "posted," they are often digitally "copied" and "pasted" on another person's "page," proliferating like cute little bunnies confined in a cage. Perhaps, they are more like viruses replicating in the minds of Christians, clogging clear Christian thinking.

These trite and cutesy minimalist messages that have enamored many Christians on social media are called "memes." The word is short for *mimeme*, referring to something that undergoes imitation (*mimesis*). The word was coined by evolutionary biologist Richard Dawkins, using an analogy between genetics and mimetics, suggesting that as genes replicate and mutate, so "memes" serve as the carriers of cultural ideas, replicating and mutating along the way. If this be the case, then the mimetic imitation of platitudinous "memes" attempting to convey concepts of Christian culture is producing many mutations.

From my perspective, this phenomenon of simplistic "meme" messages is likely producing a "dumbing down" of the gospel of Jesus Christ. When we reduce the gospel to visual-bytes of clichéd commonplace comments superimposed on inspirational images, we misrepresent and oversimply the reality of what we believe. The gospel is the living presence of the risen Lord **JESUS**, made available as the life-giving Spirit (I Cor. 15:45) to occupy our human spirits and live-out His life in the behavior of our bodies. Such a full-orbed spiritual reality of God's life functioning in receptive human beings is far superior to the vapid and inadequate portrayals of the many "meme" blurbs.

MAY 30

RELIGIOUS VENEER

We were shopping for a piece of furniture for the living room. We saw an advertisement for a cabinet that was said to be constructed of "solid oak wood." We went to take a look at the cabinet. It was a beautiful piece of furniture, but after close examination the "truth in advertising" criteria failed. It was not constructed of "solid oak wood," but instead had a thin, approximately one-eighth inch veneer of oak wood glued over inexpensive particle board. It was definitely less expensive, and probably less liable to warping, and the argument could be made for an ecological advantage of saving trees in the forest. The use of wood veneers is widely used in furniture construction today. They have some distinct advantages, and should not be despised. They should not, however, be advertised as "solid wood," and that is what we were shopping for.

The analogy of this piece of veneer-constructed furniture with one's Christian life can be very telling. Is Christianity just a thin veneer adhered to our life, a decorative covering that may only be "skin-deep," designed to give the appearance of something more substantial than it really is? When Christianity is regarded merely as a religious belief-system of assenting to a particular set of doctrines, or when Christianity is conceived of as a religious system of ethical and moral behavior modification, then such religion often becomes merely a veneer of religiosity suggesting that there is a deeper spiritual substance, when in reality it is a false impression, a counterfeiting of the Christ-life which can appear to be real, but it is really hypocrisy. **JESUS** will not agree to be a superficial and decorative religious veneer to our lives. He will only enter into the deepest spirit-core of our lives to be the substance and reality of our entire life. The Christian life must be His life *in* our life, His life *through* our life, and His life expressed *as* our life. It is only genuine Christianity when it is all of Him in all of us – fully, completely, solid-**JESUS** manifestation.

MAY 31

OBJECTIVE / SUBJECTIVE

From the earliest discussions within Christian church history there has been a necessary delineation of thought between events and actions that are *objective*, i.e. external to the Christian person, and those that are *subjective*, i.e. internal within the Christian person. The failure to differentiate between what occurs *outside* of a Christian (objective) and what transpires *inside* of a Christian individual (subjective), creates confused and misplaced categories of Christian thought, and an admixture of concepts that disallows clear understanding of the realities of the Christian faith; i.e. what God does and how man responds.

For example. Redemption was enacted historically when Jesus paid the price for the consequences of mankind's sins on the cross. Redemption was God's *objective*, universal grace-action on man's behalf without any contribution from mankind. This occurred whether people believe it or not. Regenerative conversion, on the other hand, transpires within Christian individuals when they are receptive by faith to what God has made available by His grace. Faith-receptivity allows the Spirit of the living Lord Jesus to occupy the human spirit *subjectively*, bringing divine Life to the being and function of a Christ-one.

Some theological systems of thought emphasize the *objective* work of God to the diminishment, neglect or denial of any subjective response of man. This approach tends to advocate a divine determinism that emphasizes the sovereignty of God and the total depravity or inability of humanity. Conversely, there are theologians who recognize God's objective grace-action, but tend to emphasize what human beings must do *subjectively* in order to accept and respond to God's work in Jesus Christ. These thinkers may emphasize the human response of faith, to the extent that it becomes a form of fideism wherein faith becomes an individual's contribution to his own salvation.

JUNE 1

QUIET TIMES

In some portions of the Christian community there is much emphasis placed on what are called "spiritual disciplines." These are procedures and habits of experiential devotion, encouraged of every Christian individual as the means of engagement in order to enhance one's Christian life and promote spiritual growth. Recommended activities include having a "quiet time" with God every day which involves prayer and reading one's bible, in addition to fasting, acceptable stewardship of giving, journaling the thoughts one has in times of meditation, and fellowship with other Christians. All of these can be beneficial.

What too often happens is that religion turns these actions into performance "works" with persistent admonitions for involvement therein, and a strong sense of "guilting" those who do not so engage. Just like the warnings on cigarette packages, perhaps there should be a warning to Christians about the spiritual habits encouraged by some Christian teachers. These habits may be hazardous to one's spiritual health, if one is thinking that engagement in these activities, and performing them every day for specified periods of times as a regular ritual, is a required performance necessary to grow spiritually in the Christian life. Not so! The self-effort of human "works," even those deemed "spiritual," are never the means by which genuine spiritual growth and maturity is achieved.

Spiritual growth comes via the grace-activity of God. We are to "grow in the grace and knowledge of our Lord and Savior Jesus Christ" (II Pet. 3:18). The very One who gave us life by His Son Jesus Christ is also the One who causes the development of that life. "God causes the growth" (I Cor. 3:6,7; Eph. 4:16; Col. 2:19), both in our individual Christian maturity, as well as in the collective community of Christians, the Body of Christ. Allow God's Spirit to direct your "quiet times" with the Lord **JESUS**.

JUNE 2

JESUS: CONTRASTED WITH ALL RELIGION

The contrast of the divine way of action and the actions of self-determined religion go all the way back to the Garden of Eden, where we observe the contrast between the "tree of the knowledge of good and evil" and the "tree of life." Self-determined and alleged self-actuated performance of ethical good and evil is basic to all religion. The Satanic source of all religion, the "father of lies" (Jn. 8:44), lied to mankind, saying, "You, too, can be like God, knowing good and evil" (Gen. 3:5), making yourself your own perceived center of reference for self-determining what is good and evil. The "tree of life," on the other hand, represented the life that is in Jesus alone (Jn. 14:6). Everything consistent with His character is "good," everything contrary to His character is "evil."

Fallen mankind, now "sinners" (Rom. 5:19) in terms of their spiritual identity, and united with the diabolic source of all sin (I Jn. 3:8), were graciously provided with the law-based religion of the old covenant. Despite their boast that "we can do it" (Exod. 19:8; 24:3), they were unable to do so because the Law reveals the character of God and only God can express His character. The purpose of law-based performance religion is to expose the inability of fallen mankind to function as God intends, to see their own plight as "sinners," and to see the impossibility and bankruptcy of all religion to provide the dynamic function of God.

From eternity past, God had "purposed" (Acts 20:27) to send His only begotten Son, **JESUS**, to redeem and restore humanity to their intended function by taking the death-consequences of their sin, and granting His divine life. The process of contrasting the divine life of Jesus with the performance standards of all religion is found throughout the new covenant literature. Only in deriving all from the living Lord **JESUS** do we see and experience the grace-dynamic of the divine "tree of life."

JUNE 3

REJECTING THE "WORKS" OF PERFORMANCE

I think that less than one percent of all the sermons I have heard in my lifetime have properly explained the gospel of Jesus Christ. For the most part, they have been advocating some type of performance, something that is required of the hearers that they should be or do – *be* more disciplined, *be* more committed, *be* more obedient – *do* more Bible reading and prayer, *do* more church involvement, *do* more evangelism. All of this advocacy for being and doing is not any different than the "works" that were being advocated by the Roman Catholic Church when Martin Luther could tolerate it no longer and sought reform.

If all your pastor/preacher/priest/minister talks about week after week is performing in accord with expectations of being and doing, then perhaps God is calling you to seek restoration of the grace-dynamic of the Christian life in your church fellowship, or leave that fellowship and find a congregation of believers who understand the gospel of God's grace in Jesus Christ received by faith and not by works (cf. Eph. 2:8,9). There comes a time to reject the legalistic religion of bondage to performance. The fleshly procedures and abuse of religion have to be cast out (cf. Gal. 4:30) in order to enjoy the freedom of God's grace.

Religion and God's grace are antithetical opposites. Religion always advocates the "works" of human performance, the self-effort of trying to do things for God. God's "grace was realized in Jesus Christ" (Jn. 1:17), and **JESUS** became the operational dynamic of the new covenant, with God's original intent to provide everything necessary for mankind to live as God created them to live. Paul explained explicitly to the Galatian Christians, "I do not nullify the grace of God" (Gal. 2:21) by opting for the "works" of performance. "I died to the Law" (Gal. 2:19), and any attempts to choose performance righteousness instead of grace signifies that Jesus Christ "died needlessly" (Gal. 2:21).

JUNE 4

GOD PROVIDES EVERYTHING HE EXPECTS

In the well-known "faith chapter" of Hebrews 11, we read these words, "Without faith it is impossible to please God" (Heb. 11:6). The word "impossible" in this statement is the Greek word *adunaton* (*a* = no; *dunamis* = dynamic, power). Without faith there is no dynamic or power with which to please God. So, does faith provide the dynamic empowering with which we please God? NO! Faith has no dynamic. Faith is powerless. Faith cannot energize anything. Faith merely receives from a power-source and allows that empowering to be put into effect on our behalf. The power is in the dynamic of God's grace-action in Jesus Christ.

God can only be pleased and worshipped by His own dynamic power. There is no power intrinsic within man by which to generate the action that God expects from His human creatures. God's power must be received by man in order to be redirected toward Himself. God is the empowering dynamic of His own demands. God never asks anything from man, but what He provides everything necessary to man by His own grace-dynamic to fulfill what He expects. What goes around comes around as God's grace energizes our worship, our prayer, our giving, our living, our loving. Everything God expects from us, He provides.

Man's only function is the choice of receptivity. Faith is human receptivity of God's activity, the grace-dynamic of God's grace! The grace provision received by faith becomes a cyclical "pass through" function within mankind. Humans derive the dynamic of God's character and activity out of God (*ek Theos*) in order to allow God's action to be implemented through them unto God (*eis Theos*), whereby He is glorified. "For from (*ek*) Him and through (*dia*) Him and unto (*eis*) Him are all things. To Him be the glory forever" (Rom. 11:36). Ours is the privilege as created human creatures to receive everything from God, say "thank you Lord," and return such to God for His pleasure.

JUNE 5

DISCIPLESHIP

A believer, a Christian, a disciple – are these designations of differing categories of Jesus people? No, they are simply designations of a follower of Jesus Christ who should be willing to be involved in the learning process of maturation. Jesus told His followers, "As you are going wherever you are going in life, disciplize (be engaged in discipling), by baptizing believers, and teaching them to observe what I have commanded you" (Matt. 28:19,20). Christian religion, in its typical misemphasis, has created many principles and procedures for "discipleship" with performance incentives to "go" and "make disciples" of all men.

Consider these definitions of "discipleship" from Christian religious sources: "Discipleship is teaching biblical precepts." "A disciple follows Christ, and then offers his own imitation of Christ as a model for others to follow." Once again, religion attempts to turn discipling into a necessary performance, encouraging all Christians to "make disciples." What this ends up creating is disciples of our way of thinking, disciples of our denomination, disciples conformed to our particular religious practices. Disciples of the Lord Jesus Christ must be mentored by the Spirit of Christ, the divine teacher (Jn. 14:26) within every Christian.

The "discipleship movement," so prominent in Western Christianity in the last half century, has become just another smokescreen for different varieties of performance-oriented religion. Christian religion has developed structured "programs" to run Christians through the assembly line to allegedly make them a "disciple," a first-class Christian, a mature Christian, an advanced-level Christian. Pay your one thousand dollars today for an advanced level workshop in "discipleship." May I suggest that discipling should be a spontaneous expression of the Spirit of Christ in us, sharing our lives with unbelievers and believers encouraging them to allow **JESUS** to live through them.

JUNE 6

IMAGES

I am an iconoclast because I believe that God is an iconoclast. What is an iconoclast? The word is derived from Greek *eikon* = image (English "icon") and *klan* = to break, smash, or shatter. An iconoclast is an "image-smasher" or an "idol-breaker." Human history is replete with examples of iconoclasm, whether it be the shattering of ideas, demolishing statues and temples, or defacing graphic images. There is nothing wrong with images, *per se*, but they should not replace or serve as substitutes for the reality signified. The Decalogue, for example, forbids the "making of graven images" (Exod. 20:4) or idols representing God.

Our brothers and sisters in the Eastern Orthodox churches make extensive use of graphic images in their iconography, but they constantly caution against worshipping the image rather than worshipping God in Christ through the Spirit. One might note that reality is intrinsically iconoclastic. **JESUS** is the reality (cf. Jn. 14:6), and will always attempt to move us from the symbol and shadow to the substance of Himself; from the picture that portrays Him to His own Person. As for me, I want the reality of **JESUS**. I will not be content with images that resemble Him, though I can appreciate images that are pointers to Him.

Those who live and walk in union with the Spirit of Christ (cf. I Cor. 6:17) will testify that God is constantly shattering their deficient images of Him. He will not allow us to put Him in a mental-image box that diminishes the reality of His personal and relational Being. Our mental images of God are always incomplete and inadequate, and this prompted J. B. Phillips to write his classic book, *Your God is Too Small.* Shattering our inadequate ideas of God and His ways is one of the iconoclastic marks of the Spirit's presence. When we recognize how religion has distorted our view of God, we can appreciate the iconoclastic spirit that breaks down false religious images and conceptions.

JUNE 7

FROM RESIDENT TO REIGN

Watchman Nee, in his book, *The Normal Christian Life*, tells of an elderly Chinese man who received Jesus by faith, and knew that the Spirit of Christ was resident within his spirit. Later, when he received a "check" in his spirit about an activity he wanted to engage in, he explained that "the Resident Boss" wouldn't allow him to do so. This unlearned Chinese Christian was aware that the risen and living Christ residing in His spirit was also the Jesus who was reigning as Lord to guide and lead him in the Christian life. Many Christians have not been aware that the Jesus living within them desires to be Lord of every part of their lives.

Going back one step farther, many who "sign on" as Christians, "join the church," and go through the initiation ceremonies, seem only to think they have acquired a one-way ticket to heaven when they die. They are unaware that the essential qualification of being a Christian is that the risen and living Jesus is resident within their spirit. "Do you not recognize that Jesus Christ is in you, unless you fail the test?" (II Cor. 13:5). "If anyone does not have the Spirit of Christ, he does not belong to Him" (Rom. 8:9), i.e. is not a "Christ-one," a Christian. "The Spirit testifies with our spirit that we are children of God" (Rom. 8:16).

To receive the risen and living presence of **JESUS** to reside in our spirit is to receive Him as our Savior and Lord. He does not come into the Christian only to be a Savior who erases our sins and delivers us to heaven. He does not enter into our lives merely to be an occupant or resident in our spirit. He will always function in the fullness of who He is. As the Lord of the universe, it is His intent to reign in control of every facet of our lives. As W. Ian Thomas expressed this reality, it is *All of Him in All of Us*. The living Lord **JESUS** desires that every Christian should "reign in life through Him" (Rom. 5:17), that by allowing Him to "be our life" (Col. 3:4) in every behavioral expression (cf. II Cor. 4:10,11).

JUNE 8

CHRIST-CONSCIOUSNESS

Many sincere Christians have concluded it is God's objective that Christians should have a constant Christ-consciousness, whereby at every moment in time their thoughts and emotions should be directed and focused on Jesus Christ. They view such an objective as an advanced "spiritual" ideal – but it must be questioned whether such a constant Christ-consciousness is even possible or feasible? The human mind is not made for double-mindedness, but this is not an argument for single-minded Christ-consciousness. Rather, the attention of our minds on the ordinary details of life precludes constant Christ-mindedness.

When the Spirit of Christ is received into our human spirit in spiritual regeneration there will be an inner awareness of His presence, a spiritual consciousness and assurance that we are a Christ-one, a "new creature" (II Cor. 5:17) in Christ. The Christian has "the mind of Christ" (I Cor. 2:16) in his spirit, but that does not mean that the human mind is always consciously thinking about Jesus. Knowing that we are in spiritual union (I Cor. 6:17) with Jesus, and that "He is our life" (Col. 3:4), we get on with our daily life with its necessary mental attentions, and "rest" assured in the freedom that He is living out through us.

The unrealistic and impossible ideal of continual "Christ-consciousness" sets up the Christian for a legalistic sense of failure to achieve a performance-based mindset that gives full attention to Jesus. We must avoid such condemnation (Rom. 8:1), and enjoy our freedom in Christ. Below the surface of our daily mental attentions, underlying all that we are and do, the Christian "knows that he knows" Jesus, and desires that by God's grace the character and life of the risen Lord will spontaneously manifest Himself in the midst of all things. As the spiritual heart-beat of our lives, **JESUS** functions as our life, and this is not contingent on attaining constant Christ-consciousness.

JUNE 9

LAW OR GOSPEL?

It is imperative that Christians see the contrast of law and gospel. The old covenant was based on the human performance of law regulations that humans were expected to do. The new covenant explains that the Divine Promises are fulfilled in the good news of the gospel of what God has done through His Son, by the power of the Holy Spirit. Consider these paraphrases of scripture:

Luke 16:16 - "The Law and the Prophets (with all their emphases on the performance of 'doing this' and 'not doing that') were in effect until John (i.e. until the new covenant was introduced); since that time the gospel of the kingdom of God with Jesus reigning as King in a person's life has been preached, and everyone who sees this should do everything possible to participate in that kingdom of grace."

Romans 4:5 – "For the one who abandons all trust and hope that his performance and self-actuated efforts carry any weight or count for any good in reference to his relationship with God, but instead believes that Jesus alone is the One who makes an ungodly person righteous, that person's faithful receptivity of Christ's Person and work will be reckoned, counted, and applied to him as righteousness, as the righteous presence of the Righteous One dwells in him in order to function as his life."

Galatians 2:21 – "I do not ignore, set aside, or nullify the grace of God revealed in Jesus Christ, for if being right with God and the character of God's righteousness could in any way be accomplished by my performance, self-effort, or doing anything in accordance with any behavioral laws, guidelines, or inculcations, then the death of Jesus Christ on the cross of Calvary would be rendered void, of no consequence, and unnecessary; i.e. Jesus died for the 'fun of it.'" God forbid! Christ loved me and gave Himself for me, and now **JESUS** lives in me!"

JUNE 10

CONSCIENCE

The English word "conscience" is derived from the Latin *conscientia* (*con* = together with; *scientia* = to perceive or to know). The New Testament word "conscience" is a translation of the Greek word *suneidesis* (*sun* = together with; *eido* = to perceive or to know). What does the conscience perceive together with? Suggestions have included God, an inner natural law of right and wrong, or a second-self altar-ego. It seems more feasible to explain that the human conscience perceives in conjunction with whatever attitudes are established in the human mind, either natural established attitudes or godly established attitudes.

The apostle Paul had a natural (religious) attitude that Christians were heretics and traitors to the Jewish faith. Acting on that attitude, he set out to be the hit-man for the Sanhedrin, to arrest, imprison and even kill Christians. He stood by and watched the murder of Stephen. His conscience, perceiving in conjunction with his established attitudes, had no qualms about his actions. But when he was converted on the road to Damascus, he thereafter developed godly established attitudes, recognizing that he had "persecuted the church of God" (I Cor. 15:9), and he called himself "the chief of sinners" (I Tim. 1:15).

We all have natural established attitudes acquired in our past; attitudes about activities, objects, people, ideas, ourselves and God. In order to develop godly established attitudes that align with God's perspective, we need to submit ourselves to the "renewing of the mind" (Rom. 12:2; Eph. 4:32), allowing the agency of the Holy Spirit to use the means of the inspired scriptures to provide the personal revelation of how God would have us to think. Our conscience will then function in conjunction with such godly attitudes in the mind, allowing us to freely choose to act by allowing God's character of godliness to be expressed without condemnation or guilt for our actions.

JUNE 11

A MECHANICAL GOD?

Our modern western culture seems to want everything to be robotic these days. We want to program the repetitive actions of every task in a mechanical robotic manner. By doing so, we have the mechanical action figured out (we programmed it), and we are in control of the mechanism as we control the switches to cause the robotic mechanism to do what we want it to do. Robotic military action has been utilized for several decades in drone technology, and is now moving towards autonomous automated weaponry. The RoboCop movie series projected the conceptualization of robotic law-enforcement. For many, the possibilities of robotic manipulation appear to be endless.

Robots are essentially functional machines with computer programming to perform specific tasks. They are not personal beings, and despite the many attempts to develop "artificial intelligence" in computers, they will never duplicate the complexity of a God-created human being. The physical function of humans, and to some extent the psychological function of humans may be reproduced, but the spiritual capacity of human function is incapable of mechanization. Even more far-fetched is the idea of a mechanical Robo-God, a robotic deity that would necessarily be programmed and controlled by humans.

Some Christians, however, already seem to conceive of God as a mechanized Being. When we attempt to get God figured out with our finite minds, and begin to think that we have figured out God's Being and ways, then our logical machinations project a mechanical god. Thinking that we have God figured out, we can then calculate how God will function and act in any given situation. He will always act in the immutable manner that we have Him programmed in our mind. But God is not a mechanical god, He is a personal, relational God that acts in accord with His eternal character, and not in any programmed action.

JUNE 12

DISCERNMENT

Christians should be encouraged to listen to speakers and read literature that does not necessarily concur with the particular beliefs they now hold. In the process of pondering the views of others, we learn to clarify what we believe, and we develop the ability to discern the difference between varying perspectives of a subject. Growth in discernment is a component of Christian freedom, freeing us from bondage to the opinions of others and allowing God to reveal His mind to us. An undiscerning Christian is susceptible to being enslaved to his natural established attitudes or to suggested religious interpretations.

The development of spiritual discernment comes as the Holy Spirit teaches each individual Christian how to think as God thinks. We want God's attitudes and affections to be our attitudes and affections. We want to see from God's perspective and sense the heartbeat of God for others. Every Christian has the "mind of Christ" (I Cor. 2:16). The presence of Christ necessarily includes the mind of Christ. It is when the "mind of Christ" becomes an established pattern of our human mind, developed by "the renewing of the mind" (Ro. 12:2) as the Spirit teaches (Jn. 14:26) us, then we develop practical spiritual discernment.

A person with spiritual discernment will be able to observe another person's behavior for a time, and discern whether that person has "a heart for God," a real "love of Jesus," and a desire for holiness. Discernment equips us to employ God's wisdom to make judgments about men and their message. When listening to a Christian teacher one will begin to discern their logical and theological presuppositions. When reading religious materials, one can differentiate the content of the teaching, and whether it is consistent with the revelation of God. Though some may have a special grace-gift of discernment (cf. I Cor. 12:10), all Christians should cultivate spiritual discernment (Phil. 1:9; Heb. 5:14).

JUNE 13

OVERSIMPLIFICATION

In the particular religious environment that I was brought up, they often employed an oversimplified explanation of how an individual was to respond to the gospel message (as they understood and taught such). Not only was it a simple little exercise even a child could grasp, it was an oversimplification of the human response to the life of Jesus. They utilized the "five finger exercise," pointing to each finger on one's hand and indicating that they represented (1) believing the gospel, (2) repenting of one's sins, (3) confessing Jesus as Savior, (4) being baptized by immersion in water, and (5) living the Christian life.

There were variations of the exercise. Some indicated the first finger represented "hearing the gospel," in which case the fifth incentive of "obedience," i.e. "living the Christian life," was voided or dismissed – an excision with dire consequences. Throughout the history of Christian instruction there have been many man-made explanations of the *ordo salutis*, the "order of salvation," but the "five-finger exercise" is a particularly deficient example of such. Historically, the examples always included the objective work of God in Christ, such as incarnation, redemption, regeneration, sanctification, and sometimes glorification.

The "five-finger exercise" failed to emphasize the objective work of God in Christ, focusing instead on the subjective response of what "man must do" in response to the historical presentation of Jesus almost two millennia ago. Such an emphasis often fails to account for the grace-activity of God, emphasizing instead the faith-response of the human individual. In other words, instead of being God-centered, the gospel becomes man-centered, focusing on what man does to become a Christian, rather than on what God has done, and is doing, through His Son **JESUS** Christ to provide everything necessary for the spiritual restoration of humanity to God's original created intent.

JUNE 14

THE GRACE GUARANTEE

We all want guarantees that the products we have acquired will function as intended. We will often pay extra for a warranty agreement insuring and assuring that the product will be repaired if or when it breaks down. God's assurances are not legal or logical warranties, but a relational guarantee based on the faithful character of Him who promises. God is the very definition of "integrity," as the integral oneness of His Being and character is invested in His every action. When God acts in grace via His Son, Jesus Christ (Jn. 1:17), we have the surety that He will act consistently to accomplish all that He desires.

God's promises are *guaranteed* in accordance with His grace, as we are receptive to such by faith (cf. Rom. 4:16). Writing to the Corinthians, Paul twice explained that God "put His Spirit in our hearts as a deposit, *guaranteeing* what is to come" (II Cor. 1:22; 5:5 *NIV*). This is not merely a reference to what is to come in the heavenly future, but the revealed assurance that God is going to do what God wants to do in our lives. "He who began a good work in us will carry it on to completion until the day of Christ Jesus" (Phil. 1:6). "He will bring it to pass" (I Thess. 5:24). It's not what we do, but what He has done, and is doing, in us.

God guarantees by the presence of His Holy Spirit (cf. Eph. 1:14), that He will do everything that needs doing in our lives. He will bring to fruition in us all that He desires. Why is it so difficult for Christians to accept the divine Grace Guarantee? Obviously, it is because it completely disallows any activity of man to assist or cooperate with what only God can do. Satan has thoroughly indoctrinated all men with the necessity and competency of human performance to please God. We must reject the lie! We can't; only He can! The grace of God guarantees the end result that He desires in our lives. Everything that God wants for us, He will enact! Are we willing to submit and receive it?

JUNE 15

IT'S NOT ABOUT OUR BELIEFS

Christian faith has repeatedly been cast and projected in the form of believe-right religion. This must be challenged by asserting that Christianity is not, and never was intended to be, an epistemological belief-system. Yes, the Christian religion has a long history of constructing creedal belief-statements. The Latin word *credo*, from which we get the English word "creed," means "I believe." To this day people often ask to see one's "statement of beliefs," a formal statement of ideology and doctrinal beliefs. But man-made beliefs, and the systems in which they are often formulated, are a "dime a dozen" and of little value.

Yet, we continue to observe Christians honing and fine-tuning their beliefs, developing complex charts about "false beliefs" vs. "true beliefs." Like children playing in the sand-pile of human beliefs, they argue incessantly about whose bucket contains the most brilliant rocks. Having defined their beliefs as precisely as possible, and polished them to a brilliant sheen, they then determine that anyone who believes otherwise is a "heretic." One group I am aware of claimed not to believe in creeds, declaring "we have no creed, but Christ," failing to understand that in their assertion they were stating their *credo*.

Christianity is not a belief-system. Human beliefs are human constructs of thought, and soon become idolatrous formulations carved in the concrete of inflexible minds. We must eschew the idolatry of believe-right religion. The world of mankind wants, and needs, the reality and vitality of life that supersedes their selfishness and humanistic perspectives. Christians must cease arguing about beliefs and learn to enjoy life, living by the LIFE of the One who said, "I AM the way, the Truth, and the LIFE" (Jn. 14:6), "I came that you might have LIFE, and have it more abundantly" (Jn. 10:10). Dogmatic beliefs must be set aside to simply appreciate the living Lord **JESUS**.

JUNE 16

THE RELIGIOUS AGENDA

They have been coming to my door every other week or so for approximately twenty years. Some would say that I should have sent them on their way, repudiated them, not given them the time of day, and slammed the door in their face without civil greeting or hospitality (cf. II Jn. 10,11). I chose instead to demonstrate the "fruit of the Spirit" in love, kindness, gentleness, goodness and patience (Gal. 5:22,23), knowing full well that to do so would likely encourage them with a false hope that their agenda to convince and persuade me of the correctness of their believe-right, do-right religious system might pull me in.

Religionists are but duped prisoners of thought-controlling authorities, taught to believe that they are the exclusive people of God with the exclusive message of God. They are totally unaware that they operate with the "schemes" of the Evil One (cf. II Cor. 2:11; Eph. 6:11), using underlying and under-handed propaganda techniques. Seeing everything in black or white, right or wrong categories, with no sense of dialectic balance, they major in the minors and want to argue their points vehemently. The issue they want to discuss is never relationship with Jesus; they want only to talk about such impertinent peripherals as "the king of the north" or "the despised servant," etc.

Argumentation of their belief-system is at the forefront of their agenda. They have been taught how to give "correct" responses to the usual questions, and warned to expect rejection, receiving repudiation as a sign of their correctness of thought and action – a "persecution complex." The one thing that such religionists are baffled by and do not know what to do with is how to respond to the love of the personal, living Lord **JESUS**. They will push that aside, and continue to argue incessantly in accord with their religious agenda. The one thing that we have to give the devil credit for is his persistence in his religious dupes.

JUNE 17

PARENTS WHO IMPEDE

Many parents want the best for their children, but fail to understand that their actions are impeding the natural flow of childhood, and perhaps interfering with God's providential direction in each child's life. When mothers become "helicopter moms," hovering over everything the child thinks or does, their mothering becomes smothering. When fathers become "bulldozer dads," pushing the child to excel with their projected expectations, and pressuring others (teacher, coaches, etc.) to join in the manipulations, they begin to "play god" for the child, and their fathering becomes bullying.

Children are entrusted to parents as a gift from God (Ps. 127:3). Parents are to serve as spiritual directors of the child, in order to find God's particular direction for that child's life. Parents are not to view their children as objects to be controlled or corralled, nor should they attempt to live childhood again vicariously through their children. A child does not need their parents to condescend and become their "buddy-buddy" best friends. Rather, they need relational parental love as the parent functions as the consistent authoritative guide that God intends for their children. Thus, they will participate in successful God-ordained parenting.

The parental responsibility is to "train up a child in the way he or she should go" (Prov. 22:6). Each child is unique – one may have a "natural bent" for mechanics, another for music or mathematics. Each child has different learning styles (ex. tactile, visual, oral, verbal, logical, social), even in varying subjects of instruction. Parents must allow the child to develop as the unique individual that God means each child to be. Parents want to protect their children from harm, but a most important facet of parenting is allowing the children to fail and face rejection. A great disservice is done to a child when they have not learned how to face and deal with the inevitable failures of life.

JUNE 18

THE DYNAMIC OF HIS OWN DESIRES

Perhaps you have heard someone define "grace" as God's initiative and activity whereby God serves as "the dynamic of His own demands." But God is not really interested in making any demands on the human creatures He created. He is fully aware of the inability of the human race to perform in such a manner that might serve His purposes. He created us as derivative and receptive creatures, designed to receive from Him, and express His life and character in our human behavior in such a manner that He is glorified (cf. Isa. 43:7) by the expression of His all-glorious character exhibited in His creation. Praise be to God!

Yes, there are imperative verbs in the New Testament. Someone counted more than one thousand such verbs in the Greek New Testament. But when considered carefully, the divine commands/demands are simply expressive of God's desires for His people, Christ-ones (Christians); directives to indicate where Christians should be receptive in faith to His grace-dynamic in order to allow God to be and do what God desires to be and do in our lives. Religion always seems to take the imperatives as performance dictates and duties, but to the contrary, everything that God desires in our lives, He will do.

God is the dynamic of His own desires. The onus is not on us to perform in accord with God's desires. Everything God desires, He is willing to do. "He will bring it to pass" (I Thess. 5:24). He will be our sanctification and holiness (I Thess. 3:13). He will be the provision of our love for one another (cf. I Jn. 4:9,16; Rom. 5:5; Gal. 5:22). He will be our consistent expression of integrity. All that God really desires for us is that the Son, **JESUS**, should be allowed to live out His life in our behavior (cf. II Cor. 4;10,11) as empowered by His Spirit, and all to the glory of the divine Godhead. Our only response-ability is to be available and receptive to His grace-action by faith.

JUNE 19

WHAT MUST WE DO?

Human beings always seem to want to DO something. Where does this ambition to be engaged in doing come from? Are human beings created to be activists? Is there an intrinsic restless energy within humans? Is there a dynamo of doing in every human, seeking outlet? Does this come from a Satan-inspired desire to be like God? Does the human quest to act come from an incentive to perform in order to receive accolades, or even to pat ourselves on the back for a "job well done"? Human beings are not created to be activists, but to be receptive beings, receptive to the presence and activity of a spirit-being within our spirit.

God, on the other hand, is an ever-active God, doing what He has self-determined to do, and having omnipotent energy to implement what He has determined. For God, His being and His doing are integrally combined. He does what He does, because He IS who He IS. His Being is of necessity expressed in His every action, and every action is expressive of His very Being. The prime function of God is that He acts like the God that He is. God acts in accord with His own character. God self-generates His own activity to express His own Being in every facet of His active Doing. God's active Doing is GRACE, God acting in accord with His character. God's Grace-action is through the agency of His Son, Jesus Christ (Jn. 1:17). It is Christic-grace action. Jesus is the agency through which God makes Himself known. Jesus said, "If you have seen Me, you have seen the Father" (Jn. 14:9).

Christian activity should derive from the One who has made us a new being, a "new creature" in Christ (II Cor. 5:17), His Spirit in our spirit (Rom. 8:9,16). Jesus told His disciples, "Apart from Me, you can do nothing" (Jn. 15:5). In receiving the Savior, "we are created in Christ Jesus for good works, which God prepared beforehand that we should walk in them" (Eph. 2:8-10). It's not what we do, but what Christ **JESUS** does in the Christian.

JUNE 20

TEMPORAL AND ETERNAL PERSPECTIVE

I once heard the testimony of a man who was an engineer, specializing in bridge design and construction. Sitting at his desk one day, he realized that everything he was working on would likely fall down and be of no value within approximately one hundred and fifty years. His entire life was engaged in a temporal endeavor having only temporary benefits. Many will realize that the endeavors of their lives likely have an even shorter temporal benefit than does bridge-building. The engineer gave up his career as a bridge-builder, and decided to become involved in something with eternal perspective and consequences.

The perspective of the world around us is extremely temporal. Living in the temporality of space and time parameters, the world is primarily interested in the here and now. Many cannot see beyond the end of their noses and the fulfillment of their present desires. For that reason, our culture is predominantly materialistic and consumerist, biting at the bubbles and baubles of life on earth. Paul wrote, the things which are seen are temporal, but the things which are not seen are eternal" (II Cor. 4:18). Modern man needs to figure out how to maintain an eternal perspective that transcends the visible world we live in.

Christians are "in the world, but not of the world" (cf. Jn. 17:11,14). "The world is passing away" (I Jn. 2:17), and "life is like a vapor that appears and then vanishes" (James 4:14). But "God has put eternity in the hearts of men" (Eccl. 3:11), making all men internally aware of a realm that transcends the physical world we live in. Eternality necessarily points to an eternal God, and His Eternal Son who alone is Life (Jn. 14:6) and is "the source of eternal salvation" (Heb. 5:9). Every human person simultaneously functions in the temporal and eternal realms, and must learn to prioritize their involvement. "Set your mind on things above, not on things on the earth" (Col. 3:2).

JUNE 21

IS THE WORLD GETTING WORSE?

People observe what is happening in the world, and often ask whether the world around us is getting worse, more wicked and perverse. Concluding that it must be, many take another step to surmise that this must be the "sign of the last days," prior to God's bringing final judgement upon mankind for sin. There is some very deficient theology at work in such popular thinking of concerned human beings. God has not been taken by surprise at the counter-ops of his spiritual enemy, Satan. Even before He created mankind, He knew there was going to be a constant and relentless battle for the spirits and souls of human persons.

The Evil One has been at work among mankind ever since the Garden of Eden and the first couple's wholesale sell-out to "the spirit that works in the sons of disobedience" (Eph. 2:2). His character has not changed. The devil's evil character from the beginning is the same as his evil character expressed in the world today. Sin can be quantified in its expressions, but its quality is always evil and antithetical to God's character. Sin is sin, and it will never get better, nor will it ever get worse. Satan, the "ruler of this world" (Jn. 12:31; 14:30; 16:11), is fixed in his evil character and irredeemable. He will never change for the better.

It should certainly be noted that the awareness of evil and sinfulness in the world is more explicitly "in our faces" as the events of the world are broadcast more explicitly via the media today, and the barrage of such bad news can seem overwhelming. But, the evil quality of the sin in the world is the same as it has always been. What should be the Christians' reaction to such evil? We must resign ourselves to the fact that "the world is going to do what the world is going to do," for the author of sin (I Jn. 3:8) who is "the ruler of this world" (Eph. 6:12) will inject his evil character in every situation of mankind. The world-system of evil cannot be saved or redeemed, but has been overcome in Christ.

JUNE 22

GRACE AND CHRISTIAN FREEDOM

Many Christians enjoy watching automobile racing, whether at the racetrack or on the television screen. It is exhilarating to watch the racing cars and the drivers seeking to go as fast as they can in order to win the race. Some prefer drag racing, others Indycar racing, others NASCAR, and a variety of other forms of auto racing. Although the apostle Paul could never have conceived of automobile racing, he did liken the Christian life to a foot race, advocating that we "run in such a way that you may win" (I Cor. 9:24; Heb. 12:1). This does not, however, imply that the Christian life is a matter of human performance and exertion.

The Christian life functions on the dynamic of God's grace empowering, and thereby enables the Christian "freedom for which Christ set us free" (Gal. 5:1). Grace, however, becomes a convoluted concept in the minds of some Christian racing fans. Thinking that liberty and freedom can be a dangerous opportunity for license, some perceive of grace as the "governor" or "restrictor plate" that limits and holds back full-throttle Christian freedom. Others, on the other hand, think of grace as an "accelerant" or "nitro boost" for full-throttle Christian freedom, overcoming all the limitations of religious legalism.

The analogy of automotive racing may be somewhat inadequate to explain grace and freedom in the Christian life. It is most important, however, for Christians to understand and appreciate the grace-dynamic of God in Jesus Christ, who by His Spirit provides the empowering of everything necessary for the living out of the Christ-life. The recognition of His grace-provision frees the Christian from all performance initiatives to please and appease God. Receiving and submitting to God's grace-empowering frees the Christian from all thought that we can gain victory in the race of life by finding more horse-power and giving our best exertion to enter the winner's circle.

JUNE 23

HARD TO LOVE?

We have all heard people say, or perhaps we have said, "some people are hard to love." But to indicate that someone is "hard to love" seems to imply that this is a performance action on our part that requires exertion to overcome the difficulty of trying to love certain people. From a human point of view, there is no doubt that some people do not present themselves as very lovely or loveable. They may grate against our sensitivities and established attitudes of how we think they should believe or behave. The degree to which a person is like us (or different from us) is often the criteria by which we find such a person "hard to love."

Love is not based on the thought patterns or behavior of those who would be the recipients of such love. Personal preferences and sentiment are not the prompts for love. It is a deliberate commitment to allow the character of God's love (Rom. 5:5; Gal. 5:22; I Jn. 4:7) to flow to another person without considering any reciprocal benefit we might get from such. Love only needs to be a one-way street, flowing in one direction to another without reciprocation. Some people repel and reject love, thinking that it indicts them of being a needy person, but when love is accepted by another, it can then become a loving relationship.

Who is that person who from a natural perspective you would find "hard to love"? Do you think that God in Christ finds that person "hard to love?" God so loved the world of mankind (yes, that very person whom we find "hard to love"), that He gave His only begotten Son (Jn. 3:16), **JESUS**, to die on that person's behalf. I find it hard to conceive that God's unconditional love finds anyone "hard to love." God IS love (I Jn. 4:8,16), and His love is always flowing outward from His character to every human person regardless of their personality, selfish propensities or response to Him. God's love is a constant, objective, drawing to Himself with no qualitative reservations.

JUNE 24

WHEN YOU GET TO HEAVEN

Have you ever imagined what it is going to feel like when you walk into the heavenly community for the first time? I have, and it is an exhilarating vision. "Wow! I don't think I've ever lived in such a fine neighborhood before. Nice 'digs,' they have prepared for my glorified body – all the comforts of a home, beyond my wildest expectations. People are very friendly here – no backbiting, no competition, no negativism. Don't see a single church building here, and no zealous pastors attempting to coerce you in the front door, or pounding the pulpit with their admonitions that you perform the necessary duties to qualify."

Then, I imagined Jesus taking me aside and confiding, "You won't believe what a hilarious time I had occupying your spirit, soul and body during the time you were hanging around on planet earth. I know there were people who didn't understand you, and some even thought you were 'dingy,' but you knew it wasn't you they criticized, but Me in you, so you didn't take it personal. You just let their comments roll off, like water off a duck's back. There were times when you were just 'hanging on for the ride' as you were carried in the flow of My grace, but it was "the only way to go!' "Well done, good and faithful servant!"

You can't imagine a more pleasant environment – the absence of everything miserable, and the presence of everything desirable. And the lighting – you won't believe the brilliance and purity of the Light (Edison and Tesla didn't have a clue!). And the worship was beyond compare to anything ever observed on earth. I did not observe any "pogo-sticking for Jesus," but the silence and intensity of a truly heart-level adoration for the Perfect One was palpable and pure as we all looked to and praised **JESUS**. Yes, it was the presence of **JESUS** that predominated and permeated everything and everyone. I am convinced it is correct to explain "heaven" is the presence of **JESUS** – both now and then.

JUNE 25

PERSONAL INDEPENDENCE IS AN ILLUSION

Many people in modern society have bought into the humanistic lie, thinking that they can be "independent." The idealism of youth is particularly vocal about their alleged independence, defiantly declaring, "I'm not going to be anybody's 'dupe.' I'm not going to serve anyone at any time. I am going to do my own thing, and be the master of my own fate, for I have the power to be anything I want to be!" Bob Dylan challenged such thinking in his 1979 Grammy-winning rock song, "Gotta Serve Somebody."

> "You're gonna have to serve somebody, yes indeed.
> You're gonna have to serve somebody.
> It may be the devil or it may be the Lord,
> But you're gonna have to serve somebody."

Dylan's words are consistent with scriptural teaching. Human beings were created as derivative creatures, designed to derive from either God or Satan for everything they are and do. The Evil One will repeatedly suggest that no one has a right to control you, and assert that "derivativeness is tyranny," but the truth is that all humans are dependent on one spiritual source or the other. Jesus explained that we all serve one master or another. "No one can serve two masters; for either he will hate the one and love the other, or else how will be devoted to one and despise the other" (Lk. 16:13).

When Adam and Eve believed the lie (Rom. 1:25) of self-independence (Gen. 3:5), Satan pulled the "bait and switch," and they found themselves in bondage to "the spirit that works in the sons of disobedience" (Eph. 2:2). They were not free and independent; they were "slaves of sin" (Rom. 6:17,20), sinning by deriving from the character of the devil (I Jn. 3:8). The only solution is to be "turned from darkness to light, from the power of Satan to God" (Acts 26:18) in an inner spiritual exchange.

JUNE 26

MY PERSONAL PENTECOST

In the church tradition in which I was raised and trained, there was scarce mention of the Holy Spirit. The Spirit was only a vague illuminating influence by which a person might better understand the scriptures. So, years later, when I was confronted by three pastors about my knowledge and experience of the Holy Spirit, all I could regurgitate was a misinformed theoretical ambiguity about the third person of the Godhead involved in the inspiration of the scriptures. Like the disciples in Ephesus (cf. Acts 19:2), I had no real awareness and no personal involvement with the activity of the Holy Spirit in my Christian life.

Forced to re-examine the reality of the Holy Spirit, I opened to Rom. 8:9, "If anyone does not have the Spirit of Christ, he does not belong to Him." Uh oh! Maybe I do not know what it means to have a personal relationship with the living Jesus! Then, in Rom. 8:16, I continued to read, "The Spirit Himself testifies with our spirit that we are children of God." Having never experienced such an internal testifying witness of the Spirit, I suspected that I had missed out on something important. As an unregenerate pastor, I prayed to God in the pastor's study that He might give me the Spirit of Christ and all that His presence might entail.

That day in 1973 was the occasion of my spiritual regeneration and my personal Pentecost experience, wherein I was henceforth aware that my human spirit was overwhelmed by the Spirit of God, baptized by the Spirit (I Cor. 12:13), in like manner as the Spirit was poured out at Pentecost (Acts 2:33). I knew from that point forward that my body was "a temple of God and that the Spirit of God was dwelling in me" (cf. I Cor. 3:16). That was the commencement of a trajectory which involves continuously "being filled with the Spirit" (Eph. 5:18). The Spirit of the living Christ serves as the grace-dynamic of the Christ-life within my spirit, empowering everything that God desires to do in me.

WORLDLY RELIGION

Satan is the "ruler of this world" (Jn. 12:31; 16:11). The entire world-system of evil is under the control of the Evil One. Because of the fall of mankind into sin through Adam and Eve (Gen. 3:1-7), "the whole world lies in the Evil One" (I Jn. 5:19). On the other hand, "the prince of the power of the air (Satan), is the spirit that is working in the sons of disobedience" (Eph. 2:2,3). It is important for all mankind to recognize the either/or spiritual difference and contrast between the "ruler of this world" and Jesus Christ. Jesus explicitly declared, "the ruler of this world has nothing in Me" (Jn. 14:30).

Those who have read C.S. Lewis' *Screwtape Letters* might remember the devilish Screwtape advising his nephew, Wormwood, to encourage people to be involved in religion. He commented, "the more 'religious,' the more securely ours;" "It will be an ill day for us if what most humans mean by 'religion' ever vanishes from the Earth. It can still send us the truly delicious sins." Episcopal priest, Robert Farrar Capon, wrote, "The world is by no means averse to religion. In fact, it is devoted to it with a passion. It will buy any recipe for salvation as long as that formula leaves the responsibility for cooking up salvation firmly in human hands. The world is drowning in religion, but it is scared out of its wits by any mention of the grace" of God in Jesus Christ.

Religion has, without a doubt, permeated what is known as Christianity, but the Christ-life is diametrically opposite of all religion. Christianity is not religion! Christian faith is totally invested in the person of the living Lord **JESUS**, "the last Adam who became the life-giving Spirit" (I Cor. 15:45), and now as the indwelling Spirit of life is the reality of all Christian life (cf. Rom. 8:9). **JESUS** as the antithesis of all religion, serves as the living grace-dynamic of the life of God in receptive mankind.

JUNE 28

ARE YOU COMFORTABLE WITH CHANGE?

Though some people have personalities that drive them to be "change-agents," their change maneuvers are often self-motivated to empower their self-significance. For many other people, change is quite difficult to accept. They feel like they are losing their sense of self-control as they remain "stuck in the mud" of the status-quo. Change must occur. It is inevitable. The world does not stand still. C.S. Lewis wrote, "To be in time means to change." The "change-agent" for effective change in the world and in our lives must, however, be God acting by His grace to implement His perfect character in His creation.

Those who do not like change, will find grace difficult to accept. Grace implies change! Many seem to be comfortable in their settled and sedentary religion, but God's grace will not allow anyone to sit in the rut of just enjoying the "old time religion," while chanting the mantra, "we've never done it that way before!" The ever-changing grace of God's activity by His Spirit "blows like the wind" (Jn. 3:8). Like the new wine in the old wine-skins (Lk. 5:37-39), the grace of God explodes the old religious modalities, and makes them forever unacceptable. No one who has truly experienced God's grace can be content with religion.

Grace is God in action by His Son, Jesus Christ, and by the power of His Holy Spirit. God's Being and Action are inseparable, for His Being is never static, always in action, and His ever-dynamic grace-action is invested with the entirety of His Being. Grace is risky. We never know what God is going to do, where He is going to take us, but it will always be consistent with His character. Grace is a challenging adventure wherein we "hang on for the ride." Grace is just allowing **JESUS** to live out His life in you, but that must be **JESUS** only, without any religious crutches. Grace is like walking across a shaky suspension bridge without handrails, trusting God to keep you on the bridge and upright.

JUNE 29

GOD AS LOVING FATHER

Our perspective of God can color the entire narrative of what the "good news" of the gospel is all about. Many persons throughout Christian history have had a mental picture of God as a holy and righteous Judge. They think of themselves as standing before the divine Judge, on trial for their sins. Then, just before God is about to pronounce them "Guilty as charged," Jesus the Advocate steps up and says, "Charge me instead. Put this person's sins on my account." God the Judge accepts the substitutional payment of the advocate, and declares the person standing before him, "Pardoned, Forgiven, Not guilty!" – "Next case!"

Such a perspective of God as Judge in the heavenly courtroom is regimented, impersonal and legal. As merciful and gracious as it is that Jesus stepped forward to accept the consequences for a person's sins, the redeemed culprit is led out of the courtroom, released into society, and walks down the sidewalk wondering, "What's next? I guess, I am responsible to do better, to be the kind of person God wants me to be." So, he walks into the next church building, and is told that God is a strict Moralist who expects the redeemed to conform to the ecclesiastical strictures of belief and involvement in church activities.

May I suggest a more compelling image of the scenario? Jesus, who served as my advocate, leads me out of the courtroom with His arm around me, and leads me into His Father's house until I stand face to face with His Father God. The Father is not dressed in judge's robes, but in casual attire. With tears in His eyes, He runs to me, throws His arms around me, and kisses me. He tells me that everything that is His is mine. He advises me that there are no penalties to pay, no moral codes to obey, for all will be supplied by His grace in the Son, **JESUS**. The loving Father God welcomes me into His presence and explains His desire for a loving heart-to-heart relationship that will continue forever.

JUNE 30

FREEDOM IN CHRIST

Jesus came to set men free! He said, "true disciples of Mine will know the Truth and the Truth shall make them free" (Jn. 8:32). Truth, in this context, does not refer to propositions of truth, but the personalizing of Truth in the Person of Jesus (cf. Jn. 14:6). Jesus went on to say, "If the Son makes you free, you will be free indeed" (Jn. 8:36). The Son is the Truth (the same word as Reality – Greek *aletheia*). Truth is not to be found in theological, or even biblical tenets and propositions, but in the One who came as the Reality of God Himself to be the liberator of mankind.

If Truth sets us free, what are we set free from? Christ-ones are free from the performance standards that religion inevitably imposes upon people. The law-system establishes the parameters of acceptable external behavior to keep people "in check," to keep people corralled in the fences. Law-performance served as a guardian, a *paidagogos*, a child-abusing babysitter (cf. Gal. 3:24,25). In contrast to law-performance, the dynamic of God's grace in Jesus sets us free to live as adults by means of Him. "It was for freedom that Christ set us free" (Gal. 5:1).

Freedom is scary and risky. Many are reticent to accept God's grace. Those who are enslaved find comfort in the fact that they know where the pre-set boundaries are located. Law-performance gives people the illusion of security. That is why the freedom of the Jesus-life seems like such a free-floating abstraction to many people shackled in religious confines. The freedom of living in the dynamic of God's grace, receptive to such step-by-step in faith – now, that is stepping out into the unknown in a "step of faith" wherein we do not know for sure where God is going to take us. To live free in Christ Jesus implies that we are not in control, and can no longer attempt to control where our lives are going. We "surrender all" to God's grace-activity, and totally believe that "**JESUS** is Lord" of our lives.

JULY 1

MINISTRY OVERFLOW

When many Christians think of ministry, they think of the professional minister, preacher, pastor or priest who leads, teaches and coordinates the congregation of worshippers. In the minds of many, this person is elevated to a position of knowledge, spirituality, and closeness with God that sets them apart as "God's anointed." Such a perspective has been a great detriment to the Church. The conception of ministry has been professionalized in those who have the credentials of being seminary trained, subsequently ordained and given a title by the ecclesiastical powers, thereby qualified for an ecclesial position.

God's intent is that every Christian should be a minister. The Greek word *diakonos* is translated as both "minister" or "servant" (and transliterated as "deacon"). Every Christian is to be a "servant of Christ Jesus" (I Tim. 3:6), engaged in the "ministry of the Spirit" (II Cor. 3:8), the "ministry of righteousness" (II Cor. 3:9), the "ministry of reconciliation" (II Cor. 5:18), and "ministry to the saints" (I Cor. 16:15). Every Christian is "anointed" by God (II Cor. 1:21,22) to be a vessel through which the living Lord Jesus can manifest His ministry in accord with the spiritual giftedness that He desires to express Himself in each person.

The Christian "ministry of all believers" is not what we do, but what **JESUS** does in and through us. We become the instruments and vehicles of **JESUS** ministering to others. Christ in us for others! Ministry is best viewed as the overflow of the activity of Jesus in the Christian. We are filled with the Spirit of Christ (Eph. 5:18) until we begin to overflow into the lives of others. "Our sufficiency for such ministry is from God" (II Cor. 3:5), and with Paul, we can say, "I will not presume to speak of anything except what Christ has accomplished through me" (Rom. 15:18). Genuine Christian ministry is simply **JESUS** operative in a faithful, receptive Christian in order to serve others.

JULY 2

THE JESUS-LIFE

The Christian gospel has often been presented as the availability of an "eternal life" commodity that will allow an individual to go to heaven when they die – a "go to heaven" pass. Such a simplistic understanding is inadequate, and must be expanded to recognize that "eternal life" is the divine life of Jesus, the life of the risen Lord Jesus, made available to all mankind as He continues to function in perpetuity as "the life-giving Spirit" (I Cor. 15:45). John explained, "God has given us eternal life, and this life is in His Son. He who has the Son has the life; he who does not have the Son of God does not have the life" (I Jn. 5:11,12).

"The Father gave to the Son to have Life in Himself" (Jn. 5:26), the very Life of the Godhead. Jesus declared, "I AM the resurrection and the Life" (Jn. 11:25); "I AM the way, the truth, and the Life" (Jn. 14:6). Jesus is not merely the dispenser of eternal life – Jesus IS eternal life. Eternal life is His life, raised from the dead in resurrection, and made available as the Spirit of Christ to dwell in the spirits of mankind. Eternal life is an ontological and personal reality, not a separated impersonal entity dispensed by Jesus. The presence of the Christ-life in our spirit is the reality of being a Christian. "If anyone does not have the Spirit of Christ, he does not belong to Him" (Rom. 8:9,16).

It has been a common practice of Christians throughout Christian history to develop descriptive monikers for the life they have experienced in Jesus. They seek to supply adjectives to describe and define the life granted to them in Jesus Christ. Using such phrases as "spiritual life," "Spirit-filled life," the "mystical life," "union life," "the exchanged life," "the victorious life," "the higher life," and "the deeper life," they are often attempting to differentiate the life they have experienced in Jesus from the run-of-the-mill religious "eternal life" package. We would be better served to simply speak of the "Jesus-life" or the "Christ-life."

THE MASTERMIND OF ALL RELIGION

Have you ever considered the conundrum of who is the mastermind of all religion? Since God is the Creator, did he create religion? He did set up and institute the Jewish religion for the Israelites, did He not? Or did He simply turn the Israelites over to Satan's religious system to demonstrate the ineffectiveness of such – that it does not work? Oh, it requires an abundance of human "works," but is unable to lead to relationship with God. It only served a preliminary purpose to reveal human religious "burnout," prior to the introduction of the only dynamic that would reconcile mankind by His Son, Jesus Christ.

The word "religion" implies bondage and slavery. The original Latin word *religare*, from *religio*, means to tie or to bind. Our English word "ligament," for example, is from the same source, and refers to a fibrous tissue that connects, ties, or binds together bones and/or cartilages in our physical body. Religion ties and binds people to a system of active belief or performance, and manifests itself as "believe-right" and/or "do-right" religion, falsely implying that human betterment is the objective to be pursued in order to please or appease God. Religion is Satan's specialty, as he binds and enslaves human beings to false expectations that render them "slaves to sin" (Rom. 6:6,17,20).

When **JESUS** came as the Savior of mankind, He most certainly did not come to establish another religion. He came to save us from every form of religion, and to set mankind free from all bondage to performance-based endeavors alleged to make God kindly disposed toward us. Jesus did not say, "I came that you might have religion, and practice it more faithfully." Instead, He said, "I came that you might have life (My life), and have it more abundantly" (Jn. 10:10). Jesus eschewed religion throughout His ministry on earth, and continues to do so as He is allowed to live out His life in us, for Satan is the mastermind of religion.

JULY 4

FREEDOM IS NOT FREE

Freedom is costly! It always "comes at a price." The freedom afforded to us in Jesus Christ came at the cost of beatings, injustice, mockery, and cost Him His life on a Roman cross. We are "bought with a price" (I Cor. 6:20; 7:23), the price of His taking the death consequences of sin on our behalf, in our place. Freedom always has a context. There is no such thing as "absolute freedom," without constraint or parameters. Even God's freedom is contextualized by the parameters of His own character. "It is impossible for God to lie" (Heb. 6:18). God's freedom is always in the context of His own character.

Our spiritual freedom as Christians is only in the context of the dying Savior who became the ever-living Lord **JESUS**, functioning as the life-giving Spirit in our spirit (I Cor. 15:45). Let us never forget the *cost* and the *context* of our Christian freedom. The *cost* of our freedom was that "He laid down His life for us" (I Jn. 3:16). The *context* of our Christian freedom is that "He has granted to us everything pertaining to life and godliness" (II Pet. 1:3). "I came that you might have life ... more abundantly" (Jn. 10:10). Christian freedom is always and only in the context of deriving from the life of the living Lord Jesus Christ.

"It was for freedom that Christ set us free" (Gal. 5:1). Yes, we are free from the death consequences of sin; free from habituated control of Satan's character of sin (Rom. 6:7,18,22); free from the legalistic bondage of the law (Acts 13:39); free from the "flesh" (Gal. 5:19). Yet, many have not become aware and experienced their freedom *from* religion, which is the flip-side of the freedom *to* live in God's abundant and continuous grace-life of **JESUS**. The tentacles of religion have reached deep into the crevices of our thought and experience, and we must see the cost and the context of our Christian freedom to enjoy life to the fullest by the Christ-life lived out through us.

NO SWEAT!

As a consequence of humanity's fall into sin, God said to Adam, "by the *sweat* of your brow you shall eat bread" (Gen. 3:19). So, the first mention of "sweat" in the Bible was in the curse of God toward sin. Human sweat is also mentioned in reference to the priests in the old covenant temple. "The Levitical priests shall put on linen garments; no wool shall be worn by them. They shall not wear anything that causes *sweat*" (Ezek. 44:17,18). Linen is often mentioned in the detailed recitation of the clothing of the priests (cf. Exod. 28). Linen is made from the flax plant, and is strong, absorbent, cool, and dries faster than cotton. Wool, on the other hand, is hot and causes sweaty perspiration.

The sweat of human perspiration seems to figuratively represent human effort and exertion. All Christians are priests (I Pet. 2:9; Rev. 1:6; 5:10; 20:6), serving God in the temple of their human bodies (I Cor. 6:19), and there should be "no sweat" of self-exertion. God does not want us to serve Him out of the energy and efforts of our "flesh" (cf. Gal. 5:16,17), but wants us to function in the power and strength of the Holy Spirit. Just as the work of redemption did not require our assistance, neither does the continuing sanctification of the Christian require our human efforts to assist His "finished work" (Jn. 19:30).

When living the Christian life, it should be "no sweat." It is not what we must do, but what He is doing. The Christ-life is not to be conducted by the human strength of our plans, agendas, energy, or performance. We are to "rest" (cf. Heb. 4:1-11) in the sufficiency of His grace-action. Understanding that faith is "our receptivity of His activity," our "rest" is not passive inactivity, but being available to the divine activity. "Not that we are adequate in ourselves to consider anything as coming from ourselves, but our adequacy is of God" (II Cor. 3:5). The indwelling presence of Jesus Christ is meant to facilitate the out-lived life of Jesus.

JULY 6

HIS VICTORY IS OUR VICTORY

If the Christian is not living in the abundance of Christ's victory, he is inevitably fighting a battle that is already lost. It is not the responsibility of the Christian to fight off sin. You will lose every time. When Christians attempt to battle evil by the strength of their own effort, life will be a prolonged experience of defeat. Only Jesus, as the Son of God, could overcome sin, and He has done so on our behalf, once and for all taking the consequences of our sin. Either we fully accept His victory, or we keep on living in the delusion that our best self-efforts will somehow, someday win the victory. You cannot; only He could; It is finished!

Many will remember the chorus of the song, "Victory in Jesus."

> Oh, victory in Jesus my Savior forever;
> He sought me and He bought me with His redeeming blood.
> He loved me 'ere I knew Him, and all my love is due Him.
> He plunged me to victory beneath the cleansing flood.

By faith we live in the victory of the Victor, Jesus Christ. Greater is He who is in you, than he who is in the world" (I Jn. 4:4).

What skirmish or battle do you want Jesus to be the Victor over in your present life? Is there a particular area of your life where the conflict is raging between the flesh and the Spirit (Gal. 5:17)? Is there a struggle with forgiveness? Is your battle with an out-of-control tongue (James 3:1-8)? Do you seem to have a continuous war over sexual propensities, either in the mind or acted out physically? Claim the victory of Christ over sin, whereby you can live with the peace of Christ (Phil. 4:7) and realize the full assurance that He is standing as the victor in your life. "Thanks be to God, who gives us the **victory** through our Lord Jesus Christ. (I Cor. 15:57), and by faith we participate in the victory by which Jesus has overcome the world (I Jn. 5:4).

ARE YOU PERFECT?

If someone were to walk up to you on the street and ask, "Are you perfect?" how would you respond to their question? Most people would not be so audacious or presumptuous as to affirm that they were perfect. They might respond, "No, I am not perfect; just ask my spouse." Someone, however, might respond, "Yes, I am proud to affirm that I am perfect, not on the basis of anything I do, but because the Perfect One, Jesus Christ, lives in me as my spiritual identity." These two persons are obviously speaking about two different things – one is referring to the external quality of their behavioral manifestations, and the other is referring to an internal derived spiritual condition.

The Greek word translated as "perfect" in our New Testament is the word *teleios*, derived from the word *telos*, meaning "end." *Teleios* describes something that has reached its end or objective; it is complete (Col. 1:28; James 1:4), finished (cf. Jn. 19:30; II Tim. 4:7), perfected (Jn. 17:23; Heb. 10:14; I Jn. 4:12), or mature (I Cor. 2:6; 14:20; Eph. 4;13; Heb. 5:14). As previously noted, we must differentiate between the spiritual condition or identity of a Christian, and the behavioral manifestations of a Christian. In terms of spiritual condition, every Christian should be able to affirm that they are objectively and spiritually perfect based on the presence of the Perfect One, Jesus, in the spirit of every Christian (Rom. 8:9; Phil. 3:15).

Behaviorally, Christians are in the process of sanctification and maturation, that we might "stand perfect and fully assured in the will of God" (Col. 4:12). We are not "perfected by the flesh" (Gal. 3:3) or by any human effort, but only by the grace of God as we allow **JESUS** within us to manifest the character of God's perfection in our behavior (cf. Phil. 1:6). No Christian is absolutely perfect in behavior manifestation – even the apostle Paul exclaimed, "not that I am already perfect" (Phil. 3:12).

JULY 8

DEFERENCE

When traveling with another person for any amount of time, I find it useful to pray and tell God that I am willing to defer to that person's every thought, whim, and desire during our travel together. Does this make me a lesser person? No, just a Christ-one who is willing to put aside personal preferences and desires, and willing to acquiesce and take "second-place" in order to get along in peace and unity with a friend during our travel. When we value our relationship and respect another person, the love of Christ within us compels us to set selfishness aside and defer to another in a choice for amicable social function, saying, "That's fine, let's do it your way!"

Another word for deference is submission, but this word has developed distasteful connotations in the minds of many in recent times, particularly in the social relationship of marriage. When relationships of any kind are viewed in the context of authority, power, rank, or value, the person having the alleged higher place or power is thought to be able to legitimately demand their rights of having first place, and the concept of submission is often cast as subservience or subjection whereby the alleged lesser valued person is demeaned and despised, used and abused, or even enslaved.

As love seeks the highest good of the other, we are advised to "let no person seek his own advantage, but each person seek the highest welfare of his neighbor" (I Cor. 10:24). "Do nothing from selfishness or empty conceit, but with humility of mind regard one another as more important than yourselves; do not merely look out for your own personal interests, but also for the interests of others" (Phil. 2:3,4). Ephesians 5:21 reads, "Be subject to one another in the fear of Christ" (NASB), but could just as well be translated, "Defer to one another in reverence to Christ," or "Honor Christ and put others first. (Eph. 5:21 – CEV).

JULY 9

WHO DO YOU THINK YOU ARE?

So often I hear people say, "I know God has forgiven me of my sins in Jesus, but I just can't seem to forgive myself." I repress my first response, which would be to question, "Who do you think you are? Do you realize how presumptuous it is to state your recognition that God forgives you, and then turn around and indicate that your attitudes and feelings predominate over what God has said is true of you?" You are in essence saying that despite what God says about you, your human opinion and feelings carry more weight, thus indicting God for a failed attempt in forgiving you.

In order to be kind and considerate, I usually attempt a softer, more gentle approach to allow such a person to see how their fickle feelings of self-indictment and self-judgment against themselves call into question the efficacy of the death of Jesus on the cross of Calvary. To allow one's feelings to predominate sets up a checkmate of God's divine declaration of forgiveness in Jesus Christ. Do you really want to cast doubt on the full import of Christ's redemptive sacrifice for the sins of all mankind?

If God has forgiven you and no longer remembers your sins (Heb. 10:17), then why do you keep throwing them back in His face? How dare you keep dredging up the recitation of your sins, wallowing in the self-pity of feeling unforgiven, and refusing to appreciate and appropriate the grace of God. To hang on to one's self-condemnation in an endless cycle of guilt and masochistic self-beatings is indicative of a troubled, yet arrogant, person who seems to think their sins are bigger than God's grace. "There is therefore no condemnation (including self-condemnation) for those who are in Christ Jesus" (Rom. 8:1). "Forgetting what lies behind, I press on towards the upward call of God in Christ Jesus" (Phil. 3:13,14). We must accept and receive by faith the veracity of the forgiveness of all sins in the life and death of **JESUS**.

JULY 10

CHRIST IN YOU

The central and core reality that one must be aware of in order to call themselves a "Christian" is the indwelling presence of the living Lord Jesus in the form of the Spirit in one's spirit. "Do you not recognize that *Jesus Christ is in you*," Paul asked the Corinthians, "unless you fail the test" (II Cor. 13:5) of what it means to be a Christian, and have believed in vain. Regardless of what forms of religious activities you have participated in (walking an aisle, repeating a confession of faith, submitting to water baptism, membership in a church, etc.), the single criteria of being a Christ-one is the presence of Jesus in you.

Jesus was advising His disciples of this magnificent reality of the new covenant divine presence when they were together in the Upper Room (Jn. 14-17). Preparing for His death on the cross, His resurrection, ascension, and Pentecostal outpouring in Spirit-form, Jesus told His disciples, "I will not leave you alone as orphans, I will come to you (14:28); ...the Spirit will be with you and *in you* (14:17). Abide in Me and *I in you* (15:4). They may be one just as We are one; *I in them* and You in me; they may be perfected in unity" (17:22,23)." The new covenant reality of the indwelling presence of the living Jesus is the dynamic provision of God's grace for all that He desires to be and do in us.

Christian faith is not merely an objective assent to the truth-tenets of a belief-system. Apart from the subjective, internal indwelling of the Spirit of Christ, one might be a "professor" but not a "possessor" of Jesus. "If anyone does not have the Spirit of Christ, he is none of His" (Rom. 8:9), i.e. that person cannot be considered to be a Christian. The apostle Paul explained that the "mystery of the gospel is *Christ in you*, the hope of glory" (Col. 1:26,27). More personally, he affirmed, "I have been crucified with Christ. It is no longer I who live, but *Christ lives in me*" (Gal. 2:20). The ultimate question is, "Does **JESUS** live in you?"

A GODLY MAN

A godly man is not characterized by what he does for God, but by what he allows God to be and do through him. In this case we are not using the noun "man" in its generic sense referring to "mankind," but in the gender sense referring to a human male who has received the presence of the living Lord Jesus into his spirit, and is desirous that Jesus should function in his attitudes and behavior in order to manifest godly character. Despite all of the cultural expectations of how the masculine gender of the human race should function, the godly man will desire to express godliness in all of the facets of his human life.

What will this look like? The Christian man who desires to be a godly man is often advised to control his aggression, avoid improper expressions of anger, and refrain from sensuality, but such admonitions are directed at what a man should allegedly DO to be godly. New covenant Christianity points the opposite direction, not fighting against the negatives through avoidance and resolution, but focusing on the positive of God's character and who He had made us to be as a "new creature" (II Cor. 5:17), a "new man" (Eph. 4:24) in Christ. The positive character traits of the "fruit of the Spirit" (Gal. 5:22,23) swallow up and overcome the negative character traits of the "deeds of the flesh" (Gal. 5:19-21), allowing a man to be a "godly man."

The godly character of God is expressed in the "fruit of the Spirit" – love, joy, peace, patience, kindness, goodness, faithfulness, gentleness and the godly control of oneself. The world tends to look at these as weakness and dependency, but the godly man recognizes such character traits as the strength of God operative in male behavior only by God's grace through Jesus Christ by His Spirit. The Christian male who desires to be a godly man will rely on God's grace received by faith in order to be "a man as God intends man to be."

JULY 12

A GODLY WOMAN

A godly woman is not characterized by what she does for God, but by what she allows God to be and do through her. So much religious teaching has done few favors to Christian women by the prominent admonitions to the myriad of activities that a woman should engage in and DO to be an admired godly woman. Christian women should listen to the loving Spirit of Christ within rather than to the male-dominated religious tirades about the necessity of submission to one's husband, the necessity of involvement in church activities and women's groups, what are acceptable clothing styles, how to parent one's children, etc.

A godly Christian woman who has received the Spirit of Christ in her spirit will not be afraid to resist and go counter to the world's (including religion's) cultural expectations of womanhood. Christian faith will always be counter-cultural and counter-religious. In conjunction with prior "holy women who hoped in God" (I Pet. 3:5), the godly woman will rest assured in the confident expectation that God will "bring to pass" (I Thess. 5:24) the completion (Phil. 1:6) of all that He desires to do in her life without succumbing to worldly standards or the imposition of religious rules, regulations and recommendations.

What distinguishes a godly woman from other women is the divine character that emanates from the Spirit of God within her, including empathy and compassion for others. The "Godly control" (Gal. 5:23) from within will be expressed through her attitudes, emotions, desires, speech, and actions. She will not allow the world to determine her external attractiveness, but will exhibit the "imperishable beauty of a gentle and quiet spirit" (I Pet. 3:4) which can only be supplied by the divine Spirit of Christ within her. As is stated in the wisdom of the proverb, "Charm is deceitful and beauty is passing, but a woman who fears the Lord, she shall be praised" (Prov. 31:30).

JULY 13

THE COVENANTS OF GOD WITH MEN

God is a covenant God, making agreements and arrangements with humanity that set the parameters of how He desires to and is willing to interact with mankind. He is not a capricious God who will willy-nilly impose His random expectations, but having created human beings with freedom of choice, He respects such in establishing interpersonal agreements with consequences, blessing and/or curses, for faithfulness or unfaithfulness.

The covenants of God with mankind are essentially divided into two – the old and the new. Christians know them as the *Old Testament* and the *New Testament*, because *testamentum* was the Latin word for "covenant." The initial promises for God's covenants were made to Abraham in Gen. 12-21, promises for descendants, a nation, a land, and divine blessing. Four hundred and fifty years later, after the Hebrew peoples had evidenced their unfaithfulness, God used Moses to deliver the Law guidelines for the nation of Israel to keep the covenant. God was faithful to keep His promises, but the Jewish people of the nation of Israel were disobedient and unfaithful.

God was not taken by surprise by Israel's failure, for His intention from the beginning was to fulfill His promises spiritually through the incarnation of the Son of God in the person of Jesus Christ. The new covenant implies the end of the old law-covenant (Rom. 10:4), but does not imply any change in the covenant God. God is unchangeable in essence, but He is capable of changing His operational guidelines. Established by the death of Jesus on the cross (Lk. 22:20) for the sins of mankind, the new covenant is the last covenant of God with mankind. There will never be another. The new covenant is an agreement whereby God provides the entire dynamic of His grace-action to implement the expression of His divine character in human behavior as Christ-ones are receptive in faith.

JULY 14

WHAT MAKES THE NEW NEW?

The scriptures refer to both an "old covenant" and a "new covenant." What makes the old old? What makes the new new? If the old is to be determined by chronological, historical time, then both the old and the new could conceivably be considered as old, for the new came into being approximately 2000 years ago. The old is old, not because of age, but because it was ineffectual and no longer worked (never did!). It was phased out, identified as obsolete (Heb. 8:13), rendered "null and void," and henceforth only of historical value. To prevent misunderstanding, the old here refers to what our Bibles identify as the "Old Testament."

Now, we must proceed to consider what makes the new covenant (New Testament) new. The new is new not based on chronological, historical time, or because it sequentially follows the old, but because the new covenant qualitatively includes that which was not made manifest prior to its introduction. The new is not new in the sense of a re-formed version of the old; it is not a revision or remodel of the old. The new is not the old in new packaging, for Jesus said, "you can't put new wine in old wineskins (Lk. 37:38). Ezekiel prophesied of a new covenant wherein God would put His Spirit within us (Ezek. 36:26).

The newness of the new covenant can only be identified as the living Person of **JESUS**. At the final Passover, Jesus declared, "this is the new covenant in My blood" (Lk. 22:20). The new was made available by His death and resurrection, and on Pentecost the "newness of His Spirit" (Rom. 7:6) was poured out to dwell in the spirit of human beings (Rom. 8:9,16). The new covenant (II Cor. 3:6; Heb. 8:8; 9:15; 12:24) arrangement allowed humans to become spiritual "new creatures" (II Cor. 5:17); "new men" (Eph. 4:24; Col. 3:10) having "new life" (Rom. 6:4), participating in a "new and living way" (Heb. 10:20). This is an eternal new, never to be antiquated, but forever new by the dynamic of **JESUS'** life.

JULY 15

THE BIBLE

The documents that form the compilation of the Christian scriptures were not entitled "The Bible" until c. A.D. 386 when Chrysostom compiled the then accepted books of the Hebrew scriptures and put them together with the accepted books of the more recent Christian scriptures. The resulting compilation was entitled *ta biblia,* "the books." Each of the Hebrew books was renamed with Greek names: *Genesis* meaning "to come into being;" *Exodos* (*ek*=out; *hodos*=the way) meaning "the way out," etc. The question is: Why were the scriptures of Judaic religion and the scriptures of The Way put together in one compilation?

It's understandable that Judaism was the historical womb wherein Jesus came into the world and provides historical background, however, the message of the Hebrew scriptures and the message of the Christian scriptures are as contrasted as night and day, black and white. Originally identified in Greek as the *palaia diatheke* (old covenant) and *kaine diatheke* (new covenant), the Greek was translated in Latin as *testamentum* (with more of a legal connotation). But why were the Hebrew scriptures and the Christian scriptures bound together, henceforth giving the impression that they are of equal value?

The old covenant of God was limited and temporal. It was limited in jurisdiction to the nation of Israel with whom the agreement was made through their representative, Moses. It was temporal in expected duration, and therefore not a permanent or eternal arrangement. God knew full well what He was intending to do in the Son, Jesus Christ. The new covenant, as foretold in promise to Abraham, was universal "for all nations" (Gen. 17:4,5) and was established as the permanent never-ending arrangement, intended to be the eternal covenant implemented and invested with the eternal life of the last Adam, **JESUS** Christ. Christians must focus on **JESUS** as He is revealed in the New Testament.

JULY 16

DIVIDING OF SOUL AND SPIRIT

Despite the predominate opinion among modern theological interpreters that spirit and soul are referencing the same reality, the epistle to the Hebrews explains that "the word of God is living and active and sharper than any two-edged sword, and piercing as far as the dividing of soul (*psuche*) and spirit (*pneuma*), of both joints and marrow, and able to judge the thoughts and intentions of the heart" (Heb. 4:12). This verse certainly seems to indicate that there is an identifiable and distinguishable difference between psychological and spiritual function, between the thoughts in our soul and the spiritual intentions of our heart.

The spiritual intent of every Christ-indwelt man or woman is to be a godly man or godly woman by allowing the Christ-Spirit within to manifest the life of Jesus in our mortal bodies (cf. II Cor. 4:10,11). This intent is countered again and again, though, as "the flesh sets its desires against the Spirit, and the Spirit against the flesh" (Gal. 5:17). The fleshly thoughts patterned in the established attitudes of our minds, as well as the thoughts introduced by the tempter in temptation are often in direct contradiction to what the Triune Spirit of God in our human spirits desires to accomplish in expressing the Christ-life in our behavior. As Paul states, "the good that I would I do not, and the evil that I would not that I do" (Rom. 7:19).

Hebrews 4:12 indicates that "the word of God," referring, I think, to the living Lord Jesus, the Word of God (Jn. 1:1,14), is able to pierce with His spiritual sword-like scalpel in the precise separating of the psychological and spiritual functions within a human individual. He can thereby facilitate the "renewing of our minds" (Rom. 12:2), so our attitudes might conform with God's attitudes to serve as the point of implementation of the Spirit-directed Christ-life in our behavior. Such dividing of spirit and soul exposes the real source of our human activity.

JULY 17

THE NAME OF JESUS

Many studies have been made on the names of God and the names of Jesus, seeking to examine the meanings of the various names and designations. Some people get so caught up in name descriptions that they miss the reality of the One whose names they are considering, engaging in bizarre games of "trivial pursuit." Throughout Christian history, the name of the Person of Jesus Christ has often been scrutinized and analyzed. Some have even used the name of Jesus as a mystical mantra, claiming that by repetitive verbal recitation of the name anyone can leverage God to produce supernatural phenomena.

The angel of the Lord advised Joseph, "You shall call His name 'Jesus,' because He will save His people from their sins" (Matt. 1:21,25). The given name, Jesus, means "Yahweh saves," with a possible implied reference to the deity of Jesus, that He was God in the flesh (Jn. 1:14). Jesus (*Yeshua* in Hebrew; *Iesous* in Greek) was indeed the Son of God come in a human being (Phil. 2:5-8) to be the deliverer, the Messiah (*Masiah* in Hebrew; *Christos* in Greek). "Christ" is a transliteration of the Greek word *Christos*, meaning "the anointed one," the One promised (cf. Zeph. 3:9) to be the Anointed King-Priest and Savior of Israel.

Some have objected that Christians use "Christ" as part of Jesus' proper name, arguing that "Christ" is merely a title of function. They fail to understand that the function of Jesus is so integrally united with His Being, that reference to "Jesus Christ" is a proper designation of His inseparable Person and ministry. There are at least 139 references in the New Testament scriptures referring to the person of "Jesus Christ," and the majority of such use the extended form of "the Lord Jesus Christ," evidencing more directly His divine nature and function. "What's in a name?" asked Juliet in Shakespeare's play. Paul explained, "At the name of Jesus every knee shall bow" (Phil. 2:10).

JULY 18

LEVERAGING THE BEHAVIOR OF OTHERS

Many people, professions, and institutions are attempting to leverage other people's behavior. What do we mean by the term "leverage"? Although the term is used in the world of high finance, we are employing it as used in the realm of simple physics, as the exertion of force by the use of a lever or bar to cause something to move. Many "do it yourselfers" have used crow bars, wrecking bars, and/or pry bars to apply pressure to cause something to break loose or move. It is an effective way to move large boulders that are simply too large to roll or lift. But when the concept is used in reference to psychological pressure on people to manipulate their behavior, it is outside of the parameters of Christian interaction because Christian behavior is to be energized and directed only by the Holy Spirit (Rom. 8:14).

Christian religious practitioners have often used the leverage of "the Bible says" in attempting to execute change or conformity in the lives of their participants. The claim of "pastoral authority" has also been employed to forcefully leverage people to fall into line with ecclesial expectations. The heavy-duty leverage of threatened removal from fellowship and excommunication have also been used as instruments of coercive persuasion to force Christians to behave as desired.

Some have even attempted to use the "golden rule" to leverage the behavior of another. "Do unto others, as you would have them do unto you" (cf. Lk. 6:31). What is intended to be an incentive to positive behavior taking into consideration how we desire to be treated, has been misused in a manipulative manner to indirectly force another (often one's spouse) to behave in the way one desires. "If I quit drinking, cursing, or misspending money, maybe it will shame my spouse into doing the same." Such subtle manipulations of reciprocal expectations are improper means of changing the behavior of another.

ALL YOU NEED IS LOVE

It might be termed "Beatles Theology," given the fact that John Lennon wrote the lyrics to the song, "All You Need is Love," that was popularized by the group after its release in 1967. The song was a countercultural socio-political statement, expressing an idealistic philosophical stance. Lennon explained in an interview, "Love is allowing somebody to be themselves, and that's what we need." Such an explanation of "love" is devoid of any foundational meaning, for it only expresses the humanistic idealism that inevitably slides into the social anarchy of "they all did what was right in their own eyes" (Judg. 17:6; 21:25).

The youth culture in every generation is naturally idealistic, and easily drawn into the utopian idea that "all we need is love" in order to solve all the world's problems and make the world right. Reacting to the narcissism and chaotic violence in the world around them, young people tend to view natural human kindness and cooperation as the "be all, end all" of an idealistic solution to the world's problems, and are thus led down the primrose path of humanistic social liberalism.

Definitions and descriptions of love are innumerable. Everyone has his own opinion. However, God has revealed that genuine love is derived from Him. "God is love" (I Jn. 4:8,16), and mankind loves properly only when "His love has been poured out in our hearts by the Holy Spirit" (Rom. 5:5), and expressed as the "fruit of the Spirit" (Gal. 5:22,23). Such love is the summation of Christian thought and practice. "Owe nothing to anyone except to love one another; for he who loves his neighbor has fulfilled the law. All the commands can be summed up in this saying, 'You shall love your neighbor as yourself.'" (Rom. 13:8,9). God's character of love is the starting point and end-point of Christian thought. "All we need is love," is valid, so long as God's love is the foundational source-point of understanding love.

JULY 20

ALL FIGURED OUT

It seems to be the objective of some Christians to get all the things of God figured out, all of the tenets of the Bible properly interpreted, and all the doctrines of the church carefully crafted in air-tight compartments. With finite minds they attempt to comprehend the infinite realities of God's Being and ways. Then, thinking they have it all figured out with epistemological certainty, they take an adamant stand upon their self-constructed conception of the "fundamentals of the faith" with a "know-it-all" attitude of superiority that rejects any divergence of thought. With arrogant pride, they argue that their exclusively accurate conclusions must be accepted by all.

That individuals or groups think they have the Christian faith "all figured out," in particular atonement theories, eschatological theories, or hermeneutic principles is their right. But it becomes a social issue when such people attempt to foist their belief-system as the singular and exclusive acceptable thought-pattern for everyone else. In a free society, every person has a right to think what they want, but they do not have a right to chastise, harass or demonize those who think differently. Such people are obliged to keep their elitist opinions to themselves in their exclusive enclaves or ghettos of fundamentalist thought.

No person or group has figured out all of "the deep things of God" (I Cor. 2:10). We must all come before God as humble learners of the divine mystery, as disciples of Christ. Those who think they have it all figured out are indicted by Paul's words, "knowledge puffs up with arrogance, but love builds up an interactive community in unity" (I Cor. 8:1) centered on **JESUS** Christ. The manifestation of the character of Christ is far more important than the amount or accuracy of any biblical or theological information. The Body of Christ is to be a loving relational community, rather than an accurate information dispensary.

CHRISTIAN COUNSELING

There is no doubt that Christians face personal problems in like manner as do others in the general population of mankind. Many Christians, however, do not want counsel for their problems that is based on the premises of secular humanism, denying divine and spiritual solutions and leaving God out of the equation. What is called "Christian counseling" began in the 1960s, and soon branched out into numerous approaches. Jay E. Adams, for example, introduced "Biblical counseling," using what he called the nouthetic counseling method in 1970 in the publication of his book, *Competent to Counsel*. His premise was that Christian problems result from disobedience to scriptural principles, and require Christians be admonished to increased obedience to what the Bible says in their behavioral performance.

But, if the counselor advocates human performance as the solution to one's problems, it remains a humanistic solution to one's problems. Much of what is called "Christian counseling" today is merely secular humanistic counseling premises and techniques, with a veneer of Christian vocabulary and scattered use of Biblical verses to advocate behavioral performance.

Some English translations explain that the Holy Spirit of the living Christ (cf. I Cor. 15:45) is identified as the divine Counselor (cf. Jn. 14:16,26; 15:26; 16:7 – RSV). From that basis, spiritual Christian counseling must recognize the work of the Holy Spirit, while understanding the anthropological composition of humans functioning spiritually, psychologically, and physiologically in spirit, soul, and body (I Thess. 5:23; Heb. 4:12). The grace of God in **JESUS** Christ is the dynamic that energizes the Christ-life in Christian behavior, and there are times when Christians require spiritual counsel that encourages them to remember Christ is their sufficiency, and to exercise faith in God's leading (Rom. 8:14) and empowering (Phil. 2:13).

JULY 22

WHAT IS GOD TRYING TO TEACH ME?

It is common among some Christians to ask and seek answers to the recurring question, "What is God trying to teach me in the particular circumstances that I am presently experiencing in my life?" There is no doubt that Jesus was addressed as "the good teacher" (Matt. 19:16; Mk. 10:17; Lk. 18:18), and inherent in the designation of a "disciple" is the idea of a learner (Matt. 10:24,25; 22:16), but the question might still be asked, "Is the relationship between God and man, between Christ and the Christian, meant primarily to be a pedagogical dissemination from instructor to pupil, or something more personal?

If we cast God in Christ as the pedagogical teacher in every situation, then some will soon surmise that His teaching methods are sometimes sadistic, less than compassionate, even cruel, and not conducive to good learning. If we perceive of ourselves as primarily pupils, students or scholars, then we are cast into the role of attempting to figure out the ways of God, which are past finding out (Rom. 11:33), cramming information into our craniums in order to pass the inevitable examinations, and engaging in the quest for competitive excellence to determine who will be awarded the highest score (*magna cum laude*).

Perhaps it would be more accurate for Christians to view themselves in a more intimate personal relationship with God, as "friends of God" (James 2:23), or as those who are "beloved of God" (Rom. 1:17; Col. 3:23; I Thess. 1:4). Being a Christ-one is not so much enrollment in a school of learning or an educational institution, as it is a marriage relationship (Eph. 5:32) of spiritual union (I Cor. 6:17) and intimate interaction in a love relationship. God's primary concern is not that we learn lessons from the circumstances of life, but rather that we remain relationally receptive to His desire to manifest His loving character by His grace in every circumstance of our lives.

JULY 23

PRIDE

One may make many missteps and blunders in life, and people will be likely to overlook and forgive such, but the haughty attitude of pride will always be met with public disdain. The historical philosopher, Voltaire, noted, "We are seldom proud when we are alone," thus indicating that pride is primarily an attitude of social comparison, comparing oneself with others with an attitude of superiority. The Latin word for "pride" is *superbia*, an inflated perspective of self-importance wherein one feels superb and superior to others. The Greek word for "pride" is *hyperephainos* (*huper* = above; *phaino* = to shine), referring to the mindset of "shining over and above others." "Power is what pride really enjoys: there is nothing makes a man feel so superior to others as being able to move others around like toy soldiers," wrote C.S. Lewis.

C.S. Lewis had much to say about human pride, indicating that "pride leads to every other vice" – "Pride is the mother hen under which all other sins are hatched." "It was through pride that the devil became the devil," Lewis noted, pointing to the first and original sin when Lucifer proudly exclaimed, "I shall be like the Most High God" (Isa. 14:12-14). Because pride is an inflated opinion of oneself and one's alleged self-sufficient abilities, such focus on oneself does not allow one to be receptive to God. "Pride is a spiritual cancer: it eats up the very possibility of love, or contentment, or even common sense," Lewis wrote.

In his talks on *Mere Christianity*, Lewis explained, "As long as you are proud you cannot know God. A proud man is always looking down on things and people: and, of course, as long as you are looking down you cannot see something that is above you." "Pride is an anti-God state of mind," for it is essentially the idolatry of self-deification. "God is opposed to the proud" (James 4:6; I Pet. 5:5), but gives grace to the humble.

JULY 24

HUMILITY

If it be true, as some have said, that "humility is a virtue," let it also be said that "humility cannot be achieved," lest the pride of performance preclude the possibility of humility. Humility is an attitudinal perspective that is unknown and unsought by the one having such. To the extent that one is aware of being humble, that person is likely not humble. Awareness of one's own humility evidences one's pride. If anyone thinks himself to be humble, he is likely a very proud person. The first step in being humble is to recognize one's propensity to be proud. Humility will always recognize and recoil from pride within.

The Latin word *humilitas* and the adjective *humilis*, may be translated as "humble," but also as "grounded" or "from the earth", since it derives from *humus* (earth). One who is humble will be grounded in their own insignificance. The Greek word translated "humble" is *tapeinoteta* meaning "lowly," having a modest view of one's own self-importance. The one who is humble is said to be a fit recipient of grace, "God opposes the proud but gives grace to the humble" (James 4:6; I Pet. 5:5). Those who function in their own proud self-sufficiency will seldom appreciate the grace-provision that empowers humility.

Some philosophers have described humility as the attitude of being "unselved," i.e. no longer preoccupied with one's self. This does not imply any sense of "dying to self" or self-deprecation. C.S. Lewis is quoted as saying, "Humility is not thinking less of yourself; it is thinking of yourself less." Humility is a proper perspective of oneself in reference to God and others. When we properly understand the singular holiness of God's (cf. Isa. 6:3-5) character, we are then prepared to see our rightful place in conjunction with Him. The self-focus of our self-orientation and selfish preoccupation will be overcome by God's love that seeks the highest good of others.

THE GREATEST TEMPTATION FOR CHRISTIANS

No, the greatest temptation for Christians is not chocolate, wine, or sexual liaisons. Other suggestions for the greatest temptation have included, success by the world's standards, to find security in a religious rut, to think we can have abundant life without suffering and death, and the acquisition of money with the power it brings. In 1675, Pastor John Rowe published a book entitled, *The Saints' Temptations*, declaring that the greatest temptation of Christians was to be without any temptation, finding security in the fact that they are doing quite well in life, and satisfied with their personal religious performance and goodness.

If we accept this premise that the greatest temptation of Christians is to live without any temptations, desiring that the Christian life should proceed on an even keel through calm waters with no major problems or trials – triumphal grace without any adversity – we sell ourselves short of full identification with Jesus. Jesus did not live in a vacuum-bubble of peace and calm without problems. Neither do Christians live in the unreality of an idyllic existence without trials, troubles and temptations. These are not obstacles, but opportunities to exercise our God-given freedom to receive God's sufficiency.

Jesus taught the disciples to pray, "lead us not into temptation" (Lk. 11:4), which, of course, God never does because He does not tempt anyone (James 1:13). It is the diabolic tempter who tempts us (I Thess. 3:5). Later, Jesus taught His disciples, "Pray that you might not enter into temptation" (Lk. 22:40,46); not that they should try to avoid being tempted, but that they might not succumb to the solicitations of Satan. Paul wrote, "No temptation has overtaken you that is not common to man. God is faithful, and he will not let you be tempted beyond your ability, but with the temptation he will also provide the way of escape, that you may endure it" (I Cor. 10:13,14).

JULY 26

RELIGIOUS MUDSLINGERS

In the American Western movies of the twentieth century, there were often characters referred to "gunslingers." These were usually persons with a reputation for having a "quick draw" tendency to engage in "shoot-em-up" gunfights and duels. A "mudslinger," on the other hand, is a person who tries to damage another person's reputation with verbal accusations or insults. Two primary venues where mudslingers are most active are politics and religion. They disparage or discredit another person's thoughts or actions, casting aspersions and insults at others, sometimes in very malicious attacks on character.

In the arena of religion, there are mudslingers who have a hair-trigger response for hurling invectives of "heresy" toward other persons who do not think or act as they do. Whenever they find someone who does not stack their belief-blocks in the same way they think they should be stacked, they verbally attack by charging them with being "heretics," usually meaning that one's teaching is aberrant and unacceptable to their particular version of orthodoxy. "Heresy" is a transliteration from the Greek *hairesis*, which means "to choose" from differing alternatives. Christianity as a whole was identified as an heretical sect distinct from the religion of Judaism (cf. Acts 24:5,14).

Throughout the scriptures, those propagating false teaching are identified by their attitudes and actions, more than by their beliefs. The practicum of their behavioral character expression is more telling than their belief-system. It's what they do, more than what they say. One of the "deeds of the flesh" mentioned by Paul (Gal. 5:20) was factions (*hairesis*). Mudslinging heresy-hunters fail to recognize that they themselves are engaging in heresy by their fleshly and disruptive disputes whereby they choose to stand against other Christians who may think differently than they do, and thus they create disunity.

JULY 27

DEALING WITH OUR PAST

Many Christians are filled with regrets about their past actions and indiscretions. Yes, we have "all sinned and come short of the glory of God" (Rom. 3:23). But to keep looking back at our perceived failures, and to consider ourselves as "failures" based on our behavior in the past, is simply evidence that a person has placed too much faith in themselves and their performance. God didn't expect anything more out of you! He knew full well that you were a "sinner" (Rom. 5:19) due to Adam's fall, and that you would necessarily engage in sinful behavior as the character of the Evil One was expressed in you (cf. Eph. 2:2).

Why, then, do so many keep digging around in the garbage pail of yesterday's trash? They are behavioral "dumpster divers!" When we wallow in the muck of the past, we become slaves to yesterday and its mistakes, hostages to remembrances and regrets, and unable to enjoy the freedom that Christ has bought for us. Our identity is not formed by our performances, either past or present; what we do or have done. Christians must recognize that the only performance that matters is what Jesus has accomplished on our behalf, and view themselves as the "new creature" (II Cor. 5:17) they have become "in Christ."

The God of Love (I Jn. 4:8,16) knows every transgression we have made (Heb. 4:13), and loves us anyway (Rom. 8:38,39). Out of such love, God forgives; He remembers our sins no more (Heb. 8:12; 10:17). It is an affront to God that we should keep remembering what He no longer remembers and has put aside. Paul was not proud of his past (Phil. 3:7,8), but he went on to write, "forgetting what lies behind and reaching forward to what lies ahead, I press on toward the goal for the prize of the upward call of God in Christ Jesus" (Phil. 3:13,14). It is an obvious truism: You can't live life moving forward if you're always looking backward, indicting yourself in self-condemnation.

JULY 28

I CORINTHIANS 13 – FOR PARENTS

If I speak the truisms of generations of parents, but do not have love for my children, I am but a nag or a screamer.

If I know all the mysteries of parenting, and have all the wisdom of Dr. Spock and Dr. Dobson combined, but do not love my children, I am a parental failure.

If I give myself sacrificially, giving all my time and all my money, and become a parental martyr, but do not have love for my children through it all, it all adds up to a total loss.

Loving my children involves being patient to let God work in their lives, being sensitive to their feelings, and aware of their hurts and concerns.

Loving my children means not comparing them to me or any other, not being envious of their successes, not trying to protect my reputation by governing their activities.

Love for my children is not irritable, agitated or moody.
It does not hold grudges and refuse to forgive.
It does not expect them to be perfect, or rejoice in punishment, but rejoices when they learn to walk with God.

The love of a parent is not condescending, does not demand conformity to projected expectations, is willing to admit personal failure, and is unconditional no matter what they do.

All the parenting theories will pass away.
All the lectures will blow in the wind.
All the tears and concerns will be overcome.

What remains is my faith in God, and my hope for my children, but the greatest asset of parenting is the LOVE which only **JESUS** can produce in my heart for my children.

JULY 29

THE ETERNAL

Three hombres walked into a bar. They were known around town as Past, Present and Future. The air was thick. You could cut it with a knife. It was tense! ... When the moment was complete, Past had expired; Present was hugging the Eternal; and Future was indistinguishable from Present. Don't try to figure it out; Eternal has no tense. It is a double entendré riddle.

The common and popular understanding of eternity is that "it has no beginning, and no end." Such a linear and time-bound concept of the Eternal is quite inadequate to explain the eternality of God and the eternal life that He made available to the human race in His Son, Jesus Christ. In His prayer in the Upper Room, Jesus said, "This is eternal life, that they may know You, the only true God, and Jesus Christ whom You have sent" (John 17:3). Eternal life is knowing and participating in the eternality of God's Being that is made available in the Son who is "one with the Father" (Jn. 10:30). "If you had known Me, you would have known the Father" (Jn. 14:7), Jesus told His disciples. Eternal life is a Person – the divine-human Person of the God-man, Jesus Christ. Jesus declared, "I AM the way, the truth, and the life" (Jn. 14:6), "I AM the resurrection and the life" (Jn. 11:25).

In participating in the Eternal of the presence of the living Lord Jesus, Christians have the unique opportunity of enjoying the Future-Present. The promised fulfillment of God's redemptive reconciliation and restoration of mankind is both realized and expected; already and not yet. The divine eternal life is forever actualized and realized in the NOW! The projected Future of the Eternal has been brought into the realized Present experience of the Eternal as the Resurrection-life of Jesus enlivens our spirits with His eternal life. The Eternal is personified in **JESUS**, and Christians participate in the Eternal NOW, the Future-Present, beyond time and its tenses.

JULY 30

THE GOSPEL OF THE KINGDOM

Persons living in modern democratic countries often have difficulty understanding the premises and dynamics of a kingdom. The scripture records that Jesus was proclaiming the "gospel of the kingdom" (Matt. 4:23; 9:35; 24:14). Luke, the historian, wrote, "The Law and the Prophets were preached until John; since that time the gospel of the kingdom of God has been preached" (Lk. 16:16). After John the Forerunner had announced Jesus as the Messiah, the "gospel of the kingdom" was declared to be "at hand" (Matt. 3:2; 4:17) and "in our midst" (Lk. 17:21), for the divine King had arrived to reign among men.

The "gospel of the kingdom" is once again becoming a popular theme in Christian thought, but with many misemphases. The kingdom of God does not correspond with any institutional church organization, but it does correlate to some extent with the genuine reality of the *ecclesia*. The Southern Baptist Convention once thought that the kingdom was encompassed in their organization. The Jehovah Witness organization still advocates such, and identifying their meeting places as "Kingdom Halls." Neither does the kingdom Jesus came to bring in Himself primarily refer to a future heavenly kingdom beyond this world.

The "gospel" (Greek *euangelion*) is the "good news" of **JESUS**, who as King is the kingdom in Himself (*autobasileia*). The "Gospel of the Kingdom" is the good news about the reign of **JESUS** in the lives of Christ-ones who collectively comprise the *ecclesia*, the congregation of those who are allowing **JESUS** to reign. Good news, because the world we live in is orchestrated by "the ruler of this world" (Jn. 12:31; 16:11)), whose evil character of "sin reigns in death" (Rom. 5:21). It's a dire situation indeed, remedied only by the reign of **JESUS** as Lord and King (Rev. 17:14), reigning in us and allowing us to collectively reign with Him in righteousness (Rom. 5:17) and life (Rom. 5:21).

JULY 31

DOGS AND CATS IN HEAVEN?

I was sitting out on the patio with a friend, and in the midst of our discussion he inquired, "Do you think there will be dogs and cats in heaven?" Without realizing what I was saying, I responded, "Well, I would not want to be dogmatic or categorical about the subject," and proceeded on, but my friend broke out laughing. It took me a minute to realize what I had done. I had inadvertently answered the question about "dogs and cats in heaven" with the words "dogmatic" and "categorical." I wish I had been sharp enough to have done that consciously and jestfully, but I simply stumbled into the semantic double entendré.

But, what about dogs and cats in heaven? Many Christian people have developed very close relationships with their pets, benefitting greatly from their company and companionship. If "heaven is the presence of everything desirable, and the absence of everything undesirable," as popularly stated, then why would our beloved pets not be part of our heavenly experience? Yet, we must be beware of anthropomorphically projecting our human thoughts, feelings, and capabilities upon the animal kingdom, or crossing the line into sentimentality. If heaven is a spiritual environment, do animals have spiritual capability?

The inspired scriptures do not seem to give us a definitive answer to the question we have posed. Psalm 104 has an extended passage about God's created animals, and states, "You (God) take away their spirit, they expire, and return to dust" (Ps. 104:29; Eccl. 3:21). On the other hand, in God's promised realm we find mention of "wolves, lambs, leopards, goats, lions, calves and oxen" (Isa. 11:6; 65:25). The *Apocalypse* refers to horses in heaven (Rev. 19:11,14). The Psalmist indicates that "God gives us the desires of our hearts" (Ps. 37:4). We still cannot be "dogmatic" or "categorical" about the subject, and must leave the extended outcome of our pets in the hands of our gracious God.

AUGUST 1

ADAM AND CHRIST

The inspired narrative of the scriptures portrays Adam and Christ as the only two representative men among mankind, with whom all human beings are connected in spiritual identification with one or the other. All of mankind are in one family or the other, either "in Adam" (I Cor. 15:22) or "in Christ" (Rom. 3:24; 6:11; 8:1,2; II Cor. 5:17). These two, Adam and Jesus, establish the spiritual connection and union of every human person with either Satan or God respectively, the two spirit-sources of the universe. They are in direct contrast: "As in Adam all die, so also in Christ all will be made alive" (I Cor. 15:22).

When writing to the Christians in Rome, the apostle Paul made an extended contrast between Adam and Christ in Romans 5:12-21. He explains how Adam's act of disobedience (Gen. 3; Rom. 5:15,17,18,19) at the "tree of the knowledge of good and evil" (Gen. 2:9,17) brought sin (Rom. 5:12,17) and spiritual death to the human race (Rom. 5:12), whereas Christ's act of obedience (Rom. 5:18,19) at the cross-shaped "tree" (Gal. 3:13) made available life (Rom. 5:17,21) and righteousness (Rom. 5:16-21) to receptive mankind. The "last Adam" (Jesus) henceforth "became the life-giving Spirit (I Cor. 15:45), restoring and reinvesting humanity with "the Spirit of Christ," the essential necessity for being a Christ-one, a Christian (Rom. 8:9).

Adam or Christ – which spiritual family do you trace your lineage back to? Those "in Adam" trace their spiritual origin back to the "tree of the knowledge of good and evil" and the sin-character of the Evil One. Those "in Christ" trace their spiritual origin to the "tree of life" that became the cross-shaped tree (cf. Gal. 3:13) on which the Son of God died to give us His life (I Jn. 5:20), His nature (II Pet. 1:4), and His character (Gal. 5:22,23). Unlike physical families, we can choose our spiritual descendant and family, with the everlasting consequences thereof.

AUGUST 2

PERSONAL REVELATION

God can only be known as He reveals Himself. No human being, by unaided human reason, will ever figure out God, or come to know God in a personal relational way. God has revealed Himself in an historical incarnational manner by sending the Son as the God-man, who in turn took the consequences of human sin by death on a cruel cross, and rose from the dead to ascend to the Father and be poured out as the Spirit on Pentecost. Those receiving the Spirit of Christ into their human spirit (Rom. 8:9) by the receptivity of faith, enter into personal relationship with the Triune God and enjoy the spiritual intimacy of continued personal revelation as God speaks to their hearts.

As God reveals Himself, His loving heart and holy character, to His children, those who know Him in personal relationship will cry out, as did the seraphim observed by Isaiah, "Holy, Holy, Holy is the Lord of Hosts" (Isa. 6:3). Likewise, the four living creatures observed by John in the Apocalypse were exclaiming, "Holy, Holy, Holy is the Lord God, the Almighty" (Rev. 4:8). The personal revelation of God's holiness, that sets Him apart from all others than Himself is awe-inspiring to every faithful heart having a loving relationship of spiritual union with the divine Father, Son, and Holy Spirit. We rightfully fall down in worship before Him.

Conversely and simultaneously, God's personal revelation of Himself brings a revelation of ourselves in contrast to God's holiness. The worthiness of God's character (cf. Rev. 4:11) reveals the unworthiness of our human sinfulness. Immediately after hearing the seraphim declare God to be "Holy, Holy, Holy," the prophet Isaiah declared, "Woe is me. I am ruined. I am a man of unclean lips" (Isa. 6:5), particularly in comparison to the absolute love and perfect purity of God's character. The apostle Paul's self-analysis in the light of God's grace was to identify himself as "the chief of sinners" (I Tim. 1:15).

AUGUST 3

THE AGONY AND THE ECSTASY

American author, Irving Stone, wrote a biographical novel about Michelangelo Buonarotti entitled *The Agony and the Ecstasy* (1961). Michelangelo was an Italian sculptor (creator of "The David" sculpture in Florence), a painter (who painted the ceiling of the Sistine Chapel in the Vatican), and the architect of the dome of St. Peter's Basilica in Rome. His life was full of conflicts with papal expectations and several love-interests. A film of his life, loosely based on the novel, and also entitled *The Agony and the Ecstasy,* was produced in 1965 starring Charlton Heston as Michelangelo and Rex Harrison as Pope Julius II.

The contrasts and struggles of low-points and high-points, of agony and ecstasy, evident in the life of Michelangelo, also occur in differing ways in the lives of Christians in every age. The Christian life is seldom "smooth sailing on the seas of life," but is often characterized by the ups and downs of tumultuous trials and tribulations in the midst of periodic serenity. There are times of triumph when we are receptive to God's grace, experiencing glimpses of glory as the Spirit lifts us up to fly on eagle's wings (Isa. 40:30), but also times of frustrating uncertainty, as well as defeat in succumbing to temptations.

Some Christian teachers have been less than realistic in advising Christian persons what to expect in their Christian lives. Some emphasize a defeatism that focuses on inevitable human sinfulness, and a down-cast, long-faced confessionalism of one's failures. "The good that I would I do not, and the evil that I would not that I do" (Rom. 7:19). "I am the chief of sinners" (I Tim. 1:15). Others emphasize a triumphalism focusing on all we have and are in Christ, promoting an ever-jubilant up-beat attitude touting that "His grace is sufficient" (II Cor. 12:9), "I can do all things through Christ who strengthens me" (Phil. 4:13), without recognizing problems. There will be both – agony and ecstasy.

AUGUST 4

THE SCOURGE OF HUMANITY

A scourge is something that causes great torment, affliction, burden and suffering to those who are oppressed by it. Since the Garden of Eden when the first couple opted to defy God by choosing the forbidden fruit, to reject derivation of character and action from God, and to allegedly become their own center of reference, the human "*ego*" has set itself up to be its own god, falsely believing it can engage in autogeneration of its own character and achievements. This attitude and perspective of egoism, selfism, or narcissism has become the central tenet of the philosophy of humanism that predominates in human thought.

The first-person personal pronoun in the Greek language is *ego*, translated as "I" in English. Sigmund Freud developed a theory of human behavior identifying the "ego" as the self-determinative part of every individual that volitionally chooses to suppress the "id," the instinctual pleasure-based depravity inherent in each person, while holding at bay the "superego" of superimposed moral values and religious admonitions that engender guilt. His theory was totally humanistic, positing that the human *ego* could function as its own ultimate arbiter of right or wrong, and energize an individual's self-determined behavior.

The fallacy of the humanistic scourge of human thinking is the failure to recognize, both in religious and secular thought, that human beings were created as spiritually derivative beings, who are to derive all character and motivational mobilization from a spirit-source, either God or Satan. Sinful and selfish character are derived from the Evil One, Satan; whereas righteousness, godliness, and loving concern for others are derived from the character of God in Christ. Derivativeness is not tyranny, as humanism has maintained since the Garden, but the privilege of humanity functioning as God intends. "It is no longer I (*ego*) that lives, but Christ lives in me" (Gal. 2:20).

AUGUST 5

OUR SUFFICIENCY

The world is filled with false humanistic encouragement advocating that every person has the sufficiency within themselves to be and do anything they want to be and do. Nike advertisements encourage everyone to "Just do it! Be all you can be!" Many people, however, have not been taken-in by such encouragement of self-sufficiency, and many personalities struggle with self-confidence about doing various tasks in life. These persons are often encouraged to muster up enough pseudo self-confidence to cover up their self-doubts, and play-act "as-if" they are confident enough to tackle any situation before them.

The social interactions of the world are full of such hypocrisy – putting on an "air" of confident sufficiency – while inwardly feeling miserably inept. How does a Christian go about finding a source of sufficiency and adequacy for everything they are called upon to do? Our confidence is not to be in our own abilities, but is to be based on and derived from the inexhaustible adequate provision of God's all-empowering grace in Jesus Christ. Writing to the Corinthians, Paul explained, "Not that we are sufficient in ourselves to consider anything as coming from ourselves, but our sufficiency is from God" (II Cor. 3:5).

Jesus told His disciples, "Apart from Me, you can do nothing" (Jn. 15:5). As the branch derives its life, energy and growth from the vine, so we are to derive our sufficiency for every action of our Christian lives from Jesus. It is from that assurance of sufficiency that Paul explains to the Philippian Christians, "I can do all things through Christ who strengthens me" (Phil. 4:13). It was not from self-confident or self-assurance that Paul was engaged in ministry. He explained, "God makes all grace abound, so that you have all sufficiency in everything for every good deed" (II Cor. 9:8). In the midst of Paul's weakness, God had spoken, saying, "My Grace is sufficient for you" (II Cor. 12:9).

AUGUST 6

IS LIFE A TEST?

At particular times of the year, students prepare for educational testing that measures their knowledge and skills in various disciplines. It is a time of pressure, fretting, and cramming information into their craniums in order to pass a particular test (ex. ACT, SAT, CLT, NAEP). The outcome of this performance testing of student knowledge determines their readiness for advancement, whether the student will be awarded an achievement certificate or an academic degree, and perhaps their admission and placement in the college of their choice, or even a scholarship for financing their continued advanced education.

Transferring the educational paradigm of knowledge and skill testing to our spiritual relationship with God creates a severely misconstrued perspective of how we relate to God. God is not the "Great Examiner" in the sky. Religion has falsely portrayed the Christian life as a perpetual test whereby we are attempting to "measure up" to meet God's standards of achievement or advancement. What a tragedy that so many believers conceive of the Christian life as the constant pressure of performance attempting to pass or fail the expected criteria of the behavioral tests that religion has suggests that God expects and requires.

There is no divine test that Christians are striving to pass or fail. The Christian life is not based on performance or achievement. By God's grace, we all "pass" based on Jesus' performance on our behalf. It was Jesus who faced the test, in His submission to God's intent that He take the death consequences of sin for all mankind. The only test that Christians need to be concerned about failing is the single and ultimate criteria of having received the indwelling life of **JESUS** by faith, the grace-dynamic of His life and total sufficiency (cf. II Cor. 13:5,6) for all character and ministry. Beyond that, the Christian life is not a test – merely the opportunity for **JESUS** to live out His life in us.

AUGUST 7

WHAT ABOUT THE RAPTURE?

Some will say that "rapture" is never mentioned in the Bible. What they mean is that the specific word "rapture" is not utilized in the scriptures. The basic concept of "being taken up" is certainly present in reference to the return of Jesus; "those who are alive will be caught up/taken up together in the clouds to meet the Lord in the air" (I Thess. 4:17). The original Greek word for "being taken up" is *harpazo*, translated as "snatch, take by force, or to be caught up." The Latin Vulgate used the word *rapio* or *raptus*, and was the basis of our English word "rapture," but the same root word was the origin of the English word "rape."

The earliest Christian writers used the word "rapture" for "being carried away with emotion or ecstasy," but in recent centuries the word has been used of an alleged eschatological event when Christians are "caught up" and "carried away" to avoid the tribulation on earth. In this two-phase second coming of Jesus interpretation (Jesus coming *for* the saints, and Jesus coming *with* the saints), it is conjectured that there will be a secret and silent disappearance when Christians are suddenly "snatched" from the earth, and this occurrence is to be expected at any time, i.e. it is imminent and likely to happen very soon.

Those advocating such a "rapture" usually espouse a particular theology of premillennial dispensationalism. The traditional and more prominent interpretation does not expect a bisected return of Christ, but explains that Christians are to be expectant of His unannounced impending return. Christ's second coming will not be a silent stealthy secret, but will be public and visible, with a shout and the sound of a trumpet (cf. I Thess. 4:16). Christians must beware of overemphasizing disengagement from fallen human society in an escapist mentality that seeks to avoid the trials and tribulations of life here on earth. We do expect the return of **JESUS** Christ, and our focus should be on knowing Him.

AUGUST 8

GOD-GIVEN SEXUAL DESIRES

In the infinite wisdom of God, He saw fit to create every human person with God-given sexual needs and desires. After teaching on this subject, a Christian woman who was over eighty years old came to me and admitted that she had been sexually self-stimulating herself since she was a very young girl. "What does the Bible say about that?" she asked. I explained to her that the Bible does not have any direct references to the subject of auto-sexual stimulation or masturbation. My interpretive principle is "where the Bible speaks, we speak; where the Bible is silent, we are silent," so it is improper for us to pontificate with moralistic admonitions of admissibility or inadmissibility.

That course of action has not been the norm for most religion, as they tend to manufacture moralistic and legalistic regulations of what they consider acceptable or non-acceptable. Such sexual moralism leads to logical confusion, filled with shame and guilt. All God-given human desires (ex. eating, drinking, sexuality, belonging, to be loved, for identity) can be misused in excessive fixation and indulgence, or conversely in repudiation and denial. God gave us human desires with the intent they be utilized to His glory as His character is expressed through them in the contexts where those desires were intended to be fulfilled.

God created human beings and divided them on the basis of sexual gender, male and female (Latin *sexus* = "to divide"). Sexuality should not be a taboo subject among Christians. Religion has often failed to address this subject in an open and honest manner, creating a cover-up that implies there is something sinful about the way God created us. Not so! – God declared that what He created was "very good" (Gen 1:31). God intends that we enjoy our God-given sexuality, finding God-ordained pleasure therein as the reality of the living Lord **JESUS** is realized in our human sexuality.

AUGUST 9

POWER CORRUPTS

Most are aware of the statement made by the nineteenth century British politician, Lord Acton: "Power corrupts, and absolute power corrupts absolutely." The veracity of this truism has been proven many times on the world stage of history. Many have also observed the same principle play out on the smaller stage of a local church. Numerous pastors have been led to believe, and have browbeat their leadership boards to believe, in the principle of "pastoral authority" – that pastors have a God-given right and responsibility to tell those in their congregations what they should or should not do to be submissive disciples and members.

Pastors who insist on their right to authority over those in their congregation usurp the lordship of the living Lord Jesus, and try to play Holy Spirit in people's lives. Their domineering authoritarianism often violates the apostle Peter's words about "not lording it over those allotted to your charges, but proving to be examples to the flock" (I Pet. 5:3). There is no intrinsic power inherent within the pastoral position within a local *ecclesia*. The prevalent top-down hierarchical structures of some churches do however lend themselves to heavy-handed, dictatorial and condescending pastoral micromanagers who thrive on and misuse their self-appropriated sense of power over people.

There is only one mediator between God and men (I Tim. 2:5), and that One is the living Lord **JESUS** Christ. Pastors and elders must not attempt to usurp the divine lordship of **JESUS** in Christian lives. Jesus told His disciples, "all authority is given to Me, in heaven and on earth" (Matt. 28:18), but even the authority of Jesus is not a power-based authority within a power-structure, but the personal divine lordship of the One who is the ontological life and reality of the universal Body of Christ. When the church is perceived as, and structured as, a business-model, the power of the alleged pastoral C.E.O. will corrupt the *ecclesia*.

AUGUST 10

PERSONALITY DISORDERS

The secular psychological community has established three categories of "personality disorders" (P.D.s) among the American population (cf. *DSM-5*), and projected that one in ten persons suffer from a P.D. The first cluster of P.D.s (A) includes paranoid, schizoid, and schizotypal disorders. Cluster B includes people with antisocial, borderline, histrionic, and narcissistic P.D.s. The third cluster (C) identifies those with avoidant, dependent, and obsessive-compulsive P.D.s. What should our Christian response be to these categorizations of psychological disorders? Should we reject them as unhelpful humanistic explanations, or utilize them as helpful categories of understanding?

While it is true that the inspired Scriptures do not address "personality disorders" specifically, that is not to deny that there is not realistic explanation of human thought, emotion and action occurring in human beings that is misrepresentative of the character and attitude of divinely indwelt humans functioning in normality. The norm of Christian function is the Spirit of the living Lord **JESUS** manifesting the "fruit" of His character (Gal. 5:22,23) from our spirit-core in human behavior.

Every human being has a full-set of God-given desires. In the unregenerate process of our personal development and attempts to make sense of life, those desires were patterned into action and reaction patterns of selfishness and sinfulness as we attempted to adjust to our particular families and circumstances. The new covenant literature seems to identify these selfish and sinfully formed patterns of human desires as the "flesh," contrasting such with the intents of the Spirit (cf. Gal. 5:16-23) to manifest godly character. Our "fleshly desires" (Eph. 2:3; 2 Pet. 2:18) do seem to have some correspondence with what psychology calls "personality disorders." The secular categories of P.D.s can be helpful in identifying patterns of sinfulness.

AUGUST 11

NO SPIRITUAL ALLOY

In the field of metallurgy, one can take the "nature" and essential properties of one kind of metal and combine it with the "nature" and essential properties of another kind of metal or substance, and thus create an amalgamated alloy. The resultant alloy is a combined impure substance with the admixture of two "natures" and essential properties. When the elements of iron and carbon are combined at high temperature, it creates the alloy of steel. When steel is combined with chromium the result is the alloy of stainless steel. One of the earliest alloys (3500 B.C.) was the combination of copper and tin to create bronze.

It is not possible, however, to combine two antithetical spiritual natures into a spiritual alloy that comprises the nature of a Christian person. Nor is it possible for a Christian to have two antithetical spiritual natures simultaneously. An individual can only possess one or the other, for the nature of Satan and the nature of God are absolutely incompatible and cannot coinhabit the same human spirit. Despite the prominent religious teaching that advocates either an amalgamated alloy of two natures (old/new; Adam/Christ) or dual natures that produce bipolar spiritual schizophrenia, the nature and essence of one spirit (evil) or the other (God) inhabits the human spirit.

The new covenant scriptures (*New Testament*) do not indicate that the Christian person has "two natures," as religion so commonly teaches. Paul explains, "you were by nature (Greek *phusis*) children of wrath" (Eph. 2:2). Peter later wrote, "you have become partakers of the divine nature (*phusis*)" (II Peter 1:4). The single spiritual nature that we have as Christians is the nature and essential character of the presence of the life of **JESUS** Christ, who has come to dwell in and inhabit our human spirit. This is not to deny the behavioral conflict that is operative in the Christian between the "flesh" and the Spirit (Gal. 5:16-23).

AUGUST 12

PRETENSE

Have you known people that have a hard time being "real" and genuine? They think they need to put on an air of superiority, an attitude of higher advancement, a social-face of importance or elitism. They are trying to project an appearance that they are something they are not. Seldom do they seem to realize that many who observe them can see-through their pretense, play-acting and hypocrisy. Their fleshly desire for self-enhancement fosters a misrepresentative semblance that is often recognized by others as not only hypocritical false appearance, but as a despicable farce of unreality.

This is only exacerbated when such persons engage in the pretense of superior spirituality, trying to project a "holier-than-thou" aura in the artifice of self-righteousness. Perhaps this was the case when Ananias and Sapphira came before the fledgling church (Acts 5:1-11), feigning that they were giving the entire proceeds from the sale of their property. They were charged with "testing the Holy Spirit" (5:9) by claiming to be more sacrificially "spiritual" than they really were. It is a common charade of deception among Christian people in every age. But the consequences of being fraudulent imposters are quite severe.

Jesus spoke of a similar pretense of spirituality when He noted that the scribes and Pharisees "for a pretense, make long public prayers" (Matt. 23:14). The apostle Peter, who himself once had a problem of honesty and pretense (Matt. 26:69-75), later wrote of the necessity of "putting aside all malice and deceit and hypocrisy" (I Pet. 2:1). The character of the living Lord **JESUS** expressed in Christian behavior will always be genuine, open, honest and transparent – without pretense. There is no need to engage in pretense when we recognize that the character of the Spirit of God is being manifested in who we are (identity) and everything that we do (behavior) as Christians.

AUGUST 13

"THE LORD IS MY SHEPHERD"

A group of friends and acquaintances gathered for an evening of recitations and readings of famous literature, as well as their own writings. The meeting was well underway when an actor, trained in oratory, arose and strode to the lectern to begin a recitation of the words of the Twenty-third Psalm. With polished eloquence, complete with dramatic gestures, his baritone voice projected the words of the famous psalm throughout the hall. His masterful performance was met with awe in the appreciative audience They applauded vigorously, even with a few hoots, whistles, and shouts of "bravo" emanating from the crowd.

As the din of response died down, a frail older gentleman hobbled his way slowly to the lectern using his walking cane. In a soft voice that was quaking and rather gravelly, he also began to recite the Twenty-third Psalm very slowly from memory, making poignant emphasis on the personal pronouns of the psalm. "The Lord is ***my*** Shepherd; ...***I*** shall not want. ...***He*** maketh ***me*** to lie down in green pastures; ...***He*** leadeth ***me*** beside the still waters. ...***He*** restoreth ***my*** soul; ...***He*** leadeth ***me*** in the paths of righteousness for ***His*** name's sake. ...Yea, though ***I*** walk through the valley of the shadow of death,... ***I*** will fear no evil: ...for ***Thou*** art with ***me***; ...***Thy*** rod and ***Thy*** staff they comfort ***me***. ...***Thou*** preparest a table before ***me*** in the presence of ***mine*** enemies: ...***Thou*** anointest ***my*** head with oil; ...***my*** cup runneth over. ...Surely goodness and mercy shall follow ***me*** all the days of ***my*** life: ...and ***I*** will dwell in the house of the Lord forever."

The audience was stunned in silence, experiencing the awe of reverence. There was no applause; only a few sighs, whimpers and sobs from the listeners. The actor arose, standing in place by his chair, and most graciously said, "My friends. I know the words of the Twenty-third Psalm, but this man ***knows the Shepherd***. The profound difference resonates throughout this room."

AUGUST 14

"A TIME TO DANCE"

Imagine you and the Lord Jesus walking down a sandy beach together. For much of the way, the Lord's footprints go along steadily, consistently, rarely varying the pace. But your footprints are a disorganized stream of zigzags, starts, stops, turnarounds, circles, departures and returns, but gradually your footprints begin to align with those of Jesus. Walking in unison as true friends. This seems perfect, but then an interesting thing happens; your footprints, that once etched the sand next to Jesus' are now walking precisely in His steps. Inside His larger footprints are your smaller ones. Gradually you notice another change. The footprints inside the large footprints seem to grow larger. Eventually they disappear altogether. There is only one set of footprints; they have become one. This goes on for a distance, but suddenly the second set of footprints is back. This time it seems even worse! Zigzags all over the place. Stops. Starts. Deep gashes in the sand. A disordered canvas on the sand, as both sets of footprints go every which direction. You are amazed and shocked. Your dream ends! Was it a nightmare?

So, you pray, "Lord, I think I understand the first scene with zigzags and fits. I was a new believer; I was just learning. But you walked on through the storms and helped me learn to walk with you." His response, "Correct!" "... And when the smaller footprints were inside of Yours, I was attempting to walk in Your steps." "Very good!" "... And when the smaller footprints grew and filled in Yours, I suppose that I was experiencing union with You." "Precisely." "So, Lord, what happened? The footprints seemed to separate, and it appeared worse than at first." There is a pause, and the Lord answered with a smile. "You didn't realize? That was when we danced." "To everything there is a season, a time for every purpose under heaven: A time to weep, a time to laugh; A time to mourn, and *a time to dance...*" (Ecclesiastes 3:1,4). Have you experienced the perichoretic dance with **JESUS**?

AUGUST 15

THE BURDENS OF LIFE

Sadhu Sundar Singh was a Hindu convert to Christianity, led of the Spirit to become a missionary to his people in India. Late one afternoon, the Sadhu was traveling on foot through the Himalayas with a Buddhist monk. It was bitterly cold and the blowing snow felt like sharp blades slicing into their skin. Night was fast approaching when the monk warned the Sadhu that they were in danger of freezing to death if they did not reach the monastery before darkness fell. Suddenly, on a narrow path above a steep precipice, they heard a cry for help. At the foot of the cliff lay a man who had fallen and was badly hurt. The Buddhist monk looked at Singh and said, "Do not stop. God has brought this man to his fate as a consequence of his bad *karma*. He must work it out for himself. Let us hurry on before we, too, perish." But the Sadhu replied, "God has sent me here to help my brother. I cannot abandon him."

The monk continued trudging off through the whirling snow, while Sundar Singh clambered down the steep embankment. The injured man's leg was broken, so the Sadhu made a sling out of his blanket and tied the man on his back. With great difficulty, he climbed back up the cliff, now drenched in perspiration from his effort. Doggedly, the Sadhu made his way through the deepening snow and darkness. It was all he could do to follow the path. But he persevered, though faint with fatigue and overheated from exertion. Finally, he saw ahead the lights of the monastery. Then, the Sadhu stumbled and nearly fell. Not from weakness, but he had stumbled over an object lying in the snow-covered road. Slowly he bent down on one knee and brushed the snow off the object. It was the body of the monk, frozen to death.

Years later a disciple of Sadhu Sundar Singh asked him, "What is life's most difficult task?" Without hesitation Sadhu replied: "To have no burden to carry." – What is your intercessory burden?

AUGUST 16

HAVE YOU TASTED MY JESUS?

At the University of Chicago Divinity School each year they have what is called "Baptist Day." It is a day when all the Baptists in the area are invited to the school. Each one is to bring a lunch to be eaten outdoors in a grassy picnic area. Every "Baptist Day" the school would invite one of the greatest minds to lecture in the theological education center. One year they invited Dr. Paul Tillich. Dr. Tillich spoke for two and one-half hours questioning the reality of the resurrection of Jesus. He quoted scholar after scholar and book after book, and concluded that since there was no such thing as an historical resurrection; Jesus never rose from the dead in any literal sense. When he asked for questions, an old, dark-skinned preacher with a head of short-cropped, woolly white hair stood up in the back of the auditorium.

"Docta Tillich, I got one question," he said, as all eyes turned toward him. He reached into his sack lunch and pulled out an apple and began eating it. "Docta Tillich" ... *CRUNCH, MUNCH...* "My question is a simple question." *CRUNCH, MUNCH...* "Now, I ain't never read them books you read,"...*CRUNCH, MUNCH...* "and I can't recite the Scriptures in the original Greek." ...*CRUNCH, MUNCH* ..."I don't know nothin' about Niebuhr and Heidegger." ...*CRUNCH, MUNCH...* He finished the apple. "All I wanna know is: This apple I just ate – was it bitter or sweet?"

Dr. Tillich paused, and answered in exemplary scholarly fashion: "I cannot possibly answer that question, for I haven't tasted your apple." The white-haired preacher dropped the core of his apple into his crumpled paper bag, looked up at Dr. Tillich, and said calmly, "Neither have you tasted my **JESUS**." The auditorium erupted with applause and cheers. Dr. Tillich thanked his audience, and promptly left the platform. Have you tasted and partaken of **JESUS**? "Taste and see that the LORD is good; blessed is the man who takes refuge in Him" (Psalm 34:8).

AUGUST 17

HE'S INSIDE

He does not sit on a throne on high;
Afar in the distance – way up in the sky,
Offering us benefits in the bye-and-bye.
He's Inside.

He is not a big Judge whom we must fear,
Doling out punishment – year after year.
No! His Being is present and ever so near.
He's Inside.

There's no need to beg Him as you pray,
Pleading for His help along life's way.
He's with you constantly throughout the day.
He's Inside.

You're never alone through struggle and strife
Even though your problems be painful and rife.
He's right there within you as your life.
He's Inside.

He'll handle your problems, large or small
He's always there; you need only call.
He desires to be your All-in-All.
He's Inside.

He is there within you, and He's here within me.
He desires to be our sufficiency.
Just open the eyes of your heart and see –
He's Inside.

--Adapted from a poem by Grace Ross

AUGUST 18

HANDS

The Durer family lived in the central part of Germany. Having eighteen children, the father worked many hours to support his large family. Two of the older sons had a dream to pursue their talent for art at the Academy in Nuremberg, but knew the family could not afford such. The brothers made a pact, to be decided by a coin toss. The loser of the toss would go down in the mines, and with his earnings support the other brother while he attended the art academy. After four years, they would reverse roles. Albert lost the coin toss, and went into the mines to finance his brother Albrecht's art education. Albrecht excelled, and his etchings, woodcuts, and oil paintings were soon recognized as exceptional and worthy of considerable fees and commissions.

When Albrecht had completed his art studies, he returned home to a family celebration. During the family gathering Albrecht thanked his family and friends, and made a toast to his brother who had financed his studies. His closing words were, "Now, Albert my dear brother, it is your turn to go to Nuremberg to pursue your dream, while I take care of you." Albert sat at the other end of the table, shaking his head. "No, he said, every finger on my hands has been smashed in the mine, and they now suffer from arthritis, and I will be unable to be an artist."

To pay homage to brother Albert, Albrecht drew his brother's deformed hands with palms together and fingers pointed upward. He simply called his drawing, "Hands." Those who viewed the drawing recognized it as a masterpiece and renamed it, "The Praying Hands." It has become the most well-known of all Albrecht Durer's masterful works, many of which hang in museums around the world. It is a powerful reminder of brotherly love, and the willingness to sacrifice for one we love. It is also a testimony to the fact that every man's success is facilitated not only by his own efforts, but by the help of others.

AUGUST 19

EXPECTATIONS

What do you expect? Do you have expectations, not just for the future, but for today in the midst of every situation that might occur? Do you expect God to be at work, working all things for good (Rom. 8:28) in every circumstance whether it be pleasant or unpleasant? As Christians we are assured that our destiny is determined by the redemptive work of Jesus Christ, having died on the cross in our place, and by His resurrection having made His eternal life available to us to live life every day here on earth, with the assurance that His life dwelling within us will enliven us even in perpetuity when we are in heaven eternally.

The objective expectation of eternal destiny should be an assurance for every Christian, but the subjective expectations of God's continued activity of grace in the experiences of our daily lives is a struggle for many Christians. Do we really expect God to "show up" and function by His grace and love in the midst of every occurrence and event of our everyday life? Many of us look back with 20/20 hindsight and recognize that God has worked in our lives in the past, but the foresight of expecting and appreciating God's working today and in the days to come is sometimes blurred by our own lack of vision and expectation.

Very suddenly one night, I developed an ear ache and subsequently lost the hearing in one ear. I could have easily been "bummed" about such a situation, and even blamed God for not protecting me from such a distraction. Or, I could respond in faith (the receptivity of God's activity) and hope (the confident expectation that God's grace would be working) that God would bring good and glory to Himself, even if I should have limited hearing for the rest of my life. I choose to expect the sublime action of God's grace, trusting and expecting that I will glimpse His grace at work, and see how He is working through **JESUS** to manifest His power and character in my life.

AUGUST 20

THERE'S SOMETHING ABOUT THAT NAME

In Shakespeare's lyrical tale of "star-crossed" lovers, Romeo Montague and Juliet Capulet fall in love, despite coming from two warring families. When reminded that their love-relationship was doomed to failure because his name was Montague, Juliet responds, "What's in a name? That which we call a rose by any other name would smell as sweet." Love-struck idealism may look beyond the importance of family names, but names usually convey meaning that cannot be glossed over. When someone forgets our name, either our given name or family name, they have forgotten that which designates who we are.

Prior to Jesus' birth, the angels made known the name that He was to be given, and it signified who He was and what He would do. "You shall call His name 'Jesus,' for He will save His people from their sins" (Matt. 1:21). "They shall call His name 'Immanuel," which means 'God with us'" (Matt. 1:23). The most common name designation of Jesus in the early church was "the Lord Jesus Christ" (cf. Acts 15:26); "Lord" signifying the deity of Jesus, and "Christ" signifying that He was the Anointed Messiah promised by the prophets of the old covenant.

A name has objective meaning in the identification of a person, but there is also a subjective awareness of the meaning of the name of our Lord Jesus. The Christian knows that the name of **JESUS** signifies the very Being of the One who has become our life, to be our "all in all" (Eph. 1:23). Bill and Gloria Gaither wrote and popularized the well-known gospel praise song, "There's Something About That Name."

> Jesus, Jesus, Jesus; There's just something about that name
> Master, Savior, Jesus, like the fragrance after the rain;
> Jesus, Jesus, Jesus, let all Heaven and earth proclaim
> Kings and kingdoms will all pass away,
> But there's something about that name.

AUGUST 21

"IT'S NO LONGER I WHO LIVES NOW"

Galatians 2:20 (KJV) – "I am crucified with Christ: nevertheless, I live; yet not I, but Christ liveth in me...." Approximately fifty years ago, I first heard the words of this chorus based on Gal. 2:20.

"It's no longer I who lives now, but Christ who liveth in me.
It's no longer I who lives now, but Christ who liveth in me.
I'm dead; I'm dead; Jesus is alive in me.
It's no longer I who lives now, but Christ who liveth in me."

"It's no longer I who lives now, but Christ who liveth in me.
It's no longer I who lives now, but Christ who liveth in me.
In me; In me; Jesus is alive in me.
It's no longer I who lives now, but Christ who liveth in me."

"It's no longer I who lives now, but Christ who liveth in me.
It's no longer I who lives now, but Christ who liveth in me.
He lives; He lives; Jesus is alive in me.
It's no longer I who lives now, but Christ who liveth in me."

"It's no longer I who lives now, but Christ who liveth in me.
It's no longer I who lives now, but Christ who liveth in me.
He's Lord; He's Lord; Jesus is alive in me.
It's no longer I who lives now, but Christ who liveth in me."

"It's no longer I who lives now, but Christ who liveth in me.
It's no longer I who lives now, but Christ who liveth in me.
Not me; But He; Jesus is alive in me.
It's no longer I who lives now, but Christ who liveth in me."

Via music, the Spirit often embeds a thought deeper into our minds than the non-verbal reading of a verse of scripture. The thought within this verse is central to Christians understanding the gospel truth of **JESUS** living in us as Christ-ones.

AUGUST 22

FEAR CAN BE DEVASTATING

Only after human beings had sinned and fallen under the indwelling influence of Satan, did they experience fear. Adam explained the consequence of his disobedient action to God, "I was afraid..." (Gen. 3:10). The diabolic deceiver prompts people to be fearful, portraying God to be a vindictive and punitive tyrant full of wrath and judgment. Satan "blinds the minds of unbelievers" (II Cor. 4:4) concerning God's true character and purposes, and continues to work in believers (Rev. 12:10). The harmful effects of his fear-mongering can be devastating, and thus fulfil Satan's purposes as "the destroyer" (I Cor. 10:10).

Jeremiah explained, "Fear and pitfall have come upon us, devastation and destruction" (Lam. 3:47 – Amp.). The reaction of fear to the circumstances of life can lead to anxiety, persistent and prolonged phobias, to dread and unreasonable projections of doom, and paralyzing panic. The fear that Satan inspires is a false portrayal of a god that seeks to control our thoughts, emotions and decisions in a manner that is often devastating, debilitating and paralyzing. Fear is a hope-killer, suppressing the confident expectation that God who controls all things in love is going to seek our highest good, even in distressing situations.

Paul affirmed, "Perfect love casts out fear" (I Jn. 4:18). What does that mean? What is "perfect love?" The proper question should be, "Who is 'perfect love'?" The apostle John answers that question: "God is love" (I Jn. 4:8,16). The presence of the perfect Father God, functioning graciously through the Son, Jesus Christ, and by the power of His Holy Spirit in the manifestation of His loving character, always makes available the assurance of God's love that overrides human fear. God invests His loving character within the Christian. "The love of God is poured out in our hearts by the Holy Spirit who has been given to us" (Rom. 5:5). Do we believe that God always loves us through **JESUS**?

AUGUST 23

GOD DOESN'T HOLD SIN AGAINST ANYONE

The popular Christian opinion seems to be that sin is a violation of the character of God, and God cannot tolerate sin; rather hates all sin as well as those who commit sin. Jesus the Son died for the sins of mankind, but God the Father is still mad as hell about the sinfulness of mankind and holds their sins against them if they have not received Jesus by faith. This sounds so vengeful and vindictive, and certainly questions whether God the Father and God the Son are "on the same page" concerning redemption. Is such a concept really the content of the gospel, or is it a tragic misconception of the redemptive work of Jesus Christ?

The gospel of grace explains that God the Father, and God the Son, and God the Holy Spirit, acting in full concert, determined with one mind to deal with the consequences of human sin by sending the Son to become a human who could and would die (death the consequence of sin) for the sins of every human person. He was incarnated to "put away sin by the sacrifice of Himself" (Heb. 9:26), "sacrificed once and for all to take away the sins of many" (Heb. 9:27,28). "Christ died for sins once for all, the just for the unjust, so that He might bring us to God" (I Pet. 3:18). As John the Baptist declared, Jesus was "the Lamb of God who took away the sin of the world of mankind" (Jn. 1:29).

Thereafter, God does not hold the sins of anyone against them. The death of Jesus was the satisfaction for the consequence of sin for all men (cf. I Jn. 4:10), "making peace through His blood shed on the cross" (Col. 1:19,20), reconciling all men to Himself. By His death on the cross, Jesus paid the penalty of death for the sin of all mankind. We are all "bought with a price" (I Cor. 6:20; 7:23), and God in His triune entirety holds nothing against us. Yes, universal redemption is, and has always been, the good news of the gospel. This does not eliminate the responsibility of the individual response of receptive belief for personal efficacy!

AUGUST 24

"YOU SHALL BE MY WITNESSES"

Prior to His ascension, Jesus advised His disciples, "You shall be my witnesses..." (Acts 1:8-KJV). It seems that this statement has been misunderstood and misused by Christian religion through the years. The statement has often been interpreted as a mandate for Christians to engage in human effort to promote and propagate the Christian faith and teaching. The verb in Jesus' statement is not necessarily an imperative, but is best translated as an indicative, indicating that when the Holy Spirit comes to believers, the dynamic grace activity of God's divine indwelling will function to bear witness of the Lord Jesus.

A better translation, as used in many modern translations, is "you will receive power when the Holy Spirit has come upon you, and you will be witnesses of Me... to the remotest part of the earth" (Acts 1:8). This removes the common religious emphasis on a call to Christian performance, attempting to incentivize Christians "to go witnessing" and "share your testimony" in order to build the church. Instead, to be involved in witness of Jesus is necessarily the activity of the Holy Spirit giving testimony to and glorifying (Jn. 16:14) Jesus, primarily by the outworking of the indwelling life and character of Jesus. Once again, it is not what we do to implement Christian life, but what God does!

The Greek word for "witness" or "testimony" is *marture*, from which we derive the English word "martyr." When we allow the Spirit to witness of Jesus in, through, and as us, we are laying down our lives in availability to all that **JESUS** wants to be and do in us. "Testimony" and "witness" were originally considered in a legal paradigm, but in the new covenant, the legal paradigm is put aside for a new grace paradigm, whereby the dynamic of God gives expression to the Son by the Spirit. This means that "witness" and "testimony" of **JESUS** is not what we do, but what God does by His Spirit in the practicality of living the Christ-life.

AUGUST 25

CHRISTIAN SEXUALITY

Christians must beware of succumbing to the contemporary cultural mind-set about human sexuality. The issue is not just a distinction between homosexuality and heterosexuality – genital interactions with the same (Greek *homo* = same) gender, or with another (Greek *hetero* = another) gender. Humanity is divided (Latin *sexus* = to divide) into two genders, male and female. The identification of the participants in sexual interaction does not in any way designate the encounter as "Christian." Christian sexuality necessarily involves Christ-ones allowing the character of the living Lord Jesus to be expressed in their genital interactions in a manner whereby God is glorified.

It has been suggested that we should coin another word, "hierosexuality" (Greek *hiero* = holy). That does not solve the problem, for the word *hiero* (ex. hieroglyphics) has been understood as "holy" in the sense of "religious" or "sacred" as in pagan practices (cf. Greece or Egypt). Another suggestion is reference to "hagiosexuality" (Greek *hagio* = set apart as holy). Christians are to "be holy as He is holy" (I Pet. 1:6), i.e. to allow the holy character of the Triune God to be expressed in our human behavior. But the Greek word *hagios* has also been diffused to refer to religious and moral conformity.

Christ-ones must avoid the world's tendency to define people or to base their identities in gender or genital activities. Our spiritual identity is found in **JESUS** Christ alone, not in physical criteria. As Christ-ones, we want the holy character of **JESUS** to be manifested in our moral bodies (II Cor. 4:10,11) in everything we do. Such Christocentric, Christ-activated and Christ-motivated behavior, allowing the "fruit of the Spirit" (Gal. 5:22,23) to permeate and inspire our every action, will inevitably be counter-cultural and set us apart from the world and all religion, differentiated by the holy character of God in Christian sexuality.

AUGUST 26

THE RIGHT THING TO DO

Evaluating why we do what we do is an important human function. This ability goes beyond the rest of the animal kingdom, for human beings alone seem to have the ability to be self-evaluative and engage in self-assessment. Many people fail to take the time to be self-critical, not wanting to see their own faults, but in so doing they stunt their own personal growth. Those willing to engage in self-evaluation are often able to analyze and measure where they are in their personal growth and health process. Some, however, become obsessively self-critical, preoccupied with a negative opinion of themselves.

Many people do what they do simply because they believe that what they are doing is "the right thing to do." What is the basis of this evaluation? Do they have any criteria for determining what is "right"? Somewhere in their backgrounds they usually have had some instruction concerning social propriety and morality that influences their determinations of what is "right." This may have been provided by their families or through religious and educational instruction, and they may not consciously recognize the foundational source from which they developed their concepts and perspective of "the right thing to do."

Christian individuals should be finding their basis for determining "what is right" from a more objective and absolute criteria. The "right thing to do" is elevated to a desire for righteousness before God. Righteousness is the essential character of God, and can only be derived from God. **JESUS** Christ is identified as "the Righteous One" (Acts 3:14; 7:52; 22:14), and is the basis of all true righteousness. "Christ is our righteousness" (I Cor. 1:30). Christians will desire to be "filled with the fruit of righteousness which comes through Jesus Christ, to the glory and praise of God (Phil. 1:11). We "present the members of our body as instruments of righteousness" (Rom. 6:13).

AUGUST 27

PRAYER DRUTHERS

A small (very small – usually five or less) group gathers every week to pray through the list of "prayer requests" that have been received during the previous week in our fellowship. An older gentleman who has been loyal and faithful as a "prayer warrior" has participated in that group for several years, and he brings the list of "prayer requests" when he comes to the men's bible study immediately following the prayer time. When asked to share the prayer needs of the congregation one morning, he began his recitation by saying, "The prayer druthers are as follows ..." I could hardly contain my chuckle at his choice of words.

What are "druthers"? It is a slang word for "I would rather/prefer that it would be other than what it is." That is precisely what that list of prayer requests often amounts to every week. Week after week, Christian people are writing down their solicitations imploring that situations in their lives they are not content with or pleased with might be changed to a more preferable and pleasant outcome. That strikes me as being rather self-oriented, as if they are telling God, "I want it my way!" Their prayer requests seem to be asking others to "please ply God (maybe twist God's arm) to make it otherwise than what it is."

Who's in control here? God or man? Since prayer is often viewed as seeking a change in the situation that exists, are we asking God to change? God is immutable and unchangeable, the "same yesterday, today, and forever" (Heb. 13:8). Are we asking God to change His mind and do something different in this particular situation? Or should we consider that the only one who needs to change is the one making the requests or doing the praying (the pray-er). The change that likely needs to occur is a change in the perspective of the one praying, whereby they might accept the ways of God in faith (our receptivity of His activity), and express gratitude that God's good grace is presently at work.

AUGUST 28

EXAGGERATION AND EMBELLISHMENT

Most of us have known people who would adamantly deny that they were "liars," yet their conversation is often laced with exaggerations, embellishments and excessive overstatements. They tend to misrepresent everything they speak about in an excessive manner, willing to "stretch the truth" in overstatement often by employing hyperbole that inflates the numbers to "a million times" or more. Why do they engage in such deception, dissimulation, and prevarication? They are often self-centered narcissists attempting to enhance their image among others by building themselves up via fabrication and falsification. When confronted with their hypocritical deception, they will usually attempt to dismiss such and laugh it off by claiming they were "just kidding," or "using some innocent hyperbole." It is not so innocent when we recall that Jesus told the Pharisees that they were deriving from the "father of lies" (Jn. 8:44), the devil.

In the legal system of the United States of America, a witness must swear to "tell the truth, the whole truth, and nothing but the truth." Suspicions, speculations and exaggerations are not allowed as testimony because the witness has sworn to tell "nothing but the truth." In the context of a courtroom, Pilate once asked, "What is truth?" (Jn. 18:38). True statements are those in accordance with reality. Precision of truth-telling is foundational to a fair and just society for the avoidance of social disintegration into chaos and anarchy. On a smaller scale, the facticity of our comments in our personal conversation will reveal whether we are a person who is believable and trustworthy, as well as whether we are deriving from the indwelling presence of divine Truth. **JESUS** said, "I AM the way, the truth, and the life" (Jn. 14:6). He also told those listening to Him, "You shall know the truth (**JESUS**), and the truth shall set you free" (Jn. 8:32). Christians must beware of misrepresenting the truth and reality of **JESUS** in their conversation.

AUGUST 29

IMAGINATION

Some Christians in our rationalistic world fear that imagination will take people into the realms of mysticism, myth, and make-believe. Other Christians believe that Christianity requires imagination, for the "leap of faith" requires people to go beyond the limitations of a closed rational paradigm. What place does imagination have in genuine Christian faith? Inherent in the word "imagination" is the concept of images, which range from ocular images we view with our physical eyes, to the mental images that we see with the "eyes of our heart" (Eph. 1:18). Images can be substitutes for God (as in idolatry), or images can be the means by which we see the spiritual reality of God (revelation).

Albert Einstein said, "Imagination is more important than knowledge. Knowledge is limited. Imagination encircles the world." Imagination lets us ponder "outside of the box" of our physical senses. Raw information is as dry as sawdust, unless it is steeped in imagination that allows it to become personal, relational, and transformational. Information alone does not impact us experientially, but when combined with the imagery of imagination, it becomes personal and experiential. Cerebralists choke on imagination, thinking they have to figure out everything with their mind, rather than the "mind's eye."

From *Genesis* to *Revelation*, the Bible appeals to our "mind's eye." It paints pictures using analogies and metaphors; it engages us on the imaginative level. Consider the beatitudes, the parables, the *Apocalypse* of John. The scriptures are impenetrable to many people, because they read them looking merely for information. When we approach the biblical text, instead of asking, "What does it mean?" we should ask, "How does it enter into me? How does it come alive and meaningful in my life?" "We are to "set out minds on things above" (Col. 3:2), using the "eyes of faith" to see the unseen (II Cor. 4:18).

AUGUST 30

ECCLESIA – THE FAMILY OF GOD

The institutional megachurch in America today is often like a mega-orphanage where people without genuine family relationships are housed (or warehoused), without any intent or strategic policies for reintegrating the helpless orphans into a family or into the greater society. Like regimented pawns, they march to their designated meal times, hungry for whatever morsels or gruel might be served that day, vigorously expressing their gratitude for their maintenance menu, knowing that it is far better than pandering on the street. "It's better than nothing," seems to be the general consensus of the orphans.

Jesus told His disciples, "I will not leave you as orphans" (Jn. 14:18). True to His word, He did not! By the sending of the Holy Spirit, first poured out as the new covenant fulfillment on Pentecost, the triune God established the integral community of the Family of God, the *ecclesia*, popularly known today as "the church." The intent of the *ecclesia* that Jesus promised (Matt. 16:18) was that it might be an interactive community of close intimate relationships patterned after the perichoretic personal relationships of the Father, Son, and Holy Spirit. The *ecclesia* is intended to be a spiritual family of the People of God (I Pet. 2:10).

Instead of orphans, Christians are those who are adopted into the Family of God as brothers and sisters "in Christ." It might even be noted that we are "blood-brothers" in Christ; not our blood, but **JESUS'** blood shed on the cross of Calvary on our behalf. Paul explained that "we have received a spirit of adoption as sons (and daughters) by which we cry out, 'Abba! Father!'" (Rom. 8:15; cf. Gal. 4:5; Eph. 1:5). Adoption in the Roman world was even more permanent than the process of adoption practiced in the modern world. Once adopted, the adoptee could not be rejected, disinherited or orphaned. It was truly incorporation and involvement in the "forever family" of God.

AUGUST 31

METAPHORS OF DERIVATION

Much of our Christian understanding is developed in imaginative images formed in "the mind's eye" (cf. Chaucer, *Canterbury Tales*), and viewed with the "eyes of the heart" (Eph. 1:18). This is certainly true of the mental images by which we perceive of the process whereby we depend on, and derive from, the living Lord Jesus Christ. Despite our word choices of derivation, dependency, contingency, and receptivity, the cognitive logic of our language is unable to drive home the concept to the extent that the metaphorical pictures provided in the scriptures are able to enliven and envision the spiritual reality.

The Psalmist saw the picture when he wrote that "the godly man is like a tree planted by rivers of water, that brings forth his fruit in season" (Ps. 1:3). The tree draws the moisture through the roots by osmosis to provide nutrients to the branches and leaves. This is similar to Jesus' analogy of "I am the vine and you are the branches" (Jn. 15:5), picturing the derivation and dependency of the branches on the vine in order to produce the fruit. Jesus' analogy of the Holy Spirit being like "rivers of living water, flowing from our innermost being, springing up to eternal life" (Jn. 4:14; 7:38), also pictures the divine provision.

Isaiah used the image of our being the malleable "clay" that the divine "Potter" forms into His new creation (Isa. 64:8). Paul used the picture of experiencing feminine birth-labor until "Christ might be formed in us" (Gal. 4:19). Christ is the bridegroom and Christians are the bride (Eph. 5:25-29), receptive and desirous of being impregnated in order to give birth to the character expression of Jesus. Peter switched the metaphor to our being "newborn babes receiving the milk of the word" (I Pet. 2:2) in order to "grow in our salvation." Our sufficiency is always from the divine source (II Cor. 3:5) in order to be the Christ-ones who express the derived character of **JESUS** Christ.

SEPTEMBER 1

WHO IS WATCHING?

"Big brother is watching" was a slogan used in George Orwell's book, *Nineteen Eighty-four* (1949), referring to a paranoid awareness of being surveilled at all times by an authoritarian superior. Many Christians have wondered whether family members or loved ones who have preceded them in death are looking down from heaven and observing everything they are doing on earth. To some that might be bothersome, while others might be delighted. A more important consideration is the certainty that God is watching us, for "all things are open and laid bare to the eyes of Him with whom we have to do" (Heb. 4:13).

There are no direct biblical statements that provide a definitive answer to the question of whether people in heaven can observe what we are doing on earth and see our every move, including all of our sinful actions. The verse most cited to affirm such is Heb. 12:1 – "since we have so great a cloud of witnesses surrounding us, let us also lay aside every encumbrance and the sin which so easily entangles us, and let us run with endurance the race that is set before us." The meaning of the "cloud of witnesses" is problematic. In the previous chapter in Heb. 11:4,5 the same word *marture* refers to the testimony of the righteousness of Abel and the witness that Enoch was pleasing to God. The "cloud of witnesses" may refer to the witness of the saints of old, as mentioned in the preceding chapter. Others interpret the phrase in reference to our loved ones of the modern era who have died and are now cheering us on like spectators in a stadium. If so, they are not critiquing our progress, but cheering for us to "fix our eyes on Jesus" as expressed in the next verse (12:2).

Those who have entered into the extension and perpetuity of heavenly life in **JESUS** Christ are likely preoccupied with worshipping God and enjoying the glories of heaven, and not with what or how well we who remain on earth are doing.

SEPTEMBER 2

ESCHATOLOGY

Eschatology is the study of the *eschatos*. The Greek word *eschatos* means "last" things. Many have mistakenly thought that "last" things pertain to "end" times (*telos*) or "future" events (*mello*). *Eschatos* does not necessarily refer to "last in time," but to something that is "last in a sequence." For example, the last opportunity for human beings to find relationship with God in the manner the Creator God intended is by means of the *Eschatos* Man, the "Last Adam" that Paul mentions in I Corinthians 15:45, referring to Jesus Christ. The first man was Adam in the Garden of Eden; Jesus is the last in the sequence of representative men.

God's last (*eschatos*) and final Word (Jn. 1:1,14) for the restoration of fallen mankind is His Son, Jesus Christ. God has utilized many spokespersons in the past, but Jesus is the last in the sequence. Note that the sequence goes from the *past* to the *last*, thus encompassing all of time. "God, after He spoke long ago to the fathers in the prophets in many portions and in many ways, in these last (*eschatos*) days has spoken to us in His Son" (Heb. 1:1,2). The apostle Peter quoted the prophet Joel to explain what was the occurring on Pentecost: "In the last (*eschatos*) days ... I will pour forth My Spirit on all mankind" (Acts 2:17).

God's last (*eschatos*) and ultimate work by which "everyone who calls on the name of the Lord will be saved" (Acts 2:21) is accomplished (Jn. 17:4) in the redemptive and restorative work of **JESUS** Christ, completed (Jn. 19:30) in His death, resurrection and Pentecostal outpouring. God's last (*eschatos*) action is not a series of events in the future at the end of time, but has been and is being fulfilled in **JESUS** Christ, the Last (*eschatos*) Adam by the Spirit (cf. I Cor. 15:45). Legitimate Christian eschatology will always be Christocentric, focusing on **JESUS** and avoiding the speculative projections and predictions of those selfishly attempting to see what will happen in the future.

SEPTEMBER 3

"AS HE IS, SO ARE WE IN THIS WORLD"

In what we call his first epistle, John twice indicates that "God is love" (4:8,16). In the same chapter, he subsequently writes, "As He (*Jesus)* is, so are we in this world" (4:17). We must be careful how we interpret this phrase, for John does not seem to be stating that we Christians are essentially like Jesus in this world. Jesus is the God-man, the Savior, the "one mediator between God and man" (I Tim. 2:5). Christians are not saviors or co-saviors, and do not serve as mediators between God and men. In fact, I think we should be cautious of saying, as C.S. Lewis does, that Christians are "little Christs" in the world today.

In what we call the first epistle of Paul to the Corinthians, Paul states, "The one who has been joined to the Lord (*i.e. has become a Christian*) is one spirit with Him" (6:17). Such a one-spirit union with Christ does not imply that we are essentially one with Jesus Christ, or that we are Jesus in our human form. The distinction of Christ and the Christians must always be maintained. We are relationally and spiritually one with the Spirit of the living Jesus, and thus are referred to as Christ-ones (Christians) who are identified with (spiritual identity) and indwelt by the living Lord Jesus Christ. Eastern Orthodox Christians explain that we do not become united essentially with Jesus, but we partake of the divine energies of Jesus.

The import of John's statement, "As He is, so are we in this world" (I Jn. 4:17), must be considered contextually. John has been addressing the reality of divine *agape* love (I Jn. 4:7-21), explaining that God is essentially the character of love; "God is love." Not that He has a commodity called love to distribute to others, but God is the essential source of all genuine love. The loving God has made His character available to us by means of His Son, Jesus Christ, and the presence of the Holy Spirit. "As He is (loving), so are we in this world," imaging the character of God.

SEPTEMBER 4

INTERCESSION FOR OTHERS

Many Christians think of intercession only in the context of prayer. Paul refers to several types of prayer: "I urge that supplications, prayers, *intercessions*, and thanksgivings be made for all men" (I Tim. 2:1). Intercession, however, goes beyond personal prayers to become intercessory living for another. This is not just a "spiritual gift" granted to certain people to lift others up, but is the divine character operating in every Christian. Intercession is the character of God – God's interceded for humanity by sending His Son to become a human being.

Illustrations of intercession abound in the Old Testament. Joseph endured hardship to intervene for the Hebrew people in Egypt. Moses interceded for the Hebrew people after they built the golden calf. Esther intervened for her Hebrew people when Haman sought to destroy them. After the many abominable sins of the Israelites, God said, "I looked for someone who would stand before me in the gap..., but I found no one" (Ezek. 22:30). What heartbreaking neglect – no one among the Hebrew people would intercede, intervene, act as a "go-between" and "stand in the gap" (cf. Isa. 59:16) before God.

In the new covenant of Jesus Christ, the character-action of intercession is invested with a higher revelation of God's love. The ultimate example of personal intercession is the willingness of Jesus to take our place in vicarious intervention by dying for the sins of mankind – to hang on the cross in our stead. Living now in every Christian, Christ may call us to "carry another's burdens" (Gal. 6:2) also. It may be costly to "lay down our lives" as a *marture* (martyr) for another, to "stand in the place" and exchange places with another, to be fully involved and invested for another person, but when God lays it on our heart to make the sacrifices necessary to assist another person, will we be available to "stand in the gap" as an intercessor?

SEPTEMBER 5

"THAT I MIGHT KNOW HIM"

On a natural level, the apostle Paul seems to have been an egotistical little man driven to succeed. After the Lord met him on the road to Damascus, his perspective of everything, including himself, began to be transformed. He admitted that he had "confidence in the flesh" (Phil. 3:3), but came to see that all he valued was to be counted as loss compared to the surpassing value of "knowing Christ Jesus" and "being found in Him." His foremost desire and objective now became "*that I may know Him* and the power of His resurrection and the fellowship of His sufferings, being conformed to His death..." (Phil. 3:10).

What does it mean to "know Him?" Knowing Jesus is not informational head-knowledge of "knowing about" the historical Jesus. Nor is it a lofty elitism of special gnostic awareness of spiritual things. Knowing Jesus is a relational knowing, but it is more than a mere casual acquaintance. The King James Bible reads, "Adam knew Eve, and she conceived and bore a son, Cain" (Gen. 4:1). Such "knowing" involved relational intimacy, and likewise to "know Jesus" involves an intimacy of spiritual union (cf. I Cor. 6:17) and interaction with the living Lord Jesus wherein there is a willingness to be open in transparent trust.

Trust and transparency are essential to all intimate knowing of another person. The more we trust someone, the closer we allow ourselves to get to them. We learn to trust our Lord Jesus most in the trials of life that test our faith, and these situations draw us closer to Him in intimacy. That seems to be why Paul explained his desire to "know Him, and the fellowship of His sufferings..." (Phil. 3:10). Suffering and pain are not a separate component of "knowing Jesus" – they are integrally connected. Are we willing to "know Jesus" so intimately that we are willing to suffer with Him, willing to experience the world's disdain for the One who lives in us and has become our life?

SEPTEMBER 6

WHEN VIRTUES EQUAL VICES

Religion has often commended human virtues and condemned human vices. But much of the time they are equally appalling and abominable in the sight of God. How can that be? Man's best efforts can never achieve what God intended for humanity. You may recall that the forbidden tree in the Garden of Eden was "the tree of the knowledge of good and evil" (Gen. 2:9,17). Yes, the relative "good" that human beings might achieve when they think they are generating such from their own alleged self-resource is not derived from God, and thus not the absolute good of God's character. "No one is good except God alone" (Mk. 10:18).

The "tree of life" was among the trees that the original couple were encouraged to "eat freely" from (Gen. 2:9), for it was the tree representing the choice of humanity to derive from the life and character of God. Human sin and vices obviously need to be repented of, but the human virtues of relative goodness as promoted by religion also need equally to be repented of for they do not serve God's purposes to manifest the character of the goodness and righteousness of the life of Jesus in the behavior of mankind. Jesus was clear, "Apart from Me, you can do nothing" (Jn. 15:5) – nothing that is good and glorifying to God.

The religious virtues of meritorious disciplines and good works are merely "works of the flesh" that need to be renounced and repented of as self-righteousness. Some have differentiated between "bad flesh" and "good flesh" to make the distinction between vices and virtues enacted out of the selfish and sinful patterns of our "flesh." All fleshly desires (religious or otherwise) are to be overcome by the Spirit of Christ (Gal. 5:17), allowing **JESUS** to manifest godly character and righteousness in our Christian behavior. We must not allow our fleshly vices or our fleshly virtues to draw us away from the sanctified Christ-life wherein we derive all character from Him.

SEPTEMBER 7

LAYING DOWN OUR TROPHIES

In the popular and cherished hymn, "The Old Rugged Cross," written in 1912 by George Bennard, the words of the following stanza are well-known to many Christians:

> "So, I'll cherish the old rugged cross,
> Till my trophies at last I lay down;
> And I will cling to the old rugged cross,
> And exchange it some day for a crown."

The "laying down our trophies," seems to refer to putting aside all our personal accomplishments and achievements. It is talking about laying down everything we have done and been recognized for, including (and perhaps particularly) all that we have been applauded for in our religious efforts.

In Philippians 3, Paul lists a number of religious accomplishments, sort of a religious resumé of his "trophies" that were meaningful in his life and heritage in the Jewish religion. Then he writes, "But whatever things were gain to me, those things I have counted as loss for the sake of Christ, ...and count them as rubbish, not having any righteousness of my own, ...but the righteousness which comes from God on the basis of faith" (Phil. 3:5-9). What Paul previously considered to be achievement "trophies," he now considers as junk compared to the knowing of Christ Jesus, his Lord and Savior.

What are the "trophies," the achievements that religion assured us were so valuable, that you are holding on to? It may be serving on committees or assuming various positions in the church. It may be a doctoral degree diploma, or a pastoral ordination certificate, or a library of Christian books. Are we willing to consider that all these things and endeavors have no real value compared to the dynamic of the living Lord **JESUS**? We do not have to wait until death to lay down our "trophies."

SEPTEMBER 8

RELATING TO YOUR PASTOR

Pastors come in all shapes and sizes, genders and personalities, gifts and talents, as well as organizational and speaking abilities – and even spiritual maturation levels. For those who have been part of hierarchical church structures, there is often a tendency to have an elevated perspective of the pastor and the position – even elevating the pastor to "six feet above contradiction" when occupying the pulpit. I saw a quip recently that said, "Do not put your pastor on a pedestal where he or she might be knocked off. Instead, put your pastor on your prayer list where he or she might be lifted up to God's care and grace."

Pastors are simply human beings who have availed themselves to be "shepherds of the sheep" in your particular congregation. They are not necessarily "more spiritual" than any other person in the congregation. Though some claim to have a spiritual gift of shepherding and a "call to ministry," all pastors are fallible persons subject to temptation and choices to misrepresent who they are "in Christ" by sinful behavior. Pastors are particularly vulnerable to temptations of pride of position, of assuming a sense of power whereby they might take advantage of others, and even to develop bonds that can lead to sexual temptation.

When a pastor makes a claim to have "pastoral authority" and seeks to dictate or condescend to others, that pastor is stepping beyond the role of a legitimate under-shepherd and attempting to usurp the power of the Shepherd, **JESUS**, who has been "given all authority in heaven and on earth" (Matt. 28:18). All pastors need personal friends, but some have been taught to avoid personal friendships with people in the congregation in order to stand apart as "holy." This is not a healthy attitude in the Family of God, the *ecclesia* of Jesus Christ. If you sense that you are led of the Lord to befriend your pastor, reach out to explore whether a genuine friendship might develop.

MIND YOUR OWN BUSINESS

Some Christians are overly concerned about what others are thinking or doing. Whether those being observed are non-Christians or Christians, these judgmental saints set themselves up as self-appointed thought guardians and fruit inspectors, attempting to determine whether people's thoughts and behaviors are inspired by the devil or by the Lord Jesus. They make determinations whether such a person is, or is not, a Christian – i.e. whether the person being observed is a genuine Christ-one or just a religious slave deriving from the "father of lies" (Jn. 8:44) and duped by the "angel of light" (II Cor 11:14).

These brethren need to be advised to cease trying to "play Holy Spirit" in the lives of others. It is a role too big for any of us. Self-determinations fueled by zeal and self-righteousness are not going to convince our acquaintances to adopt our faith. Yes, Christians are called upon to "bear one another's burdens" (Gal. 6:2), and to intercede in prayer (I Tim. 2:1) for others. But, we must not become meddlesome, argumentative, and judgmental, thereby falling into the ditch of "believe-right religion" with its demands for doctrinal agreement. We must understand that God loves these people more than we do, and love allows for latitude.

This "must make it right" syndrome is particularly evident among those who began their pilgrimage in the Roman Catholic Church, and then were introduced into a personal relationship with the living Jesus. Zealous that others caught in religion might also find life and freedom in Christ, their surveillance antennae are tuned to confrontation. These hyper-vigilant proctors are usually unaware that when they focus their eyes on the behaviors of other people, they inevitably take their eyes off **JESUS** (Heb. 12:2) and how He is attempting to work in their own lives so they might "grow in the grace and knowledge of the Lord Jesus" (II Pet. 3:18). MYOB – mind your own business!

SEPTEMBER 10

GOD, YOU WON'T BELIEVE WHAT I HAVE DONE!

Some Christians act so shocked when they sin and misrepresent their new identity in Christ. Even more so when they get caught in sin. They often come before God exclaiming, "God, You won't believe what I have done this time." God must chuckle, thinking, "I didn't really expect anything else out of you. I know what you are capable of – nothing of any consequence in My sight. Didn't Jesus say, 'Apart from Me, you can do nothing' (Jn. 15:5)?" The fallacy of fallen humanity is that they humanistically think they can self-generate character and active expression that pleases God, and they refuse to give up on their alleged self-potential.

"Not that we are adequate in ourselves to consider anything as coming from ourselves (*ek autos*), but our adequacy is from God (*ek Theos*)" (II Cor. 3:5). No, our sinful character is not derived from God but from the opposing spirit-source, the diabolic deceiver. "The one who practices sin is of the devil (*ek diabolos*)" (I Jn. 3:8), i.e. derives what he does from the energizing of the Evil One. What the humanist mistakenly believes is generated by himself is really generated by Satan, the character source of all selfishness and sin. Sin and selfishness are not intrinsic to humanity, as many think, but is character derived from the devil.

Humans do not self-generate character of any kind – neither righteousness or sinfulness. Humans are derivative creatures designed to receive from a spirit source, either God or Satan. We cannot save ourselves from our fallen spiritual condition: salvation is "not of ourselves (*ek humon*), it is the gift of God" (Eph. 2:8,9). The power to do as God desires is from God, not of ourselves (*ek humon*)" (II Cor. 4:7). "Yes, but I am a Christ-one; why is the character of selfishness and sinfulness still manifested in my thoughts and behaviors?" Every Christian still retains fleshly patterns of selfishness and sinfulness in the desires of their soul, which must be overcome by the Spirit (Gal. 5:17).

SEPTEMBER 11

"I CAN'T"

Time and again, when one of our children were asked to do something, they would wail, "But, I can't!" There may have been times when they did not feel competent to do what they were being asked, but most of the time it was simply because they were disinclined to do what they were being asked to do. My wife's response was usually, "'Can't' is not an acceptable answer; I would not ask you to do what you are incapable of doing." The same interchange continues as she gives music lessons to young people. When asked to play something, the student says, "I can't." My wife says, "I don't accept 'can't' as an answer."

As Christians, we are God's children. "As many as received Him, He gave the right to become children of God" (Jn. 1:12). "The Spirit testifies with our spirit that we are children of God" (Rom. 8:16). There may be times when we complain that we can't do something because we are disinclined to do what God asks of us. But, when we honestly and seriously come before God and say, "I can't," God is undoubtedly excited that we are admitting our inadequacy, and conversely willing to accept His adequacy. "Not that we are adequate to consider anything as coming from ourselves, but our adequacy is from God" (II Cor. 3:5).

When we come before God and say, "I can't," God must be saying to Himself, "Thank goodness! I never thought you could. In fact, I knew you could not do what only I can do." But when we try to do what only He can do, God is grieved when we are so frustrated in our inability and failing to rest in His peace. When we think we can do something for God, we will never let God do what God wants to do in our life. Oh, the frustration of religious efforts. God rejoices when we come with a repentant heart, saying, "I can't; only You can, and I am willing to let You." Those are words of faith – of our receptivity to His activity. As always, it is not what we do, but what God does!

SEPTEMBER 12

THE LEAP OF FAITH

Soren Kierkegaard may not have coined the phrase, "the leap of faith," but he certainly popularized the concept, and it is often identified with his thought. The meaning of the phrase has received diverse interpretation, but we will be using it as many others have, in reference to the personal conversion of receiving God's grace to become a Christ-one. The "leap of faith" is not like jumping off of a cliff into the unknown in an irrational and absurd manner. Nor is it an act of no return whereby one loses their freedom and right to choose in a punctiliar surrender of absolute total commitment to an ideal or set of beliefs.

Western civilization thinks with the linear logic of Aristotelian objectivism, positing a certitude to their rational conclusions. Kierkegaard suggested a "leap of faith" from such mental rationalism to the subjective relationality of personal interactive love wherein we entrust ourselves to another. It is a "leap" from the deification of our own mental ability and reason, to the acceptance of the deity of God, inclusive of the mystery of infinity beyond finite reasoning. Truth or reality is to be found in the internal subjectivity of reckoning on the God who is love (I Jn. 4:8,16). The "leap" is a choice to function counterintuitively and overcome the objective doubt based on sterile logic.

A human being is more than just a mind operating with objectivity; we are also created with internal heart that enlarges human function with subjectivity. Reality must be considered with both. To become a Christ-one is not a rejection of reason; it is simply the willingness to go beyond the limits of reason in order to know God in Christ in genuine relationship. The "leap of faith" frees reason from the presumptuousness of exclusive certainty, recognizing that the absence of subjective faith is not reasoned certainty of knowledge, but questioning, confusion and despair concerning what reason cannot understand.

SEPTEMBER 13

WHEN YOU BECAME A CHRISTIAN

Let's take a moment for personal reflection concerning when you became a Christian. Some think it important to know the date, time and place of one's conversion. Many times, however, we cannot recollect when we commenced a relationship with another person. Some testify of an emotionally moving or ecstatic experience associated with their conversion, while others indicate that they just slipped into a new relationship with Jesus apart from any bells, whistles, or external accompaniments. What really matters is the spiritual reality of the Spirit of Christ coming to indwell and function in the spirit of an individual.

Those who experienced a conversion in the context of the institutional church likely recall a connection with baptism, eucharist or church membership. Others came to relationship with Jesus in nature or in a quiet place, just between them and God. Some reached out to God in the midst of desperation. There are some who might say, "I don't know when or if I had a conversion experience; it just seems that I have been a Christian all my life." Could it be that a person is a Christian and doesn't know it? They may question such because they do not seem to meet the prescribed criteria that some regard as necessary.

Personally, I gave mental assent to the Jesus of history when I was a young boy of twelve, but it wasn't until I was twenty-seven that I subjectively accepted the Spirit of Christ to live in my spirit (Rom. 8:9,16). There are those who consider themselves Christians because they have always participated in the church, but they may simply be nominal Christians, in name only, and not experiencing the full spiritual reality of the Christ-life. There are some who have tragic misconceptions that hinder them from becoming a Christian, thinking that they need to be more perfect, or that they must have total commitment without mental reservation. Not so! Jesus wants to know you just as you are!

SEPTEMBER 14

GOD IS SEEKING F. A. T. CHRISTIANS

An initial response to the title of this reading might be, "Well, He sure has plenty to pick from." It is not our objective, however, to consider the physical girth of contemporary Christian persons, but to employ the word "FAT" as an acrostic to represent the characteristics of being **F**aithful, **A**vailable and **T**eachable.

Faithful – "As you received Christ Jesus (by faith), so walk in Him (by faith)" (Col. 2:6). A regular and consistent pattern of such receptivity to Christ's activity will develop a settled disposition of faithfulness. Those who are faithful are those who persevere (abide under the difficulties), endure and "stay put" in a pattern of constancy and trustworthiness. Such steadfast fidelity and dependability will lead to the Lord's commendation, "Well done, good and faithful servant. You have been faithful over a little; I will set you over much" (Matt. 25:21).

Available – A faithful person will be an available person. It is not ability that God is looking for, but availability to His ability. God has a plan; He seeks Christian persons who are yielded to Him and open to His grace action; Christians who will respond like Isaiah, "Here am I Lord, use me" (Isa. 6:8). Christians are to be servants who are willing to be there when God calls, willing to be used of God, and available to be the vessels of God's expression.

Teachable – There are plenty of haughty Christians who have convinced themselves that they know all that God wants them to know, that they have God and His ways all figured out. The "ways of God are past finding out" (Rom. 11:33), for the divine mystery cannot be comprehended with finite human reason. The objective is not correct systematizing of the fundamental biblical and doctrinal opinions, but the willingness to be disciples who are learners and followers of **JESUS**. Part of that process will be to "listen under" the instruction of God in prayer.

SEPTEMBER 15

"O YE OF LITTLE FAITH"

Despite the perfect faithfulness of God day after day in our past lives, there is still the human tendency to question or doubt that God will continue to do as He promised in the future. "He who promised is faithful" (Heb. 10:23). With 20/20 hindsight, we recognize God has been at work and His grace has always been sufficient, but our foresight of faith is often weak and faltering. We often have a degree of fear and angst concerning God's continued faithfulness in our lives in the future. Why are we so skeptical that God will continue to be the faithful God that He has proven Himself to be time and time again in our lives?

On several occasions when Jesus was training His disciples, He used the phrase, "O ye of little faith!" In the boat when a storm came up on the Sea of Galilee, the disciples panicked. Jesus said, "Why are you afraid, you men of little faith?" (Matt. 6:26). Peter walked on water, but turned his attention to the wind and the waves, and cried for help. Jesus said, "Ye of little faith; why did you doubt?" (Matt. 14:31). On the far side of the sea, faced with a hungry crowd, the disciples were discussing their options. Jesus said, "You men of little faith; do you not remember the loaves and the fishes, and how all was provided?" (Matt. 16:8).

Our senses often tell us the seen situation is too overwhelming; the waves are too high; the task is too large. The tempter introduces skeptical thoughts that God is impotent, unaware, unloving and unfaithful. Not only is the devil the "accuser of the brethren" (Rev. 12:10), he is also the accuser of God before the brethren, attempting to cause us to doubt God. We must "fix our eyes on Jesus" (Heb. 12:2), recognizing the presence and sufficiency of the living Lord Jesus in the midst of the situation. We do so, one step at a time. God is not likely to map out the rest of our life, for then we would trust in the map and not in Jesus. It is always a bit humbling to hear Jesus say, "O ye of little faith!"

SEPTEMBER 16

WEAKNESS – THE NECESSARY QUALIFICATION

God's *modus operandi* is to capitalize on our weaknesses, so that our weakness will highlight His strength. When God called Moses to go to Egypt and confront Pharaoh about letting the Israelites depart, Moses was quick to plead his inadequacy (Exod. 3:13–4:12), and asked God to please send someone else (Exod. 4:13). Moses was very aware of his weaknesses and limitations, but he needed to see that God was not calling him to pull this off in his own strength. He needed to understand that God would be at work through his weakness to do what He, God, wanted to accomplish. Moses just needed to be an available instrument.

In the new covenant, it is the apostle Paul who had to learn the qualification of weakness. He wrote to the Corinthian church, "God has chosen the weak things of the world to shame the things which are strong" (I Cor. 1:27). In his second epistle to the Corinthians, he lists that which "commended him as a servant of God: ...afflictions, hardships, distresses, beatings, imprisonments, tumults, labors, sleeplessness, hunger" (II Cor. 6:4-10). Then he wrote, "Most gladly, I will boast about my weaknesses, so that the power of Christ may dwell in me. Therefore, I am content with weaknesses, with insults, with distresses, with persecutions, with difficulties, for Christ's sake; for when I am weak, then I am strong" (II Cor. 12:9,10).

Personal weakness is the necessary qualification to be used of God. Nothing forces us to depend on God like the desperation that comes from being asked to do what we are incapable of doing apart from God. Then, we begin to recognize that faith is our receptivity to His activity. The ministry resumés of ministry candidates usually record their abilities and accomplishments. Can you imagine what a ministry committee would do if they received a resumé listing the candidate's weaknesses and inabilities, culminating in "My only strength is **JESUS**"?

NEW HEAVEN AND NEW EARTH

Religion always clamors to engage in speculations about the details of that which God has not chosen to reveal. References to "new heavens and a new earth" (cf. Isa. 65:17; 66:22; II Pet. 3:13; and Revelation 21:1) seem to refer to the perfect contextual environment wherein we will experience the life of Jesus forever. We should beware of thinking of geographical or even cosmic locations of placement, and instead approach the metaphorical images of "new heavens and new earth" as ontological realities picturing the presence of the risen **JESUS**. The "new heaven and new earth" will be the new environmental context wherein we eternally enjoy the life of the living Lord Jesus in our imperishable (I Cor. 15:42,52), immortal (I Cor. 15:53,54), spiritual (I Cor. 15:44), heavenly (I Cor. 15:39,40) and glorified (I Cor. 15:43) bodies after our earthly physical bodies pass away. Christians have already been given the "new life" of Christ (Rom. 6:4) when we became "new creatures in Christ" (II Cor. 5:17), and the "new heaven and new earth" are simply the perpetuated extension of His life in a new contextual environment suited to our new embodiment as "citizens of heaven" (Phil. 3:20) after our earthly "house" (II Cor. 5:1) is done away with.

An alternative understanding is found among those who employ the hermeneutic grid of premillennial dispensationalism. They think that the old earth and heaven will be rejuvenated, renovated or refurbished (remade rather than made new) so that Christ will reign on earth in the "renewed heaven and earth," after the one-thousand-year millennium along with the redeemed souls. They misunderstand that the "new" is *kainos* (new in kind or reality), rather than *neos* (new in time).

In order to keep our focus on **JESUS**, it is better to understand the "new heaven and the new earth" in the metaphorical sense of the perfect context of His life for eternity.

SEPTEMBER 18

PRAYER: OPPORTUNITY AND OBEDIENCE

Most Christians I have visited with are not totally satisfied with their prayer life. Why? For the most part, they have not been able to shed the legalistic expectations about prayer that have been hammered into them by their religious training. Just think of the hang-ups that our marital and other close relationships would be plagued with if the strictures of our personal communication were strictly proscribed in the manner that religion has tried to do with prayer: you can only talk to the one you love at certain times, in particular places and positions with acceptable pious words of commencement and conclusion.

Our personal prayer life should not be constricted in a legalistic strait-jacket of stilted posture and constraint. Prayer should be an extremely free interchange of personal communication with the One we love. I think prayer should be similar to the personal conversations a couple engages in as they sit across from one another in the morning conversing over their coffee, or even the intimate talk that a husband and wife have as they snuggle together in bed. Prayer should be an opportunity to share one's heart openly, even whisper "sweet nothings" in God's ear, by repetitive expressions of our love for the divine Lover, and His declarations of love for us.

Prayer should be the opportunity to explore our common-union, the communion of spirit-union (I Cor. 6:17) with our bridegroom, **JESUS** Christ. Older theological writers used to refer to prayer as "intercourse with God," a term that modern writers shy away from. Prayer involves an intimacy of relationship with the Persons of the triune God. It is in prayer that we have an opportunity for obedience, an opportunity to "listen under" the direction and leading of the Spirit of Christ (Rom. 8:14) to ascertain how the Lord, the Bridegroom, desires to take our relationship to ever-greater depths of loving oneness.

THE MOST DANGEROUS THREAT

A zealous Christian young man excitedly asked me one day, "Do you know what is the most dangerous threat to the world today?" Before he could tell me his opinion, I responded, "Yes I do!" Brought up short, he impatiently queried, "What do you think it is? I pointed in the direction behind him and said, "Do you see that steeple of a church building rising up on the hill? I think that is the most dangerous threat to the world today." He was flummoxed, and did not know what to say next. But when he caught his breath, he responded, "No, I think the Muslims are the most dangerous threat to the world today. They must be stopped before they overcome us." In our subsequent conversation, I went on to explain that the church steeple represented the impotent belief-system of Christian religion that was faking out the world of fallen mankind with a sterile message that lacked the life of the living Lord Jesus dwelling within true believers. Being an impressionable young man, having "zeal without knowledge" (Prov. 19:2; Rom. 10:2), he was unable to comprehend what I was saying.

Very few people seem to be able to differentiate and distinguish between the vital dynamic of the living Lord Jesus dwelling as Spirit in the spirits of faithfully receptive persons, and the religious system of what is called "Christianity" that has developed over the centuries using biblical vocabulary but "denying the power" (II Tim. 3:5) of the gospel. It was Soren Kierkegaard, the extremely insightful Danish Christian thinker, who wrote these words, "The established church is far more dangerous to Christianity than any heresy or schism. We play at Christianity. We use all the orthodox Christian terminology – but everything without character. There is something frightful in the fact that the most dangerous thing of all, playing at Christianity, is never included in the list of heresies and schisms." Putting religion in the place of **JESUS** is a dangerous threat.

SEPTEMBER 20

HOLY TROUBLEMAKERS

Where did Christians ever get the idea that God intends for them to "fit in" and be "normal" in the world; that they are to meld into society around them, make no waves, and be, as it were, "invisible saints"? That is not the objective advocated in the new covenant. Christ-ones are not intended to be passive, to "roll over and play dead," or to "put our light under a bushel" (Matt. 5;14-16). Jesus said He came to "set the world on fire" (Lk. 12:39). Early observers explained that Christians had "turned the world upside down" (Acts 17:6). Later reports were that Christians were cannibals (because they were eating the body and blood of Jesus), and lawbreakers (they would not serve as soldiers).

Christians were, and always should be, regarded by the world around them as "holy troublemakers." Christians will always make a ruckus in the world, and cause holy acrimony (even between mother, father – Matt. 10:35,37). Why? Because the *dunamis* of God's grace in Jesus Christ is always counter-intuitive, counter-productive and counter-cultural to the world's ways. When Paul went to Philippi and cast the demons out of the young lady being merchandised, thus shutting down their cash cow, the slave owners were livid. A ruckus ensued that led to Paul and Silas being incarcerated and beaten (cf. Acts 16:16-24).

French Christian sociologist and philosopher, Jacques Ellul, wrote "Christians were never meant to be normal. We have always been *holy troublemakers*; we have always been creators of uncertainty, agents of dissension that is incompatible with the status quo. We do not accept the world as it is, but we insist on the world becoming the way that God wants it to be. And the Kingdom of God is different from the patterns of the world." When the living Lord **JESUS** is active in Christ-ones in antithetical opposition to the world system, they will be regarded as unconventional troublemakers and revolutionaries.

SEPTEMBER 21

HUMAN FREEDOM

Determinism precludes freedom. Human freedom precludes determinism. If something is determined by an outside force or person, then we do not have any freedom in the matter. For example, your human being was determined by the conjugal interaction of your father and mother. You had no choice in the matter of your physical conception or birth. As a human being, you do now, however, have a choice in your continued existence as a human being, as well as a choice in the quality of the existence of your being. Yes, it was determined by the choice of Adam and Eve that you would be physically born spiritually dead and deriving from the selfish and sinful character of Satan, a "sinner" (Rom. 5:19) in spiritual condition and identity. It is not determined, however, that we must remain in such state, and we therefore have the freedom to choose to respond to what God has made available to all mankind in His Son, Jesus Christ.

The apostle Paul explained that he was called to minister to the Gentiles by offering them the choice "to turn from the dominion of Satan to God, and receive forgiveness of sins" (Acts 26:18). Apart from and beyond any diabolic or divine determinism, human beings have the freedom of choice to exchange one spiritual source for the other in spiritual conversion.

But human freedom is not a static punctiliar action. Our freedom is always dynamic, and must be exercised to be maintained. The moment an individual person ceases to exercise their freedom of choice, the forces of determinism will immediately take the opportunity to make that person a slave. Those most precarious to enslavement are those who think they are settled in a state of freedom and cease to exercise their ongoing freedom. The continuing choice of faith is dynamic, and Christians cannot rest on their laurels in "once saved, always saved." "As you received Christ **JESUS** (by faith), so walk in Him (by faith)" (Col. 2:6).

SEPTEMBER 22

CHRISTIAN PRINCIPLES

Many people conceive of Christianity as a compendium of principles – principles pertaining to correct belief or principles pointing to proper behavior. Christianity is not a matter of principles. A "principle" is defined as "a foundational truth on which one builds a system of belief or behavior." As such, it is a human construct of logical thought processes to develop a chain of reasoning. Christianity is not founded on static principles of human thought, but is formed by the dynamic reality of the living Person of Jesus Christ who came as the Son of God incarnate to bring the life of God for the restoration of mankind.

We must eschew all conceptualization of the Christian faith as formed by so-called "Christian principles." When we reduce Christianity to a compendium of principles which can be logically deduced and declared, we allow the gospel to be deformed into theological and philosophical thought-doctrine, or into a legal system of ethics that can allegedly be performed by the exertion of self-effort in moral conformity. Such bastardization of the gospel is in large part the reason why much of the world looks at Christianity today as nothing but another belief-system or moral code they do not seem interested in considering.

The gospel is the "good news" of the revelation of **JESUS** Christ Himself, who by His life, death, resurrection and ascension became the life-giving Spirit (cf. I Cor. 15:45), providing the vital dynamic of divine life to empower humanity to function as God intended. Christ is not a mere principle by which human function is to be shaped and explained. Rather, He is the God-man who by His "finished work" (cf. Jn. 19:30) became the living Lord providing the grace-action of God to all receptive human persons, the dynamic whereby Christians live the Christ-life in the world today. This reality is incomparably different from a sterile philosophy with impotent principles of belief and behavior.

SEPTEMBER 23

THE POWER OF GOD

Despite how we view God's power, the foremost perspective should not be of an absolute and Sovereign Master in control of all that exists, an Almighty God with ultimate authority to judge and determine. The power of God is most clearly evident in the action of God as He self-limits Himself, and puts Himself on our human level. It is the power of an incarnated God, who in the Son "emptied Himself, taking the form of a bond-servant, being made in the likeness of men, and being found in appearance as a man, He humbled Himself by becoming obedient to the point of death, even death on a cross" (Phil. 2:7,8). Yes, it is counter-intuitive, but the power of God is not in forcefulness, but in humility, lowliness, and even weakness.

When we think of a power-based God who implements His will in fiat and by force, we often neglect many of the more distinctive features of God's character. An authoritative power-based God, acting in force and might, is indicative of the god proposed by the religion of Islam (Allah), but does not describe the triune God of the Christian faith that commences with the "God who is love" (I Jn. 4:8,16), who "so loved the world that He gave His only begotten Son" (cf. Jn. 3:16). The power of Love is ultimately more effective than the power of might and strength.

God's power was made perfect in weakness (Heb. 2:9,10). The ultimate display of strength or power through humiliation and weakness is the crucifixion of Jesus Christ. By all the world's standards of evaluation Jesus' death would seem to evidence weakness and failure, but the paradoxical reality of God's ways allowed Him to manifest power in and through the weakness of death – the redemptive death of **JESUS** on the cross, resurrected in power (Rom. 1:4; Phil. 3:10), made available the restoration of God's life to dwell in the spirits of mankind. The power of God continues to be manifested in our weakness (cf. II Cor. 12:8).

SEPTEMBER 24

THE POWER OF THE WORLD

Where does the power of the world come from? What is the source from which all the powers of violence and destruction and death and evil are derived? It is not conceivable that these arise spontaneously "out of nothing," or that such power of evil is intrinsic to humanity at large. Humans are not devils. God created human beings and declared, "It is very good!" (Gen. 1:31). God has revealed there is a source of power antithetical and antagonistic to His power. The Evil One (II Thess. 3:3) is "the ruler of this world" (Jn. 12:31; 16:11), and God has allowed him to have power, the "power of darkness" (Lk. 22:53), the "power of death" (Heb. 2:14), the "power of the Evil One" (I Thess. 5:19).

This diabolic power is invested in all that pertains to the world system around us: Governmental power, political rancor, the biased educational-system, and yes, even (or especially) religious confusion. All of this is derived from and empowered by "the powers and forces of wickedness" (Eph. 6:12), the "power of the enemy" (Lk. 10:19). There is a cosmic spiritual war taking place, and most seem to be oblivious or blinded to what is transpiring. We have been deceived by the Deceiver (II Jn. 1:7) into thinking that the world system is a natural, neutral, and spontaneous expression of well-meaning but misguided people.

When the devil offered Jesus "all the kingdoms of the world" (Matt. 4:8,9), Jesus did not contest his ability to do so. Jesus did not say, "No, you do not have power to make such an offer!" Jesus refused the offer of worldly power because it came with the contingency requirement that He fall down and give worship and give abeyance to Satan (Matt. 4:9). The response of Jesus reveals the real issue: "You shall worship the Lord your God, and bow down to Him only" (Matt. 4:10). The early Christians fully understood that what we call "the State" belonged to the devil, and was empowered by his evil character.

SEPTEMBER 25

INDIFFERENCE

A young man met a young lady, and they seemed to get along quite nicely. There appeared to be those tingly-sparks of sentiment between them. He subsequently proclaimed loud and clear, far and wide, that he was in love, that he had a girlfriend who meant the world to him. But when time and distance briefly separated them, the young man expressed indifference concerning the young lady, as if she did not matter to him. What love is this? Was it a momentary infatuation fueled by temporary emotion, that hardly deserved to be called "love"? Could such sentiment ever result in a relationship of "'til death do us part?"

Let me warn you that I have set the reader up with this speculative scenario. Let's turn the topic at hand from love to faith. Many have proclaimed with utmost zeal the faith and love they have experienced in a newfound relationship with Jesus Christ. But in time, whether brief or lengthy, such persons often make it known, whether in action or verbal expression, that they have lost interest in Jesus. They are indifferent toward Jesus, neither hot nor cold, just ambivalent. The question is again, "What love is this? Does such a person really have faith? Can such an indifferent person truly be identified as a Christ-one?

Indifference reveals the lie to professed love and faith. The apostle John explained, "if a man says, 'I love God,'" and it is not expressed in personal relationship, "he is a liar" (I Jn. 4:20). James, the brother of the Lord Jesus, indicates that professed faith without the outworking of the character of the One who is the object of that faith is useless, dead, and does not qualify as faith (cf. James 2:17-26). If faith be defined as one's "receptivity of the activity of God in Christ **JESUS** by the Spirit," then the absence of the activity of the expression of Christ's character necessarily reveals the illegitimacy of any profession of faith. Love and faith without continuing expression are meaningless.

SEPTEMBER 26

THE SPIRIT IS NOT SPOOKY

People who were raised in church fellowships using the *King James Bible* often have some funny, fuzzy thinking when it comes to the Holy Spirit. Reference to the "Holy Ghost" has produced correlative thoughts of "Casper the Friendly Ghost," as well as questions about "Ghost-busters." One Christian lady tells of her misconceptions about the "Holy Ghost" as a young girl in church. She thought that the Holy Ghost had something to do with Halloween and the receiving of candy. Gifts from Santa Claus at Christmas; eggs from the Easter Bunny at Easter; and candy from the Holy Ghost on Halloween. A sadly mistaken perspective!

The Holy Ghost is not an inexplicable smoky and spooky apparition that may jump out and yell "BOO!" at any moment. It is regrettable that the Greek word *pneuma* (English "spirit") was ever translated "ghost." Jesus explained that "God is Spirit" (Jn. 4:24). Paul indicated that "the Last Adam (Jesus Christ) became life-giving Spirit" (I Cor. 15:45). The Holy Spirit is one of the Persons in the three-in-One Godhead, but all are Holy and all are Spirit. The Holy Spirit in conjunction with the Father and the Son dwells within the Christian (cf. I Cor. 6:19; II Tim. 1:14; Heb. 6:4). "If anyone does not have the Spirit, he is none of His (i.e. not a Christ-one)" (Rom. 8:9). When the Holy Spirit within our spirit "bears witness with our spirit" (Rom. 8:16), we have the witness that we are children of God.

The point that needs to be made is that the Holy Spirit is not just a vague and nebulous (even spooky) divine influence used by God. The Holy Spirit is one of the divine Persons of the Godhead. His Personal Being is evidenced in that He speaks (Acts 8:29; 13:2), teaches (Jn. 24:26); makes decisions (Acts 15:28), can be grieved (Eph. 4:30), and even outraged (Heb. 10:29). The three Persons of the Trinity are distinct as Father, Son, and Holy Spirit, but are united as the One Holy God.

SEPTEMBER 27

THE DEVIL

Have we out-grown the idea of a personal devil? Have we so bought into the Enlightenment model of rationalism that allows only empirical evidence and what makes sense to our minds, that we have adjudged the presence of the "Evil One" to be mere myth? People can laugh all they want about the "antiquated, outmoded" idea of a personal devil, for by such action they only reveal that the Deceiver has spun his web in their mind to "blind the minds of the unbelievers" (II Cor. 4:4), and they are totally unaware that they "are held captive in the snare of the devil, doing his will unbeknownst" (II Tim. 2:26).

We need to give due credit to our Christian brethren from the Pentecostal and Charismatic movements of the Christian community for their emphasis on the ontological reality of a personal devil over the last century. Mention of the devil had become almost a laughingstock in the mainline denominations of the institutional church, and the Spirit-filled brethren clearly testified of their experiential awareness of the activity of the Evil One in the world around them, as well as in the temptation of their own lives. How can a Christian "resist the devil that he might flee from us" (James 4:7), if regarded as a mere fiction?

There is a cosmic conflict occurring between the Absolute, Righteous, Loving God and the antithetical spirit (Eph. 2:2; I Jn. 4:6) of Satan (*satanos* meaning "adversary - Acts 26:18; II Cor. 11:4), who as the "Evil One" (I Thess. 3:3; I Jn. 3:2; 5:18,19), serves as the Enemy (Lk. 10:19; Acts 13:10) and Adversary of God (I Pet. 5:8). We must not allow ourselves to be deceived (Acts 13:10; II Cor. 11:3; Rev. 12:9; 20:2) about the devil's real personal existence and wiles (Eph. 6:11). He is "the accuser of the brethren" (Rev. 12;10), and constantly tempts (Matt. 4:3; I Thess. 3:5) Christ-ones to adopt his evil character. "Greater is He [Jesus] who is in you, than he who is in the world [*the devil*]" (I Jn. 4:4).

SEPTEMBER 28

APOLOGETICS

Apologetics has nothing to do with being apologetic for our Christian faith – not in the sense of being embarrassed or regretful. The classification of "Christian Apologetics" is derived from the Greek word *apologia*, as used by Peter in his first epistle: "Always being ready to make a *defense* to everyone who asks you to give an account for the hope that is in you, with gentleness and reverence" (I Pet. 3:15). Though translated as "defense" or "argument," the Greek word *apologia* is best understood as an "explanation." This is not a call for man-made logical reasonings to "defend" the Christian faith, as if the Christian faith needed to be defended by man. Christianity is not a corpus of history and doctrines needing logical defense, but the dynamic Person and life of the risen and living Lord Jesus.

Never known for understatement or disengagement, the Danish thinker, Soren Kierkegaard, wrote, "He who first invented the notion of defending Christianity is *de facto* Judas #2; he also betrays with a kiss, only his treachery is that of stupidity." The "good news" of Jesus does not need the logical defense of men. The use of apologetics as human defense of Jesus is mindful of Peter's ill-fated attempt to defend Jesus in the garden when the authorities came to arrest Him prior up to His God-ordained crucifixion. "Then Simon Peter having a sword drew it, and smote the high priest's servant, Malchus, and cut off his ear" (Jn. 18:10).

So much for our misguided attempts to bring out our logic-swords to defend Jesus. God in Christ by the Spirit does not need our measly attempts to defend Him. Perhaps the best translation of *apologia* (*apo* = from; *logos* = word) is to "explain" what **JESUS** means to us. We simply share **JESUS**, usually avoiding all the intellectual and philosophical arguments about Jesus, and we share Him with "words from" our heart, explaining how He, the Word, drew us into loving personal relationship with Himself.

SEPTEMBER 29

THE JOY OF GIVING

"Oh no, the preacher is going to be speaking on 'The Stewardship of Giving'." Why do I have such a negative reaction of aversion? Because on every occasion I have heard someone speak on monetary giving in the context of the institutional church, it has been a castigating exhortation to increased performance of working harder by digging deeper to give more in the collection. I do not recall hearing a preacher address the subject of Christian giving from a perspective that incorporates the grace of God, the source of all genuine giving, and the dynamic of the indwelling presence of the Triune God in the spirits of believers.

The essence of being a Christ-one is the indwelling presence of the Spirit of Christ (Rom. 8:9; II Cor. 13:5). That means that the Divine Giver lives within the Christian, and is to be the primary impetus of Christian giving. Christian giving is not determined by percentages of income to calculate a "tithe," nor is it motivated by emotional yanks on one's sympathetic heartstrings. Christian giving is motivated by the inner prompting of God, the Divine Giver, to give what He desires, to whom He desires, when He desires. "God loves a cheerful (Greek *hilaros*) giver" (II Cor. 9:7); we can be hilarious givers when we recognize that it is not what we are doing, but what God is doing through us. God is giving what really belongs to Him, temporarily entrusted to us as trustees, to whom He desires to give it, and it is all to His glory.

Writing to the Corinthian church about Christian giving (II Cor. 8,9), Paul encourages them to excel in "the grace of giving" (II Cor. 8:7). He mentions the word "grace" of God eight times in this excursus on Christian giving. It is only when our Christian giving is motivated by God's "grace of giving" through us that we can begin to experience the "joy of giving" as we enjoy being the conduits of God's grace-giving. With hilarious joy we have the pleasure of observing God's grace operative through our lives.

SEPTEMBER 30

FREE TO LIVE BY GRACE

Religion is built around shame-based, guilt-producing calls to do and perform in accord with certain expectations of behavioral conformity. Such human "works" are 180 degrees opposite of the operational premise of the new covenant gospel of God's grace in Jesus Christ implemented by the power of the Holy Spirit. It's not what we do, but what God has done and is doing that is the basis of genuine Christian thought. Grace is "God in action." Grace is the dynamic power of God's provision to manifest His character, the very life of **JESUS** (II Cor. 4:10,11) within the Christian, to the praise of His own glory (cf. I Cor. 10:31).

"It was for freedom that Christ set us free" (Gal. 5:1). "Christ sets us free from the law" (Rom. 7:3) – "free from the law of sin and of death" (Rom. 8:2). By the provision of Christ's sufficiency of grace, He sets us free from all of the expectations of the human performance of religious laws; all of the "thou shalts" and "thou shalt nots" whereby we are bound to behavioral modification guidelines to produce and effect our own good behavior under the guise that such self-effort constitutes righteousness. By the provision and power of the indwelling **JESUS**, we are free to BE and DO all that God intends for His human creatures.

It is by God's grace in Jesus Christ that Christ-ones are free to manifest His character and activity. We are free to re-present **JESUS** in the world today – not just represent as examples, but allow Jesus to live out His life and character in all that we do. We are free to live by grace, by the impetus and impulse of the direction of the Spirit of Christ, "led by the Spirit" (Rom. 8:14), demonstrating that we are the "children of God." The divine gift of grace in Jesus Christ allows for the restoration of righteousness to mankind by the presence and provision of the grace-life whereby the human race is restored to function as God intended by God functioning in human individuals.

OCTOBER 1

DO GOOD PEOPLE GO TO HEAVEN?

Why is it that Christian people are so concerned whether this person or that person is going to heaven? Is the objective of the Christian life to go to heaven? Or is the objective of the Christian life that a person might know Jesus in vital spiritual union to the extent that the living Christ dwelling within one's spirit becomes that person's life (Col. 1:27)? Jesus did not say, "I came that you might go to heaven." What He did say was, "I came that you might have life, and have it more abundantly" (Jn. 10:10). "I am the resurrection and the life" (Jn. 11:25). Having the spiritual life of **JESUS** is more important than an otherworldly destination.

A relatively new Christian was participating in a Bible study, and he was questioning why Christian people were so keen on making the determination as to whether particular people were going to heaven or hell. The rigid, inflexible either/or attitude that Christians were displaying in his group did not seem to evidence much compassion. He asked the question, "Does someone like the Dali Lama stand any chance of going to heaven in your opinion?" "Oh no, the reply came back. He is not identified as a Christian, and is therefore identified with the devil, and is necessarily going to suffer eternal damnation in hell."

The newcomer was flabbergasted at the judgmentalism that could so quickly and proudly assert that someone whose life was characterized by a global mission of doing good for others would summarily be unsuitable for heaven and condemned to hell. "Do you mean to tell me," he asked the group, "that if any person does not believe in Jesus, and believe the doctrines that you consider to be the essentials of the gospel in the manner that you folks do; that such person is going to hell, and has no chance of going to heaven?" They affirmed that to be their belief. Many honest searchers after God are put-off by narrow, exclusivist attitudes that think they have the ways of God all figured out.

OCTOBER 2

PASCAL'S WAGER

Blaise Pascal was a brilliant French mathematician and philosopher during the seventeenth century (1623-1662). He is credited with several mathematical theorems, as well as being the inventor of one of the first mechanical calculating machines. His Christian faith was sympathetic to the Jansenist movement within the Roman Catholic Church, a rigid Augustinian system of determinism. His most famous Christian work was left unfinished at his death, simply entitled *Pensées*, meaning "thoughts," and it was comprised of fragments of thoughts and pensive considerations pertaining to faith and philosophy.

At the forefront of the arguments in the Jansenist sect was the attempted explanation of God's determinative grace in conjunction with human freedom of choice. This led also to the contrastual juxtapositioning of faith and reason. These themes appear in Pascal's writings, and may have been his own personal struggle to balance his thinking as a mathematician and scientist with his own Christian faith. He wrote, "Faith embraces many truths which seem to contradict each other," but "contradiction is not a sign of falsity." It appears that this was his attempt to explain the reality of dialectic contrasts in Christian thought.

"We know the truth, not only by reason, but also by the heart," Pascal wrote. There is both objective and subjective approaches to truth. He also wrote, "All our reasoning comes down to surrendering to feeling," to what we cannot fully comprehend, but feel nevertheless and know it must be real." One of Pascal's best-known concepts is called "Pascal's wager." He explains, "Belief is a wise wager. Granted that faith cannot be proved, what harm will come to you if you gamble on its truth and it proves false? If you gain, you gain all; if you lose, you lose nothing. Wager, then, without hesitation." Belief in **JESUS** cannot be empirically verified, but you can bet your life on Him.

OCTOBER 3

SHOULD WE "ASK FOR FORGIVENESS"?

It is a very popular concept and phrase in Christian religion, that encourages Christian people to "ask God for forgiveness" of their sins. The question must be asked, "Is that a biblical admonition or suggestion? It will surprise many Christian people to realize that such an admonition is not found in any of the new covenant writings of the New Testament. Can you believe it? Such a phrase of admonition is never found in the Christian writings. The misunderstanding arises from a theological deficiency that fails to grasp that our human action of solicitation or request does not prompt God's action of forgiveness.

This is not to say that there is not an ongoing process of forgiveness in the Christian life, but it is not predicated, prompted or appropriated on the basis of our solicitation for divine forgiveness. God continues to be the forgiving God, but He intentionally purposed to forgive all of mankind's sin in the once-and-for-all act of His Son, **JESUS** Christ, dying for all of the sins of all human beings on the cross, where He exclaimed, "It is finished!" (Jn. 19:30). The redemptive death of **JESUS** satisfied the just consequence of death for all sin, past, present and future. Christians must cease to beg and harangue God for that which he has already fully done in the death of His Son. To do so is to deny the efficacy of Jesus' substitutionary death.

Yes, Christians continue to misrepresent who they are "in Christ" by sinful expression (cf. I Jn. 1:8), and we are "to confess our sins" to God (I Jn. 1:9) and "to one another" (James 5:16), but confess (Greek *homologeo* means "to say the same thing" as God about our sins; to call sin "sin"). "To confess" is not the same, nor does it imply, "asking for forgiveness." We appropriate God's forgiveness that is given through the death of **JESUS** by simply recalling the cross and saying, "Thank you, Lord!" That will likely be a repetitive process until we die, or until Jesus returns.

OCTOBER 4

DEALING WITH PERSONAL REJECTION

The community of mankind was designed to be a community of love and acceptance, manifesting the character of God in His human creatures as people took the time to get to know one another and interact by encouraging one another. When the first couple rejected deriving loving acceptance from the Triune God in the garden, instead of becoming independent (the Lie), they inevitably began to derive character from the Evil One. Satan's character of sin and selfishness is always a socially rejective character because when our focus is on ourselves, we reject others in order to address our own wants.

The social interaction of fallen humanity is rampant with personal rejection. Interpersonal rejection is so pervasive in the fallen world that a genuine community of love seems for many to be idealistic and surreal. We have all been rejected in one way or another, in multiple ways. The pop-psychological explanation is that we have all been part of dysfunctional families and a dysfunctional society. So much so, that it might be said that what I am writing here is "just one reject addressing a bunch of rejects." The universality of sinful personal rejection is something that every human person is acquainted with today.

Some persons have been severely wounded by personal rejection in their lives. This often occurs in families, in both parental rejection of children (especially fathers), and adult children's rejection of their parents. Fathers often exasperate their children (Eph. 6:4), and children fail to honor their father and mother (Exod. 20:12). Such rejection is both hurtful and causes long-term damage. Satan is the diabolic destroyer of families and friendship, and one of his foremost techniques is personal rejection. "My father and mother may abandon me, but the Lord will take me up" (Ps. 27:10-*GNT*). **JESUS**, the essence of God's love, counters and overcomes the rejection of Satan.

OCTOBER 5

FULFILLMENT THEOLOGY

I received a long-distance call from a foreign country. It was the rabbi I had met and become acquainted earlier in the year soon after he had visited the United States to attend the President's Prayer Breakfast with a pastor he had befriended from his home country. While in Washington D.C., he took the opportunity to go to the Holocaust Museum. There, he took his time to view the exhibits, and was so moved that as he exited the facility he dropped to his knees and sobbed, "The Christians didn't do it to us!" Throughout his upbringing and rabbinic studies, he was told that the Christians were responsible for Jewish persecution, including the Holocaust. The outcome of this traumatic revelation in contrast to all of his religious training, was that the Jewish rabbi received Jesus as the Messiah, and received the living Lord Jesus into his spirit as his personal Lord and Savior. It was a costly decision, for he lost his career and position as a rabbi, and his wife and children repudiated him.

He was calling me to inquire whether it was part of historic and traditional Christian teaching to assert the validity of "replacement theology," or "supercessionism." The rabbi interpreted such thinking to mean that God had rejected, repudiated, and replaced the Jewish race and religion *en masse* because of their rejection of the Messiah and participation in the crucifixion of Jesus, thereby allowing for and justifying the antisemitism that has been a blight on human relations for centuries. Such an understanding was abhorrent to the rabbi, for he was and would remain a Jewish person for his entire life. I advised him that such an interpretation was not a valid part of orthodox Christian thought, and he would be better served to think in terms of "fulfillment theology" with the recognition that **JESUS** had fulfilled all the promises of the old covenant, and was indeed the Messiah promised to the Jewish people and all mankind – the Son of God, the Savior for all men.

OCTOBER 6

THE STORY OF A SOUL

The Story of a Soul is the title of a brief autobiography written by Thérèse of Lisieux, combining three smaller documents written between 1895-1897. She suffered a painful death from tuberculosis in 1897 at the age of 24 years. She had joined the Carmelite order at age 15, to join her sisters who had previously joined. Thérèse was nicknamed "the Little Flower of Jesus." She made a powerful impact by her simple practical spirituality during her brief life. The process for her canonization began in 1914, and she was recognized as a Saint by The Roman Catholic Church in 1925. Together with St. Francis of Assisi, she is one of the most popular saints in the history of the church. The Basilica of St. Thérèse in Lisieux, France has become a center for pilgrims from around the world, second only to Lourdes.

Thérèse was a young lady of deep prayer. She commented, "Prayer is an aspiration of the heart, it is a simple glance directed to heaven, it is a cry of gratitude and love in the midst of trial as well as joy; finally, it is a supernatural experience which expands my soul and unites me to Jesus." In her constant communion with God, Thérèse learned to live spontaneously in the moment, explaining" If I did not live from one moment to another, it would be impossible for me to be patient. But when I only look at the present, I forget the past, and I take care not to forestall the future." In the quietude of the convent, Thérèse appreciated the writings of St. John of the Cross and Thomas à Kempis, but explained that she best loved the New Testament gospels because she could focus on **JESUS**. The short and simple autobiography of Thérèse of Lisieux draws the reader into her personal humility and simple spirituality. Appropriately entitled, it is the *Story of a Soul* possessed with a sweet spirit, lovingly united with the Spirit of the living Lord **JESUS**. On one occasion, she wrote ""I have at last found my vocation; it is love." Many have sensed her love in reading Thérèse's autobiography.

OCTOBER 7

THE USEFULNESS OF USELESSNESS

The life of the living Lord Jesus lived out in the Christ-one (Christian) will inevitably be counter-productive to the productivity objectives of the world. Jesus told a parable about a servant who recognized he was under obligation to his master and did not expect to be treated like a king. He served his master, and summarized his action, "We are useless slaves; we have done only that which we ought to have done" (cf. Lk. 17:7-10). No time off. No award banquets. The slaves knew their proper place and their expected service, and the slave's comment was a self-diagnosis of accepted placement, available for the master's use.

Christians are bond-slaves of Jesus Christ, intended to be receptive and available to the Lord for whatever purposes He desires to utilize them to express His life and character. It is not our place to tout our usefulness, but to recognize our proper place of humble uselessness as servants for the Master's use. When asked to serve in whatever way the Master desires, our dutiful response should be, "Yes, Lord, whatever you say!" If we are going to be useful to Christ's purposes of what He desires to be and do in us, we must come to a recognition of the "usefulness of uselessness" wherein we are available to the Lord.

The flipside of this relationship is the awareness of "the uselessness of usefulness." All we think we can do for the Lord; all of our self-affirmed productivity and "works" is useless for God's purposes – just "wood, hay and stubble" (I Cor. 3:12). If God is not doing it, it is not worth doing. Christian life and ministry are what God does, not what we do. Jesus told His disciples, "Apart from Me, you can do nothing" (Jn. 15:5). The Christian servant has an added dimension, recognizing that any useful endeavors are empowered by the God's own grace-dynamic. Paul declared, "I do not presume to speak of anything except what Christ has accomplished through me" (Rom. 15:18).

OCTOBER 8

ABORTION WOUNDED HEARTS

"My body, my choice" has been the mantra of the "pro-choice" lobby encouraging young mothers to abort their unborn children for their own convenience. The young women who listen to and act upon this self-centered cultural advice of the world seldom have any real awareness that their "choices have consequences," and the severity of those choices. The psychological community has been forced to admit the mental and emotional scars often leading to long-term personality disorders in those who have experienced the unnatural extrication of a preborn child. They have noted that the adverse effects of an abortion are similar to "post-traumatic stress disorder," like that suffered by military veterans after involvement in the atrocities of warfare.

The internal personal affects in those who have chosen abortion include denial, grief, guilt, shame, self-condemnation, depression, obsessive thoughts, and even suicidal ideas (to name just a few). These can lead over time to self-hatred, loneliness, helplessness, sadness, accusing voices, difficulty concentrating, sleep disorders, anxiety attacks, relationship problems, and attempts to escape in drug use and alcoholism. Those who have chosen abortion often end up seeking treatment for mental health issues. In addition, one must add the spiritual heartbreak of thinking God rejects them and does not love or forgive them

Abortion is sin, but not the unforgivable sin. "We have all sinned, and come short of the glory of God" (Rom. 3:23). The sin-source and death-dealer (Heb. 2:14) temporarily tempts us to sin. The Spirit of God is ever ready to draw us to Himself in love, forgiveness of sin, and intimate relationship. Christians, as a whole, must realize the immense mission field of ministry to the 60 million ladies (young and old), in the United States alone, who have made the choice to take the life of their child while still in the womb. We extend the LOVE-LIFE of **JESUS**, the Son of God.

OCTOBER 9

THE ROOT OF BITTERNESS

The Mother Goose nursery rhyme begins: "Mary, Mary, quite contrary, how does your garden grow?" She might have answered, "With weeds aplenty having bitter roots, producing gall, I let no one know." Paul's comment about the "root of bitterness" in Heb. 12:15 brings to mind the concept of a pernicious weed, the poisonous root of which begins to grow like a cancer in our heart. We have all experienced bitterness growing in our emotional garden. Living in Satan's rejective world-system, we have all been wronged, slighted, mistreated, hurt, and rejected. We feel sorry for ourselves. Bitterness is inevitably a self-concern, a character and attitude implanted by Satan.

What kinds of bitterness have we harbored in our garden? Ponder for a moment what persons or situations periodically arise in your mind and emotions, even in your dreams, wherein you "replay the tape" of being hurt. The "root of bitterness" produces the long-term fruit of grudging resentment and moody hypersensitivity, as well as continuing self-justification. Paul notes the weed cluster, "Let bitterness, wrath, anger, clamor, and slander be put away, along with all malice" (Eph. 4:31). Peter refers to "the gall of bitterness and the bondage of iniquity" (Acts 8:23). Hatefulness and holiness are incompatible (Heb. 12:14).

If anyone might have responded with bitterness it could have been Jesus. In the midst of rejection and injustice that led to death, He was "like a silent lamb led to slaughter" (Acts 8:32). His reply, "Father forgive them, they know not what they do" (Lk. 23:34). That same living Lord Jesus, risen and serving as the life-giving Spirit (I Cor. 15:45), now lives in us as Christ-ones. **JESUS** Christ, the divine Forgiver lives in us. The only antidote to bitterness is to live in the GRACE provision of God in **JESUS** Christ, manifesting His life and character of acceptance. "See to it that no one fails to obtain the grace of God" (Heb. 12:14).

OCTOBER 10

INDIVIDUAL HUMAN BEINGS

God relates to man by means of individual human beings. Having created human beings as choosing creatures with individual freedom of choice, God desires to engage in a faith-love relationship with human individuals, a personal relationship between divine Being and a human being. Such a Person-to-person relationship must be freely chosen by a human being, without any coercion or imposition from the Greater Being, else it becomes a mechanical relationship. The human individual must be willingly receptive, by faith, to the relational presence and active function of the Personal triune God, willing to derive all being and action from God in Christ by the Spirit.

In the impersonal and mechanical relations wherein mankind is deriving and drawing from the antithetical spirit-source of Satan, we observe a contrary *modus operandi*, a sweeping inclusion to deal with humanity-at-large, *en masse*, as a collective or corporate group. It is declared, for example, that "in Adam all die" (I Cor. 15:22), a universal imposition of spiritual death brought about by "the one having the power of death, that is the devil" (Heb. 2:14), energizing within fallen humanity as "the spirit that works within the sons of disobedience" (Eph. 2:2). The remainder of the declaration states, "In Christ all will be made alive" (I Cor. 15:22). The caveat, the proviso of differentiation that must be noted, is that God's grace activity to restore all individual human beings "in union with Christ" is not a wholesale imposition of inclusion, but is predicated on a freely chosen receptivity whereby an individual human being chooses to receive **JESUS** by faith, to be spiritually united with Him (cf. I Cor. 6:17), and to function by means of His life (cf. Jn. 14:6; I Jn. 5:12). Beware the theology that would declare that there is an at-large and arbitrary determination of imposing God's action in Christ on mankind (whether to a limited or comprehensive designated collective of "elect") without individual consent and reception.

OCTOBER 11

PASTORS PROMOTE ABORTION

Most Christians believe that taking the life of an unborn child in the gruesome process of abortion is a sin, contrary to the character of the living God. Most pastors consider it their responsibility to expose and preach against sin of every kind, but why are the overwhelming majority of pastors so silent about the sin of abortion? Are they fearful of violating the world's standard of "political correctness?" Are they concerned that it will cause the thirty percent of the women in their congregation who have had abortions to be uncomfortable? The silence of the leaders in the churches concerning abortion has indirectly condoned and promoted abortion among Christians.

How so? The contemporary Western Church has been hesitant and squeamish about addressing the subject of sexuality as a whole, often treating this important facet of human experience as a taboo subject to be kept under wraps in a code of silence. Everyone in our culture is quite aware of the "in your face" prevalence of sexual emphasis and stimulation. When the church fails to explain how Jesus relates to the totality of life, inclusive of sexuality, we subtly enhance the curiosity of young people about the forbidden subject, and our silence promotes exploration, and then we hypocritically chastise with "tsk, tsk!"

Pastors and churches must clearly state how they will express love and compassion toward young ladies who get pregnant. It's not enough to simply explain our stance toward abortion and the killing of unborn babies. We must also have a clearly stated church policy of how we will express love and compassion to pregnant women, and assist them in their plight. Failing to do so, we indirectly promote abortion by our silence, and many Christian ladies will continue to choose abortion to terminate their pregnancies because they are unsure that the church will receive them and their child with the love of **JESUS**.

OCTOBER 12

SEXUAL SIN

Sexual sins seem to be particularly pervasive as they stubbornly lodge in our conscious or subconscious minds. Despite the levels of purity or impurity in our sexual thoughts and actions of the past, seldom does an individual not carry some baggage concerning sexual indiscretions. We might ask whether God is as concerned about such as many Christians seem to be. In the poignant story of Hosea (whose name means "salvation"), the sixth century B.C. prophet married Gomer who proved to be unfaithful, just as God had promised, for the storyline was to be an analogy of the unfaithfulness of God's people.

The real story is about a compassionate and loving God, who despite an unfaithful spouse who prostituted herself with other lovers, continued to love and forgive her even to the extent of buying her back (redemption) out of the illicit sex trade to be His "beloved" wife once again. Finding her naked, forsaken, and enslaved in a bed of impurity and lewdness, Hosea spoke tenderly to her, persuading her to come home and be his wife again. When cleansed with redemptive love and forgiveness, the adulteress wife was once again regarded as pure and virginal as the renewed bride of Hosea.

When our sins (sexual and otherwise) are cleansed in the blood of the Lamb (cf. Rev. 7:14; 12:11), we are "new creatures in Christ; old has passed away, all has become new" (II Cor. 5:17). Paul explained to the Corinthians, "You were washed, you were sanctified, you were justified in the name of the Lord Jesus Christ and by the Spirit of our God" (I Cor. 6:11). The "new man" (Eph. 4:24; Col. 3:10) is righteous, perfect, pure and virginal, made new by the presence of the Spirit of Christ (Rom. 8:9). The "spirit of promiscuity" (Hosea 4:12; 5:4) can be overcome by the redemption of **JESUS** Christ and the continuing restoration and sufficiency of the grace of God.

OCTOBER 13

KNOWING THE WILL OF GOD?

Christian people have gone through all kinds of machinations in their attempts to ascertain and discern the "will of God." Some seem to think that finding the will of God is somewhat like trying to find a needle in a haystack, or searching through a maze to find the hidden object. This perspective identifies the "will of God" as an entity that is detached and separated from how God has revealed Himself in the new covenant. God has revealed Himself in the Son, Jesus Christ, and everything about God is to be seen in and through Jesus. Jesus is the love of God, the salvation of God, the will of God for every situation.

The will of God is **JESUS**. Knowing the "will of God" is much more than "knowing about" a projected direction to pursue in life, or about the selection of a particular object to be used in our lives. Whatever the object, whatever the direction, God desires and wills that the life and character of the living Lord Jesus be operative and exhibited in every action of our Christian lives. The "will of God" should be perceived not merely as *informational* details, but as personal, *relational* "knowing" of Jesus in deep spiritual oneness and intimacy, whereby we spontaneously allow Jesus who has "become our life" to function in and through us to express God's character in everything we do.

The "will of God" is always that **JESUS** be lived out in every situation of our lives. Should I buy that car? Should I take that new job? Should I marry that person? "My sheep hear My voice" (Jn. 10:27), Jesus said. The Christian who "listens under" the voice of Christ within, obediently desiring to know how God in Christ by the Spirit wants to function in his/her life, will ascertain and know the "will of God" in Jesus, and can thus freely choose to implement the various options of behavior that will allow the character of **JESUS** to be "manifested in our bodily behavior" (II Cor. 4:10,11) to the glory of the triune God.

OCTOBER 14

CHRISTIAN MARRIAGE

When two cats have their tails tied together, and they are hanging over a clothesline wire, it can be said that they are "married," i.e. joined. But you can be sure that they are not happy about the situation, and are attempting to claw each other's guts out. That is not the picture of marriage that God intended for a man and a woman. There is much more to marriage than two "cats" getting their tails tied together. The marriage union that God intends for Christians within the new covenant arrangement, wherein the living Lord Jesus indwells both a husband and a wife, is a deep spiritual union like no other relationship on earth.

It can only be called "Christian marriage" when the living Lord Jesus is operative as Lord in both partners, thus creating a spiritual relationship of oneness. Two persons, a man and a woman, in whom the Spirit of Christ lives and functions and draws into unity with one another and with the triune God. The "two become one," not essentially (for he is still he, and she is still she), but relationally in a single unit of spiritual oneness. A "mystery" indeed (Eph. 5:32), revealed only by the presence of Jesus and His divine love that always gives sacrificially for the highest good of the other without self-concern.

The "one spirit" union of Christian marriage can only be effected in a man and a woman who have experienced the "one spirit" union wherein their spirits are "joined to the Lord Jesus" (I Cor. 6:17) as Christ-ones. This internal spiritual union necessarily disallows as absolutely incongruous any external sexual intimacy with another other than one's spouse, for such would create an inner connection that boomerangs in lethal consequences (I Cor. 6:15-18). In "one spirit" union with Christ and with one another, the participants in a "Christian marriage" become a conjugal temple of the Holy Spirit (I Cor. 6:19), whereby they together manifest union as no other relationship on earth can do.

OCTOBER 15

THE QUESTION OF SOURCE

Billy Preston wrote and recorded a song that became a #1 *Billboard* hit in October, 1974. It began with the words, "Nothin from nothin leaves nothin." Billy Preston was not a philosopher, but the words of the song lead us to a consideration of the source of all things. Some of the foundational questions of speculative philosophy are ""Where did this thing, or being, come from? How did it come into being? What is its origin or source? Everything should be traced back to its source of derivation, for nothing comes into being via a spontaneous "puuuf," and nothing functions without an originating and sustaining energy source."

In the Greek New Testament scriptures, the issue of "source" is conveyed by the preposition *ek*, meaning "out of," which pertains to source, origin or derivation. Despite the age-old theological argument that the world was created *ex nihilo*, "out of nothing," a more biblical explanation is that all things find their created origin and source *ek Theos*, "out of God." I Cor. 8:6 refers to "one God, the Father, out of (*ek*) whom are all things." The Amplified and Passion translations refer to "the one God who is the Source of all things." II Cor. 3:5 states, "not that we are adequate to consider anything as coming out of (*ek auton*) ourselves, but our adequacy is (*ek Theos*) out of God" (derived from God).

Everything in the created order, and everything in the new creation order of the new covenant, has a source from which it derives its existence and function. Without such etiological consideration of originating source, we end up with the absurdities of self-generative perpetual motion, purposeless existential vacuum, and teleological nihilism. The source of the Christian life is derived from the regenerative presence of the living Lord Jesus dwelling in the spirit of a Christ-one, and the functional out-living of the Christ-life as God provides everything necessary by His grace to manifest His divine life.

OCTOBER 16

DIY CHRISTIANITY – AN OXYMORON

"Do it yourself" (D.I.Y.) endeavors became popular in the twentieth century, when individuals chose to build, modify or repair their homes or equipment without relying on the expertise of professionals in the field. Particularly prevalent in the area of home improvement, the DIY emphasis was popularized in television programs, and spread even more rapidly after the introduction of the internet and such websites as diynetwork.com. The proliferation of YouTube videos showing step-by-step how-to instructions to accomplish almost any task imaginable has continued to fuel the DIY movement.

But to refer to "DIY Christianity" is to create an oxymoronic phrase using incongruous or self-contradictory terms. Christianity, by definition, implies the life and action of the living Lord Jesus. "Do it yourself" self-effort is inconsistent and contrary to the grace-dynamic of God in Christ which is the essence of Christianity, *sola gratia*. Such incongruity has been repeatedly misunderstood throughout the history of Christian religion. The trademark of all religion is to focus on the "works" of human performance by which mankind seeks to please and appease God, and earn meritorious credit toward future benefits.

Only Christ can live the Christ-life. Only as the living Lord Jesus Christ, by the Spirit (I Cor. 15:45) lives within the Christian and is allowed to function by the receptive faith of the believer will the Christian life be manifested via the "fruit of the Spirit" (Gal. 5:22,23). It's not what we Christians think we can do for the Lord, nor is the Christian life to be conceived as a "fixer-upper" project. Everything that we think and attempt to accomplish by our own "works" for advancement in our Christian lives amounts to nothing more than superfluous "wood, hay and stubble" (I Cor. 3:12) or "rubbish" (Phil. 3:8). DIY Christianity is a contradiction in terms – only **JESUS** lives the Christ life.

UNDERSTANDING THE SCRIPTURES

The scriptures (Greek *scriptura*, meaning "writings") were inspired by the Holy Spirit (II Tim. 3:15,16) and providentially preserved through the centuries by means of repetitive copying and translation into our native languages. Scripture is not an end in itself, but an objective means of conveying truth statements, which by the agency of the Holy Spirit can speak to our inner spiritual being. It is possible to read the words of the scriptures and have no understanding of their meaning (cf. Matt. 22:29). Philip asked the Ethiopian eunuch, "Do you understand what you are reading?" (Acts 8:30). He did not understand, because "the natural man does not understand spiritual things" (I Cor. 2:14). The "eyes of one's heart must be enlightened" (Eph. 1:18) by the Holy Spirit. Jesus had to "open the minds" of His disciples "so they could understand the scriptures" (Lk. 24:45). Without such personal revelation, reading the scriptures is like reading someone else's mail. It is the only book in the world that requires the reader to know the author in order to understand the book.

The purpose of understanding the scriptures is that we might more intimately know **JESUS** (Jn. 5:39), and understand the spiritual realities of God in Christ (I Cor. 2:12,13). As we do so, we are encouraged to persevere and have hope (Rom. 15:4), and progress in our "obedience of faith" (Rom. 16:26). We must not deify the scriptures or equate them with the living Lord Jesus. Christianity is not a book-religion; it is the dynamic grace-provision of the living Lord **JESUS**, and His reception by faith in the lives of Christ-ones. It is imperative that we recognize the difference between the personified Word of God, the living Lord Jesus (Jn. 1:1,14), and the secondary use of the written "word of God" in the scriptures. We should not diminish or deprecate the scriptures in any way, but neither do we want to deify the scriptures or allow the scriptures to displace the reverence that is due to **JESUS** Christ alone.

OCTOBER 18

I CORINTHIANS 13 – FOR TEACHERS

If I teach with the best educational techniques, and provide stimulating and motivational lessons, but have not love,
I am but a time-wasting information processor.

If I spend hours preparing my lesson plans with the clearest instructional objectives, but have not love,
I am just an over-organized ideologue.

If I utilize the most eye-catching visual aids and the latest classroom technology, but have not love,
I am just a high-tech visionary.

A loving teacher is kind and patient with every student,
regards each student as an important individual,
and treats their personal problems with confidence.

A teacher's love is not condescending, does not play favorites,
does not gossip, does not publicly humiliate, is not easily agitated
or discouraged, and does not give-up on misbehaving students.

A teacher's love bears the responsibility of instruction,
Believes that students' minds should not be wasted,
Hopes that every student will achieve their potential,
and endures all disturbances in the process.

The latest textbooks will soon be out-of-date.
Contemporary teaching methods will become outmoded.
Educational technology is obsolete before we know it,
but a loving teacher can affect a student's life forever.

Now abideth preparation, instruction, and love, but the greatest of these is a teacher's love for the students.

OCTOBER 19

"MADE FOR ANOTHER WORLD"

Clive Staples (C.S.) Lewis wrote, "If I find in myself a desire which no experience in this world can satisfy, the most probable explanation is that I was made for another world." We must first question the legitimacy of the argument Lewis is making. He seems to be setting up an argument for life beyond this life in an eternal dimension or context. Logically, this seems to be an *aposteriori* argument commencing with an observation on which one draws a theory or conclusion. Psychologically, this appears to be an argument from "felt need" to necessary fulfillment, and it must be noted that "felt needs" are notoriously questionable.

Whether the basis of the argument is valid or not, the statement does serve the purpose of causing people to consider a realm beyond the natural (and even rational) parameters of mere scientific thought. Lewis' comment suggests that human beings should consider a dimension beyond the physical and temporal, since metaphysical ponderings of the spiritual and eternal realm are obviously conceivable to the human mind.

Simultaneous with the suggestion of our being "made for another world," we must remember that humans were made for this world. We are human creatures made for physical existence and life on planet earth, but we are physical, human creatures with spiritual capacity and the opportunity for eternal participation in **JESUS**. While we may be "made for another world" eventually, our present calling is to live in this world as "strangers and aliens" (I Pet. 2:11), "citizens of heaven" (Phil. 3:20), functioning "in the world but not of this world" (Jn. 17:11,14). As Christians, believing as we do in an existence and life beyond this life, we must be cognizant of both the physical and spiritual realms of our existence, not becoming overly worldly-minded and engaged in the matters of this world, but not becoming "so heavenly-minded, that we are of no earthly good."

OCTOBER 20

SHARING THE GOSPEL

There was a time in my life when I tried my hand at direct sales. I was selling both insurance and real estate. I enjoyed visiting with people, but could not engage in any coercion to pressure someone to buy what I was selling. The broker I was working for kept harping, "you're here to sell, not tell." My comeback was, "I am a teacher; I am here to tell people about the product, and if the product doesn't sell itself as necessary or desirable to a person's life, then I am willing to respect the choice the prospective buyer has made." The broker was beyond frustrated, and needless to say, my career in sales was short-lived.

My approach to sharing the gospel corresponds to my philosophy of sales. I refuse to engage in the high-pressure coercion of trying to push Jesus down the throat of an unsuspecting victim. I abhor and am appalled at the aggressive so-called "evangelism" that many fundamentalists employ. I have likened their techniques to criminal assault and rape. When dealing with people who are God's creatures, having freedom of choice, we must build relational bridges and treat each person with respect, not using them as an ego-building stepping-stone of success that is self-justified as serving their eternal good.

The gospel is relational from start to finish, commencing with the eternal loving community of the triune God, who has graciously chosen to invite us to participate in that community. I have no impersonal agenda to capture a person and make a "convert," nor will I attempt to use a person for my own ends – that is not love. If the genuine love of **JESUS** does not captivate a person as something desirable and necessary for their lives, then they are free to keep searching. But if a person is interested in what makes my life different from others, I am quite willing to share that **JESUS** Christ is the essence of my life, willing to make an *apologia* for the hope that is in me (I Pet. 3:15).

OCTOBER 21

THE TWIN TOWERS

Many who see such a reference to "the twin towers," first think of the twin towers of the Financial Trade Center in New York City that were destroyed when planes were deliberately flown into the towers on September 11, 2001. That senseless tragedy might be countered by the "twin towers" of Christian fellowship that Paul refers to when he writes, "speaking the **truth** in **love**, we are to grow up in all aspects into Him who is the head, even Christ" (Eph. 4:15). Truth without love can be cold and calculating without any heart. Love without the stability of truth can be ooey-gooey, sentimental mush that has no backbone.

The twin towers of essential Christian fellowship involve **truth** and **love**. When we think of "truth" we often think of truth propositions, the formulation and content of Christian doctrinal teaching and instruction. There are some Christians who are so focused on cerebral assent to accurate theology that they fail to understand the personal and relational interaction of love in the Body of Christ. Paul writes, "The goal of our instruction (*of **truth***) is **love** from a pure heart and a good conscience and a sincere faith" (I Tim. 1:5). The personification of truth is in Jesus Christ (Jn. 14:6), who always operates in love (Rom. 8:39).

The progressive world system in which Christians necessarily live, but are not to be of the same mindset as, believes that "what the world needs now is love, sweet love," but perceives such love as tolerance and diversity without consideration of any truth-stand that provides necessary unity and stability. Christians must be cautious not to subjugate the truth of Christ to a false and foggy notion of love. Paul explains that genuine "**love** rejoices in the **truth**" (I Cor. 13:6). Christian love derives from the character of God (I Jn. 4:8,16), and is expressed by the Spirit (Gal. 5:22). Truth is the foundation of love; love is the expression of truth. Both are personified and exemplified in **JESUS**.

OCTOBER 22

WORLDLY RELIGION

The religion of worldliness is rampant today. Religion has adapted to worldliness and adopted the character, attitudes, and agendas of Satan's world-system. When it does so, it no longer seeks to effect any real change in people's live, but simply encourages their selfish pursuit of materialistic acquisition and personal well-being. Any spiritual concerns become merely physical health concerns. The popular religion of many mainline denominational religious institutions has sold out to the world; it has pawned itself to the world's hock shop. Religion has become part of the world-system; it is the devil's playground.

Christian religion has sealed its pact with that worldly wisdom which it originally professed to contradict and renounce. Though still mistakenly identified as God's enterprise, religion (of all varieties) is part of Satan's world-system. Can it be any clearer? "Do not love the world nor the things in the world. If anyone loves the world, the love of the Father is not in him" (I Jn. 2:15). "You adulteresses, do you not know that friendship with the world is hostility toward God, Therefore, whoever wishes to be a friend of the world makes himself an enemy of God" (James 4:4).

Brennan Manning stated, "The greatest single cause of atheism in the world today is Christians, who acknowledge Jesus with their lips, walk out the door, and deny Him by their lifestyle. That is what an unbelieving world simply finds unbelievable." The misrepresentation of those who profess to be Christ-ones, Christians, while the character of **JESUS** represented by "the fruit of the Spirit" (Gal. 5:22,23) is not manifested in their lives, proclaim a lie. We can talk until we are "blue in the face" about the intricacies of our ecclesiastical doctrines and practices, but unless the character of the living Lord **JESUS** Christ is expressed in the lives of Christian people it is all meaningless tongue-wagging and hypocritical haranguing.

OCTOBER 23

THE INCONGRUITY OF MERITOCRACY

Michael Young wrote a book in 1958 entitled, *The Rise of the Meritocracy*, in which he criticized the merit-based structure of British education. Perhaps it is time for someone to write another such book questioning the extent to which such meritocracy has permeated and infected the operational function of the modern Western evangelical church. What do we mean by the term "meritocracy"? It is the power and authority of those who evidence their merits of ability and competency, and are selected to lead based on their talents, their proven efforts of leadership performance in their positions in the world.

Too much of the leadership in the churches today is merely the transference of the world's standards of leadership, and the selection of individuals who have proven abilities and records of accomplishment in their positions outside of the church. Churches and denominations then pragmatically vest them in church positions based on the merits of their proven performance and achievement in the world. This is a recipe for failure, leading to a tragic misrepresentation of church function.

The Church is the Body of Christ (Rom. 12:5; I Cor. 12:12,27; Eph. 4;12), and is to be viewed as a collective spiritual organism. The function of the Church is counter-intuitive to the function of every organization in the world. Meritocracy, the rule of those chosen on the merits of their accomplishments, has no place in the Church. The living Lord **JESUS**, operating as the life-giving Spirit (I Cor. 15:45) is the head (Col. 1:18) of the church, and human leaders are to be selected who are receptive to allowing the living Christ to lead His Body through them. The only merit is what Christ accomplished in His redemptive work, and what He continues to do by His divine authority and power in receptive Christ-followers, willing to say, "I can't, but I believe that the living Lord Jesus can do what He wants to do through me."

OCTOBER 24

THE TALKING DONKEY

Some readers will be able to reach back in their recollection to remember the television series in the 1960s about "Mister Ed, the Talking Horse." The tagline was, "A horse is a horse, of course, of course, and no one can talk to a horse, of course." But Mr. Ed could converse with his hapless owner, Wilbur. Earlier, in the 1950s, Walter Brooks had written, "Francis, the Talking Mule," and a series of children's books about "Freddie, the Talking Pig." Long prior to all of these stories of the twentieth century, there was recorded the rather off-beat story of "Balaam, and the Talking Donkey" as recorded in Numbers 22-24.

Balaam of Peor was known as a seer, a type of a prophet who could allegedly foretell the future, and issue oracles of blessings or curses upon other people and groups. Balaam, however, was a duplicitous prophet who was really in it for the profit. He could be influenced – bought and sold – and would sell himself out to one side or the other, or even both sides simultaneously as a double-crossing dual-agent. He was being solicited by King Balak of Moab, who was offering him sizeable money, to utter curses against the nation of Israel, and God had told him not to go. But Balaam, riding his trusted donkey, was on his way to see Balak in Moab and collect his mercenary bounty.

On the way, the donkey, more spiritually attuned than Balaam, saw the angel of the Lord standing in the way with a sword, and turned aside. Balaam was angry with the donkey, and beat him severely. Then the donkey spoke, "What have I done to you to cause you to beat me? Haven't I been dutiful and faithful?" Later, Balaam sold out Israel enticing them into sexual immorality and idolatry (Numb. 25:1-9; Jude 11; Rev. 2:14). In contrast, **JESUS** was (and is) the true voice of God, revealing the Father throughout His life, saying, "If you have seen Me, you have seen the Father" (Jn. 14:9). "I and the Father are one" (Jn. 10:30).

OCTOBER 25

LOVE AND SUFFERING

Frank Sinatra released the song, "Love and Marriage" in 1956. The lyrics stated that "love and marriage, go together like a horse and carriage ... you can't have one without the other." As a corollary of the former, I would suggest that love and suffering are so intertwined that "you can't have one without the other." Many people seem to have an idyllic perspective that deep love should allow for a serenity devoid of pain and hurt – a euphoric ecstasy. But the facts are that the people we love most deeply are likely the very people that will hurt us most deeply. Inherent in unconditional love is the risk that those we love might reject such love and cause deep pain.

Genuine human love does not imply the absence of hurt and pain. To the contrary, such love is almost an inevitable trajectory to experiencing hurt and pain. Some who have known human love most intimately will even tell you that they have a healthy fear of love. Love can be hurtful, and we eschew such relational pain. For some this has even led to an unhealthy aversion of such love.

Even divine love can experience pain and suffering. "God is love" (I Jn. 4:8,16). "God so loved the world of *fallen* mankind that He gave His only begotten Son" (Jn. 3:16). "The Son so loved us that He gave Himself (*dying on the cross*) for us" (Gal. 2:20). God in Christ knew the pain of betrayal, and the suffering of injustice. Because He is love, He chose to suffer in our stead. "Jesus, because of the suffering of death was crowned with glory and honor" (Heb. 2:9). In conjunction with His love, we can "consider that the sufferings of this present time are not worthy to be compared with the glory that is to be revealed to us" (Rom. 8:18). The deepest suffering comes out of the deepest love, and apart from such love we will never know the glory that comes from such suffering. As we "share the suffering of Christ, we will rejoice at the revelation of His glory" (I Pet. 4:13).

OCTOBER 26

THE SLAVERY OF RELIGION

Most modern people seem to eschew slavery in its many forms, whether it be slavery based on race, nationality, economics, or the contemporary sexual slavery. Human beings deserve the dignity of functioning in the manner God created humans to function with genuine freedom of choice, and the freedom to pursue life, liberty and the personal pursuit of self-chosen objectives. No human being has a right to buy, sell, manipulate or otherwise enslave another person to do his bidding, thus disallowing another human being to be a fully functioning individual enjoying the freedom of a self-determined life.

May I suggest that one of the cruelest forms of slavery on planet earth today is religious slavery. The slavery of religion enslaves more people than all the other forms of slavery. Religious slavery goes far deeper than physical use and abuse of another person (although that has occurred). Religion enslaves people's minds, emotions, and decision-making. Religion twists people's desires, and enslaves their spirit to "the devil, held captive to do his will" (II Tim. 2:26). Religion is a pervasive force that people equate with God and allow to control them. "By what a man is overcome, by this he is enslaved" (II Pet. 2:19).

The Israelite people were enslaved by the Egyptians. God called Moses to be the deliverer of his people by confronting the Pharaoh, saying "Let My people go!" Where is the Moses of our day, who will stand up to all religious authorities, and say, "Let God's people go!"? Quit enslaving people in the confines of performance "works" to build your edifices, to enhance your prestigious positions of prominence, and to pad your statistical successes. It's time to declare an emancipation proclamation whereby people are set free from religious slavery in order to engage in genuine spiritual union with the living Lord **JESUS** Christ. It may require the decimation of all religious enterprises.

OCTOBER 27

FREEDOM TO BE IMPIOUS?

Is it possible to have too much freedom? Those who remain bound up in legalism, seem to think that any degree of freedom is too much freedom. But those who have jettisoned the legalism of religion, and are enjoying the freedom of participating in the relationality of God's grace in Jesus Christ, sometimes have to face situations where their actions may collide with what others consider the propriety of piety. Yes, these people's opinions may be legalistic adherence to religious rituals or narrow ethical constraints, but does our grace-freedom give us the permission to trample on the tulips of others' fragile opinions?

Let us consider some examples in the New Testament. One of the major issues among the early Christians as they integrated both Jewish and Gentile believers in Jesus Christ was the question of whether the God-given food laws of what was kosher in the old covenant were still binding. The Jewish Christians wanted to maintain conformity to the Law, and the Gentile Christians considered such to be legalism not required by God's grace. In his epistles to the Corinthians and to the Romans, Paul mentions the "weak brother" who was not convinced of his convictions, and advises, "Whatever is not of faith is sin" (Rom. 14:23).

Another example: Paul was peeved at the legalistic Judaizers who followed him wherever he went seeking to undermine his teaching of God's grace in Jesus Christ, by declaring that the old covenant mandate of male circumcision remained in force for Christians. Writing to the Galatians, Paul indicates that if the Judaizing false teachers were so "knife-happy," why don't they go all the way and "cut it off" (Gal. 5:21). No doubt, the legalists thought Paul was being impious – that in his grace-freedom, he was being blasphemous and heretical, much less inconsiderate. "It's not nice to kick the religious crutches out from religious cripples who need them! Where's your respect for others?"

OCTOBER 28

THE DEATH OF RELIGION

"If God could, or would, die tonight, what would happen to Christian religion in the days thereafter?" The answer is simple: "Nothing!" Christian religion, along with all other forms of religion, would continue as usual, with the well-oiled machinery functioning to produce ever-so-slightly varying performance inculcations for the myriad of workers who keep the machinery lubricated in order to crank out the "product" that keeps them in business. Religion is a perpetual motion machine that usually (not always) seems to have an abundant supply of workers willing to contribute and volunteer for the ethereal "cause."

The demise of religion is inherent in the gospel of Jesus Christ. As the Swiss theologian, Karl Barth, wrote in his voluminous *Church Dogmatics*, "The Revelation of God – the Abolition of Religion." When the reality of the God-man, the "Word made flesh" (Jn. 1:14); when the "truth and the grace of God" (Jn. 1:17) were realized in personal incarnational manifestation, religion in all its forms (man-made and divinely inaugurated) could never legitimately "hold water" thereafter. God's Self-revealing in the Son, Jesus Christ, indicts all religion as but hopeless counterfeits. The presence of the Christ-life is the death-knoll of all religion.

The entirety of the *New Testament*, has an underlying theme of the illegitimacy of religion due to the advent and redemptive action of **JESUS**. In the gospel narratives Jesus repeatedly indicates that the old wineskins of religion would explode due the new wine of the vital dynamic of His life. His parabolic teaching exposed religion in various analogies. The epistle to the Hebrews warns against reverting back to religion. The Revelation of **JESUS** observed by John is a major indictment upon religion, calling her a whore (Rev. 17:15,16; 19:2), a prostitution of the intended relationship of Christ and His people (Eph. 5:23). The whore is killed! Religion goes to hell (Rev. 19:11–22:5).

OCTOBER 29

ABANDONMENT

French Christian, Charles de Foucauld (1858-1916), wrote a "Prayer of Abandonment" that has been meaningful to many Christians. Here are some words of his prayer: "Father, I abandon myself into your hands; do with me what you will. Let only your will be done in me. Into your hands I commend my soul: I offer it to you with all the love of my heart, for I love you, Lord, and so need to give myself, to surrender myself into your hands without reserve, and with boundless confidence, for you are my Father." The deepest depth of love is the abandonment of yourself to another – becoming a love-slave to the one you love.

Another classic of Christian literature is the book by Jean-Pierre de Caussade, another French Christian (1675-1751), entitled *Abandonment to Divine Providence*. Listen to his words, "I submit in all things and absolutely to Your good pleasure for time and eternity; and I wish to do this, Oh my God. I renounce my own will to follow Yours in all things; dispose of me, Oh my God, according to Your good will and pleasure. In the state of abandonment, the only rule is the duty (*obedience*) of the present moment." Jean-Pierre did admit that "Those who have abandoned themselves to God always lead mysterious lives."

Abandonment implies that we are not in control of our life – no self-sufficiency. It only occurs in a life of love and faith, wherein we trust that the Other will love us no matter what, and trust that such love will seek our highest good, and do us no harm. In total openness and transparency, we surrender and relinquish control with no thought of self-protection or reservation, indicating "You can do anything you want with me or to me – anything!" We need only look at **JESUS** in order to see the epitome of personal abandonment. "I do nothing of my own initiative" (Jn. 5:30; 8:42; 14:10). "Not my will, but Thine be done" (Lk. 22:42). "Father, into Your hands I commend my spirit" (Lk. 23:46).

OCTOBER 30

DO I HAVE TO GO TO CHURCH?

Many a child has asked their parents, "Do I *have to* go to church?" Many adults today, those who have begun to recognize the reality of Christianity in the vital dynamic of a personal relationship with the living Lord Jesus, are likewise asking the same question, "Do I *have to* go to church?" Regardless of the answer your parents gave to your question when you were young, I want to give a resounding "NO" to the question being asked. No one *has to* go to church (with the exception of the children who are required to do their parents bidding). Church attendance is not a required performance effort imposed upon all Christians in order to appease God, and keep one in God's good graces.

The problem with all of the "do I *have* to ..." questions is that the focus of our consideration is on ourselves, a self-perspective and concern about requirements of Christian activity or involvement. The question for the Christ-indwelt Christ-one is not necessarily about what I *have to* do, or even about what I *want to* do or *don't want to* do, but what does the living Lord Jesus Christ who dwells in me *want to* be and do in me? Is the Lord's intent and desire to act being transferred to the personal desires within us in order to allow Him to act through us? Has His *want to* become our *want to*? By "listening under" the Lord Jesus in Christian obedience, we ascertain what He *wants to* do in us. We can be sure that Christ in us *wants to* love and encourage other Christians in our *koinonia* fellowship. Christian gathering in the *ecclesia* is not about our own whims, but about allowing **JESUS** to minister to others.

Someone will ask, "What about Hebrews 10:25: 'Do not forsake assembling yourselves together...'"? The context of that verse is that Hebrew Christians in Jerusalem were being tempted to jettison their Christian faith and revert to Jewish religion. Paul encouraged them to gather together and encourage one another in mutual perseverance.

OCTOBER 31

RESENTMENT

If you take an honest look inward to evaluate whether you have any resentment or animosity toward another person or group of persons, what comes to your mind? Is there some unresolved hurt or sadness that generates discontentment or irritation as that memory "tape" plays in your mind? The context of such grievances may be any interpersonal interactions we have been involved with. We might have lingering resentment against employers, fellow workers, neighbors, churches, social clubs, parents, siblings, and even against our marital spouses.

Resentment is often a reaction to a real or perceived attitude or incidence of personal slight or injustice. "I've been wronged. What that other person did is not right! I do not like what happened. I take offense at what the person said or did. I do not deserve to be treated like that." It must be noted that such resentment is usually an affront to our sense of ego-worth. It is often a self-oriented reaction of self-concern, that may stem from a sense of envy or a sense of personal entitlement. The primary concern will be how we choose to react to such affronts. Retaliation and revenge will never resolve the situation, but always exacerbate the problem.

A positive, though counterintuitive, response is to bless the one or ones who have hurt us by seeking their highest good in love. There is no resentment in love; only acceptance of the other person and the willingness to forgive with a genuine empathy that puts oneself in the other's place, even to the extent of being willing to be poured out and used up *by* and *for* the other. If anyone had cause for resentment, it was **JESUS**, as He was unjustly persecuted to the point of a gruesome death, but His response from the cross was, "Father forgive them, for they know not what they do" (Lk. 23:34). Resentment dissipates as we cease to ponder the alleged wrong, and express love for the other.

NOVEMBER 1

SOCIAL CONFLICT

How is one to make sense of the social conflict and unrest in our world today – neighbor against neighbor; brother against brother? The underlying fuel of populism is resentment – we're going to "drain the swamp" to do away with the power-brokers. The overwhelming driver of elitist progressivism is disdain of those "ignorant delorables" who do not know what is best for them. They clash in the polarized ideological perspectives of a divided society, often producing the spark-point that leads to civil war –the sad tragedy wherein the closest of friends and neighbors are set against one another in mortal combat.

It is extremely difficult to moderate these conflicting passions, either in the sense of refereeing the conflict they generate, or attempting to diminish the intensity and tension of the contrary settled attitudes. Ideological passions run so hot that reason is jettisoned, much less any concern for an alternative viewpoint that transcends the temporal hostilities in the attempt to see an eternal perspective. Neutrality does not seem to be an option. Disinterest slides into the indifferent detachment of the *idiotes* who had no concern for the good of the whole. Are we left only with "choose your side" and "fight, fight, fight"?

So much for the utopian optimism of everyone working together to make things better and better for all. The "conflict theory" of fallen human social interactions has prevailed again, with its opposing antagonism of "us vs. them," and the fallacious skewed incentive that "God is on our side." Those who are Christ-ones want to explain that **JESUS** is the "prince of peace" (Isa. 9:6), but it will often seem they are a voice crying in the wilderness. We can proclaim the need to "love one another" (Jn. 13:34,35), and "love your enemies" (Lk. 6:35), but it will often seem like we are in an echo chamber and no one is listening. That is often the case when we are "in the world, but not of the world" (Jn. 17:11,16).

NOVEMBER 2

PERSPECTIVES ON SUFFERING

There seems to be a great divide between the perspective of suffering in the old covenant and the attitude toward suffering in the new covenant. In the Jewish old covenant of law performance, human suffering was predominantly regarded as something punitive, a curse of God for disobedience, to be avoided at all costs. When the people of Israel encountered suffering, the reaction was often "God is angry with us. Please God, deliver us from this painful predicament." Suffering was to be avoided. Job's advisors are representative of the attitude that suffering was the consequence of God's discontent and wrath.

The new covenant perspective is so different. Jesus embraced suffering. Jesus "learned obedience through the things he suffered" (Heb. 5:8). By His "suffering of death, He is crowned with glory and honor, that by the grace of God He might taste death for everyone" (Heb. 2:9). God "perfected the author of salvation through sufferings, in order to bring many sons to glory" (Heb. 2:10. The people of Israel, however, were unable to entertain the idea of a suffering Savior. Such a concept was incongruous with their expectation of a victorious conqueror who would restore the nation of Israel to its former glory.

In the new covenant, God privileges His Christ-ones to identify with and participate in the suffering of **JESUS** as part of the Christian experience. Christians can embrace suffering, knowing that Christ suffered for us, and we follow in His steps (I Pet. 2:21). With Paul, we are to "consider that the sufferings of this present time are not worthy to be compared with the glory that is to be revealed to us" (Rom. 8:18). Thus, we can "exult in our tribulations, knowing that tribulation brings about perseverance" (Rom. 5:3). In the new covenant, suffering is the opportunity to demonstrate that God's grace in Christ **JESUS** is sufficient, regardless of how difficult the situation might be.

NOVEMBER 3

SUBTLETIES OF CHRISTIAN THOUGHT

Narrow-minded dogmatism cannot tolerate subtleties. Such thinking demands *prima facie* interpretation – direct, obvious, face-value, "literal" understanding of a text. The conclusions of such interpretation must be formatted in formulaic straight-line linear logic, in black and white categories capable of rigid systematization with no latitude of understanding. By such simplistic assertion of propositional truth, they seek to control correct doctrinal formulations. When confronted with diverse subtleties of thought, they refer to such as "incoherent sophistry" that attempts to "play with my mind."

"The ways of God are past finding out" (Rom. 11:33) by utilizing simple human logic. "Our thoughts are not His thoughts" (Isa. 55:8,9). Spiritual realities concerning "divine mysteries" require subtleties of spiritual understanding employing God's wisdom. Jesus often used the subtlety of indirect teaching in His parables, metaphors and analogies. The disciples struggled to grasp what He was referring to – the meaning was not obscure, just not obvious and self-evident. It is in the subtleties of Christian thought that we begin to see the fine points, the nuances, the innuendos and the variegated shades of meaning – even the dialectic thinking that can accept both sides of any issue.

Subtleties of Christian thought must be understood with the spiritual understanding (Col. 1:9) of "the mind of Christ" (I Cor. 2:16). As Christians, ""we have received the Spirit who is from God, so that we may know the things freely given to us by God" (I Cor. 2:12). Even so, Paul prayed that "the eyes of our heart might be enlightened ... that we might know the surpassing greatness of His power toward us who believe" (Eph. 1:18,19). Spiritual subtleties are not obvious and explicit, often incapable of definitive human formulation, necessitating allowance for variance and disagreement of thought and interpretation.

NOVEMBER 4

SEEING FROM GOD'S PERSPECTIVE

Gideon needed a change of perspective (cf. Judges 6 and 7). He had heard of God's powerful acts for the people of Israel in the past, but questioned whether God was concerned about His people, and powerful enough to protect His people from their plight of being oppressed by the Midianites. The angel of the Lord came to Gideon, and after a couple of "dew miracles" to show Him God's presence and power, Gideon was convinced to lead his people in battle against the enemy armies. After God thinned the troops to only three hundred men, they approached the Midianites with only trumpets and torches in jars. Such unconventional warfare frightened the intruders, causing them to flee, evidencing God's powerful preservation of His people.

Our human point of view is so often limited by myopic self-centered perspectives and self-doubts. Some focus on their human inadequacy, while others have grandiose opinions of human potential. Both fail to consider God's perspective and God's power by which all human endeavors are rendered effectual. "'My thoughts are not your thoughts, nor are your ways My ways,' declares the Lord" (Isa. 55:8). In order to be successful, we must see as God sees, from God's perspective, and understand that our sufficiency is only in the power of His grace. Thereby, we can be "in on" what God is "up to," allowing Him to function in us.

God's ways are inscrutable and unfathomable (Rom. 11:33), and to see from God's perspective requires that He reveal His will and His ways via His Son, **JESUS** Christ, and by His Spirit. We want to see as God sees in order to participate in His divine action. How does God view what is happening in our family? How does God view what is taking place in our faith community? How does God view what is taking place in our country? "The eyes of our heart must be enlightened to see the surpassing greatness of His power toward those who believe" (Eph. 1:18,19).

NOVEMBER 5

RESTLESSNESS

Most of us have known persons who cannot sit still to enjoy what is transpiring in their lives in the present time, in the NOW. There is a restlessness in their soul – their thoughts, emotions, and decision-making – that is evidenced in the constant forward propulsion of their physical bodies to attempt to do what they think they need to do. What is the motivating source that creates such relentless drive to go full-speed ahead until they burn-out or drop dead?

Driven by humanistic cultural incentives to "give it your best" and "be the best you can be" – "just do it!" – some have a developed personality pattern driven by significance and success. They go, go, go and do, do, do until their body breaks down, they have a heart attack, or a nervous breakdown diagnosed as a "anxiety disorder." This is sometimes exacerbated by religious admonitions and inculcations of "doing for Jesus" and "serving Jesus," which are inevitably interminable quests because the devotee can never do enough in order to convince themselves that they have pleased God. The diabolic task-master of all religion, who is also identified as "the destroyer" (I Cor. 10:10), constantly prompts religious dupes with the lying incentive to perform and do more "works" to reach the elusive goal of receiving an "Atta-boy" reward in heaven. Culture and religion are both used by Satan to drive people to exasperation and desperation.

Those who have discovered the all-sufficient grace of God in **JESUS** Christ can learn to rest in the Sabbath Rest (Heb. 4:1-11) provided for all Christians in Christ. Such divine Rest is the antidote to all performance-based restlessness. "God has blessed us with every spiritual blessing in the heavenly places in Christ" (Eph. 1:3), "granting us everything pertaining to life and godliness" (I Pet. 1:3). May we all find our Rest in Him.

NOVEMBER 6

DEGREES AND PEDIGREES

Satan has certainly gained a foothold among religious professionals by introducing the subtle temptation of vanity and pride in credentialed degrees and pedigrees. There is such a clamoring in the academic and ecclesiastical environment for ever-higher academic lineage and credentials by which the recipients acquire social prominence and advanced professional positions. Additional academic degrees allow for increased "letters" behind one's name (B.S.; M.S.; Ph. D.), which can confer various prefixes and titles such as Reverend, Bishop, Father, Doctor, etc. A common acquisition among pastors is a D.D. degree (Doctor of Divinity), snidely referred to by others as "donated dignity." The entire system of religious tiers dividing a "clergy" class from an inferior "laity," is an abominable aberration of God's intent. Ray Stedman referred to all Christians as "claity," for we are all "clay pots," earthen vessels, in which the treasure of Jesus' life is available to occupy (cf. II Cor. 4:7).

Jesus exposed and denounced the Pharisees for their proud jockeying for public position and prominence, telling His disciples, "They love the place of honor at banquets and the chief seats in the synagogues, and respectful greetings in the market places, and being called Rabbi by men. But do not be called Rabbi; for One is your Teacher, and you are all brothers" (Matt. 23:6-8).

When recently asked why I did not use my earned academic monikers, I explained that I considered such titles and credentials divisive and not conducive to unity. They set people apart from one another, one higher than another, and fail to facilitate the awareness that we are all "one in Christ Jesus" (Gal. 3:28). Our identity is not to be found in titles or labels, but only in the person of **JESUS** Christ. I only want to be identified and introduced as a "Christ-one," a Christian who knows and loves the risen and living Lord **JESUS** – a "brother in Christ."

NOVEMBER 7

CHRISTIANITY IS NOT AN ...ISM

When we use the suffix ...ism to describe and refer to a distinctive ideology or system of thought, or to patterned practices that have become a sociological movement, even to the point of being institutionalized, we have encapsulated the phenomenon being described into a man-made package of thought capable of human analysis and dissection. Is Christianity, capable of being "boxed" or "bottled" in such static thought categories? It is inconceivable that Jesus, during His redemptive mission on earth, had any intent to establish an ...ism. He came to make Himself available to humanity.

The French sociologist, Jacques Ellul, pointed out that the French word for "christianity" is *christianisme*. Increasingly, the term English word "christianity" is understood as but a religious "...ism," a man-made institutional organization often called "Christian religion," that clamors for a "hearing" of its ideological agenda. It seems that we have come full circle: When the term "Christian" was first employed (Acts 11:26), it apparently began as a pejorative moniker of derision, and now it is regarded as such again, but this time the Christian institution and its programs have brought the negative perspective on itself.

Christianity is not to be considered as merely an ...ism. If we Christians are going to continue to use the term "Christianity," we must begin to explain the term with more precision. We must make it clear that **JESUS** Christ is a risen and living divine/human Person active in His people who are called Christ-ones. Some have defined Christianity as Christ-in-you-ity. We are obliged to counter the misconceptions of our Christian faith as merely a system of ideological thought, or as one particular type of religious adherence and practice among the various world religions. Christianity is the vital dynamic of the Spirit of **JESUS** Christ in the spirits of persons receptive to Him by faith.

NOVEMBER 8

EVANGELISM

In some Christian groups, the foremost responsibility of every Christian and the church at large is thought to be evangelism, i.e. to be engaged in active sharing of the gospel message with nonbelievers. The stated incentive for such activity is usually the "Great Commission" of Matthew 28:19,20 where Jesus told His disciples, "Go and make disciples of all the nations, baptizing them in the name of the Father and the Son and the Holy Spirit, teaching them to observe all that I commanded you." The primary verb is not "go," and the objective is not to share an ideological message in order to "make disciples."

Notice the suffix "...ism" on the end of the word "evangelism." Are we not obliged to ask, "Is evangelism just another one of the many man-made ...isms of thought and practice that Christian people have developed into a procedural and manipulative practice to cajole people into association with their group? Is evangelism a marketing ploy of the evangelical church as it seeks to develop a larger "base" by recruiting new members and increasing its numbers? Do those engaged in the ploy of evangelism serve as salespersons seeking to "seal the deal" by encouraging people to make a "decision for Christ," join the church, and assure themselves a place in heaven?

Evangelism procedures in the evangelical church too often "miss the point." The living Lord **JESUS** is shoved to the side, and viewed only as a means to an end – the objective of getting souls into the fold of their institution, and eventually into heaven, meanwhile disingenuously failing to disclose the expectations of church membership and its concomitant expectations of commitment to financial giving, regular attendance and ministry participation. **JESUS** is the evangel, the only "good news" whereby humans can be redeemed, regenerated and restored to the godly function that God designed for mankind.

NOVEMBER 9

THE WORSHIP SERVICE

Many churches refer to their Sunday morning assemblies as "worship services." How much worship is taking place, and who is being worshipped in the midst of these gatherings? The worship leaders, the pastor, worship director, song leader, and musicians are often the actors who are the focal point for the audience who sits in the pews. Are these center-stage persons to be the object of the attention, admiration, awe and worship of the audience?

The Danish Christian thinker, Soren Kierkegaard, likened what happens in ecclesiastical worship services with theatre-goers attending the theatre, being entertained by the actors on the stage. His observation was that the assembly of the *ecclesia* should be absolutely contrary to the theatre. Rather than our attending the service to be an audience of the action performed by actors on center-stage, Kierkegaard suggested all Christian persons should be the actors, allowing the Spirit of God (through the pastor and other worship assistants) to be the prompter of our lines and actions, while the audience to whom all worship is to be directed is the Triune God – an audience of One.

While Kierkegaard's observation is helpful in recognizing that the focal point of our worship is not to be directed towards those on the stage, the whole scenario of a theatre, actors, and an audience may be inadequate to illustrate Christian collective and corporate worship. In our participatory relationship with Father, Son, and Holy Spirit, wherein all things are to be derived from God, God should be the Actor, the actuating prompter, and the audience. Once again, it is not what we do, but what God does! It is the all-glorious character of God expressed in Christ-ones to the glory of God. The worship of our daily lives will be the determiner of the authenticity and legitimacy of our assembled worship services, wherein **JESUS** is to be praised and revered.

NOVEMBER 10

OUT OF ... THROUGH ... UNTO

Paul's concluding statement, prior to addressing the practical themes beginning in chapter twelve of Romans, is: "For *from* (*ek* – out of) Him and *through* (*dia* – through, by means of) Him and *to* (*eis* – directed unto) Him are all things. To Him *be* the glory forever. Amen!" (Rom. 11:36). This brief rhythmic statement seems to summarize the operational model and process of everything in the Christian life. Everything 'Christian' is derived "out of" God in Christ; dynamically energized "through" God in Christ; and manifested "unto" the glory of God in Christ. The living Lord Jesus is the source, energy, and objective of everything called "Christian."

The sequence of prepositions in Paul's statement to the Romans provides the cyclical, closed circle sequence of divine action, which comprises the entirety of what we call "the Christian life." "We do not know how to pray as we should, but the Spirit Himself intercedes for us with groanings too deep for words" (Rom. 8:26), to dynamically direct our communion with God. Our worship commences with God's provision of grace, dynamically expressing the "worth-ship" of His all-glorious character in praise to the Father. All Christian living has its origin in the One who is Life (cf. Jn. 14:6; I Jn. 5:12), dynamically manifesting His life (II Cor. 4:10,11) to the glory of God. Jesus is the "faithful Witness" (Rev. 1:5; 3:4), who lives out and lays down His *marture* life in the midst of our being witnesses (Acts 1:8) of Him.

Every action of the Christian life, prayer, worship, living, witness, etc., is but the empowering and out-working of God in action by the Son, **JESUS** Christ, by means of the Spirit – the closed circle, cyclical action of God in the Christian. Everything "Christian" commences with the indwelling Christ in the spirit of a Christ-one, re-presenting His life in the context of our lives, whereby we might "do all things to the glory of God (cf. I Cor. 10:31).

NOVEMBER 11

WHAT ABOUT DOUBT?

Those who are dead-sure of the certainties of their belief-system are those who most loudly proclaim the evils of all doubt. But in so doing, they reveal their uncertainties concerning the tenability of their own belief-system, thus exposing the back-door to their own doubts. There is a chasm of polarity between absoluteness of belief and the uncertainty of conviction that comprises the questioning stance of doubt. In other words, settled belief cannot tolerate doubt. Christian faith, on the other hand, is quite content to accommodate doubt, viewing such as the springboard to progressive relational faith.

French philosopher/theologian, Jacques Ellul, proposed such a distinction between belief and faith in his book, *The Living Faith: Belief and Doubt in a Perilous World*, explaining, "Faith presupposes doubt, while belief excludes it." Belief is suspicious of all questioning, fearful that it might undermine the solidity of the belief-structure. Faith welcomes questioning, realizing that uncertainty serves to strengthen the process of dynamic and vital faith. In the unique words of Frederick Buechner, "Doubts are the ants in the pants of faith. They keep it awake and moving." Faith is a living reality, not a concretized substance.

Doubt is the continued questioning that allows for amplification and intensification of operative faith, beyond empirical objectification. Doubt is an ongoing component of faith for it prods and spurs us in our receptivity of the activity of God, while trusting and confidently expecting that the divine dynamic of God's grace will continue in the same manner as He has been faithful to act in the past. Faith without the catalyst of inquisitive doubt always risks becoming the idolatrous and deified certitude of an inflexible belief-system that tolerates no challenges or uncertainty. The living Lord **JESUS** is not a static object of belief, but embodies the relational life of God unphased by perplexity.

NO DISTINCTION OF VALUE OR FUNCTION

Perhaps the chief culprits for making divisive social distinctions (racial, gender, class, etc.) are the belief-systems of religion. These are the very institutions that should have been emphasizing the unity of all people and the spiritual character of deference essential for all cooperative social unity and function. The Christian religion has from its commencement fostered cultural biases of gender function, indicating that women are not allowed to function in certain roles in the church. That despite the fact that not one of the categories of spiritual giftedness for Christian ministry (I Cor. 12:4-31) has any gender specification.

In the context of an indictment of all legalism (Gal. 3:1-25), Paul explained that "we are all children of God through faith in Christ Jesus, having been clothed with Christ" (Gal. 3:26,27). "There is neither Jew nor Greek, there is neither slave nor free man, there is neither male nor female; for you are all one in Christ Jesus" (Gal. 3:28). It seems clear that social distinctions of gender, race, and social class are irrelevant to Christian evaluation and function in the church. We are to avoid all legalistic formulations whereby such distinctions determine placement of subordination or superiority of function among Christians.

The issue in Christian fellowship and ministry is not gender, race, or social class, but whether the character of the living Lord **JESUS** is displayed in loving deference that puts another ahead of oneself. Mutual deference is not gender specific. Both men and women are to put aside their selfishness in order to act lovingly toward others in every kind of social situation, be it the workplace, church function, or interpersonal relationships such as marriage. "Regard one another as more important than yourselves; do not merely look out for your own personal interests, but also for the interests of others" (Phil. 2:3,4). "Defer to one another in reverence to Christ" (Eph. 5:21).

NOVEMBER 13

COMMUNITY

There is a lot of talk these days among Christian people about developing "community" in the context of the *ecclesia*. The word "community" combines the two words "common" and "unity." This leads to the question of what constitutes the "common unity" that is being popularly sought. The answer often given is a common uniformity of belief or practice that will reinforce the "believe-right" and "do-right" religion presently established. But is such uniformity really the basis of genuine community? Or is there a sense of social connectivity wherein people are connected in similarity of oneness and concern for one another?

The apostle Paul does not seem to have been all that concerned about orchestrating and building "common unity," but advised the Ephesian Christians to "be diligent to *preserve* the unity of the Spirit in the bond of peace. There is one body and one Spirit, just as also you were called in one hope of your calling; one Lord, one faith, one baptism, one God and Father of all who is over all and through all and in all" (Eph. 4:3-6). The common unity was already established and needed only to be "preserved." That is not to say that a mutual sense of social community could not continue to be developed in the unified fellowship.

The traditional church model for developing community has been: 1) Present the message, 2) Call for personal decision, 3) Welcome into fellowship based on uniformity of belief and performance of initiation standards. The Celts of Ireland developed a different revolutionary approach: 1) Develop social community, 2) Serve and engage in loving fellowship with one another, 3) Invite community participants into Christian belief, 4) Welcome continuing maturation and an ever-deeper sense of community. This leads to a much more natural sense of relational and social community where people can be honest about their own relationship with **JESUS** and with one another.

NOVEMBER 14

"I WANNA SEE GOD AT WORK!"

It was the plaintive cry of a man who had been a Christian and served in his local church for many years, but he was throwing up his arms in frustration. He had worked hard, alongside of many others, to support the programs of the church. He had seen the best that man could do in dedicated commitment to serving God, and the programmed productivity of church involvement did not seem to be bringing forth any supernatural results. In exhaustion and exasperation, he cried out, "I just want to see God at work in His people." What this man was seeking was a visible manifestation of the Grace out-working of divine activity.

Was this man wrong in desiring and seeking to see "God at work"? No, he was not! Granted, God is always at work, and what He is doing in people's hearts is not always visible in obvious manifestations, but if God is present in His Christ-ones, we can expect that He will be exhibiting His character and His power. He is never a passive God. "God is at work in us, both to will and to work for His good pleasure" (Phil. 2:13). "We are His workmanship, created in Christ Jesus for good works, which God prepared beforehand that we should walk in them" (Eph. 2:10), "equipped in every good thing to do His will" (Heb. 13:21).

It is a sad indictment upon the modern institutional church that the predominant emphasis of its preaching and teaching has been to promote the performance of human "works" of involvement and maintenance. In the sixteenth century, many joined Martin Luther in decrying the "works" orientation of the church, leading to the Reformation. Perhaps now, after five hundred years, is the time when concerned Christians need to join their voices in saying, "We wanna see God at work!" We want to see the Grace of God in action. We want to see what God can and will do, not just what man can and has done. **JESUS** wants to "work out in us what is pleasing in His sight" (Heb. 13:21).

NOVEMBER 15

AN UNKNOWING CHRISTIAN?

Is it possible to be an "unknowing Christian"? Many might immediately respond and say, "Is there any other kind of Christian?" No Christian is all-knowing – that is an attribute of God alone, His omniscience. Every Christian lacks knowledge in various areas. Every Christian has limitations of general knowledge, as well as limited biblical and theological knowledge, and no one knows everything about God and His ways – "His ways are past finding out" (Rom. 11:33). There is a difference between informational knowing of God and relational knowing of God – the latter being inexhaustible in its depth of intimacy.

Allow me to switch gears in this consideration of an "unknowing Christian." Instead of focusing on what a Christian knows or doesn't know, let us ponder this question, "Is it possible to be a Christian and not know it?" To this question, many will immediately reply, "No, to be a Christian is to know that you relationally know the living Lord Jesus, and to be secure and assured about such a relationship." They might even quote Romans 8:16: "The Spirit bears witness with our spirit that we are a child of God." Or I John 5:10: "The one who believes in the Son of God has the testimony in himself."

Ponder this! Many have been involved in Christian community for some time, and then realize that they are not a Christian. Is it not possible that others may have been involved in Christian community, but have been unwilling to claim or affirm that they are a "Christian," perhaps because they have mistaken ideas of what is necessary to become or be a Christian? Some have misconceptions about the necessity of having one's biblical and theological knowledge "all figured out," about the need for "absolute surrender," or the mistaken notion that to be a Christian one has to be "perfect." We must beware of trying to determine what is transpiring within the heart of another.

NOVEMBER 16

FELLOWSHIP WITH LOVED ONES IN HEAVEN?

Christians have long asked whether we will recognize, know and enjoy fellowship with our loved ones in heaven? There is no explicit denial or affirmation of such in the scriptures. Some have denied that we should be concerned with such, citing lack of "flesh and blood" physicality (I Cor. 15:50), while others have indicated that we will be so focused on worshipping Jesus that we will not be seeking out friends, acquaintances and loved ones. Those answers are unsatisfactory. We presently communicate with people without physical presence via telephone, internet, etc. Worship of Jesus necessarily involves his divine love and concern for participation with others.

Many scriptural allusions have been cited as affirmation of continued fellowship in heaven: Hebrew peoples often referred to one's death as being "gathered to his people" (Gen. 25:8; 35;29; 49:29). David looked forward to being with his son who died (II Sam. 12:23). Jesus spoke of sitting down with the patriarchs in the kingdom of heaven (Matt. 8:11). The rich man recognized both Abraham and Lazarus (Lk. 16:19-31). Peter, James, and John recognized Moses, Elijah and Jesus in the transfiguration (Matt. 17:3,4). Such citations are not definitive for some, so we proceed to the Theo-logic of the gospel.

Relational community is integral to what Jesus came to bring in Himself in the gospel – participation in the eternally loving interpersonal fellowship of the Trinity. Why would that be terminated? Intrinsic to the gospel is the person-to-person intimacy of fellowship – an eternal interactive and intimate community in spiritual union with **JESUS**, and with all those who are "in Him." Heaven is simply the extension, continuity and perpetuity of the life and fellowship that Christians enjoy in the Body of Christ – "on earth and in heaven" (Matt. 6:10; Eph. 1:10). The present is the foretaste of eternal fellowship with the saints.

NOVEMBER 17

DEATH PENALTY?

Not wanting to deceive any readers, I hereby state at the outset that I am not addressing the social phenomenon of imposing a "death penalty" on individuals who have committed grievous crimes against others in a given society. The Bible certainly mentions the practice of capital punishment (cf. Gen. 9:6; Numb. 35:16-21) in the old covenant, but new covenant Christians are divided about the advisability of employing such execution measures in modern society.

The real concern of this article pertains to theological rather than social analysis – to consider whether God has in the past, or ever does, impose a spiritual death penalty upon human beings because of their sin. Popular evangelical theological discussion has often referred to "the death penalty for sin." The discussion turns on the meaning of Genesis 2:17. God tells the first couple in the Garden of Eden, "in the day that you eat from it (the tree of the knowledge of good and evil), you will surely die" (Gen. 2:17). Is this to be understood as a divine threat of punitive consequence for disobedience? Or is this simply an indicative statement of alternative? If you eat from the "tree of life," you will be deriving life from the living God, allowing for the divine out-working of the divinely in-breathed life of God (Gen. 2:7), whereas partaking of the "tree of the knowledge of good and evil" will necessarily imply that you have chosen to derive death from "the one having the power of death, that is the devil" (Heb. 2:14).

The living God is the life-giver (physical and spiritual). All divine spiritual life is His life. Jesus said, "I AM the life" (Jn. 11:25; 14:6). The devil, the Evil One, is the death-dealer, "the one having the power of death" (Heb. 2:14). The gospel explains that by His death, **JESUS** destroyed the power and "the works of the devil" (I Jn. 3:8), allowing Christians to pass out of spiritual death into spiritual life (Jn. 5:24; I Jn. 3:14).

NOVEMBER 18

ARE YOU READY FOR THE SECOND COMING?

The young fellow, having far "more zeal than knowledge" (Rom. 10:2), approached me on the street, asking excitedly "Are you ready for the second coming of Jesus?" The questioner was a bit nonplussed by the surety of my answer, "Yes, I am without a doubt ready for the return of Jesus Christ." Not quite sure where to go next, he continued, "What makes you so sure that you are ready if He should come again tonight?" I responded, "My surety is based on God's faithfulness, having revealed Himself in His Son who died in my stead and returned in Spirit-form to be my life. My confident readiness for Christ's second coming is entirely based on the reality of His first coming."

The young man was a bit befuddled by my response, but caught his breath and began to recapitulate what he had been taught by his religious advisors about "the signs of the times" necessitating the "imminent return of Jesus any day now, like a thief in the night," and how the temple was going to be rebuilt in Jerusalem, and the Jews would reign in their kingdom. "Do you believe all that?" he queried. "Can't say that I do!" I replied, not wanting to burst his balloon, but carefully proceeding to explain that the impending return of the risen Lord Jesus in a second coming was entirely predicated upon acceptance of His first coming.

Unsettled that I did not fit his paradigm of zealous futuristic belief, and unsure how to carry the conversation any farther, he may have determined that I was a hopeless cause and scurried on his way to confront another unsuspecting listener. The "second coming" of Jesus is not the focal point of the gospel, though many have attempted to make it such. The gospel is focused on the incarnation, life, crucifixion, resurrection, and Pentecostal outpouring of **JESUS** during His redemptive and restorative mission to earth to re-life human beings in spiritual regeneration – such life is His "eternal life," to be enjoyed NOW.

NOVEMBER 19

GUILT AND SHAME

When Adam and Eve disobeyed the prohibition of eating the fruit from the forbidden tree (Gen. 3), there was the objective guilt of transgressing God's prohibition, and likely the personal subjective guilt from violating their internal attitude that God's determination was valid. After some self-justification, they found themselves in a social situation wherein they recognized their physical nakedness before one another and God, and sought to hide themselves in shame by covering themselves with leaves. Such an attempt at hiding revealed their shame-based attitudes built upon the false-guilt of violating the fallacious mental thinking that nakedness was contrary to God's intent.

Guilt and shame are closely allied, but need to be carefully distinguished in light of the abundant use of the terms in pop-psychology today. Both guilt and shame were originally used in noun form, but have in recent times morphed into verb forms of "guilting" and "shaming" other people. Objective guilt is the result of transgressing a law. Subjective personal guilt is the internal result of one's conscience objecting to the behavioral transgression of an "established attitude." Shame is the result of socially imposed expectations of personal being and doing that a human individual or group may seek to avoid by conforming to the external social expectations.

In popular verb form, both "guilting" and "shaming" have become manipulative tools of social leverage, used by those with a personal agenda to force people to think and behave in social conformity to their thoughts and standards. Religion has become particularly adept at using such techniques to manipulate the thought and behavior of people who are concerned about being right with God. Christ-ones must learn to dismiss such tactics, for our only legitimate concern is what the living Lord **JESUS** wants to be and do in each individual.

NOVEMBER 20

"THE GREAT DIVORCE"

Marital divorce is not an unforgiveable sin. Though it may diminish the best earthly picture of divine spiritual oneness, Jesus recognized that human marriages can degenerate into nonviability and the action of divorce should be handled in a civil and loving manner. C.S. Lewis' book, *The Great Divorce*, does not deal with the dissolution of human marriage, but instead considers the dichotomy of the either/or polarity of those who are lost in the delusion of humanistic attribution of the deification of their own mental constructs and those who have received the Spirit of Christ and become receptive Christ-ones.

Using the analogy of a busload of denizens from the nether world of hell travelling together with a group of citizens from heaven, Lewis constructs the fantasy conversations of the diverse residents as they travel together to make a visit to heaven. The "ghosts," as Lewis refers to those from hell, are generally indicative of those who have elevated their academic thinking to a deified end-all of religious belief. The "spirits," on the other hand, symbolically represent those persons who believe in a personal living God, known through the Son, Jesus, and they have received His Spirit into their spirit, willing to submit all to Him.

A "ghost" voices his concern that heaven might be "a place where I shall find a wider sphere of usefulness, and scope for the talents God has given me, and an atmosphere of free inquiry." A "spirit" traveler responds, "There will be no sphere of usefulness, for you are not needed there at all. There will be no scope for your talents; only forgiveness for having perverted them. And no atmosphere for inquiry, for you are being taken to the land, not of questions but of answers, and you shall see the face of God." Continuing the discussion, the Christian "spirit" explains, "We know nothing of religion here in heaven. We think only of Christ." Such is the "great divorce" of humanism and Christian reality.

NOVEMBER 21

"LET THERE BE LIGHT"

Early in the creation record of Genesis 1, prior to the reported creation of the direct light of the sun and the reflected light of the moon (vss. 11-16), God is recorded as saying, "Let there be light!" (vs. 3). Human explanations of that comment have been numerous and varied. Those coming from a more recent scientific orientation have suggested that this might refer to the friction-energy of the "big-bang" dispersion of all matter, prior to the development of the sun and the moon in the Milky Way Galaxy of the universe wherein humans exist today. Thereby they integrate the creative and evolutionary explanations.

Those approaching from a more mystical perspective have speculated that enlightenment must precede appreciation of the physicality and tangibility, i.e. the forms of creation. God was creating the illumination that "brings to light" His divine Being in His creation. "The heavens declare the glory of God, and the firmament shows His handiwork" (Ps. 19:1). Creating all things *ek Theos*, "out of Himself," God wanted to permeate the created world with the Light of His Being. "God is light, and in Him there is no darkness at all" (I Jn. 1:5). God was desirous that He, Himself, should be the light of the created order, just as He will be in "the new heavens and new earth" (Rev. 22:5).

A more Christ-centered explanation is suggested by others. Paul seems to key off of the phrase in Genesis 1:3 when he wrote to the Corinthians, "God, who said, 'Light shall shine out of darkness,' is the One who has shone in our hearts to give the Light of the knowledge of the glory of God in the face of Christ" (II Cor. 4:6). During His earthly redemptive ministry, Jesus self-declared, "I am the Light of the world; he who follows Me will not walk in the darkness, but will have the Light of life" (John 8:12). John identified Jesus as "the true Light which, coming into the world, enlightens every man" (Jn. 1:9).

PASTORAL SPIRITUALITY

It is a tragic indictment of most Christian training schools to note that they offer almost no training in Christian spirituality. This lack of instruction in *pneumatikoi*, "spiritual things," is becoming increasingly evident in the spiritual deadness of contemporary western churches. Young Christian leaders are *not* being taught what it means to "grow in the grace and knowledge of our Lord and Savior Jesus Christ" (II Pet. 3:18); they have no depth of spiritual understanding, and consequently, they cannot teach and mentor the persons within their congregations on what it means to "grow up in all aspects into Christ" (Eph. 4:15).

In place of personal spirituality and a close walk with the living Lord Jesus as one listens to the divine Spirit, church leaders have adopted the "business model" of implementing the procedures of success in an institutional organization. The numerical and statistical success factors of the world, calculated by considering which church has the highest number of the "three big B's," buildings, budgets and baptisms, have become the criteria of ecclesiastical success. By means of calculable methodologies, leadership styles, and strong pastoral personalities, churches are focused on growing into megachurches of renown.

When pastors have no depth of spirituality, churches degenerate into "the blind leading the blind," and the flock follows the "Pied Piper Pastor" over the precipice into the abyss. Participants in the *ecclesia* of Christ are not intended to be a slice of lemmings. Every Christ-one having a personal relationship with the living Lord **JESUS** is intended to be obediently "listening under" the directional "Head of the Body," Jesus Christ (Col. 1:18; 2:19; Eph. 5:23), and drawing ever closer into intimacy of union with Christ the Lord. The pastoral responsibility in such a spiritual organism (not organization) is to lead by spiritual example into an increasing awareness of "the deep things of God."

NOVEMBER 23

THE EYES OF FAITH

The world says, "I wouldn't have believed it if I hadn't seen it." Their operative premise is "seeing is believing," as was expressed by Jesus' disciple, Thomas, "Unless I *see* the nail prints in His hands, I will not *believe*" (Jn. 20:25). The Christian perspective is counterintuitive to that of the world, "I wouldn't have *seen* it if I hadn't *believed* it," based on their faith that God is at work. "Believing is seeing" is the Christian perspective. In the context of bringing the entombed Lazarus out from the grave, Jesus said to Lazarus' sister, Martha, "Did I not say to you that if you *believe, you will see* the glory of God?" (John 11:40).

The natural man, a humanist, sees only his own abilities and trusts only in himself. A Christian, a "new creature in Christ" (II Cor. 5:17) has spiritual eyes to see what God by His Spirit is able and willing to do. "We walk by faith, not by sight" (II Cor. 5:7), seeing the invisible possibilities of God. The eyes of faith see what others cannot see; they provide "the conviction of things not seen" (Heb. 11:1), and open up our participation in the "paradigm of the sublime" whereby we "see the unseen" (II Cor. 4:18,19) of God's glory. Believing that God specializes in the impossible, we can exercise receptivity of God's activity, availability to His ability – that is faith!

When the seventy disciples returned after having seen God working miraculously, Jesus said to them, "Blessed are the *eyes which see the things you see*" (Lk. 10:23). Day by day, we are to "fix our *eyes* on Jesus, the author and perfecter of faith" (Heb. 12:2). Paul prayed for every Christian, "I pray that the *eyes of your heart may be enlightened*, so that you will know what is the hope of His calling, what are the riches of the glory of His inheritance in the saints, and what is the surpassing greatness of His power toward us who believe" (Eph. 1:18,19). Having spiritual "eyes of faith," we believe and rejoice (I Pet. 1:8).

NOVEMBER 24

THANKSGIVING

Does God cause, or allow, the unpleasantries of life? God is never the blameworthy or culpable cause of that which is contrary to His character. He always acts "in character." However, this does not mean that He cannot utilize situations and people who evidence evil character for His own purposes. Remember Joseph, sold into slavery by his brothers, ended up in Potiphar's house, and when his brothers came in need, he responded, "you meant it for evil, but God meant it for good" (Gen. 50:20). Paul wrote, "God causes all things to work together for good to those who love God, and are called according to His purpose" (Rom. 8:28).

Thanking God for the unpleasantries of life is difficult for many believers. They seem to think that a good God will only allow good circumstances for the good people who believe in Him. God's perspective of what is good or best for our lives often involves painful and unpleasant circumstances. Such unpleasantries, even suffering, are not to be regarded as "evil," but the orchestrations of God's love for our highest good. "Those whom the Lord loves He disciplines, and He scourges every son whom He receives" (Heb. 12:6; Prov. 3:12). It is often in the crises of life that we reach out in dependence upon God.

The Greek word translated "to give thanks" (thanksgiving) in the New Testament is *eucharistia* (*eu* = good; *charis* = grace). Yes, it is the root word for Eucharist (I Cor. 11:24). Thanksgiving is to recognize the "good grace" of God in every situation. This requires that we see God's immensity, sovereignty and His character of love. The apostle Paul learned to "see from God's point of view" as he suffered from "a thorn in the flesh" (II Cor. 12:7), which he identified as "a messenger from Satan," but could see God's purpose in the inconvenience, "to keep me from exalting myself." In the midst of such, he could see God's "good grace" and "be content with weakness" (II Cor. 11:10).

NOVEMBER 25

THE GOSPEL IN A NUTSHELL

Jesus died on the cross to give Himself **FOR** *us.* This is the Christian doctrine of *Redemption,* whereby Jesus' action of crucifixion on the cross "paid the price" for the consequence for human sin. "Christ died **for** sins once for all, *the* just **for** *the* unjust, so that He might bring us to God" (I Pet. 3:18). Christ "gave Himself **for** us, to redeem us from every lawless deed" (Titus 2:14). Jesus took the consequence of death on our behalf.

Jesus rose from the dead to give Himself **TO** us. This is the Christian doctrine of spiritual *Regeneration.* God, by His great mercy "has caused us to be *born again* to a living hope through the resurrection of Jesus Christ from the dead" (I Pet. 1:3). When we receive the Spirit of Jesus we become children of God, "born of God" (Jn. 1:12,13). We receive the provision of the very resurrection-life of the living Lord Jesus into our spirit. We are "partakers of the divine nature" (II Pet. 1:4).

Jesus died on the cross to give Himself **AS** us. This is the Christian doctrine of the vicarious *Substitution* of Jesus "in our place." When Jesus died on the cross, He died there **as** us. Paul explained, "I have been crucified with Christ; it is no longer I who lives but Christ lives in me" (Gal. 2:20). "You have died, and your life is hidden with Christ" (Col. 2:3). "The old has passed away; all things have become new" (II Cor. 5:17).

Jesus rose from the dead to live His life **THROUGH** us. This is the Christian doctrine of *Sanctification,* whereby the Christ-life given *to* us is for the purpose of His life being lived out *through* us. The holy character of Jesus is to be re-presented in our behavior. Paul explained, "I do not presume to speak of anything, except what Christ has accomplished **through** me" (Rom. 15;18). The life of the risen Lord JESUS is to be lived out **through** us to the glory of God.

NOVEMBER 26

THE FATHERHOOD OF GOD

Fathers, in general, have gotten a bad rap in modern social thought. The feminist agenda has often faulted and charged fathers, and all males, with being the cause of suppressing women over the centuries, thereby inciting the need for all women to stand up and assert their rights to assume their rightful place in families and society. Some counsellors have referred to "the father wound" suffered by both men and women during parenting. Some (both male and female) have rejected the Christian gospel based on their repudiation of the idea of God as Father, due to bad memories of their human fathers.

It is not legitimate to formulate one's thoughts of the Fatherhood of God based on less than adequate human fathers. The Fatherhood of God is established by and revealed in the Son, Jesus Christ, who said, "If you have seen/known Me, you have seen/known the Father" (Jn. 14:7). Think about it – the divine Father is known as "Father" because He has a Son, and sent that Son to be the revelation of Himself, and the Son provided the redemptive bridge by which fallen mankind can enter into personal relationship with God as Father. The gospel is essentially a relational invitation to participate in the family of God wherein God is accepted and enjoyed as the loving Father.

Every human person is created with a need to relate to and be loved by a Father, i.e. God. No human father can ever fulfill the deep spiritual need that every human being has for father-relationship. Human fathers are "not up to the job" of serving as divine spiritual Father. Only by the grace of God in Jesus Christ can we who are fathers manifest God's loving heart to our children. The longing of every child's heart is to be loved and accepted by their father, and to hear from their father the words that **JESUS** heard from His Father, "This is my beloved Son (daughter, child), in whom I am well-pleased" (Matt. 3:17; 17:5).

NOVEMBER 27

GROWING OLDER

Human aging is inevitable as we live in this space/time human context of planet earth. Everyone is growing biologically older day-by-day, nanosecond-by-nanosecond. We cannot turn back the clock. There are no time-machines that transport us back in to give us another opportunity to go through the same circumstances, and try to do a better job next time. There is no "fountain of youth" to keep us from the progression of getting older, despite the myth of Juan Ponce de Leon's search for such in the location he called "Florida," which apparently convinced thousands of others to search for it there, even to this very day.

The technical term for aging or growing old is "senescence." The term has nothing to do with getting senile, but is derived from the Latin root word *senescere* meaning "to grow old." The first question might be, "Why do human beings grow old?" Did God create and design men and women with planned obsolescence? Is there a natural entropy of biological organisms? Scientific senescence research is ongoing, examining genetic, hormonal and environmental factors of aging. Genome research of DNA variations as well as divergent stem cell theories are being examined. The quest continues as we seek to understand why human beings grow older and eventually die.

Meanwhile, the production of anti-aging pills, creams, and potions are proliferating, and being marketed to susceptible and gullible people, along with a myriad of procedures alleged to reverse the aging process and prolong longevity of life. People are willing to grasp at straws in overcome the inevitable process of human aging. It is estimated that approximately two-thirds of the human beings who die every day around the globe, die of age-related causes of one kind or another. The most important consideration is not how to stifle human aging, but to consider the spiritual life of **JESUS** that transcends physical life.

NOVEMBER 28

CHRISTIAN HOPE

What makes Christian hope different and distinct from any other basis of hope? Hope looks forward with confident expectation of desirable outcomes yet to be. Worldly hope looks forward with optimistic anticipation that things are going to get better when humanistic ideas are implemented to form an idealistic society. Such cultural hope has great faith in human goodness and intelligence, governmental capability for change, health care advances, development of educational systems, political promises, the legal justice system, economic policies, etc. Such human means are not proven to produce the desired outcomes.

The Jewish people of the old covenant (Old Testament) were a people of hope with confident expectation that Yahweh-God was going to fulfill His promises in a future geographical nationalism that brought particular blessing to them as an ethnically favored people. Jewish hope always looks forward to the future when the promised Messiah-Deliverer might come and establish a promised Jewish kingdom. Such futuristic hope of what might be has not materialized, in large part because of their biased misconceptions of the how God would fulfill His promises. They failed to understand the spiritual fulfillment.

Christian hope is comprised of the confident expectation that the "better" (cf. Hebrews) has already come and been fulfilled in **JESUS** Christ. This realized expectation allows for our confident hopeful expectation that the Christ-life can be re-presented through us in a manner that is totally sufficient and satisfactory for every situation we might confront in life. Christians have Christ in them, the hope of glorious (cf. Col. 1:27) participation in the divine grace that brings total fulfillment in life. We "hope in Christ to the praise of His glory" (Eph. 1:12). Christian hope realizes fulfillment in **JESUS** Christ, and confidently expects our indwelling Lord to provide everything to God's glory.

NOVEMBER 29

DO YOU HATE WHAT GOD HATES?

Does God hate? Yes, he hates and cannot tolerate any character that is not consistent with Himself. God hates sin! In other words, He loves us so much that He hates and abhors all evil character that destroys the good creation He has brought into being. When God hates, He exhibits the necessary flip-side of His love. The question is: Are we in unity with God in hating what God hates? The attitudes of the world, which the Evil One controls as its ruler (Jn. 12:31; 16:11), so subtly suck God's people into cultural adaptation and acceptance of attitudes and expressions of evil character that are contrary to the character of God.

To what extent have we gradually succumbed to the attitudes of our culture, to accept expressions of character that are contrary to the character of God. The time is coming when we will be called to align ourselves with God's character of righteousness, and take a stand against all character expression that is contrary to God's character. Such a stand will be countercultural because most of our society, including most of the culture's religion, have deemed it narrow-minded and less than loving to take such a stand. Are we willing to be ostracized for standing with God and His character and refusing to accept what is unacceptable to God – to call sin "sin"?

Why is it so difficult to get people who call themselves "Christians" to take a stand against abortion, homosexuality, the idolatry of materialism, the self-absorbed quest to "do our own thing" in the haughty selfishness of self-deification? It is not people that God hates. We are to love our brother (I Jn. 4:20) and neighbor (Lk. 10:27-36) with His love. God hates the abominable acts that express the destructive character of the Evil One (Deut. 12:31; Ezek. 33:11; Prov. 6:16-19; 8:13). "Keep the charge of the Lord your God, to walk in His ways, to keep His statutes, and His testimonies, that you may succeed in all you do" (I Kings 2:3).

NOVEMBER 30

DO INFANTS WHO DIE GO TO HEAVEN?

Christians have long desired a definitive answer to the question whether infants who die go to heaven without having heard the gospel and responding to such in personal acceptance, and without being baptized. There does not seem to be a definitive answer in the scripture, but we will take a look at what the scripture does say, as well as some Christian explanations that have been proffered. The passage most often cited is that where David is dealing with the death of the infant that he and Bathsheba had conceived in adultery. David laments, "I cannot bring him back. I will go to him, but he will not return to me" (II Samuel 12:23). Though the child will not be restored to life, David believes that the infant is in a place where he can eventually join him, generally considered to be heaven.

Some Christians are backed into a corner by their theological position. Those who accept the thesis of "original sin," that all humanity is corrupted by Adam's sin, even in the womb, with the consequence of being inherent "sinners" damned to hell unless they believe, are hard put to explain how that can transpire in an infant (unborn or born). Through many contrived and convoluted arguments, some would explain that God in His foreknowledge already knows how that child would have responded to the gospel of Jesus Christ should he have lived, so it is not for us to conjecture. Others have argued that a child must reach the "age of accountability" (who knows when?) to understand sin and salvation and accept Jesus. Prior to that time, they are not accountable. Still others would explain that all family members, including children, are brought into the covenant kingdom under the authority of the family head.

The God I have come to know in Jesus Christ is loving, merciful and gracious. I do not have figure out His ways. He loves to receive children unto Himself (Matt. 19:14; Lk. 18:16).

DECEMBER 1

DON'T JUDGE A BOOK BY ITS COVER

The man's clothing and hair were disheveled and bedraggled. The way he comported himself seemed to evidence that he did not have much confidence; probably a poor self-image. He had no doubt suffered much rejection in his past, and did not want to subject himself to more. He hung his head and shoulders, did not look people in the eye, and appeared to be another case of hopeless humanity. People passed him by, suspicious of such a destitute and homeless person, not wanting to get involved in his problems, fearing that such a scruffy and unkempt individual might have mental health problems and be unpredictable.

It is so easy to jump to unsubstantiated conclusions about people by the way they look. What goes through your mind when you encounter a person who is obese, a person whose hair is in long dreadlocks, a lady who is wearing a Muslim burka, a person whose appearance and actions are obviously gay, or a parent who is not overseeing their out-of-control children? Do you make the effort to interact with such people, or do you shy away from association with them? Samuel had to learn that "the Lord does not see as man sees; for man looks at the outward appearance, but the Lord looks at the heart" (1 Samuel 16:7).

I am suggesting that we all might make it a point to pick out the persons who look most uncomfortable in the situation where we find ourselves. Select those who don't look like they fit in the group or social situation where you are. They may be social misfits who do not know how to dress in a manner that makes them more presentable, and they may have an unpleasant odor. Sometimes they talk too loudly, and may encroach on that bubble of space that should be maintained in social conversation. I am suggesting that we make an intentional effort to strike up conversation with such people, befriend them, and do so regularly, willing to assist them in whatever way we can.

DECEMBER 2

CONTENTMENT

Most people are pleased when circumstances seem to be going their way, and they are getting what they want in life. But that is simply the chance-happiness of taking delight in the selfish fulfillment of one's desires. When the situation turns sour, these same people are often quite discontent. They may be frustrated, irritated, and complain incessantly about what they dislike and hate. Focusing on themselves and their selfish aspirations, they are unwilling to accept adverse circumstances. Instead of experiencing contentment, they are often contentious, engaging in conflict with anyone unwilling to cater to their wants.

Contrasted with the self-oriented happiness based on pleasurable circumstances, there is a settled contentment with life in the midst of all circumstances. This is far more than the unconcerned passivism of "what will be, will be" – who gives a damn? There is a positive, even supernatural, contentment whereby we are willing to accept all circumstances because we believe that God is in control of life, Christ is Lord, and the divine peace of the Holy Spirit is greater than any problems the world can present. This is the contentment that accompanies godliness (I Tim. 6:6), expressing God's character in our attitudes.

There is great freedom in contentment when a person is free from selfish aspirations, free from striving, free from reaction to circumstances – willing to accept what transpires (Phil. 4:11), and content with what we have been given (Heb. 13:5; cf. Matt. 5:5 *Message*). Godly contentment even goes beyond such. Can we be content with being overlooked, unrecognized, or rejected? Can we be content with obscurity or being unknown? Paul said, "I am content with weaknesses, with insults, with distresses, with persecutions, with difficulties for Christ's sake; for when I am weak, then I am strong (II Cor. 12:10). Yes, there can be Godly contentment and serenity in the midst of all storms.

DECEMBER 3

THE SON OF GOD BECAME ...

Every Christian is quite aware of the great Christological statements in the first chapter of John's gospel. In the prologue of his gospel, John writes, "in the beginning was the Word, and the Word was with God, and the Word was God" (Jn. 1:1). Who was the "Word," the *logos*, that John refers to? In Christian thought, the "Word" referred to by John has always been considered as a reference to the Son of God, the second Person of the Triune Godhead. Later in the first chapter of John's gospel, we read the great incarnational statement where John (by the Holy Spirit) explains that "the Word (the Son of God) became flesh and dwelt among us, and we saw His glory, glory as of the only begotten from the Father, full of grace and truth" (Jn. 1:14). When the angel of the Lord told Joseph about the child in Mary's womb, he explained, "you shall call His name **JESUS**, for He will save His people from their sins" (Matt. 1:21). The first "becoming" of the Son of God was His "becoming flesh," a human being, in the incarnation of the individual personage of **JESUS**. This incarnational "becoming" has been a foundational teaching of Christian thought from the beginning.

That, however, is not the only "becoming" whereby the Son of God took on a different form. Many Christians have never seen the second reference to the Son of God "becoming." In the context of emphasizing the resurrection of **JESUS** from the dead, Paul explains that "the Last Adam" (the incarnated **JESUS**) became "living Spirit" by means of the resurrection (I Cor. 15:45). In order that the resurrection-life of **JESUS** might be made available for the regeneration and restoration of God's life in fallen and estranged humanity, the resurrected Son of God became "the Spirit of Christ" to indwell receptive humanity. "If anyone does not have the Spirit of Christ, he is none of His" (Rom. 8:9), i.e. not a Christ-one. There was a "becoming" in the incarnation, and also a "becoming" in the resurrection of **JESUS**.

DECEMBER 4

AMBIGUOUS GRACE

Does anyone know what the word "grace" means in Christian thought today? Religious conversation often mentions "grace," but it is in ambiguous half-definitions and misnomers. "Grace" has become a much misused and abused term in contemporary Christian discussion. It has become a meaningless and gratuitous word that everyone is expected to know what it means, but no one can clearly define. Here are a few descriptive examples of how it is used:

Grace is the primer on God's pump
Grace is the lubricant of God's love
Grace is an attribute of God's mercy
Grace is the initial availability of God's action
Grace is the universal favor and blessing of God
Grace is the pardon that gets you off the hook
Grace is God's permission to do anything you want
Grace is courteous goodwill and forgiveness
Grace is unmerited clemency and reprieve
Grace is divine assistance in sanctification
Grace is the attitude of propriety and refinement
Grace is a commodity conferred on the basis of obedience
Grace is God's leverage to coerce human action

Some of these may touch on meanings that have scriptural support, but for the most part they do not lead to an acceptable Christian understanding of grace. I would define the term in this way: "Grace is God in action in accord with His character, implemented by means of the Son, JESUS Christ (Jn. 1:17), and the power of His Holy Spirit (Heb. 10:29). Since God's character is always love and righteousness, grace is the active willingness and dynamic of God to manifest His character in Christian lives. Such grace-action of God is to be received and made personally efficacious by faith (Eph. 2:8,9).

DECEMBER 5

PASSION FOR THE LIBERATION OF MANKIND

Jesus can legitimately be viewed as the liberator of mankind. He came to set men free from every thought and power that might enslave them. Jesus came to liberate human beings from the enslavement that results from human ideas and every form of earthly human power that men are so willing to follow. Whether it be political power, nationalistic power, ideological power, economic power, military power, religious power, or spiritual power, Jesus came to free us from all the powers of this world (cf. Rom. 8:38; Eph. 6:12). We are to be single-minded in our desires to submit only to the Power of God (Rom. 1:16; I Cor. 1:18).

The deepest form of slavery comes as Satan enslaves and ensnares humanity (II Tim. 2:26). "The whole world lies in the power of the Evil One" (I Jn. 5:19). Fallen humans are "slaves of sin" (Jn. 8:34; Rom. 6:6); only freed from sin (Rom. 6:7; 8:2) in Christ. Though once in "slavery to corruption" (Rom. 8:21), we are set free to the glory of God. "Through fear of death," mankind is "subject to slavery" (Heb. 2:15), and in Christ we are "set free from the body of this death" (Rom. 7:24).

Jesus told the Jewish followers, "You shall know the Truth, and the Truth shall set you free" (John 8:32). "I am the Truth (Jn. 14:6), He later told His disciples. "When the Son sets you free, you are free indeed" (Jn. 8:36). Paul explained, "it was for freedom that Christ set us free" (Gal. 5:1), so since we are "called to freedom" (Gal. 5:13), do not be enslaved to fleshly desires, and "do not becomes slaves of men" (I Cor. 7:23).

Paul wrote, "For though I am free from all men, I have made myself a slave to all, so that I may win more (I Cor. 9:19). Christ-ones should have a passion for the liberation of all men, in ways that eschew all forms of enslavement that encroach upon the freedom that we have been given in Christ.

DECEMBER 6

THE STATUE IN THE CITY PARK

Many seem to attempt to model the behavior of their Christian lives after the statue in the city park. Isn't that statue admirable and outstanding? It doesn't get intoxicated by consuming too much alcohol or taking drugs; it doesn't chase the opposite gender or engage in immoral sexual escapades; it doesn't make false accusations and engage in gossip about others; it doesn't get involved in any mayhem or criminal activity. So, the statue is sober, chaste, discreet and law-abiding. Isn't that what comprises Christian behavior? NO! What one does or does not do, never causes anyone to be righteous, loving, kind, and pure.

Granted it's a dirty job the statue does, with all those pigeons coming and going, but somebody needs to do it – or not do it. But the Christian life is not a calculation of what we DO NOT DO, our abstentions and passivity. Nor is it a summary of what we DO, our virtues and disciplines, such as read our Bibles, pray every day, or attend church. The Christian life is solely the extent to which we allow the living Lord **JESUS** who lives within every genuine Christian to re-present and manifest His perfect character in our behavior. The Christ-life is what we allow JESUS to DO through us – His life lived out through our bodies.

In some religions the "golden rule" reads, "Do *not* do to others what you would *not* have them to do to you." Such is merely negation and privation – not doing. The Christian version reads, "Do unto others, as you would have them do unto you" (cf. Matt. 7:12), but few Christians seem to know the source of such doing, that all Christian "doing" is to be the "doing" of the Lord Jesus in the Christian. "Apart from Me, you can do nothing" (Jn. 15:5). Our desire is to be living expressions of the risen Christ, not just "do nothing" statues in the city park or in the stained-glass sanctuary of a church building, or "do-gooder" activists engaging in ridiculous religious repetitions of self-effort.

DECEMBER 7

BE RECONCILED

Our worship of God cannot be divorced from our down to earth relationships with other people. In the *Sermon on the Mount,* Jesus states, "If you are presenting your offering at the altar, and there remember that your brother has something against you, leave your offering there before the altar and go; first *be reconciled* to your brother, and then come and present your offering" (Matt. 5:23,24). In Corinthians, Paul advises a woman to be "*reconciled* with her husband" (I Cor. 7:11). To reconcile to "to be brought together again" in the relational interaction of harmonious and peaceful fellowship with one another.

Genuine reconciliation of broken human relationships is not merely to overlook or gloss over the issues of estrangement; it is more than the acquiescence that says, "Forget it, act like it never happened, let bygones be bygones." Reconciliation implies a restored relationship of trust that leads to joint action together. The process of reconciliation often requires personal forgiveness, which for Christians necessitates the Forgiver, Jesus Christ, living and functioning in us. It only requires one person to forgive another, but it takes two or more to remove the suspicions, reestablish trust, and engage in reconciled relationship.

Is there anyone who has "anything against you" (Matt. 5:23) that you are aware of? Are there persons that you are estranged from due to previous misunderstanding, emotional issues, hurtful words, financial transactions, etc.? Most people have some relationships where they are "at odds" with others, where estrangement and ostracism has occurred; someone may be holding grudges, and you have gone long periods of time without speaking to these persons. Perhaps now is the time to "bury the hatchet" of hostility, and clear up any differences you have with such persons. Paul's words are pertinent: "As far as it depends on you, be at peace with all men" (Rom. 12:18).

DECEMBER 8

THE WORLD IS NOT OUR RESPONSIBILITY

Most can recall where they were when they first heard the news that planes had been flown into the twin towers of the World Trade Center in New York City on September 11, 2001. It was shocking to soon realize that these were deliberate acts of terrorism attributed to a group called Al Qaeda. I was a couple of thousand miles away from home, and could not return for almost a week. But my first response to what had happened, knowing that there would be retaliation, was to declare, "the world is going to do what the world is going to do!" The ways of the world are somewhat predictable – "tit for tat!" "If you hit me; I will hit you in retaliation."

Some readers likely had a negative reaction to the title of this article. They were probably thinking of the world of human persons, and the universal responsibility we all have for our fellow-men. Perhaps you have now figured out that this article is addressing the world-system of which the Evil One, Satan, is the ruler (Jn. 12:31; 16:11). This antagonistic system of evil is beyond the responsibility of any Christian to change, to convert, to save, or even improve. Only God in Christ can challenge Satan, and indeed Christ has defeated the devil (Heb. 2:14; I Jn. 3:8), and has "overcome the world" (Jn. 16:33). Though the serpent's head has been crushed (Gen. 3:15), he is still writhing and wreaking havoc via his world-system and personal temptation (cf. I Pet. 5:8,9; Rev. 12:12). He will remain "the ruler of this world" until he is cast into the abyss (Rev. 20:3). In the meantime, the world is going to do what the world is going to do, because the character of Satan is fixed in antithesis to God.

Christians are "in the world, but not of the world" (Jn. 17:11,13), and must be concerned that the world of humanity is loved by God (Jn. 3:16) in **JESUS** Christ. It is our responsibility to share with the world of mankind the good news of the gospel.

DECEMBER 9

WILL-POWER

The world likes to talk about employing "will-power" to overcome negative and unhealthy behaviors in one's life, as well as using "will-power" as the impetus to do what we know we ought to do to be better persons. Many Christians also speak of having "free-will" to make choices that can then be implemented with "will-power" to achieve the spirituality they desire. Although I know I am bucking the humanistic trend of modern thought, I must question whether human beings in general have the "free-will" to determine their self-chosen course of action or the "will-power" to enact what they have determined to do.

Even the 12-step anonymity groups such as AA, NA, OEA, SA, etc. recognize that human "will-power" is insufficient to overcome the addictive tendencies of people. Steps 1-3 address the admission of the problem, the need for a power beyond themselves to manage the problem, and a surrender to that power. The volitional choice mechanism of human will does not have power in itself to implement such behavioral changes. The "power beyond ourselves" is a spiritual power that will either be the "power of the Evil One" (I Jn. 5:19) or "the power of God" (I Cor. 1:24), but there is no independent "will-power" by which human beings can determine and self-generate their behavior.

The myth of will-power as a self-generative mechanism of human behavior is not consistent with the new covenant scriptural teaching of "derivative humanity." God created human beings, not as independent selves who by self-discipline and self-control can conquer temptation and manifest positive and constructive righteousness. Rather, He created us as derivative creatures who will necessarily derive our motivation and character for all behavior from one spiritual source or the other (God or Satan). Humans do have freedom of choice in the human will to decide the source from which we will derive.

DECEMBER 10

THE DARK FACTOR

A broad international psychological study is being conducted to measure what researchers are calling "the dark core" in human persons. This "D quotient," as it has been called, is intended to calculate and provide clinical measurement of the selfishness and sinfulness characteristics in human personality. They want to assess "traits related to antagonistic, malevolent, and socially aversive behavior," and how they affect disutility in social situations. I find it very interesting that secular behavioral and social specialists are recognizing and attempting to evaluate "the dark core" in human personalities.

This psychological study does not take into account the spiritual function of mankind, but from a spiritual perspective it is not difficult to see some equivalence of "the dark core" designation with the diabolic inducement of spiritual depravity in human beings. In fact, the "D quotient" might be a measurement of the "diabolic-orientation" and serve as a "depravity indicator" in human persons. This would serve to document the scriptural statement that "the prince of the power of the air (the devil) is the spirit that is at work in the sons of disobedience" (Eph. 2:2). Paul proceeds to explain "our struggle is against the powers, against the world forces of this *darkness*, against the spiritual forces of wickedness in the heavenly places" (Eph. 6:12).

Throughout the new covenant scriptures, we read of directionless people wherein "*darkness* has blinded their eyes" (I Jn. 2:11), but these persons are "called out of *darkness* into His marvelous light" (I Pet. 2:9), and "transferred from the domain of *darkness* to the kingdom of His beloved Son" (Col. 1:13). Such a transfer requires a spiritual conversion from "*darkness* to light," from "deriving from Satan to deriving from God" (Acts 26:18), a turning from "the dark core" to the "light core" of union with "the Light of the Lord" (Eph. 5:8), **JESUS** Christ.

DECEMBER 11

HOW ABOUT YOUR DIET?

"Diet" is not a four-letter, dirty word, as some might surmise. A general definition of the word "diet" is simply the variety of foods that a person or group of persons regularly eats. Since it is necessary for everyone to eat, we all have a diet of various foods that we eat. The English word "diet" is derived from the Latin word *dieta*, meaning "daily regimen." The more limited definition of a "diet" is a plan for a restricted course of foods undertaken for weight-loss or medical reasons. The word "diet" began to be used as an adjective in the 20th century referring to "diet soft drinks" and "diet pills" intended to reduce calories and overeating.

Many entrepreneurs jumped on the diet bandwagon, providing their opinions for diet plans, and charging for the advice. It is reported that Americans today spend more than $60 billion annually on weight-loss programs and products. Surveys also show that Christian persons are more apt to be obese than the general population. Why is that? In light of that phenomenon, many different religious diet plans have been marketed. One of the more well-known religious diet plans is called "The Daniel Diet" or "The Daniel Fast," based on Dan. 1:12, and it is essentially a vegetarian diet plan for a particular period of time.

Diet plans can so easily become law-based legalistic procedures to encourage the self-effort of performance for selfish objectives. Christians are no longer "under law" (Rom. 6:14,15), but "it was for freedom that Christ set us free" (Gal. 5:1). Paul wrote, "food does not bring us near to God; we are no worse if we eat, and no better if we do" (I Cor. 8:8). How, then, would God have us to eat? We must personally listen in obedience under the Lord **JESUS** Christ, to ascertain His priorities for our life, and eat responsibly under the dynamic of His grace. That being said, this acrostic of the word "diet" might serve as an effective weight-loss diet: **D**ecrease • **I**ntake • **E**xercise • **T**enaciously.

DECEMBER 12

FALSE TEACHERS

Throughout the inspired scriptures, both old and new covenants, there are abundant references to "false teachers." After examination of these many biblical references, it appears that God's concern is not always about a "false message" that is aberrant and inconsistent with the teaching of God's truth, but even more so, the warning about false teachers has to do with the "false methods" utilized to deceitfully dupe and manipulate their listeners. When the message is not lived out in accord with the character of God who they claim to represent, then "what they *do* speaks so loud, that what they *say* is dispelled."

Some of the misrepresentative methods used by false teachers include the demand to be regarded as an authority, in an attempt to develop a dependency of their followers upon them, whereby the listeners become followers of the teacher, rather than followers of Jesus Christ. Such false teachers often emphasize faith in the teacher, or faith in various principles or promises, or faith in faith, rather than proper faith in Christ. In addition, they may seek the limelight, evidence pride in their teaching or spirituality, advocate legalistic performance to please God, engage in financial or sexual exploitation.

Contemporary reference to false teachers usually identifies their message and their methods as "cultic," i.e. aberrant and misleading. The root of such a designation is to indicate that what they *say* and what they *do* does not lead people into pure worship of the perfect, loving God, revealed by and in the divine Son, **JESUS** Christ. The Latin word *cultus*, from which our English word "cult" is derived, meant "worship." One should be aware, however, that a contemporary synonym of the word "cultic" is the word "religious." Religious methods are cultic methods as they do not operate from the dynamic grace of God, but instead use man-made methods (cf. Col. 2:16-23) of manipulation.

DECEMBER 13

BARGAINING WITH GOD

Despite how long we have known and experienced the grace of God and been growing in "the grace and knowledge of the Lord Jesus Christ" (II Pet. 3:18), when we have a lapse in our focus on the all-sufficient Lord Jesus, and slip into "slack-abiding" (what Baptists often call "backsliding), and fail to pay attention to our faith-receptivity of God's activity, we often revert back to attempting to bargain with God. "God, I know I need your blessing in my life, and if I *do* this action or *do not* engage in that activity You are likely to withdraw Your blessing from my life, so I need to be more faithful in performing the works You expect of me, so I can continue to expect Your blessing upon my life."

Such a prayer is based on the false premise that God's grace action is based on a reciprocal bargaining negotiation. The naturalistic "if ... then" premise is a pre-grace perspective. The "natural man" (I Cor. 2:14) thinks, "If I do my part, then God will do His part, therefore I must do my best, so God can do the rest." It is sometimes difficult to remember that God's blessing is not contingent on what we might do for Him or abstain from doing. "God has blessed us with every blessing in heavenly places in Christ Jesus" (Eph. 1:3). We do not need to plead for, pray for, work for, or negotiate for God's blessing or good will.

The bargaining paradigm of relationship with God does not have any validity. We have no "chips" with which to bargain ("apart from Me you can do nothing" – Jn. 15:5), and God has already expended all His "chips" in the Son, Jesus Christ, having "granted us all things pertaining to life and godliness" (II Pet. 1:3), in order that we might become "partakers of the divine nature" (II Pet. 1:4). We have nothing to bring to the table; God has everything, and all that He has He has already given to us in His Son, **JESUS** Christ. Jesus declared from the cross, "It is finished!" – no more negotiated bargaining deals. Just live by His GRACE!

DECEMBER 14

RELIGIOUS DO-GOODERS

There are thousands upon thousands of people in the churches today for whom the designation "religious do-gooders" aptly describes their approach to their religion. In fact, most local churches would not survive if it were not for the "religious do-gooders" who consistently respond to the repetitive calls to be involved, to be committed, to serve, to give time, energy and money for the continued operation of the local institution. The problem comes when these naïve volunteers idealistically think that they are "serving the Lord" and thereby ever so subtly think that they are earning points with God or stars in their crown.

They are put to work like indentured servants, doing everything from dusting the furniture, sweeping the walkways, mowing the lawn, weeding the flower gardens, maintaining the landscaping, painting the walls of classrooms, folding the bulletins, watching the children in the nursery, filling and washing the communion cups, serving as greeters or ushers, and any other menial job the powers that be want completed. They are often undiscerning in their quest to "go, go, go and do, do, do for Jesus," failing to understand that Christian life and ministry is to be accomplished by the dynamic of God's grace in Jesus Christ.

Hold on now! We must avoid being snide or cynical, and looking down with contempt on hard-working Christians. Paul did write, "We are God's handiwork, created in Christ Jesus to do *good works,* which God prepared in advance for us to do" (Eph. 2:10). Even earlier, Paul wrote, "Let us not grow weary of *doing good,* for in due season we will reap, if we do not give up. So then, as we have opportunity, let us *do good* to everyone, and especially to those who are of the household of faith" (Gal. 6:9,10). It should be our desire, however, that such people will develop spiritual discernment that realizes they are only called to be and to do what the Lord **JESUS** wants to be and do in and through them.

DECEMBER 15

FAITH IS NOT THE GIFT OF GOD

Many Christians have the mistaken notion, because they have been taught such, that "faith is the gift of God." Those who maintain such a tenet, end up logically denying all human responsibility to respond to what God has done, and what He wants to continue to do in their lives through Jesus Christ. The end result of such thinking is that man is simply viewed as an automaton, a puppet on a string being manipulated by a sovereign puppeteer enacting His predetermined intentions in the actions and behavior of human beings.

Now, it is accurate to explain that God has given all human creatures the freedom of choice by which they can make responsible choices. As choosing creatures, human beings are responsible to make choices in response to what God has done, and is doing, in Jesus Christ. Such choices that a human makes by using his God-given freedom of choice is called "faith." Faith is the freely chosen human receptivity of God's activity of Grace, both initially in response to God's redemption in Jesus (cf. Jn. 1:12,13) and continually (Col. 2:6) with the Christian life.

The misunderstanding that "faith is the gift of God" comes from faulty exegesis of two primary verses in the New Testament. Paul wrote, "For by grace you have been saved through faith; and that not of yourselves, it is the gift of God" (Eph. 2:8). "That" which is the gift of God is "salvation," not the human response of faith. The second verse is also a very familiar verse: "I have been crucified with Christ; and it is no longer I who live, but Christ lives in me; and the life which I now live in the flesh I live by faith in the Son of God, who loved me and gave Himself up for me" (Gal. 2:20). The King James Bible reads, "the life I now live in the flesh I live by *the faith of* the Son of God," as if it was Jesus' faith. Not so! Faith is not the gift of God. It is a human being exercising his God-given freedom of choice to respond to God's grace in Jesus Christ.

DECEMBER 16

ARE YOU DEVOTED TO YOUR DEVOTIONS?

Millions of Christians have had admonitions preached at them and drilled into them that they should be involved in "daily devotions." This usually entails a specific time each day set aside to commune with God, a place to engage in this practice, and a plan for daily bible reading and personal prayer. Such "spiritual disciplines" have long been advocated in the church, and can no doubt be beneficial to personal spiritual growth. The problem comes when such disciplines are enacted in mechanical and legalistic engagement, and are regarded as "means of grace" whereby an individual is alleged to become more "spiritual" and closer to God. The only "means of grace" is **JESUS** (cf. Jn. 1:17).

Jesus made it explicitly clear to the Jewish leaders, "You search the scriptures, thinking that in them you have eternal life, and it is these that testify of ME, and you are unwilling to come to ME so that you may have life" (Jn. 5:39). The living Lord Jesus is our life (Jn. 14:6; Col. 3:4; I Jn. 5:12,13), and we must not seek life apart from Him, even in personal devotions, "Quiet Time," or a "Daily Watch." The disciplines of devotion are not an end in themselves. We must remember that the real objective is to know **JESUS** in deep spiritual intimacy, listening in obedience to the Spirit of Christ to lead and direct our lives (cf. Rom. 8:14).

We must beware of developing a devotion to devotions, rather than "devotion to Christ." Writing to the Corinthians, Paul explained that He wanted to promote "devotion to the Lord" (I Cor. 7:23), and did not want them to be led astray from "the simplicity and purity of devotion to Christ" (II Cor. 11:3). Many mature Christians will tell you that they are no longer bound to daily devotional techniques, preferring instead to spontaneously be involved in personal relationship with the living Lord **JESUS** throughout every day. Beware of concentrating on the peripherals rather than on the living Person of **JESUS** our Lord.

DECEMBER 17

RESPONDING TO THE CIRCUMSTANCES

A saintly lady in our congregation suffered greatly throughout her life. She was afflicted with polio at a young age, and bore the effects of that disease throughout her life. She did not let that slow her down, however, and went on to earn a doctoral degree, become a teacher as well as a pastor's wife. Later in life, the post-polio symptoms were severe, and she was consigned to a wheelchair. Despite later developing cancer, she had a sweet character and attitude that attracted many people to seek her counsel. People would ask how she maintained such a positive attitude in the midst of difficulties. Her response was, "What happens to me is not nearly as important as how I respond to it."

This woman's approach to the situations of life is a lesson for us all. We must not let the circumstances of life define us. The Christian's desire should be that the character of the living Lord **JESUS** might define us. That is why we are identified as "Christ-ones," because the living "Christ is our life" (Col. 3:4). We want the character of Christ, "the fruit of the Spirit" (Gal. 5:22,23), to be manifested in our behavior, despite and in the very midst of, whatever trials we might encounter. Christians are not escapists seeking deliverance from what life might bring. We are "in the world, but not of the world" (Jn. 17:11,14), to let His light shine.

Yes, we often initially react to incidents in life with self-concern with subsequent attempts to control the situation by our best self-effort. But such humanistic endeavors to do things "man's way" seldom solve the problems we encounter. Moving beyond self-reaction, Christians have the provision of God's grace that allows them to respond in faith to any circumstances we might confront. "God's way" of responding to the situations of life is to allow the provision of the life of **JESUS** who lives within the Christian (cf. II Cor. 13:5; Gal. 2:20) to exhibit the power of the Holy Spirit to God's glory.

DECEMBER 18

"WHAT I NEED IS PATIENCE"

The young mother was quite exasperated with her children, who were running off in several directions, and not responding to her disciplinary admonitions. Nothing was going right for the auto mechanic that day, when pieces broke while he was removing them, and the new replacement parts would not fit. Profits were down and the business manager was feeling the pressure to turn the business around without taking it out on the employees around him. Though their tasks were quite diverse, they were quite united in being at their wits end on how to deal with their situations, and exclaiming, "What I need is patience!"

What is patience? The Greek word means "long-suffering, i.e. accepting the situation and enduring it without an impetuous outburst of hasty irritation or anger. Is patience a virtue, as many have explained? Since virtue is often thought to be the meritorious performance of moral standards, the Christian response should be, "No, patience is not a performance virtue," for Paul explains that patience is included in "the fruit of the Spirit" (Gal. 5:22,23). Patience is part of the cluster of dynamic character traits that only the Spirit of the risen Lord **JESUS** can activate by His grace in our attitudes and behavior.

One person, in the midst of a frustrating moment exclaimed, "What I need is patience!" My response was, "Have you not received Jesus in your spirit?" He assured me that he had received Christ within. I replied, "If you have Jesus, you have all the patience that you will ever need. The entire character of Christ is inherent in "the fruit of the Spirit," and you need only call on the patience of Christ in any situation that "Jesus Christ might demonstrate His perfect patience" (I Tim. 1:16). Patience is not a stand-alone commodity that should be sought only in difficult situations. We must not be a fruit-picker, but allow the complete cluster of Christ's character to be exhibited at all times.

DECEMBER 19

WHAT'S THE OBJ?

I don't know about you, but I often have to develop some helpful mind games to keep myself on course. I find it all too easy to let the monotony of the mundane dull my mind and senses to the big picture of what life is all about. It is so easy to get in the rut of routine in our regular lives so we fail to remain focused on the ultimate goal of life. I find this to be particularly true when I am tempted to react to something relatively insignificant like a slow driver in the fast lane, a person who has cut in front of me in a line, or when I am in a hurry and everything seems to be slowing me down. When I feel my emotional temperature rising, and hopefully before I erupt, I have to pull myself up short and ask myself, "What the OBJ?" What's the real objective of my being here on earth and in the midst of this situation? When the Israelites were frustrated with the obstacles preventing them from entering the promised land, God reminded them of "everyone whom I have created for My glory" (Isa. 43:7). I must continually be reminded that the objective of any moment in time is that God might be glorified through me, as the life of **JESUS** is manifested in my life and behavior (II Cor. 4:10,11). As I have been forced to admit repeatedly, time after time, the issue is **JESUS** in the midst of every experience of my life.

Why is it so difficult for me to remember the OBJ when the circumstances threaten to overwhelm me, just as the waves threatened to overwhelm Peter on the Sea of Galilee (Matt. 14:29-31)? God has "called us unto sanctification" (I Thess. 4:7), "for the purpose of godliness" (I Tim. 4:7), to "love from a pure heart and good conscience and a sincere faith" (I Tim. 1:5), and all of this is part of "the eternal purpose which He carried out in Christ Jesus our Lord" (Eph. 3:11). Quite aware of my redemption and regeneration in Christ, I will, no doubt, have to answer my own question about "what's the OBJ" many more times as I bounce through life like a pinball against the bumpers.

DECEMBER 20

DOES GOD HAVE GENDER?

The polytheistic religion of the Greeks had both male gods and female goddesses, with such mythological speculation even allowing for gods with combined male and female bi-gender. The gods and goddesses were speculatively thought to cavort with one another and procreate children who were also gods. The triune Christian God, Father, Son, and Holy Spirit, is not identified in scripture as having any inherent gender, but the translators of Christian scripture have generally used masculine pronouns to refer to each of the three persons of the Trinity. Only in recent history has pronominal gender reference been challenged.

Through the years of English bible translation (since the fifteenth century), the three Persons of the Triune Godhead have traditionally been referred to using masculine pronouns. Changing gender trends in the twentieth century produced gender-agendas that would attempt to influence the translation and interpretation of the Christian scriptures. The feminist and sexist agenda wanted to address God as "she," and change references to "the sons of God" as inclusive of both "the sons and daughters of God." The homosexual and transgender advocates were more comfortable with gender-neutral translations.

The truth of the matter is that God is a divine being and has no personal gender. He transcends gender. Gender is introduced in the biblical creation account when God created human beings, "male and female created He them" (Gen. 1:27). The original biblical languages of Hebrew and Greek both employ grammatical gender for nouns, verbs and pronouns, but such use does not imply or necessarily align with sexual gender. References to God as "He" have traditionally been considered as metaphorical, and references to the Son of God becoming a "man" always employ the generic word for "human" instead of the gender specific reference to Jesus becoming a male.

DECEMBER 21

"IT'S OBVIOUS YOU'RE RELIGIOUS"

The neighborhood ladies were visiting, and one lady said to another, "Well, it's obvious you're religious." What did she mean by such a comment? Was this a compliment or a derisive comment? What made it so obvious? It might have been her attire if her hair was in a bun, she covered her head with a scarf, she never adorned herself with makeup, and she always wore ankle length cotton dresses. It might have been that she always carried a large black Bible. It may have been that with consistent and conscientious regularity, she frequently loaded the children in the car on various days of the week and drove away.

Religion is all about routine human action. The religious adherents are encouraged to go, go, go and do, do, do in performance exercises for the deity and the hierarchy. They are expected to attend all the gatherings regularly, to serve faithfully in endeavors that promote the group, and to give generously of their monies to finance the building and the leaders. Such performance activities are the foremost expectation of most religious groups, so much so that without such they would cease to exist. Religion uses and abuses people for its own ends. Religion is a fallen human enterprise, energized by Satan.

Many genuine Christian persons have succumbed to the pressure to be involved in religious activities, expending great energy and personal resources in the parasitic hyperactivity of religion. Christians must be cautioned to not let doing religious things and engaging in institutional church activities take the place of knowing and loving **JESUS** Christ in an intimate and ever-deepening relationship. Our desire must be to make it obvious that we are a Christ-one, indwelt by the living Christ, based only on the fact there is something different and positive about our attitude and behavior as we allow the character of the Lord **JESUS** Christ to be evidenced in our daily behavior.

DECEMBER 22

"I DON'T MEASURE UP!"

An active Christian leader, a minister, said, "I just feel like I don't measure up to what God expects of me. I feel like I fall far short, like I am a failure." Many others likewise have the nagging feeling that they're not doing enough to please God, and are constantly asking, "What else should I be doing?" Such people are often exhausted from their active endeavors and nearing physical and emotional burn-out. One person exclaimed, "Just when I think that I am nearing the goal of what I should be doing, it seems like they move the goal-line and there is so much more that I should be doing." My question: "Who is setting these goals?"

These goals of expectation have often been set up by performance-oriented religious authorities. So much false guilt has been fostered by the performance paradigm of religion that views God as a taskmaster with never-ending expectations that we should jump through the hoops progressing toward undefined measurement criteria, all the while belittling and berating oneself for not measuring up. Religious people just can't believe it when you tell them that God doesn't have any expectations for what they can do. He knows that "Apart from Jesus, they can do nothing (cf. Jn. 15:5) of any consequence in the kingdom. Just BE who you are "in Christ."

The issue in our Christian life is the living out of the life of Christ, not our progression on some scale of religious measurement. The only measurement is **JESUS**, and He is not measuring our performance. Our Christian life is not based on what we DO, but on what He has done (Jn. 19:30) and what He wants to continue to do by His grace (II Cor. 3:5; I Thess. 5:24). Everything He would desire to do in us, He provides the divine dynamic to accomplish through us by His grace. Since the only measurement is His character, then His divine doing of grace is quite sufficient as He manifests His life in and through us (II Cor. 4:10,11).

DECEMBER 23

THE IDOLATRY OF KNOWLEDGE

Within the Christian community, wherein all devotion and adoration of worship is to be directed to God in Christ alone, and all forms of idolatry are eschewed and forbidden, there is a subtle and pernicious form of reverence verging on worship for the false-god of knowledge. Paul warned that such idolatrous "knowledge makes one arrogant" (I Cor. 8:1). There have long been those engaged in academic philosophy, those claiming to know and perceive (*scientia*) natural and supernatural realities, those with advanced degrees from esteemed universities, and those with baffling vocabularies who "have a way with words" people admire and want to listen to. Paul warned Timothy about "avoiding the worldly empty chatter and opposing arguments of what is falsely called 'knowledge'" (I Tim. 6:20).

The Greeks had several explanations of knowledge and wisdom. *Noesis* was the intellectual understanding via the mind (*nous*). *Sophia* referred to the skilled use of wisdom, and was identified as a Greek god, becoming the basis of philosophy (*philosophia*, "love of wisdom"). *Gnosis* was the general word for personal knowledge, but in philosophical Gnosticism referred to a transcendental knowledge that could arrive at the "divine spark" of the divinization of humanity. *Theoria* was divine contemplation, leading to communion with the gods.

All of these influenced early Christian thought, but Christians are encouraged to have personal and relational knowledge of the living Lord **JESUS**. Paul wanted to "know Christ as Lord…and the power of His resurrection" (Phil,. 3:8,10), emphasizing "a true knowledge of God's mystery, that is, Christ Himself" (Col. 2:2). Peter advised us to "grow in the grace and knowledge of our Lord and Savior, **JESUS** Christ" (II Pet. 3:18). There is a knowledge at the heart of our personal worship of God in Christ, but we must eschew the idolatrous human knowledge that fosters pride.

DECEMBER 24

THE GOD-MAN

At the heart of Christian thought is the understanding that Jesus was, and is, the God-man. Early in Christian theological thought, the Greek word *theanthropos* was used to describe how deity and humanity were combined in the person of Jesus Christ. The word is a Greek compound, *theos* = God; *anthropos* = man. In Latin theological discussion, the phrase *deus homo* (*deus* = god; *homo* = man) was utilized. More precise explanation of the God-man reality was developed at the Council of Chalcedon in A.D. 451, where Christian theologians affirmed that Jesus had two natures, divine and human, combined in *hypostatic* union.

Christian teaching through the subsequent centuries has affirmed that the second Person of the Godhead, the Son of God, was incarnated as a human individual in the person of Jesus Christ, born as an infant in Bethlehem. The "Word became flesh" is the apostle John's expression (Jn. 1:1,14), while Paul explains that the Son of God "although He existed in the form of God, did not regard equality with God a thing to be grasped, but emptied Himself, taking the form of a bond-servant, being made in the likeness of men" (Phil. 2:6,7). In the *kenotic* self-emptying of Himself, Jesus did not empty Himself of deity or divine glory, but of the right and prerogative of exclusively divine function.

The assertion of Jesus Christ as the God-man has been the core of Christian thought through the centuries of the Church. There have been aberrations wherein some emphasized the humanity of Jesus to the neglect of His deity, and others have emphasized His deity to the neglect of His humanity. They must be held together – **JESUS** was, and is, fully God and fully man. A more recent aberration is the assertion that the incarnational hypostatic union applies not just to the person of Jesus, but since Jesus represented all mankind, all human persons universally, without exception, have been made god-men through Jesus. NO!

DECEMBER 25

"THE WORD BECAME FLESH"

Theologically, one must avoid pushing the concept of incarnation beyond what the scriptures indicate. The Son of God became a human, was incarnated and became flesh in the individuated personage of the man, Jesus Christ. To push that to a generalized statement that "God became mankind" is to go beyond the revealed statements of scripture. The incarnation was not a subsuming of humanity into the Being of the Godhead as some have indicated. The Son of God, the second person of the triune Godhead, assumed human personage as the singular God-man who could thereby be the Savior of mankind.

"The Word" (Greek *logos*), referring to the divine Son of God, "who was with God, and was God" (Jn. 1:1) "became (Greek *egeneto*, came into being as) flesh (physical human body form)" (Jn. 1:14). Paul explains that "Christ Jesus, although He existed in the form of God (deity), did not regard equality with God a thing to be grasped (held on to), but emptied Himself, taking the form of a bond-servant, being made in the likeness of men (humanity)" (Phil. 2:5-7). What did the divine Son "empty Himself" of in order to be enfleshed or incarnated into the human person of Jesus? Not His deity, for He could still say "I and the Father are one" (Jn. 10:30). Not His divine glory, for when He became flesh His glory was evident (Jn. 1:14). It is best explained that He emptied Himself of His divine prerogative to function independently as God, in order to function as a dependent human creature who would rely upon the indwelling spiritual presence of the Father (Jn. 14:10), by faith, to take the initiative (Jn. 5:30; 8:28) to empower and express His character in every human action.

In becoming the incarnated God-man, **JESUS** was not balancing his deity and humanity schizophrenically, for these two aspects of his being were hypostatically conjoined. Neither did the Word have to commit divine suicide when enfleshed in human form.

DECEMBER 26

ACCEPTING THE UNACCEPTABLE

There are some activities that are glossed-over and deemed "acceptable" in the Christian community, that are definitely unacceptable in the sight of God. Specifically, we will address the toxic talk of personal gossip that shares information about another when the one talking and the one listening are not part of the problem or the solution. Even non-Christians have noted how Christian people tend to speak judgmentally behind each other's backs, engaging in defamation and verbal assassination rather than straight-forward honest conversation that is constructive and upbuilding to those they say they love.

What a tragic indictment. Why is gossip so common among Christian people? Idle talk and sharing of rumors, what Paul calls "worldly and empty chatter which spreads like gangrene" (II Tim. 2:16,17), soon becomes slander (Rom. 1:29,30) and "talking about things not proper to mention" (I Tim. 5:13). It is usually based on the pride of "being in the know" about someone, and feeling superior by being in control of sharing a juicy detail in the game of "one-up-man-ship" wherein "I know something you don't know, and I can't wait to share it with you." "The words of a whisperer are like dainty morsels" (Prov. 18:8).

Gossip is a cancer in the Body of Christ. It is unacceptable because it is so misrepresentative of the character of the living Lord **JESUS**. To tear another down to build yourself up is so contrary to the character of divine Love that "seeks the highest good of the other, without thought of what I get out of it." Paul wrote, "Let no unwholesome word proceed from your mouth, but only such a word as is good for edification according to the need of the moment, so that it will give grace to those who hear" (Eph. 4:29). Satan, the father of lies (Jn. 8:44), is the slanderer who accuses the brethren (Rev. 12:10), and the source of all gossip that tears holes in the fabric of the church of Jesus Christ.

DECEMBER 27

THE LIAISON OF LOSERS

The Christian community was never intended to be a country-club of those who were successful in life, where they could gather to enjoy their positions and acquisitions, by slapping each other on the back to celebrate their success. Instead of such a "society of the successful," Jesus seems to have likened the kingdom of God to something more like a "liaison of losers" who are quite aware of their flaws and failures, their inabilities and inadequacies, but are willing to reach out in humility to grasp the hand of God's grace to be lifted up to an adequacy and sufficiency that is derived out of God's Being and action.

Have you noticed the many parables that Jesus told about the lowly, the lost, the losers, and "the least of these," indicating that the kingdom of God would be comprised of such persons? In the parable of the lost sheep, the Shepherd is willing to leave the remaining flock of ninety-nine grazing to seek the one who was lost. In the parable of the lost coin, the woman searches in every crack and cranny to find the coin that rolled away. In the parable of the lost son, best known as "the prodigal son," the Father, representing God, joyously rushes out to welcome home the lost son, and incorporate him into the family.

It should be patently obvious that the modern "health and wealth gospel" is such an antithetical contrast to the composition of the kingdom of God that Jesus intended. The riches of God's grace are extended to the have-nots, the needy, those who are quite aware of their various forms of poverty, and are willing to reach out to accept God's provision. The good news of the gospel is that the lost have been found in **JESUS** Christ, and the losers who have humbly recognized their inability cooperatively collaborate in a "liaison of losers" who are now "seated in the heavenlies" (Eph. 1:20; 2:6) in Christ, constantly grateful for the restorative provision of God's abundant love and grace in Jesus Christ.

DECEMBER 28

THE DEVIL'S PLAYGROUND

Some might identify "the devil's playground" with such places as Hollywood, Las Vegas, New Orleans, New York City, Rio de Janeiro, etc. May I suggest that "the devil's playground" is much more pervasive than such geographical locations of sinful and debaucherous behavior. The devil's playground is located in every city and village in every state, for in the institutions and buildings of religion in every location, as well in the hearts and minds of the religious people who gather there, Satan has a heyday perverting the attitudes and actions of religious people to cause them to behave in misrepresentative ways.

In his classic book, *Screwtape Letters*, C.S. Lewis conjectures that the senior devil, Screwtape, is giving a speech at the Annual Dinner of the Tempter's Training College for Young Devils, declaring, "It will be an ill day for us if what most humans mean by 'religion' ever vanishes from the Earth. It can still send us the truly delicious sins. The fine flower of unholiness can grow only in the close neighbourhood of the Holy. Nowhere do we tempt so successfully as on the very steps of the altar." Three centuries earlier, Blaise Pascal wrote, "Men never do evil so completely and cheerfully as when they do it from religious conviction."

The Apostle Paul referred to his religious detractors by writing, "For such are false apostles, deceitful workers, transforming themselves into apostles of Christ. And no wonder! For Satan himself transforms himself into an angel of light. Therefore, it is no great thing if his ministers also transform themselves into ministers of righteousness, whose end will be according to their works" (2 Corinthians 11:13,14). Paul was stating that Satan is a master of disguise, masquerading as deceptive counterfeits in religious teachers. It is so imperative that Christian people develop spiritual discernment to differentiate what is of the Evil One and what is derived from the Lord **JESUS** Christ.

DECEMBER 29

WHEN TRAGEDY STRIKES

Christians are not immune or exempt from experiencing the common tragedies of life. Such painful situations will affect our human thinking, feeling, and decision-making (and even our bodies) in the same manner as it does every human being. Everyone is prone to ask "Why?", knowing that such a question will seldom have a satisfactory answer. Rabbi Kushner's book, *When Bad Things Happen to Good People*, asked that question so many ask, and offered soothing sympathy to those are suffering, but could not definitively answer the "why?" question. Often the only encouragement is "the way out is through," as it was for the Israelites struggling in the Arabian wilderness.

Yes, when tragedy strikes, we may feel numb from the shock; our mind and emotions may be temporarily frozen or paralyzed; and we may be tempted to give up and take flight. Such reaction is often accompanied by fear and/or anger. These reactions of fight, fright, and flight are natural human reactions, and are not to be despised as weakness. Those persons who are Christ-ones do, however, have spiritual resources to rely on during and following the shock of such a difficult situation. The presence of the indwelling Spirit of the risen Lord **JESUS** provides the power of God's grace to offer comfort (cf. II Cor. 1:3-6) and strength to navigate through the trial and tribulation of the tragedy.

The apostle Paul's encouragement to the Corinthians Christians might be translated, "No tragedy has overtaken you but such as is common to man; and God is faithful, who will not allow you to be tested beyond what you are able, but with the tragedy will provide the way of escape also, so that you will be able to endure it" (I Cor. 10:13). The Christian is encouraged to respond to tragedies by trusting in God, and that by allowing for the receptivity of His activity of grace to be operative within and through the difficult circumstance.

DECEMBER 30

"JUST AS I AM"

The lyrics of the familiar hymn, "Just As I Am," were originally written by Charlotte Elliott in 1835. They have often been used as an invitation hymn in churches, and became quite famous when so used by the Billy Graham crusades.

> Just as I am, without one plea,
> But that Thy blood was shed for me,
> And That Thou bid'st me come to Thee.
> O Lamb of God, I come! I come!

Many persons made decisions to receive Jesus when this hymn was being sung. You may be one of them.

An irony often results when those who receive the living Lord Jesus become part of a church fellowship of evangelical Christians. Such Christian fellowships often have very tightly held beliefs and attitudes of doctrinal conformity, of behavioral acceptability, of the type of clothing suitable for attendance at worship, of a respectable lifestyle testimony, and even political opinions. They expect everyone who is part of their group to be like-minded, thinking that the key to unity is uniformity.

Those who might begin to attend such a fellowship, and do not meet the unspoken criteria of acceptability are often not afforded the "Just as I Am" welcome for social involvement. They are looked at askance and expected to conform prior to social acceptance in the group. Such people might be accepted into union with **JESUS**, but we cannot accept you unless you look like us, talk like us, think like us, and act like us. Strangers who are different find it very difficult to break down the artificial barriers for inclusion in the fellowship. The Body of Christ, the Church, often misrepresents in social practice the **JESUS** they claim to be identified with as Christ-ones.

DECEMBER 31

YEAR'S END

Many people write a poem at the end of the year, remembering, reflecting, and contemplating what has transpired in the past year, and sharing their emotions about the losses, the joys, and their anticipations for the future. Poetry is a good vehicle for such review and evaluation, for it requires time to intentionally put into words our inner thoughts and feelings. Year's end is a time to ponder the mile-marker of another year of trials, friendships, and circumstances planned or unplanned. It can be a time to evaluate where we have been during the past year, and where we would like to go next year.

In business and the world of finance, the end of a fiscal year is a time to "close the books," but in general human life we never really "close the books" because the memories of the past year remain as markers of life's experiences, and hopefully serve as springboards to what is yet to come. Did we make some mistakes in the past year? If not, it's likely that we have not been adventurous, willing to be vulnerable and take risks. Do not be afraid to fail, for it is from the foibles and failures of life that we learn the most important lessons. Whatever transpired, we must ask ourselves, "Has this year been used to the glory of God?"

Tomorrow will commence the first day of a new year, a new calendar year of opportunities to be the person God intends us to be. We should be cautious about making promises and resolutions of what we intend to **DO** in the next year. It is far more important to simply set out to **BE** who we are "in Christ" during the next year. It is best to let God chart the course and trajectory of our lives in the coming year, and allow Him to pilot us through the inevitable circumstances that the new year will bring. God knows the future, but has not seen fit to give us such foresight – probably for our own good. So, we set out to walk each day, step by step, looking to **JESUS** as our sufficiency.

Indices

SCRIPTURAL INDEX

TOPICAL INDEX

Other Books by Jim Fowler

Man As God Intended: A Study in Theological Anthropology. This book, the first that Jim wrote, lays the foundation for the remainder of his writing and teaching. The themes of theological anthropology, derivative humanity, and Christocentric theology are introduced in this book. Though filled with theological content, it is written in an easy-to-understand manner that will not intimidate the reader. If you haven't read Jim's writings before, this is a good place to start.

Christ at Work in You: The Continuing Function of the Risen Lord Jesus. This volume is a good sequel to *Man as God Intended*, for it transitions from the theological groundwork of the indwelling Lord Jesus to the practical outworking of Christ's life in our daily lives. Jim considers the inevitable behavioral conflict of the Spirit and the flesh (cf. Gal. 5:16-18), explaining that the "flesh" pertains to the residual selfish and sinful patterns that remain in the soul of a Christian.

Spirit-union Allows for Soul-rest. Beginning with the recognition of the Christian's spirit-union with the livng Lord Jesus (cf. I Cor. 6:17), this volume explores the behavioral implications of His life in our soul and body. Living, as we do, in a restless world, it is important that we understand that the true "rest" that Jesus intends for us (cf. Matt. 11:28) can only be experienced in spiritual union with Christ and allowing His life to be lived out through our behavior.

The Issue is JESUS: Daily Thoughts for Thoughtful Christians. This book is the prequel to the book in your hands. Like this book, it is comprised of 365 daily readings that cause the reader to focus on **JESUS** every day, while also rethinking other topics and themes as they relate to the One who is the central reality of our Christian faith. Religion has so often "majored in the minors," and it is important to be reminded daily that *The Issue is Jesus*, Christianity is Christ.

The Triune God in Christian Thought and Experience. Christian teaching on the Trinity has been both confusing and controversial. This is partially due to early Christian thinkers developing their thought on the basis of Greek philosophy rather than on the revelation of God in Jesus Christ. Using the theological categories of *theologia*, *oikonomia*, and *koinonia*, Jim seeks to take the reader into the practical experience of the Father, Son, and Holy Spirit.

Two Sides of Every Coin: The Dialectic Formatting of Christian Thought. Just as every coin has two sides, every topic within Christian thought also has at least two contrasting perspectives. These contrasts form both/and dialectics necessitating a balanced tension of complementarity between the two tenets. In this volume author Jim Fowler seeks to illustrate the dialectic formatting in various categories of Christian thought by utilizing one hundred and thirty dialectic charts.

Derivative Man: Man As God Intended. Taking John 15:1-8 as his primary text, Jim seeks to explicate that in like manner as the branch derives everything from the vine, the Christian is to derive everything from the life-source of the living Lord Jesus. Jesus explained to His disciples, "Apart from Me, you can do nothing." It is only as we are deriving everything from Jesus by faith, by means of our receptivity of His activity, that we can allow the Christ-life to be expressed.

A Commentary on the Epistle to the Galatians: The Gospel Versus Religion. Jim believes that "Galatianism" is pervasive and prevalent in the churches today, as religious legalists have duped Christians with the didactic declarations of "how-to" Christian religion in prescribed procedures, formulas, techniques and duties. The Church today is in dire need of the message of "grace and liberty" in Christ. Jim has three other commentaries in the Christocentric Commentary Series.

These and twenty other volumes authored by Jim Fowler are available on Amazon.com. Jim Fowler's Amazon author page can be viewed by going to: https://www.amazon.com/-/e/B00LWU9CHE.